YOU WILL

—First sensed   of the men wh

—Read the note by James McCord that opened up the can of worms.

—Listened with growing outrage to the secret Nixon tapes and searched for the true cause of the mysterious 18-minute erasure.

—Met with Henry Kissinger and William Simon as they pleaded for John Mitchell.

—Decided to levy a possible fine against Nixon because "the President loved money."

—Discloses what Nixon's fate might have been in his court had the ex-President not been pardoned.

These are just a sampling of the revelations in a book that is both the fullest story ever of Watergate and the incredibly moving life story of a man who thought himself merely ordinary until history demanded more.

SIGNET and MENTOR Books of Special Interest

JOHN J. SIRICA

TO SET THE RECORD STRAIGHT

THE BREAK-IN, THE TAPES, THE CONSPIRATORS, THE PARDON

A SIGNET BOOK

NEW AMERICAN LIBRARY

TIMES MIRROR

To my wife *Lucy,*
and *Jack, Tricia,* and *Eileen*

Copyright © 1979 by John J. Sirica

SIGNET TRADEMARK REG. U.S. PAT. OFF. AND FOREIGN COUNTRIES
REGISTERED TRADEMARK—MARCA REGISTRADA
HECHO EN CHICAGO, U.S.A.

SIGNET, SIGNET CLASSICS, MENTOR, PLUME, MERIDIAN
AND NAL BOOKS are published by
The New American Library, Inc.,
1633 Broadway, New York, New York 10019

First Signet Printing, April, 1980

1 2 3 4 5 6 7 8 9

PRINTED IN THE UNITED STATES OF AMERICA

Contents

Foreword

From beginning to end, the Watergate case took five years to work its way through the United States District Court in Washington. From the fall of 1972, when indictments were first returned against the original suspects, until late in the fall of 1977, I was involved in nearly every phase of that proceeding. Although, at times, the work load was too much for one judge and other judges on our court took important parts of the case, I devoted five full years of my life, my last five as an active, full-time judge, to Watergate.

Before the case was finished, various accounts of it had already appeared in book form. Defendants, prosecutors, staff members from the congressional investigation, historians, and journalists have contributed to the growing body of literature on the subject. Even the chief actor in this nasty drama, Richard Nixon, has written his version of the events of 1972 and after.

Both because I had already spent so much of my life with Watergate and because so many others had written on the subject, I was not eager to add to that literature. At first, I must say, I found the idea of reliving those years almost too burdensome to contemplate. I felt I had done my share.

But I received scores of letters from friends and from the general public urging that I set down my own impressions of that crucial period in our national history. Many friends in the legal profession, judges and lawyers alike, also encouraged me to write this book, mostly because they wanted to see the story of the judiciary's role told more completely than it had been before.

I found those pleas very persuasive. I also found that many of the previous accounts were self-serving. I felt I had an obligation to set the record straight. After waiting until the very last of the Watergate matters had passed through the courts, I agreed to undertake this book, feeling that if the story was to be told, I would rather tell it myself.

For more than a year, I have reflected on my life both during the case and before. I have tried to tell the story of the Watergate case as I saw it from the bench. And I have tried to tell something of my own life's story so that people may know a bit about the kind of person I am, the experiences I brought to the bench, the events and people who influenced me and made me what I am.

Far from being a burden, this work has been a pleasure. The luxury of spending so much time reflecting on this case and on my whole life has, I sincerely hope, produced a book which not only tells the Watergate story from a unique perspective—that of the judge who tried the whole case—but will also, years from now, when historians are piecing together the events of our times, add significantly to understanding of the grave constitutional crisis through which we passed.

I have deliberately avoided making this a book for lawyers alone, although I think members of my profession will learn a good deal from it. Rather I want the case and the judiciary's responsibilities in it to be understood by everyone. Most of all, my desire is that the young people in this country learn two things from this book. First, I hope they will see that our system works as the Founding Fathers hoped it would, and that it must be nurtured and preserved; and second, I hope young Americans will realize the kinds of opportunities this country affords its citizens.

Washington, D.C.   JOHN J. SIRICA

Acknowledgments

I am indebted to a number of people whose assistance was vital to this project.

First, I must thank John F. Stacks, whose writing skills made my job so much easier. John took valuable time away from his duties at *Time Magazine*, where he helped direct coverage of Watergate in 1973 and 1974, to work with me. His considerable knowledge of the case and his perspective on those events was of enormous help as I organized my own thoughts. We have spent hundreds of hours together and have become more than just collaborators on this book. We have become close friends.

I must also thank Todd Christofferson, now practicing law, who graciously consented to review the manuscript. He has shared many of his own reflections of those hectic days. More important, however, was Todd's aid and support during those difficult days of the trials and hearings. Richard Azzaro, Lynn Wardle, and Mrs. Alease Holley also shared those long days and nights in the courthouse with us, giving freely of their talent and time. My son Jack Sirica, a reporter for the *Nashville Tennessean*, offered his advice on the manuscript.

I would also like to thank George Brockway and the editors at W. W. Norton & Company for their encouragement and editorial advice.

Charles Artley, my deputy United States marshal from 1957 through 1975, was a faithful aide and companion to me through all the major events of Watergate. His successor, Deputy United States Marshal William "Dutch" DeLodovico was with me on February 5, 1976, when I suffered a severe heart attack. His quick and expert aid, and his knowledge of the techniques of cardio-pulmonary resuscitation, saved my life. There is no way to thank him enough.

Prologue

During the five years I was involved with the Watergate case, more than 25,000 letters poured into my office. Most of those letters praised me, congratulated me, supported me, and urged me to follow my conscience and instincts in handling the matters that came up, one after another, in what seemed an endless nightmare of official misconduct, criminal behavior, suspicions, and charges and countercharges. There was a time in the middle of the case when it seemed a close question whether the country could take any more revelations and shocks. And there was a time when I wondered too whether I could take any more. The letters were very important to me. They made me realize how many people had placed their faith not so much in me, but in the courts, and in our system of justice. At a time when the very word "politics" seemed tainted, when many of our governmental institutions were regarded with deep cynicism and distrust, the law and the courts offered, judging by the letters I got, something for people to believe in.

Some people, of course, didn't like what the courts were doing. The mail that was unfavorable was often laced with attacks on me personally. During those years I got five letters threatening my life, and by the end of the case I had to have around-the-clock protection at my home in Northwest Washington so that we could relax without worrying that some psychopath would strike in the middle of the night.

Not all of the personal references were bad. One earnest fellow in California, in the fall of 1975, established the John J. Sirica Presidential Draft Committee. He circulated petitions and inspired a series of letters and telegrams urging me to run in 1976. I was at first amused by his efforts, and then touched by his apparent sincerity in feeling that I could help the country out of a tight spot by running for president. I became concerned, however, when several friends said they'd heard about his campaign on the radio. When he finally wrote me in early January, 1976, to announce his plans to go to New Hampshire to prepare a write-in campaign in my name, I realized he was serious. I had Bob Ruyak, my law clerk, send him a stiff note asking him to stop his efforts on my behalf. That was the last we heard of him, but I must confess I still have a black bumper sticker with bright orange letters saying "Sirica for President."

A strange combination of accidents, circumstances, luck, and—I suppose—Divine Providence, has controlled my life. The enormous distance from a nomadic childhood in a poor and constantly struggling family to a career in the law, and then to the federal bench and to a critical confrontation with the most powerful man in the world, is nearly incomprehensible. I think back over the failures I've had, the mistakes I've made, and the wrong turns I almost took. I think of the chance encounters with the people who helped shape my life—those who cared for me, gave me advice and counsel, helped me in difficult times, those who were my friends and mentors, guiding me in the right directions. I think of what I was and what I became, and I can't believe it. I know this country is full of people like me, people who have lived Horatio Alger lives, and I thank Heaven I was born here. Still, the knowledge that many others have traveled a long way in their lives doesn't take away from my own amazement at what has happened to me. I have to pinch myself still when I think that so many thousands of people cared so much about what I did, when I think that some actually wanted me to be president, and some others wanted me dead.

Both my parents were the children of Italian immigrants. My mother, whose maiden name was Rose Zinno, was born in New Haven, Connecticut, where her parents had settled after the trip to America. My father, Ferdinand, called Fred, was born in the small town of San Valentino, about eighteen miles from Naples. He came with his father to this country when he was about seven. His mother died in Italy when he was very young. I remember his talking about the long journey to America in the steerage of a ship and about the thrill of seeing the Statue of Liberty as they docked in New York City. It is a familiar story. Like a lot of other people at that time, Dad got very little formal education; he said he did not go beyond the second or third grade. He took up the barber trade when he was very young, beginning as an apprentice, standing on a box to lather the customers before their shaves.

I was born in Waterbury, Connecticut, in 1904, and lived there until I was six or seven years old. At that point, my father began a sad sort of odyssey, moving from city to city, from Dayton to Jacksonville to New Orleans, and then back to Jacksonville and, in 1917, to Richmond, Virginia. In each place, the story was much the same. My father would attempt to earn his living with one kind of business or another. Each time, he would fail. In several cities he purchased small enterprises, only to discover that the income they produced was much less than had been promised by the seller. In 1918 we were uprooted once again, moving to Washington, D.C.

Moving around kept me from ever having any close childhood friends, but it didn't hurt my health. Especially in the summers on the Florida beaches, I developed a tremendous appetite. I remember to this day the large plates of grits with two or three fried eggs on top that my mother used to prepare. I really loved this dish. That, and the Italian pasta my mother made, fattened me up to a rather large 185 pounds by the time we got to Washington.

It was difficult in those days, with our financial situation, to find a place to live. We wound up in a little two-room flat on D Street, NW, between Ninth and Tenth streets, where the new FBI building is now. There was a shoemaker's shop on the first floor. Compared to our times near the ocean in Florida, summer in Washington was stifling. There was of course no air conditioning then. Along with thousands of other people, on especially hot nights we used to sleep in the parks or down at Haines Point, along the Potomac River, just to get a breath of fresh air.

My father preached constantly about the virtues of an education, but I wasn't much impressed. When I was fourteen years old, I was fascinated with automobiles. I had learned to drive a friend's car in Richmond, and I decided that instead of continuing in school, I'd become an auto mechanic. Very shortly after we arrived in Washington, I found a job at the Gish Garage, at Seventeenth and U streets, NW. I was a mechanic's helper and my main job was to grease cars. It was a rather unpleasant task. I'd crawl under the cars as best I could, overalls covering my pudgy body. In those days, the lubrication systems were primitive, and you had to clean out the hardened old grease from the grease cups with your hands and a screw driver before packing new grease into the cups. I figured out that I could shortcut the whole process simply by smearing some fresh grease on the outside of some of the cups, leaving the appearance, I thought, of a well-done job. But before long some of the customers with squeaking cars began to complain to the boss, and one day he caught me in the act. He unscrewed a couple of the grease cups, saw the old grease, and bawled me out right in front of the mechanic I was supposed to be helping. I was humiliated and could hear my father's warnings about honesty and integrity ringing in my ears. I was so embarrassed that I hid out in the men's room at the garage and had myself a good cry. A few days later I quit the job, thinking I would eventually be fired anyway. That ended my career in auto mechanics. But I'll never forget the experience.

In the fall of 1918, we were visited by a cousin from Waterbury. He was in his early twenties and was named Alphonso Sirica; we called him "Fonsy." He was determined to make something of himself, and to get an education. He encouraged me, as my father did, to go back to school. Largely because of his advice, I entered Emerson Preparatory School, a small school with only two or three teachers and extremely low tuition costs. I went to classes there at night and worked during the day. I struggled along, since with all our previous moves from city to city, my grammar-school education had not been very good. After going to Emerson for a year or so, I transferred to Columbia Preparatory School. There were about twenty students there in a two- or three-story building on I Street, NW. More important than the school was a friend I made at Columbia. Henry K. Jawish became like a brother to me, and I was greatly influenced by him. By the spring of 1921, Henry and I had been graduated from Columbia. I suppose I had the equivalent of two or three years of high school by that time. But Henry had been talking about getting into law school and I followed along. At the same time, my cousin Fonsy had entered law school, and he visited again, repeating his urgings that I go further in my education.

In those days, it was possible to go directly from high school into law school, without getting an undergraduate degree in college. I didn't have any particular desire to become a lawyer. I was only seventeen years old, but with my father's preaching in mind, Fonsy's advice, and the example of Henry Jawish to follow, I applied to George Washington University Law School. Henry was accepted and, amazingly, so was I.

I started law school that fall. In just about a month, I realized what a mistake I had made. I couldn't begin to understand what the professors were talking about; it was like being in a foreign country. I got discouraged and quit. But I had resolved that summer to do something about my body and weight. After giving up law school, I joined the YMCA and began to exercise regularly. I learned how to box that fall and found that once I had lost all the extra weight, I was pretty good, or at least I thought so. I boxed almost every day with local professional welterweights and middleweights. By the next spring I had lost about thirty pounds and had begun boxing at local clubs in exhibition bouts with the professionals. I thoroughly enjoyed my new life as an athlete and felt I had finally found something at which I could excel. In the summer of 1922 I worked as a lifeguard at a bathing beach located where the Jefferson Memorial now stands. Every day, the lifeguards would get together and run the three and a half miles around Haines Point. We would box four or five rounds before our lunch. I thought it was a wonderful way to spend the summer until one day a swimmer came over to my rowboat and said he thought he had discovered a body lying on the bottom. I dove out of the boat and began feeling around the muddy floor of the Tidal Basin. Suddenly, I touched the body. It frightened me so much I didn't know what to do. I gave the body a push and it floated slowly to the surface. Along with the other lifeguards, I tried to revive the young man. But it turned out he had had a heart attack and was dead. I felt responsible for his death because it happened in the area I was patrolling. I nearly quit my job. My friends talked me out of it, however, and I finished the summer there.

After a year at George Washington University Law School, Henry Jawish transferred to Georgetown University Law School for some reason, and I decided to make a fresh start with him. I was now eighteen years old, but I was not any better prepared for law school than the year before. Even though my physical condition had improved tremendously, and I had learned how to handle myself in the boxing ring, I was terribly timid and shy. I feared being called upon in class and would frequently avoid school altogether rather than risk the embarrassment of having to answer questions I didn't understand. As long as I live, I'll never forget the night Professor Charles Keigwin picked me out of the class and began asking questions about the course work. He was a brilliant man, a great professor, and the author of several law books. I had no idea what he was talking about. I was flustered, blushing and perspiring as he grilled me. Finally, he just threw up his hands and said, "Mr. Seereeca, I do not think you understand the etymology of this word." My God, I didn't even know the meaning of "etymology." My classmates were getting a big kick out of my humiliation.

By this time, my father, in another of his attempts to better himself, had bought a small poolroom with two bowling alleys and a snack bar. He had spent all his savings on the business, and soon realized that he had sunk his money into a very rough place. He wasn't making any profit to speak of and didn't like the type of people who frequented the establishment. I used to help out in the evenings, racking up balls for the pool players and setting pins for the bowlers. But my father was again in despair. As he had so often before, he had trusted someone only to be deceived. We lived in rooms above the place. I remember Dad coming upstairs one night after closing. He poured himself a drink as the tears rolled down his face. He was again facing the fact that his hopes were being dashed.

I guess my father wanted to hold on long enough to sell the place and recover his money. But things just got worse. One evening a particularly unpleasant group came in. Many of them had been drinking, even though this was during prohibition. My father decided to close early, about 9 P.M., to get rid of the roughnecks. But one young man was angry that we were closing. He called me a "goddamned wop" and threw a punch. By this time, I knew how to handle myself. I side-stepped the punch and clipped him on the jaw with a left hook. He landed flat on his back and had to be carried out. When word of that incident spread around, it got a bit easier for us to control things in the poolroom.

I don't think my father owned the place quite a year. He knew that a lot of gamblers and bootleggers came in, but he also knew that if he threw out all the undesirables, he'd be without enough customers to make any money at all. Men from the Government Printing Office, just down North Capitol Street, would come in after work, order a soft drink, and then mix in a little hard liquor from the pints in their pockets. The low point in that whole experience came one night when the city police, aware of the kinds of people who visited the establishment, made a search of the premises. Stashed in the men's room, they found a small quantity of bootleg liquor, apparently left there by one of my father's customers. The police took my dad to the police station and charged him with violation of the Volstead Act. He was not locked up, and the next day, when he appeared in police court with his lawyer, he explained that the liquor must have belonged to a customer and that he didn't even know it was there. No charges were filed, but the incident embarrassed the whole family.

Finally, about a month after my second try at law school, Dad found a buyer for the poolroom. As he had done so often before, he set out to find a new place to start his life over again. This time, he decided to try California. With my recent humiliation in law school still fresh in my mind, I was ready to go along. He wanted me to stay in school, but I told him I'd find a school in the West after we got there. Dad had a four-cylinder Hupmobile, and with my mother and my younger brother, Andy, we headed for Los Angeles. We made St. Louis, about a thousand miles away, in four days.

West of St. Louis, however, the roads were terrible. It took us nine days to get through Missouri and Kansas. Several times a day we'd get stuck in the mud and have to ask farmers or road builders with tractors to pull us out. A few days later, we reached the desert of the Southwest. As it was getting dark one evening, we drove into some water-filled ruts in the road. The car sank right down to the running boards. There didn't seem to be any way to get out. Before long, an Indian drove up behind us and stopped. His wife and several children were with him. He got out of his car, walked over to us, and told us not to worry. Then that poor fellow went to work. He shoveled and dug and gathered stones to jack up the wheels. Finally, he got us out. We drove on, following the Indian and his family, hoping to find a small town with a little hotel. But there was nothing on that road. We finally gave up and spent the night in the car in the desert. Even though my brother was carrying a gun with him, the howling of the coyotes scared us all to death. I'll never forget the kindness that Indian showed us.

Twenty-one days after leaving Washington, we arrived in Los Angeles. We had no friends there. My father found work, but I didn't. His job wasn't much, though, and the whole family was lonely and discouraged. After three months in California, we all agreed to head back east. This time, we set off for Miami, where one of my mother's sisters was living. All the way east my father preached to me about the necessity of going back to law school. "You can see what a tough world this is," he said. "You can see how difficult it can be without an education." For the first time, I really believed him. When we got to Miami, I contacted Georgetown Law School and was readmitted. In January 1923, I began law school for the third time.

It wasn't any easier now than on the two previous tries. I still shivered nervously when the professors called on me. I turned nineteen that March, and I was in a class with many men who were twenty-five or twenty-six years old, had been through World War I, and were just getting started again. Though I was not the only student who had come directly from high school into law school, many of the older men had received their college degrees before going into the army. My preparation was simply not adequate. I still found it very difficult to comprehend what the professors were teaching and to understand the books on contracts, real property, negotiable instruments, torts, and the like. Perhaps because of the unhappy experience in Los Angeles or because I had seen my father disappointed and frustrated so many times, I had made up my mind to stick with law school. I had a certain amount of determination, but that was mixed with a continuing feeling that I was not cut out to be a lawyer. I was still very timid. It was a real effort to stand on my feet and express myself.

Money was another problem. By this time, my parents were able to help me a little, but I needed to work to pay for my studies. I was lucky enough to get a job at the Knights of Columbus gymnasium as a physical-education and boxing instructor. The job paid about a hundred dollars a month. I would go there three nights a week to teach calisthenics to a group of men and to help some of them learn something about boxing. One night a week, I taught a class of women. On Saturday mornings I had the children's class.

As has happened to me so often, the people whom I met and who befriended me made an enormous difference in my life. While I was working at the Knights of Columbus, I met several men who would help shape my future. I used to spar and train with an assistant United States attorney named Leo A. Rover. He was an excellent trial lawyer and later became U.S. attorney and then chief judge of the Municipal Court of Appeals for the District of Columbia. He gave me a lot of encouragement and advice, and eventually the relationship became like that of a father and son. Boxing had become more than a sport for me. It gave me confidence and courage and introduced me to people who became good friends. Another man who advised and encouraged me a great deal was Morris Cafritz. Morris was at that time becoming one of the most prominent and successful real-estate developers in Washington. He later built up a huge personal fortune, but that never seemed to affect the way he treated people. He was always the same, whether dealing with a millionaire or with a person of very small means. He somehow took a liking to me.

I was graduated from Georgetown Law School in June 1926. I ranked, I believe, somewhere in the middle of the class, but I was still unsure about becoming a lawyer. I was tempted by the idea of becoming a professional boxer since I felt more confident of my ability as a fighter than as a lawyer. I couldn't decide whether or not to take the bar exam. Most of the graduates of our class enrolled in a bar review course right after law school and then took the exam while the subjects were still fresh in their minds. I had not taken the bar review course.

On the morning the bar exam was to be given, I had breakfast with Morris Cafritz. I had pretty well decided to skip the bar exam and head for Florida to see my mother and father. I told Morris I was not too eager to proceed with the law but really didn't know what I was going to do. He knew I was thinking about becoming a professional boxer. "Don't be foolish," he told me. "Even if you're not prepared, take the exam. It will be good experience for you, even if you fail it." In those days, taking the bar exam cost twenty-five dollars. I had a little more than that in my pocket, but Morris offered to lend me the money. I thanked him, but told him I was probably not going to take the exam. He persisted, however. "Remember," he said, "you may want to come back to Washington some day. Wouldn't it be nice, if you're lucky enough to pass, to have that behind you?" I went to the law school that morning to return some books I had borrowed. When I saw the other students lined up to pay their exam fee, I suddenly decided to give the exam a try.

The bar exam lasted three days. Each evening after the test sessions, my friends and I would gather to compare answers. I headed for Miami prepared for the worst, certain that I did not have a chance of passing. I moved in with my father and mother and brother Andy and began making the rounds of law firms to see if I could get located in some capacity while waiting for the bar exam results. I knew no one in Miami connected with the law, so it was a matter of going from one firm to another, just knocking on doors, trying in vain to find a position.

I figured that if I couldn't get a job with a law firm, I could at least stay in shape and keep up my boxing. One day I stopped in at the downtown YMCA to get a little exercise. A man with a cauliflower ear asked if I would play a game of handball. After the game, he asked me if I would put on the boxing gloves and spar a few rounds. We boxed four or five rounds, and he wanted to know where I had gotten my experience in the ring. He introduced himself as Jack Britton. It turned out that Britton, who had held the world welterweight title twice, was training for a comeback. He was regarded as one of the most "scientific" boxers ever to fight in his division and had made a considerable amount of money. He had invested all of it in Florida real estate, however, and had lost it in the land bust, about 1925. Now, needing to earn more money, he was ready to go back to professional boxing.

I did not have anything else to do, and I was impressed with Britton and liked him instantly. So when he asked me to become his sparring partner, I agreed right away. We worked together all summer. Jack had three or four bouts, earning about $1,500 for each. Out of his prize money, he'd pay me $100 or $150 for training with him for each fight. Our sparring sessions were often attended by local sportswriters, who began to notice me. "Who is that little black-haired fellow who's giving Britton such a good workout?" one asked. At the same time, Jack was urging me to give up on the law for a while. He knew how frustrated I was about trying to find a position in Miami. He said to me one day that I boxed very well. "You don't get hit often, and when you do, you're always going away from the punches." He said he would like to see me try the game for a couple of years. He thought I would do well and could earn some money.

I never really said yes or no, but one day Britton told me that a local promoter needed someone to box in a semi-windup at Douglas Stadium, a local boxing arena. Jack said I'd get $100 to box ten rounds with a fellow named Tommy Thompson. Thompson was a six-foot-tall welterweight who was known for having fought one of the roughest bouts ever staged in Miami. Jack said he didn't think Thompson was a very good boxer, however, and urged me on. "He won't hit you a solid punch in ten rounds," Jack said. I decided to take the fight.

It was scheduled for July 1926, and I started to train like hell. I ran four or five miles a day on a golf course in Miami Beach and boxed every day with Jack and other professionals. Back in Washington, I had fought about thirty exhibitions, lasting four or five rounds, with local professionals and had boxed ten rounds in the gym, but nothing I ever did worried me as much as that oncoming fight. I'll never forget the day Thompson and I weighed in. I made the welterweight limit of 147 pounds. Thompson was a few pounds heavier. I stood about five feet six, and Thompson towered over me, it seemed. He was the toughest, meanest-looking human being I had ever seen. He hadn't shaved for a week or two and gave me a hard stare to frighten me. It worked. Before the fight, I kept seeing Thompson's unshaven face glaring at me. To reassure myself I repeated over and over Jack Britton's words: "He won't hit you a solid punch."

I was still nervous when the fight began. I had a shaky first round, trying to feel out Thompson, trying to learn how he punched and moved. The second round brought me more confidence, and I began to think Jack had been right. Thompson was a vicious puncher but he was not a good boxer. I found I could hit him and then block or avoid his punches. The fight went the full ten rounds and I won a unanimous decision and $100. I was elated. Here it was, my first ten-round professional bout, and I had won. The write-ups in the newspapers the next day were all good, even though they didn't spell my name correctly. The *Miami Herald* headlined: "Serici: Great Little Mitt Artist." I was on my way as a professional boxer—that is, until my mother heard about the fight.

A few days before the bout, a friend had wired me the incredible news that I had passed the bar exam in Washington and that one of the best students in the class had failed. I really didn't believe the telegram, so I called another friend to check on it. It was true. I had more or less put the bar exam out of my mind while worrying about Tommy Thompson, but my mother hadn't. She really hit the ceiling when she heard about the fight: "Your father and I struggled and slaved trying to send you a little money from time to time to help you finish law school so that you might be somebody. And now all you want to do is be a prize fighter. Are you crazy?"

I tried to explain that I hadn't been able to find a job with a law firm and that I didn't think I'd get hurt boxing. "I've just got to do something, and I'm only trying to earn a few dollars," I told her.

My mother wasn't convinced. I felt I had really let my parents down. I was ashamed of myself. My brother had been fighting some, too. In fact, Andy and I used to spar a good bit together. I remember one day he sort of walked into one of my punches and fell back against the metal pole supporting the ropes around the ring. He was unconscious for a while and when he came around he was still dizzy and disoriented. This scared the hell out of me. Britton and I drove Andy around town for hours, waiting for his head to clear.

My parents never seemed too concerned about how my brother would turn out. I remember my father predicting that he would become a successful businessman. He was right; Andy wound up years later running a large fleet of taxicabs in Washington. But the prospect of my turning away from the law and toward boxing was just too much for my parents. I agreed to return to Washington and the law. Shortly after Labor Day, I took a ship back north. It was a combination freight and passenger ship that docked in Baltimore. I remember we left Miami just before a terrible hurricane devastated much of the Florida coast, killing more than a hundred people.

Through the fall of 1926, I repeated the job-hunting routine I had started in Miami, with the same result. Among the law firms unwilling to give me a chance was Hogan and Hartson, where years later I was to become a partner. I never really understood my failure to find a job, since I had managed to finish at a fine law school and had been admitted to the District of Columbia bar. I turned again to my friend Morris Cafritz. Morris had just opened a new co-operative apartment house on Fourteenth Street and offered me a job there, selling apartments on a straight commission basis.

I soon learned I wasn't much of a salesman. I could never think of a clever sales pitch, so I'd simply conduct the prospective buyers on a tour of the apartment. "This is the living room," I'd say. "This is the bedroom; this is the kitchen." Any fool could plainly recognize the kitchen, the bedrooms, the bathroom. It was little wonder that by December I had managed to sell a grand total of one efficiency apartment. With the holidays coming, I headed back to Miami to visit my family and to try again with the law firms there. I was fast becoming as much of a gypsy as my father had been.

Jack Britton was still in Miami, so I hooked up with him again. He was working at the Roney Plaza Pools, at Twenty-third Street and Collins Avenue, training several wealthy men who had taken up boxing to keep in shape. Jack offered me fifty dollars a week to help him out, and I went to work. One of the men who came by regularly was Bernard F. Gimbel, the department-store owner. I used to train with Mr. Gimbel every morning in the hot sun. He was about forty-two years old, but was in excellent condition and was a good boxer. He also became a good friend and adviser. He counseled me not to get discouraged with the law, to keep trying, and he offered to help me get located in Washington. Shortly after the holidays, Gimbel had to return to New York. He let me use the upper berth in his train compartment, thus saving me the fare to Washington, where I would make another stab at getting started in the law.

Again I encountered the same problems. To pass the time, I went back to the Knights of Columbus gym to box and work out. There I ran into an old friend, Ray Neudecker, with whom I had boxed and trained while I was in law school. Ray was an assistant United States attorney. One of Ray's former colleagues in the United States attorney's office was a man named Bert Emerson, who had gone into private practice. Ray recommended me for a place in Bert's office. At the time, Bert was one of the outstanding criminal lawyers in the city. His office was on Fifth Street, the center of the legal profession in those days.

The practice of law in Washington in the mid-1920's was nothing like today's formal, specialized government and corporate practice. Most lawyers were generalists, taking whatever cases came their way, and usually—it seems—having a lot more fun than lawyers do now. Some of Washington's best attorneys began practice on Fifth Street. Washington was really a small town then, and the community of lawyers was small, close-knit, and quite friendly. Most lawyers worked together nearly every day, running up against each other in police or criminal court. The important work was usually finished by noon. Some of the lawyers would spend their afternoons playing handball or boxing, often with delightful people like Milton Kronheim, then a bail bondsman on Fifth Street and later Washington's largest wholesale liquor dealer and a great friend of mine.

Because of Ray's recommendation, Bert Emerson offered me my first job as a lawyer. He was practicing with two brothers, Joe and Russell Kelly, and an associate named Nita Hinman. He had a beautifully furnished, second-floor suite. The office space was all occupied, but out of kindness, Bert said I could hang around the office and help out. He pointed to a rack in the corner of the outer office where I could hang my hat and coat. I would be a sort of messenger, and he promised that I could have a case now and then to get some experience. It wasn't much, there was no regular pay, but it was a start and I was very happy to be in Bert Emerson's office.

Getting this job was one of the luckiest breaks of my life. I admired Bert Emerson. He was tall, slim, handsome, and wore custom-tailored suits. I was still very sensitive about the fact that I had not gone to college. Bert hadn't been to college either. Like me, he had gone directly from high school into law school, but he had nevertheless become a very successful trial lawyer. I began to feel there was some hope for me. Every day, I would show up bright and early at Bert's office. When he went to court, I would go along, sitting beside him, watching him question the witnesses and argue to the jury. Bert was an artist at talking to the jury. He told me thousands of times that the worst mistake a lawyer could make was to underestimate the intelligence of a jury, to try to fool them. I studied his mannerisms, the way he spoke, the way he could rise to great oratorical heights in arguing his case, and the way he could achieve a tone of great sadness in explaining some unfortunate aspect of a defendant's life. He reassured me about my own nervousness in court, pointing out that everyone was nervous in the beginning, and that with experience, it would go away.

Bert was besieged with clients at the time. Once, when he was out of the country, one of the Kelly boys and I were in police court trying a case when word came that another judge had called up one of Bert's cases. Kelly asked our judge to excuse him so he could appear in the other courtroom. He told the judge he could only try one case at a time. The judge, John P. McMahon, looked down at me and said, "What's the matter with that little black-haired fellow? Let him take the other case." Kelly explained that I had never tried a case before. "Now is a good time to start," the judge said. And off I went. That was on July 7, 1927.

Downstairs in the other courtroom, I found that my friend Ray Neudecker was the prosecutor. The case involved a defendant charged with violation of the prohibition laws. There really was not much of a defense to offer. But my new client refused to plead guilty. We spent the morning on the case and took a break for lunch. Joe Kelly and I had lunch together. One of the things he said was, "Don't forget to tell the jury that this is your first case." He figured that would get me some sympathy. Of course, I didn't have to tell anybody it was my first case. I was literally shivering in my shoes. After lunch, I went back to court for my argument to the jury. I spoke a full two minutes, which seemed like two hours to me, and then announced to the jury, "Well, I guess I've taken enough of your time." They retired to the jury room and in ten minutes came back with a guilty verdict. The judge asked me if I wanted the sentence to be pronounced right away. "Might as well," I answered, being too naïve to know that it's always better to wait a few days to let the case cool down before sentencing. The judge threw the book at my client.

I stayed in Bert's office for three and a half years. I tried fourteen court-assigned felony cases in that time, losing every one except the last. In that one, the prosecution's case was so weak, there was no way to lose it. Indeed, after the trial, the judge told the prosecutor that had I asked for a directed verdict of not guilty before the jury received the case, he would have granted it. But I didn't know enough to ask for a directed verdict. I also tried many other civil and criminal cases during that time.

Poor Bert Emerson. Even while I was with him, he had started to drink heavily. He would often tell his wife Ruth that he and I were going out to interview witnesses in the evening. Instead, we'd hit the night spots around town. At times Bert would wind up too inebriated to drive. I would have to take him home. He never was able to get away from liquor and some years later this totally ruined his practice. He died at forty-eight, weighing about sixty-five pounds and suffering from acute alcoholism. He was like a brother to me, and I shall always be grateful to him.

Sometimes, when I think back over those days, I don't know how I got as far as I did. But I know I couldn't have gotten anywhere without people like Leo Rover, Morris Cafritz, Milton Kronheim, Jack Britton, Bernard F. Gimbel, and especially Bert Emerson. Without Bert, I would not have remained in the practice of law.

After I had served about three years as an apprentice in Bert Emerson's office, my old friend and adviser Leo Rover offered me a job as one of his assistants in the U.S. attorney's office. He had been appointed by President Hoover, and he asked that I get two endorsements from Republicans to assure approval of my appointment. Up to that time I had taken no interest in politics whatsoever. I didn't know a Republican from a Democrat. Of course, I was only twenty-six years old. The only way I knew to find some support was to ask my relatives in Connecticut to see what they could do. A cousin, Mrs. Gertrude Bowes, happened to be active in local Republican politics in Waterbury, and she introduced me to Congressman Edward Goss and Senator Hiram Bingham. They agreed to write the necessary endorsements. Although I got valuable trial experience as an assistant U.S. attorney, prosecuting and handling about two hundred cases in three and a half years, the importance of that period of my life lay in the political affiliation I developed. The Republicans had done me a favor. I never forgot it. It's hard to say whether my political views were conservative before I got that job through the Republicans or whether they became conservative because of the association, but in any event it was the start of a long relationship. I never had much use for people who switched back and forth between parties. Nor did I ever believe that one party had a monopoly on honesty or integrity.

I stayed in the U.S. attorney's office until the beginning of 1934. With the Democrats in office, it was clear that Leo Rover was going to be replaced, so I quit the prosecutor's job on January 15, 1934, to start my own practice.

By then my parents had moved back to Washington from Florida. My dad was barbering again and his financial situation had improved somewhat. He had managed to buy a little house on Fourteenth Street, NW, and I lived there during my years in the U.S. attorney's office. Thank Heaven I was able to stay there after I started practicing; without that free lodging, I would have gone under. I had a little two-room office in the Shoreham Building, on Fifteenth Street, NW, for which I paid ninety dollars a month rent. I had a secretary whom I paid about ten dollars a week. It seemed there was never any money left over after those outlays. It also seemed the phone never rang. This was the beginning of what I call my "starvation period," when I really lived from hand to mouth. The period lasted, essentially, until 1949, when I joined the firm of Hogan and Hartson. Had it not been for staying at my parents' home, and for the few cases friends sent my way, I would have had to quit the law altogether. I earned my biggest single fee by successfully defending Walter Winchell against a defamation suit. But that case took the better part of a year. It was my friends that kept me going. And I never had a better or closer friend than Jack Dempsey.

Dempsey and I met in 1934 in Washington. Congress had just legalized professional boxing in the District. I was still quite interested in the sport and so Goldie Ahearn (a local prize fighter) and I decided we'd set up a boxing club. The idea was that we'd promote professional fights in our own little boxing arena, make some money, and stay close to the sport we both liked so much. For our opening, Ahearn prevailed on his friend Max Waxman, Dempsey's business manager, to have the former heavyweight champ referee the main bout. We figured the crowds would come to see Dempsey, if not the fighters themselves.

The boxing arena turned out to be a failure, but my friendship with Dempsey developed steadily after our first meeting. I occasionally went to New York for weekends, and Dempsey took me into his circle of friends. He always introduced me as his Washington lawyer. Eventually, we got closer than two brothers. At times when I didn't know how I'd make the next rent payment on my little office, some client would suddenly show up, at Dempsey's suggestion.

In early 1940, my father suffered a heart attack while he

was visiting Miami. I went down to see him in the hospital and found that he was very upset about the care he was getting. He felt he was being ignored by the medical staff and nurses. He asked me if my friend Jack Dempsey could help out. Jack was operating a hotel in Miami Beach at the time and quickly agreed to come over to see my father. After his visit, there was an incredible change. The nurses and doctors couldn't do enough for Dad, apparently impressed that we knew someone famous. Jack would stop by each day to see my father. On February 10, Jack came by, and my father stuck his hand outside his oxygen tent to shake Jack's hand. Shortly after that, Dad died. We brought him back to Washington to be buried. We were all terribly upset, but Jack just took over. He made all the train and funeral arrangements and was a great comfort to us all.

Jack and I had some great times together. In 1942, he was touring with the Cole Brothers Circus and wanted some company. I met the circus in North Carolina and spent three days with Jack on the circus train. I'll never forget Jack charming the ladies, making the clowns laugh, playing poker with the circus workers.

One day in 1945, Jack dropped by my Washington office, where, as usual, I was drinking a lot of coffee and waiting for the telephone to ring. He had been made a lieutenant commander in the Coast Guard and was setting off on a cross-country tour to sell government savings bonds. He urged me to come along to help him out. At each stop there would be a large rally with a variety of entertainment. Jack's job was to come on stage at the end of the show to be interviewed and, in the process of talking about his boxing career, to urge the audience to buy bonds. In Richmond one night, the local sportswriter who was supposed to interview Jack got drunk and Jack asked me to take his place.

After that night, we appeared together in about eighteen cities and towns from the East Coast to the West. I'd ask Jack questions like "What was your toughest fight?" and "Do you think you could have beaten Joe Louis?" Jack would never answer that last question, except to say he wished he were still young enough to try. We sold millions of dollars' worth of bonds, and while thoroughly enjoying myself, I also felt I was doing something important for the country. We visited Charleston and Columbia in South Carolina, Atlanta, Birmingham, New Orleans, and Austin. I remember stopping in Omaha and meeting Father Flanagan at Boys Town, where Jack and I had the privilege of talking to about three hundred orphans. In Portland, Oregon, General Jonathan ("Skinny") Wainwright was staying in the same hotel, just home after being liberated from a Japanese prison camp. I remember he came by our suite to meet Dempsey. He was truly one of the great heroes of World War II. The tour went on through Oregon and California, and then to Minneapolis, where the mayor, Hubert Humphrey, greeted us. It was the most exciting and interesting trip I ever made. When Lucy and I were married in 1952 in Fort Lauderdale, Jack was my best man. He was present when I was sworn in as a judge in 1957. He is my best friend.

Like many lawyers, I found that politics became a sort of hobby. I never thought of seeking elective office, but after the Republicans helped me get into the U.S. attorney's office, I wanted to help them out in return. I didn't want them to think I was ungrateful. My father was a red-hot Democrat. He disliked Herbert Hoover with a passion and couldn't understand how I could be a Republican. But most of my friends were Republicans and I felt comfortable there.

In 1936, Leo Rover, who had made me an assistant in the U.S. attorney's office, became Republican State Committee chairman for the District of Columbia. When he and his slate of delegates to the 1936 convention in Cleveland were challenged, he asked me to come and help him in the fight before the credentials committee. We lost, but I had my first taste of national politics there.

I was later elected a member of the Republican state committee in the District and in 1940 campaigned for Wendell Willkie. I was used mostly to speak to Italian-American groups and remember making speeches for Willkie in Buffalo, Newburgh, and Syracuse, New York, and in Trenton, New Jersey. In 1944, I was chief counsel to a congressional committee and, under the Hatch Act, couldn't participate in electoral politics. In 1948, I again spoke in cities in New York State, this time for Thomas Dewey. I had it in the back of my mind that some day I'd like to be a federal judge, and thought that my work in politics might help.

In 1952, my old friend Mabel Walker Willebrandt, a former assistant attorney general of the United States, was working actively for Senator Robert Taft. At her request, I went to the Chicago convention to help her round up delegates for Senator Taft, who lost, of course, to General Eisenhower. While in Chicago, I ran into Senator Joe McCarthy. We had been friends for several years, double-dating once in a while and going to the race track together from time to time. I liked Joe a lot in those days. Dempsey and I had attended his wedding. "He's a real barroom fighter," Jack would say approvingly.

I made a number of appearances for the Eisenhower-Nixon ticket in 1952, again concentrating mostly on Italian-American organizations. I spoke in several cities in New Jersey and also spoke in Bridgeport, Connecticut, and in Cleveland. Then in 1953, Joe McCarthy offered me the job of chief counsel to his Senate subcommittee which was investigating Communist influence in government.

I must say that I found the offer very attractive. What appealed to me most was the fact that Republicans controlled Congress, and therefore, as chief counsel, I could run my own investigation. I wasn't especially excited by McCarthy's charges about Communist infiltration, but it seemed at the time to be an important matter that needed further examination. By the time McCarthy made his offer, I had moved over to Hogan and Hartson and was finally earning a decent living. But I was still intrigued by his proposal.

Lucy and I talked a long time about the idea of my going back up to Capitol Hill. She was strongly opposed, feeling that since I was now a partner in a good firm, I would be foolish to leave. Joe stopped by our apartment one evening and I told him I felt I had better stay where I was. He agreed that it would be a mistake to leave a good firm like Hogan and Hartson. He told me that since I wasn't going to take the job, he was probably going to hire a young New York lawyer named Roy Cohn. One of the reasons for hiring Cohn, he said, was "that it might convince people I am not anti-Semitic."

It wasn't long before McCarthy ran amok, making ever-wilder charges and finally humiliating himself in the Army-McCarthy hearings in 1954. I have often wondered what I would have done had I been his counsel. I don't know whether I could have controlled him. Perhaps he would have listened to me. But most likely I would have gone down with him. Herbert Brownell had it right years later when, after I was appointed to the bench, he told me I would never have been a federal judge had I taken that job with Joe McCarthy. I'm sure, looking back, that had I still been single, I would have done so. Thank God for Lucy Camalier Sirica.

In 1956, I was the acting national committeeman for the District of Columbia and an alternate delegate to the convention in San Francisco. I worked again that fall for the Eisenhower-Nixon ticket and served as a member of the Republican National Finance Committee. It was my work in the two Eisenhower elections that made me the friends who finally helped me get on the bench. Leonard Hall was then Republican National Committee chairman. In 1953 he had asked me if I would accept the job of commissioner of immigration. Leo Rover advised me to turn it down and I did, but I mentioned to Len Hall that I would like to be a federal judge some day.

In the fall of 1956, Henry Schweinhaut, a judge on the United States District Court, retired. I was then serving on the Republican State Committee for the District, and another lawyer, George Hart, was the Republican state chairman for the District. I knew Hart wanted that position on the bench. Still another local lawyer, Fontaine Bradley, of the firm of Covington and Burling, was also interested. I asked Hart if he would get the State Committee to recommend all three of us to Attorney General Brownell. Instead, the State Committee submitted only Hart's name. The District of Columbia Bar Association endorsed David Bress, a Democrat, as well as Hart and myself.

During the 1952 campaign, I had met a fellow named Anthony Russo, an assistant to Brownell and one of his very close friends. I now sought an opinion from him about my chances. He told me that the job was wide open. So I got Len Hall to support me in the White House. William Rogers, whom I had known for a long time, was then deputy attorney general. One of his duties was the screening of judicial nominees. I learned years later that he was one of my strongest supporters. I'm sure now that without his help, I would not have received the appointment to the federal bench. Ever since, I have been most grateful to Rogers and the others who were in my corner when I was seeking the judgeship. Rogers, of course, was later Richard Nixon's first secretary of state.

On April 2, 1957, I was sworn in as a federal district

judge.* I had never been so proud and happy in my life. I had realized my dream. From my office in the federal courthouse, I could see Bert Emerson's old office on Fifth Street. I could easily remember my days as a kid lawyer trying cases in the police courts. It seemed like a long, long way—a big jump from Fifth Street to the bench for a guy like me.

---

* In 1958, George Hart was appointed by President Eisenhower to the next vacancy on our court. And when I stepped down as chief judge in 1974, he succeeded me.

1

Preparing for
the First Trial

The work of a federal judge in Washington was once quite different from that of most federal judges around the country. Until Congress reorganized the court system in the District of Columbia a few years ago, our district judges acted both as federal judges and, in some ways, as state-court judges. Because Washington is technically a federal territory, our court heard many criminal cases that in other places would have gone into the state courts.

This peculiar allocation of judicial functions was still in effect in the spring of 1972. As a result, I was presiding over one of the most grisly murder trials imaginable. The case involved a former employee of the federal government, a white man, who had schemed to have his wife raped and murdered by an accomplice, a black man, in order to gain control of her money. The two men first agreed that she would be killed after a shopping trip. But the husband called that off, apparently because his son was to come along. He didn't want the boy to witness his mother's murder.

Instead, a second plan was put into effect. The man and his wife had dinner at a waterfront restaurant, and as they were leaving the parking lot, the accomplice held them up at gun point. He instructed them to drive to the East Capitol Street Bridge. While they drove, the wife reassured her husband, who of course already knew the scenario, that they would be unharmed if they co-operated with what she assumed was simply a robbery attempt. At the lonely bridge site near the Potomac River, the accomplice took the wife out of the car, raped her, shot her twice in the head, and then fled the scene. The husband drove to a nearby gas station to report the crime.

Brilliant work by the Metropolitan Police Department and the U.S. attorney's office broke the case and produced separate first-degree-murder and conspiracy indictments against the two men. Prior to his trial, the husband claimed that the accomplice had been blackmailing him by threatening to disclose his extramarital affair and that the murder was then planned to get the money to buy off the accomplice. In his own defense, the accomplice said that he did know the husband but had not conspired to murder the wife. The prosecutors wanted to let the husband plead guilty to a reduced charge in exchange for his testimony against the accomplice, who would then likely be convicted of premeditated murder and, at a minimum, spend the rest of his life in jail. I rejected the plea bargain, however, relying upon the legal axiom of "equal justice under law." The law states that conspirators are culpable in like degree even if one goes further in carrying out the conspiracy than the other. The two men were equally responsible for this brutal killing, in my view. And another problem was also on my mind. The husband was white; the accomplice was black. I shuddered to think what might be the reaction of Washington's large black community if the white man who planned his own wife's death was let off with a fifteen-year-to-life term while the black man might have to pay with his life. In separate trials each was convicted of first-degree murder. On appeal, my rejection of the husband's guilty plea was overturned and the case was remanded to me to accept a second-degree plea. I sentenced him to the maximum jail term for second-degree murder.

In mid-June, 1972, I was faced with sentencing the accomplice, and I wasn't getting much sleep thinking about it. I have always had mixed feelings about capital punishment, but the facts in this case were so disgusting, so horrible, that it seemed made for the death sentence. Still, having the power to take a person's life is an awful thing. On the weekend of June 17, it weighed very heavily on my mind.*

At the time, I was serving as chief judge of the district court, a position based on seniority of service. In addition to

---

* On June 22, I sentenced the accomplice to death. But he was never executed. Later that year, the Supreme Court invalidated the kinds of death-penalty statutes under which he had been sentenced. He is now serving a life sentence.

hearing cases, it was my responsibility to handle much of the administrative work of the court, to assign special cases to particular judges, and to oversee the work of the federal grand juries. I had always made it a practice to read the local newspapers carefully to anticipate the work load the court might have and to get a preliminary understanding of the kinds of cases I might have to assign for trial. My interest was immediately aroused on Sunday, June 18, by a little story in the *Washington Post* about a burglary at the Democratic National Committee's headquarters in the Watergate office building.

It wasn't much of a story, but it was a little out of the ordinary. Five men had been arrested inside the headquarters carrying sophisticated electronic equipment and rather large sums of money, mostly in hundred-dollar bills. "Politics," I thought immediately. The average felon doesn't look for money in offices, especially in political offices, so the incident seemed odd even though the Watergate complex was also a popular in-town residence for rich Washingtonians. The apartment building adjacent to the offices was home for Attorney General John Mitchell and his wife, Martha, for chief Republican money raiser Maurice Stans, and for President Nixon's personal secretary, Rose Mary Woods.

The break-in itself occurred early on the morning of June 17. The story of how the burglars were discovered is well known, but I've always wondered what would have happened had Frank Wills, the private security guard at the Watergate offices, not seen the tape covering the locks on the doors inside the office complex.* Wills did spot the tape, called the city police, and within minutes, five men were arrested inside the Democrats' office. Their leader was James McCord. The four others were Bernard L. Barker, Frank A. Sturgis, Virgilio Gonzalez, and Eugenio R. Martinez, all from Miami. A grand jury investigation was quickly set in motion by the principal assistant U.S. attorney, Earl Silbert. It was clear that this was a matter with which I would have more contact.

* H. R. Haldeman has suggested that by placing the tape on the doors so it was visible to the guard, the burglars showed they actually wanted to be caught. That is nonsense. There was no other way to tape the locks open effectively. Indeed, his entire theory that the Watergate break-in was a Democratic setup is, to put it mildly, ridiculous.

What wasn't clear, however, and would remain a secret for nearly a year, was just how the five men came to be spying on the Democrats and their chairman, Lawrence F. O'Brien. When the four men from Miami were asked at their arraignment what their occupation was, they answered, "Anti-communist." McCord identified himself as a former CIA agent. There was some thought that the bugging which was found to have occurred was a misguided adventure by a group of superpatriots. But there were suspicious ties between the burglars and President Nixon's re-election committee. McCord was on the payroll of this committee as a security co-ordinator. G. Gordon Liddy, counsel to the fund-raising branch of the committee, and E. Howard Hunt, once an employee of White House aide Charles Colson, were soon tied to the break-in. Officials of the committee, including its leader, John Mitchell, who a few months earlier had resigned as attorney general to run the president's campaign, quickly denied any knowledge of the break-in plans. They blamed Liddy and Hunt for the operation.

Only a few people in Washington that summer knew that the break-in was really just one act in a long series of White House-inspired attempts to circumvent the law. Intense concern about continued protests against the Vietnam War and about leaks of sensitive foreign-policy information embarrassing to the president and to his chief diplomatic adviser, Henry Kissinger, along with the president's own concern about his political future, had led to a series of illegal operations planned inside the White House. In 1969, a group of reporters and administration aides were illegally wiretapped in an attempt to discover the source of leaks about the secret bombing of Cambodia and other unannounced policies. The so-called "Huston plan," which included burglaries, wiretaps, and illegal domestic intelligence gathering by the CIA, was formulated in 1970 in response to the antiwar movement. When Daniel Ellsberg leaked the Pentagon Papers the White House sent Liddy and Hunt to break into Ellsberg's psychiatrist's office and steal information that would discredit Ellsberg. The pair recruited Barker and Martinez, as well as a third Miamian, Felipe DeDiego, to do the actual breaking and entering.

Concern for "national security" was the rationale that supported these actions. That concern was matched in the White House by worries about President Nixon's political survival.

In 1970 the Republicans did rather poorly across the country, despite, or perhaps because of, hard-hitting and divisive performances by Vice-president Agnew and by the president himself. Senator Edmund Muskie, who had run as the vice-presidential nominee in 1968, appeared to be the Democratic front-runner. By 1971, he was ahead of the president in some public-opinion polls.

In recent presidential contests, the candidates have tended to have only the loosest of relationships with the national party committees, preferring to run their own campaigns. So the Nixon group established the Committee to Re-elect the President (CRP). Nixon critics immediately dubbed this committee "CREEP." Attorney General Mitchell, even though still in the Justice Department, was put in charge of the president's political operation. No effort was to be spared. Huge sums of money were raised by Maurice Stans, the finance-committee chairman, who also operated apart from the Republican National Committee. New and stricter campaign-spending rules were coming into effect on April 7, 1972, and Stans and his group made every effort to raise large amounts of money before that date, so that donors could remain anonymous and so that huge individual gifts, many nearly coerced out of corporate leaders by Stans, would not have to be reported fully.

Anxiety about demonstrators and the obsessive desire to eliminate all political dangers to the president merged in the spring of 1971 when Nixon himself demanded that his campaign officials improve their political-intelligence capabilities. This demand bred attempts by his subordinates to learn more about Senator Muskie's campaign plans and to delve further into Senator Edward Kennedy's car accident on Chappaquiddick Island, in which a young woman companion was killed. The president himself, according to some aides, also initiated an attempt to link Democratic National Committee Chairman O'Brien with billionaire Howard Hughes, who was said to have kept O'Brien on a large retainer. Throughout 1971, a number of high-level White House officials attempted to satisfy the president's wish for better undercover work against the Democrats.

In December 1971, G. Gordon Liddy was named general counsel to the CRP. He was responsible for advising the committee on the complicated election laws, and was also expected to provide more of the political intelligence that the

president was demanding. It was the latter responsibility that
Liddy took more seriously. Liddy himself was a strange duck,
once stunning White House counsel John Dean by showing
him a burn on the palm of his hand which, he explained, had
resulted when he deliberately held his hand over a candle
flame to prove his tolerance for pain.

In January 1972, Liddy proposed a massive intelligence operation against the Democrats. At a meeting in the attorney
general's office, Liddy suggested establishing mugging squads,
forming kidnapping teams, procuring prostitutes to compromise delegates to the Democratic convention, and in-
stalling a system of electronic bugs to spy on the candidates
at the convention. In what John Dean later told the Senate
Watergate committee was a "mind-boggling" million-dollar
plan, Liddy suggested bugging O'Brien's Watergate office and
his headquarters suite at the Democratic convention in Miami
that summer. Mitchell was unimpressed, except by the size of
Liddy's budget, and told the former FBI man to "revise" his
plan. Liddy did revise it—down to a half-million-dollar
budget. Still Mitchell wouldn't approve. Dean and Jeb Stuart
Magruder, Mitchell's deputy at the CRP, later testified that
considerable pressure was then applied to Magruder by White
House aide Charles Colson and by Gordon Strachan, an aide
of Nixon's chief of staff H. R. Haldeman. Finally, at a meeting in Florida on March 30, Mitchell, according to
Magruder, approved a $250,000 budget for Liddy's plan,
which had been dubbed "Gemstone" by its cloak-and-dagger
originator.

Liddy wasted no time. He had already enlisted the help of
James McCord, then working as a bodyguard for Martha
Mitchell and as a security consultant protecting the CRP offices. Hunt, with whom Liddy had worked on the Ellsberg
break-in, recruited his friends from Miami.

To pay the recruits and to finance purchase of the necessary equipment, Liddy eventually drew a total of $199,000 in
cash from Hugh Sloan, Maurice Stans's deputy in the committee's finance office. By sheer coincidence, some of the cash
Liddy drew and handed out to the burglars had been given to
the committee by Miamian Bernard Barker. Some time before the break-in, Liddy had been asked to convert several
campaign contribution checks into cash so that the origins of
the gifts could not be traced. One of those checks, drawn for
$25,000 in the name of Republican fund raiser Kenneth

Dahlberg, actually represented a gift from a Democratic friend of Hubert Humphrey named Dwayne Andreas, who wanted to conceal the fact that he was giving to the Nixon campaign. Liddy had sent the checks to Barker, who deposited them in his own account, then later withdrew the cash and sent it back to Liddy. Barker "laundered" a total of $114,000 for the committee this way, including $89,000 in checks drawn on a Mexican bank.

On Sunday, May 28, McCord and the four men from Miami broke into the Democratic headquarters in the Watergate office building and installed electronic bugs in the phones of Larry O'Brien's secretary and of O'Brien's deputy, R. Spencer Oliver. They left undetected. The bugs sent radio signals across the street to the Howard Johnson motel, where they were monitored by Alfred Baldwin III, another former FBI agent. But when the transcripts of these phone conversations reached Magruder and Strachan—and later, by Magruder's account, John Mitchell—they were judged worthless. Liddy and his team planned another break-in, to tap O'Brien's own phone and thereby prove that their operation was worth the extraordinary amount of money the committee was paying for it. That second break-in, June 17, resulted in the arrest of McCord and the Miamians, and subsequently of Liddy and Hunt. Baldwin was eventually tracked down by the FBI, and, under a grant of immunity from prosecution, became the prosecution's chief witness.

The obvious connection of Hunt, Liddy, and McCord to the Republican campaign organization immediately set off investigations by reporters seeking to find out who had authorized and paid for the bugging and break-in. Before long, the *Washington Post* connected the money the burglars were carrying with CRP funds by tracing the bills back to Barker's account. The government prosecutors also had been investigating the matter. On September 15, in my courtroom, indictments were returned against the seven defendants, charging them with conspiracy, burglary, and violation of the federal laws against electronic interception of oral communications. Attorney General Richard Kleindienst said the next day that the investigation leading to the indictments was "the most intensive, objective and thorough . . . in many years, reaching out to cities all across the United States as well as into other countries." Yet there was no mention in the indictments of the origin of the money the defendants carried.

With the election coming up, and Senator George McGovern's candidacy in desperate trouble, charges about Republican responsibility for the break-in were being made more frequently. It was clear this case was going to be difficult and perhaps time-consuming. It was going to require special handling. As public interest increased, I began to think more seriously about how to assign the case for trial. I had several options. I could let the case be assigned randomly—that is, listed in the clerk's office and given to the first available judge. But our court rules at the time provided that if a case promised to be protracted, "such case shall be specially assigned to a Judge for all purposes by the Chief Judge." The chief judge of our district court, as I've explained, has responsibility for a variety of administrative duties, in addition to his own caseload. Hence he usually hears fewer cases than the other fourteen active judges on the court and has more time to devote to difficult trials. I thought that perhaps I should try the case myself.

Several days before the indictments were returned, I began consulting with some of my colleagues on the bench. I found Judge Howard Corcoran one day near the first-floor elevator. I have always felt comfortable with Howard. He's a fair, objective judge who was appointed by President Johnson. His brother Thomas ("Tommy the Cork") Corcoran was a close adviser to President Roosevelt. Howard, too, is a Democrat; he was at one time acting United States attorney in New York City. I asked Howard what he thought about my taking the case since I had the time as chief judge and since it was obviously going to have political overtones. I reminded him of my own background in Republican politics. We chatted for about fifteen minutes, and his advice was that I should assign the case to myself. He felt that if a judge appointed by a Democratic president had the case, the way might be open for charges of political bias, should the break-in prove embarrassing for the Republicans. "That's what I've been thinking," I told him. "I've been through these things."

I went on to see Leonard Walsh, a former chief judge of the Municipal Court in Washington, who had been appointed, like myself, by President Eisenhower. He agreed that I should take the case. Edward Tamm, another Democratic appointee, also agreed. Finally, I stopped by to see my friend and neighbor Matthew McGuire.

McGuire, who was appointed by President Roosevelt, is a veteran of Massachusetts politics, and has a great Irish wit. I respect his judgment and admire his sense of humor. Once a defendant about to be sentenced announced to McGuire that his lawyer had taken $500 from him, ostensibly to bribe McGuire to throw the case out. McGuire didn't miss a beat, announcing simply, "I'm sorry, I didn't get it," and sent the man to jail. Another time, McGuire was trying to assign a public defender to an indigent defendant. The defendant said he didn't need a lawyer because he was being advised by Jesus Christ. "I'm sorry," said McGuire, "you need local counsel."

McGuire agreed with my decision to assign the case to myself. At the time of the indictments, the prosecutors asked that the case be specially assigned. On September 18, I designated myself as presiding judge. I didn't really know what I was getting into. I didn't have a hint that it wouldn't be until five years later that I would finally see the last of this case.

With the press and the Democratic politicians throwing charges at the White House, alleging involvement of higher-ups in the break-in, and with the White House and Republican politicians charging unfair treatment by the press and by their opponents, it seemed to me that the first danger was that the rights of the defendants could be damaged by pretrial publicity. The prosecutors were concerned, too, that their case against the seven men would be lost if the defendants could show that their chances for a fair trial had been tainted by all the attention the case was getting. So on October 4, 1972, I issued a so-called "gag order" to prevent the case's being tried in the newspapers, and on television. The order enjoined "the Department of Justice, the Office of the United States Attorney, the FBI, the defendants, their lawyers, witnesses and potential witnesses including alleged victims . . . from making any extrajudicial statements to anyone, including the news media, concerning any aspects of this case. . . ."

Like a lot of other actions I would take later in the case, the gag order provoked an immediate controversy. The Democrats in Congress were eager to get to the bottom of the Watergate "caper," as it was then called. The General Accounting Office, an arm of Congress, had made several attempts to investigate the Republican campaign spending patterns, without getting very far. In the House of Representatives, Congressman Wright Patman, the outspoken Texas populist, was determined to launch an investigation of the campaign contribution checks that had moved through defendant Barker's account and of other Republican money that had been "laundered" in Mexico to conceal its origin. But his requests for Justice Department witnesses were refused. The Department officials said they wanted to "protect the rights" of the Watergate defendants, taking a position that John Dean says he urged on Henry Petersen, the head of the Department's criminal division. The White House had also leaned heavily on Congressman Gerald R. Ford to help head off the investigation. The day before my gag order was issued, Patman's committee voted against giving their chairman subpoena power. The restriction on public comment about the case obviously strengthened the hand of the administration in stonewalling Patman. The congressman was understandably frustrated. He still planned to call witnesses at a public session, so he dispatched a five-page letter asking that I reconsider the order.

Looking at his letter now, I must admire his instincts about what was going on in this case. The key paragraph stated:

> In discussing this case, we might as well face the practical situation as it actually exists. It is a fact that the Justice Department is an arm of the Administration about which most of this investigation centers. It is a fact that the futures of the high officials of the Justice Department are dependent upon political events and there is nothing to be gained by pretending that this situation does not exist. The Justice Department has, in recent days, attempted to intervene in matters before the Banking and Currency Committee and has attempted to use issues which are before your Court as an excuse to block and to encourage others to block proper legislative investigations. This heightens the probable damage from a broad interpretation of your order and it heightens the need for you to limit your order to those very specific charges in the indictments and not allow your order to be used for broader political purposes.

I agreed completely with the congressman. I had no intention of impeding in any way an investigation by Congress. I therefore modified the gag order, on October 6, making it clear that congressional activity and news media reporting were not meant to be affected. But it was too late for Patman. Hobbled by the vote denying him subpoena power, he was reduced to lecturing empty chairs, symbolizing the refusal of Mitchell, Stans, Dean, and Clark MacGregor, head of CRP, to testify. The United States District Court was left as the only branch of government trying to get to the bottom of Watergate.

In the absence of a congressional investigation, there was heavy pressure building to have the Watergate case tried before November, to get the facts out in the open before the American people cast their ballots in the presidential election. I have heard speculation that had the trial been held before the election, the results in November might have been different. I doubt that. With indictments returned in mid-September, the earliest we could have gone to trial would have been late October and as it turned out, the trial lasted about four weeks. To put it bluntly now, the cover-up was firmly in place that fall, and pushing the trial forward would not likely have broken the case before the election.

To me, furthermore, the important consideration was to have a fair trial, not a quick one. Despite the protests, I set the trial date for November 15. (More postponements became necessary and the trial did not actually begin until mid-January.) I was determined that the court procedures not get fouled up in the election campaign. And there were still a lot of problems to be straightened out before a trial could begin. The Democrats had filed a million-dollar civil damage suit against the Committee to Re-elect the President for alleged involvement in the bugging. The case was assigned, at random, to Judge Charles Richey of our court. I told Judge Richey directly that I didn't want him to hear that case until the criminal matter had been settled. I didn't think it was fair to have the civil case tried before the criminal case.

After the election, there were attempts to move the case out of the District of Columbia, based on the fact that the people of the District (along with the people of Massachusetts) had been the only ones to choose Senator McGovern over President Nixon. The intense press interest in the case, especially by the *Washington Post*, was also cited. I denied the motion. The idea that the way people voted would influence their judgment as jurors in a criminal case was nonsense to me. The defense attorneys, lacking much else to work with, also objected to my initial decision to use the big, ceremonial courtroom on the sixth floor of the courthouse for the trial. They argued that it would give the case a "dimension that doesn't normally exist in a trial," that having more spectators and press than usual present would be prejudicial to the defendants. That, too, was nonsense. Defense counsel thought that sequestering the jury would have the same effect. I overruled them again, hoping to insure that the trial would not be tainted by what the jurors read or heard.

A more serious problem was raised by defense counsel concerning an interview given to the *Los Angeles Times* by the government's key witness, Alfred Baldwin, the man who had monitored the bugging equipment from the Howard Johnson motel. Throughout the fall, the defense had tried first to get Baldwin to turn over a tape recording of the interview and then, when it was found that Baldwin had erased the tape, to get the newspaper itself to turn over its notes and recordings. The attorneys had a valid point. Baldwin had apparently spent five hours talking with reporters from the *Times*. The newspaper had printed a long story based on that interview. Defense counsel wanted to know if there were any inconsistencies between what Baldwin had told the newspaper and what he was going to testify to in court. In October, I issued a subpoena for the newspaper records. The paper, however, decided that under the First Amendment, guaranteeing a free press, they were protected from disclosing their sources. That didn't seem to me to be the issue. The source of the material was known—Baldwin himself. I felt the defendants had the right to try to impeach the credibility of their chief accuser. By December, the *Times* still hadn't complied with the subpoena. So just before Christmas, I found the *Times*'s bureau chief, John Lawrence, in contempt of court for failing to produce the requested material. I ordered Lawrence held in custody until he purged himself of the contempt, denying his lawyer's request that he be set free while my ruling was appealed. I felt strongly that the paper was putting its own constitutional rights ahead of the rights of the accused. The court of appeals freed Lawrence in a few hours. Several days later, Baldwin released the *Times* from an agreement to keep the notes and recordings secret, and the issue became moot.

I was much angrier about a problem that arose because of the aggressiveness shown by the *Washington Post*'s pair of investigators, Carl Bernstein and Bob Woodward. As the two later described the incident, Woodward went one day to the clerk's office in the courthouse and asked to see the lists of jurors and grand jurors. He was permitted to read them, but told to take no notes. He didn't take notes in the clerk's office, but instead memorized the names and sneaked off to the men's room to write them down. Early in December, the prosecutors—the only officials present at the grand jury hearing—reported to me that one grand juror had complained that he had been contacted at home by one of the *Post* reporters. Years and years ago, in the first sensational and highly publicized criminal trial I participated in as a young lawyer, I felt that the jury was influenced improperly by seeing newspaper accounts of the trial just as they began their deliberations. Ever since, I have been very sensitive about protecting juries from outside influence. When we finally went to trial in the Watergate case, I was to warn my marshals that if anyone said anything to the trial jurors, or let them see newspapers or any account of the trial, they, the marshals themselves, would go to jail. When I heard about the *Post* reporters' actions, I was ready to take them to task for their tampering. The newspaper had performed an invaluable public service in keeping the spotlight on the Watergate case, but now they had gone too far, interfering, I thought, with the administration of justice.

But the prosecutors urged me not to punish the reporters. They pointed out that the grand juror who was contacted had been faithful to his oath not to discuss the case and had turned the reporter away without saying anything. The newspaper's attorney, Edward Bennett Williams, assured me that the *Post* management had admonished the eager young reporters and that no further incidents like this would occur. I settled on a stiff lecture in open court, reminding everyone present that to approach a grand juror and solicit information about a case being investigated was to ask for a citation for contempt. I praised the grand jurors for their refusal to cooperate and recessed the proceeding to let the message sink in. In their later book about their reporting efforts, Woodward and Bernstein said that after that lecture, "they felt lousy . . . they had sailed around it [the law] and exposed others to danger. They had chosen expediency over principle. . . ." I agree. Had they actually obtained information from that grand juror, they would have gone to jail.

Six months had now gone by since the break-in. Despite all the pretrial problems, I was eager to get the case moving. We had gone beyond the original trial date because in late October I had hurt my back. While in New Orleans to attend a meeting of judges I had dinner one evening with my wife, Lucy, and some other judges and their wives in a French Quarter restaurant. Suddenly I felt a sharp pain in my lower back. I managed to get back to the hotel, but the next morning I could hardly get out of bed. When I returned to court the next week, my back hurt so much I had to pace back and forth behind my chair while on the bench, instead of sitting through the session. My doctors said I had a pinched nerve. Reluctantly, I had to put the Watergate trial over to January to give my back a chance to mend properly. When that delay was announced, I got my first taste of the kinds of public emotion this case was raising. I got a letter from a doctor in Philadelphia who called my delay of the trial "incredible." "I have seen and treated hundreds of patients," he went on, advising me that my back ailment could "be treated and cured . . . and does not prevent an ordinary citizen—a judge is, of course, not an ordinary citizen!!!—from attending to his business. If you can't do your job and perform your judicial duties—get out."

I suppose the doctor's anger was aroused by his desire to get to the bottom of the Watergate case. I shared his concern, even if I didn't accept his medical and career advice. There were still simply too many unanswered questions in the case. By that time, thinking about the break-in and reading about it, I'd have had to be some kind of moron to believe that no other people were involved. No political campaign committee would turn over so much money to a man like Gordon Liddy without someone higher up in the organization approving the transaction. How could I not see that?

These questions about the case were on my mind during a pretrial session in my courtroom December 4. In the course of a discussion about exhibits to be offered by the prosecutors, I asked Earl Silbert whether there was going to be any effort to trace the money found on the defendants.

"Yes, there will be, if the court please," he answered.

"Are you going to offer any evidence in this case—I take it

that everybody has read all of the newspaper items that are a matter of record in this case. I have read them in connection with the motion for a change of venue. Are you going to offer any evidence on the question of how the $25,000 check got into the possession of Mr. Barker?" I asked.

"Yes, Your Honor," Silbert said.

"You are going to trace that?" I asked.

"Yes," he said again.

"That is all in these exhibits, correct?" I asked.

"Not the $25,000 check as part of the hundred [exhibits] that have been premarked. We still have about fifty to one hundred further exhibits to mark and that will be part of those exhibits, if Your Honor please," he said.

"Are you going to try and trace, I think there is an item of $89,000?"

"Not necessarily from the source, but we will trace it part of the way through the system," Silbert said.

"Why don't you trace it from the source?" I asked. "Isn't that part of the case?"

Silbert said that getting a full accounting of the $89,000 Liddy obtained from Hugh Sloan would involve testimony of a person out of the country, over whom he didn't have subpoena power. He seemed to be backing away from that problem. I tried a more direct approach.

"Now on the question of motive and intent in this case, as you know there has been a lot of talk about who hired whom to go into this place. Is the government going to offer any evidence on the question of motive and intent for entering the Democratic National Committee's headquarters?" I asked Silbert.

"There will be some evidence if the court please," he responded.

"What do you mean by 'some evidence'?"

"Well there will be some evidence introduced. It is a question [on] which the jury will make the proper inference, it is up to the jury to accept or reject the evidence that we propose to offer, but there will be evidence we will offer from which a jury may draw, we think, an appropriate inference as to perhaps a variety of interests," Silbert said carefully.

I felt I was putting the prosecutors on notice about what the problems were going to be with their case. The indictment they had prepared was very narrowly drawn, and of course I don't criticize them for that. You should charge only what you can prove. And it's also true that, technically, they didn't have to prove a motive, only that the seven men were guilty of the charges against them. But the public was growing more and more suspicious. There had to be some reason these men had gone into the Watergate. Why not develop it? Why not get all the truth out and settle the question once and for all?

The point I was trying to make still didn't seem to be clear to the prosecutors. I returned to the question a few minutes later and was as direct as I could be: ". . . this jury is going to want to know somewhere along the line what did these men go into the headquarters for? What was their purpose? Was it their sole purpose to go in there for so-called political espionage or were they paid to go in there? Did they go in there for the purpose of financial gain? Who hired them to go in there? Who started this thing? There are a myriad of problems in this case that I can see coming up and so can you. They are going to want to know these things. . . . This is going to be one of the crucial issues in this case—why did they go in there? Who hired them, if somebody did hire them? And a whole lot of things are going to come out in this case in order to enlighten the jury—at least should come out as to the purpose for entry into the Democratic national headquarters. It is that simple."

The questions were obvious, but the answers weren't simple. I had no idea just how complicated it all was, how complex were the barriers being thrown up not just to keep the prosecutors and the court in the dark but to prevent the entire nation from finding out what had really happened.

I like Earl Silbert. I think he's a good lawyer. I wanted to be helpful, to share with him some of my experiences which I felt might give him some guidance through what was obviously a tough situation.

A few days before the trial started, he was in my chambers discussing an administrative problem unconnected with the Watergate case. I said to him, "Earl, look, you've got a great opportunity in this case if you go right down the middle, let the chips fall where they may. Don't let anybody put any pressure on you."

Before he left my office, I gave him a bound copy of the hearings conducted back in 1944 by a select committee of the House of Representatives into the activities of the Federal Communications Commission. I wanted the young prosecutor to know just how whitewashers were engineered. And I wanted him to know that I had had direct experience with cover-ups while serving as chief counsel to that committee.

The committee investigation included an examination of the FCC's role in the sale of two radio stations, one in New York City and one in Fort Lauderdale, Florida. In both cases, there were serious allegations that commission employees and others had misused their offices and power to force the transfer of the stations at lower than fair market prices.

I spent the better part of a year working on the case. And by the fall of 1944, I had brought enough witnesses and evidence into public hearings to establish a strong case against some former commission personnel, and others. But the hearings were proving increasingly embarrassing to friends of the Roosevelt administration. Rather than encourage a full airing of the facts, some New Dealers apparently decided to use their political muscle on Capitol Hill and, in fact, managed to convince a majority of the select committee to close the hearings to the public.

In my view, the purpose of the closed hearings was to cover up the true facts of the New York case. When the decision to move the hearings behind closed doors was made, I felt that my role as chief counsel had been compromised. It seemed to me that a majority of the committee was no longer interested in a real investigation and so during the last open session I announced my resignation.

"There is only one way I can try a case," I said then, "whether before a congressional committee or in a courtroom, and that is to present all the facts and let the chips fall where they may. . . . There is great public interest in this case. The press is going to print this. I know what is going to happen, and I don't want it on my conscience that anyone can say John Sirica, a resident of the District for many years, is a party to a whitewash. . . ."

The hearings continued in closed sessions after I left, but the majority found nothing wrong with the FCC's conduct in the New York case. I felt my prediction was correct: there had been a whitewash and a cover-up.

2
The Trial Begins

The ceremonial courtroom on the sixth floor was packed on the morning of January 10, 1973. Every available seat in the huge, high-ceilinged room was filled. The defendants and their attorneys crowded around two tables to my right; the government prosecutors, Silbert, Seymour Glanzer, and Donald Campbell at a table to my left. Artists from the television networks, with their large sketch pads and colored pencils, crowded in among the scores of reporters gathered to hear the beginning of the trial of the seven Watergate defendants. The usual rustling and shuffling caused by my marshal's call, "All rise," was magnified by the unusual number of people assembled to watch the proceedings. I felt very much alone as I took my place on the bench. Behind me on the raised second tier of the bench was the long row of now empty chairs used by the judges of the court when they sit in special sessions. From the massive gray marble wall behind those empty chairs, the stone figures of Moses, Hammurabi, Justinian, and Solon stared over my shoulder, adding to my own loneliness, but reminding me of the tradition of law I hoped would be upheld.

I was anxious to get started. We had picked a jury in two days, and they were now seated in the jury box to my left, waiting to hear the facts in the case. I was anxious that they hear *all* the facts. From the beginning, it was my hope that the trial would bring out the truth, that, within the framework of the law, the trial would be the forum in which the unanswered questions of Watergate would be answered. There was in Washington by then a strange mixture of cynicism and curiosity about the trial result. The case already had strong political implications, what with all the allegations about the involvement of people close to the Nixon campaign, including some in the White House itself.

The president, though not yet inaugurated for the second term he had won so easily over Senator McGovern, was acting very much like a man sure of his future. Only weeks before, he had ordered the Christmas bombing of North Vietnam. That action had provoked more protests against the war and had caused Senate Democrats to vote to cut off any further money for the war in Southeast Asia. The president had in turn warned the Senate that criticism of his efforts would only prolong the conflict. The president and his closest aides were in the midst of an attempt to centralize within the White House their control of the government, provoking protests from the affected government departments and agencies. And Nixon was asserting his right to "impound" funds voted by Congress for various spending projects with which he disagreed. The president was making few public statements, but when he did appear, Nixon sounded belligerent. That tone, coupled with his actions, led *Washington Post* columnist David Broder to describe Nixon as "tough and taciturn." Broder wrote in early January, "One cannot avoid the feeling that the tough Mr. Nixon may ultimately find he has made it tough on himself."

Although I had no feeling that the break-in case could involve the president himself, my instincts told me that if the truth came out, things could be difficult for some of the president's friends and assistants. And so, with my advice to Earl Silbert still fresh in my mind—and I hoped in his—I was eager to hear his opening statement. It is in those remarks that the prosecutors lay out, for the first time in public, their whole theory of the case they will try to prove. It provides the framework on which they will later place the evidence and the testimony they present to the jury.

For more than an hour that morning, Earl Silbert outlined his case. His presentation was a competent recital of the break-in events themselves. But, frankly, I was disappointed.

When Silbert got around to discussing the money found on the defendants and the source of that money, I hoped he would unravel some of the mystery of this case. Instead, Silbert told the jury:

Now the evidence that we will produce before you will show that Mr. Liddy from the time he received the assignment [to gather intelligence] until June 17 received about $235,000.

What did Mr. Porter [Herbert Porter, Magruder's deputy at the Committee to Re-elect the President] and Mr. Magruder receive in exchange or in return for that expenditure of funds? Mr. Porter received some information about an anticipated demonstration in Manchester, New Hampshire, from the left-wing group. He received a second piece of information about an anticipated demonstration in Miami, Florida, from a right-wing extremist group.

Mr. Magruder received some information from Mr. Liddy that instead of the 100,000 demonstrators they might expect at San Diego they could expect about 250,-000. And this caused a good deal of concern and was relied on partially by the Republicans as to why the convention site about the first week of May was transferred from San Diego, California, to Miami, Florida. That is the information they received.

We don't have any records, the government doesn't have any records as to what happened to the rest of that money given to Mr. Liddy but as you will listen to my opening statement you will listen also to the evidence received in court, the testimony of the witnesses, we will be able to account to you for approximately $50,000 of that money. We cannot account for the rest.

The money question lay at the heart of the case, naturally. Silbert made it clear, as everyone had already read in the newspapers, that the defendants had been paid by the president's campaign committee. Porter and Magruder and Hugh Sloan, the deputy at the finance committee, had all known about Liddy's assignment to gather intelligence. But Silbert said not a word about whether or not they had known in advance about the break-in and bugging. And the fact that only a small fraction of the money Liddy had been given had been traced signaled to me that Earl Silbert and the prosecutors hadn't yet found out the full story of the Watergate affair.

Silbert went on, leaving the impression with the jury that Liddy had somehow gone off on his own, had in effect misused the money and the authority that the president's campaign aides had given him. "Liddy was the boss," he repeated several times.

Silbert then turned to the question of motive, as I had urged a month before.

"Obviously, it was a political motive, political campaign," he said. "The operation was directed against the Democratic party, particularly Senator George McGovern, because of his alleged left-wing views. . . . The interests of the persons, the defendants in this case may vary, that is, the motivation of the defendant Hunt and defendant Liddy may have been different from the motivations of the four defendants from Miami, and they in turn may have had a different motivation than defendant McCord. Certainly the facts will suggest . . . to you, based on the information that we produce before you, it was a financial motive here, financial motive."

Silbert was now way off the mark. He went on to suggest that the Miamians were in bad financial trouble and needed the money Hunt offered them. He told the jury that McCord's private security company was in the red and that without the break-in money he would have "had a tremendous deficit in his business." The idea was apparently that these men had gone into the Democratic headquarters for the same reason a robber goes into a bank—they needed the money. This was the most limited view of the case it was possible to take, and it frustrated me. I recessed the trial for lunch.

When the afternoon session began, McCord's lawyer, Gerald Alch, a member of the Boston firm headed by the famous defense attorney F. Lee Bailey, got to his feet to speak for his client. He said that he was not going to dispute the fact that McCord was caught at the Watergate the night of June 17. "The question," Alch told the jury, "is why was he there? What was his intent in being there? What was his motive in being there? . . . The evidence will not show that Mr. McCord was present at the Watergate on the night in question for any type of financial reward or gain. . . . The existence of a criminal intent is a necessary ingredient of every crime. We will show that Mr. McCord had no criminal intent. We will show that Mr. McCord was not aware of all of those facts which might make his conduct criminal."

I had never met Gerald Alch before he appeared for McCord. He seemed to be a competent attorney, even though he was a bit theatrical and always seemed to be wearing heavy make-up to improve his appearance for the television cameras outside the courthouse. I thought that the question of motive that he raised was the right question. Alch's reference to McCord's not having all the facts was an interesting hint that perhaps Alch was ready to argue that McCord had been misled by higher-ups as to the purpose of the break-in and the authority behind it. Or perhaps he would contend that McCord was being made a scapegoat. That argument wouldn't excuse McCord's action, but it might get him some sympathy from the jury. I had used a similar argument myself years before, when I defended an officer of the Union Electric Company of Missouri who was caught red-handed making illegal payments to politicians and other public officials out of a company slush fund that had been organized by his superiors. But to make the argument work, Alch would have to name some names, to point the finger at others, higher up. He never did.

When Alch finished his opening statement, Henry Rothblatt rose. Rothblatt was representing the four Miamians, and he came to the job with a good reputation. He had successfully defended Colonel Oran Henderson against charges stemming from the Mylai massacre in Vietnam. Rothblatt was even more flamboyant than Alch. He wore a toupee and had a thin mustache that almost seemed to be drawn onto his upper lip with a pencil. He was given to great melodramatic speeches in the courtroom, and was the kind of lawyer who needs a tight rein from the bench to keep him from taking over the proceedings. He quickly painted his clients as the underdogs in the trial, men of little means, men with patriotic motives. He got so wound up that I had to urge him to get his emotions under control. "Keep on an even keel and don't let your blood pressure go up," I cautioned him.

Like Alch, Rothblatt raised the question of motive. This time, I took advantage of the opening and asked Rothblatt, "Is it your defense that they were taking orders from somebody, were ordered to go into the Watergate? Is this what you are going to show? . . . I wish you would get down to the basic issues here: why did they go into the Watergate? Tell the jury what you think the evidence is going to be."

Rothblatt, at a disadvantage either because he didn't know the full story or because his clients didn't want it told, continued to dance around the idea that the Miamians were simply following orders (Judge J. Skelly Wright, of the court of appeals, later described them as "footsoldiers" of the plot). The trial was only a few hours old, but I was already annoyed. Rothblatt took off on a rhetorical binge about "this temple of justice" and the "hysteria of overwhelming publicity" that brought an objection from the prosecutors.

"I think you have gone about far enough," I told Rothblatt. "If you want to argue these things later on and get dramatic about it, that is your business, but I don't want you to do it in the opening statement. . . . Let's get down to it. You have talked about motive. The government talks about motive. Of course, the jury is going to want to know why the men went in there. Let's get down to the details and find out why they went in there if you have some evidence as to that. That is one of the crucial issues in the case. *Who paid them?* Did they get any money to go in there? Was it purely for political espionage? What was the purpose? I think these are the things that might be discussed in a case like this."

Rothblatt ended with a little flourish, pleading for "a sense of objectivity and justice . . . the spirit of justice" and the "help of our supreme intelligence, the power that all of us have faith in," and then sat down.

3

Searching for
the Truth

"At this time, Your Honor," Howard Hunt's lawyer said after Rothblatt had finished, "Mr. Hunt wishes to withdraw his plea of not guilty and enter pleas of guilty to counts 1, 2, and 8."*

The attorney, William Bittman, announced that the prosecutors had agreed to the change of plea and were supporting it. Silbert said that after the plea was accepted, Hunt would be called before the grand jury for further questioning about "the involvement of others." I called a recess for fifteen minutes to think about the plea change. When I returned I advised Hunt—and the other defendants, in case they were thinking about pleading guilty—that my policy was usually to commit a defendant to jail, not release him on bond, after a guilty plea.

When we resumed the next day, Thursday, January 11, I announced that I was unwilling to accept Hunt's plea to only three counts of the indictment. My unstated feeling was that the government had a good case against Hunt on all the counts in which he was named. But just as important, I felt, was the way the partial plea would look to the public. The trial was the only place, at that time, where we could learn the truth of the Watergate case. If Hunt simply pleaded guilty, took his medicine, and went to jail, the chance that we

---

* The first two counts charged Hunt and the others with conspiracy and with burglary. Counts 3, 4, 5, and 8 related to the bugging of the Watergate office. Hunt was not named in counts 6 and 7, which charged McCord and the Miamians with possessing illegal eavesdropping equipment.

would ever find out what was going on in the case would be reduced.

"The court sees as an element of its discretion and as part of its duty proper representation of the public interest in justice. The court and the public have an interest in the just administration of the criminal laws and the court believes that such interest encompasses not only the substance of justice but also the appearance of justice," I said.

Bittman quickly said that Hunt would plead guilty to all six of the counts against him. I called Hunt before the bench and advised him of his rights, of the charges to which he was pleading guilty, and of the possible jail sentence he was facing in making the plea. Hunt appeared defeated. His wife had been killed in an airplane crash only a few weeks before. He was a pathetic figure standing there, a former CIA agent, a man of some literary talent who had produced a small library of spy novels, the father of four children and a resident of the posh Potomac suburb. Now, he was facing a long term in jail.

"Now, in your own words, I would like you to tell me from the beginning just how you got into this conspiracy, what you did, various things that you did so I can decide whether or not you are knowingly and intentionally entering this plea voluntarily with full knowledge of possible consequences," I told Hunt. Bittman objected, on the ground that Hunt would be going before the grand jury and that was the proper forum for more detailed questioning about his role. He was correct, so I asked Hunt if he waived his right to say in court all he knew about the case. He did, and another chance to get to the bottom of Watergate was gone.

"Has anyone threatened or coerced you into making this guilty plea?" I asked Hunt.

"No, Your Honor," he said.

"Has any promise of any kind been made to induce your plea of guilty?"

"No, Your Honor," he answered.

Because Hunt had fled after the break-in, was accustomed to foreign travel, and had used aliases while engaged in the break-in, I set bond at $100,000.

As he left the courthouse, Hunt told reporters who cornered him that as far as he knew, no higher-ups were involved in the affair.

The rest of that day's session was taken up with the beginning of the government's case against the remaining defendants. But there was a more important drama being played out behind the scenes. It came to my attention Friday morning. The four Miamians—Barker, Sturgis, Martinez, and Gonzalez—had been insisting that their lawyer, Rothblatt, assist them in pleading guilty. Rothblatt had refused. In court Friday, they asked me to permit them to replace Rothblatt with an attorney appointed by the court, who, they presumed, would follow their instructions. As the story was later told, Rothblatt was resisting the guilty pleas because he felt his clients were being pressured into following Hunt's example. I called Alvin Newmyer, a long time friend of mine and one of the leaders of the bar, to take over from Rothblatt. We adjourned for the weekend to let Newmyer get on top of his case.

Over the weekend, the *New York Times, Time Magazine,* Jack Anderson, and then the *Washington Post* ran stories alleging that Hunt was behind the proposed guilty pleas by the four men from Miami and that they were still being paid by someone, in return for their loyal silence. When we resumed the trial Monday morning, I cut off all newspapers for the jury; I could not trust that the marshal's editing would catch all of the growing number of Watergate stories. But I was eager to hear what the government would have to say about them. Seymour Glanzer declared that the news stories contained "certain innuendos and insinuations." He said the prosecutors had asked the defendants whether "in any manner, shape or form, directly or indirectly, or suggestively, they were coerced in any manner to enter this plea." They, of course, denied that they were coerced.

As with Hunt, I had no choice but to accept full guilty pleas, but the sudden departure of five of the seven defendants, especially in light of the published suspicions that they were being paid off to plead guilty, made me angry. I asked the four men to come before the bench. As I read the charges against them and advised them of their rights and of the possible sentences they faced, they all nodded nervously and answered "yes, sir" in chorus to my questions. I was determined that despite the pleas, I would make an attempt to find out what else they knew about the case. With the jury out of the room, I began.

"I want you to be straightforward with these questions. I want you to come forward in a truthful manner. I don't care who they might hurt or help, it doesn't make any difference to this court who you might mention or who it hurts or helps, just so you don't involve any innocent people. Do you understand that?"

"Yes, sir," they said in unison.

Turning to Martinez, I asked how he had become involved in the break-in. "I want to know specifics," I said. I asked whether he had broken into the headquarters for money, as Silbert had suggested in his opening statement.

"Money doesn't mean a thing to us, Your Honor," Martinez said.

"Do you know of anybody else that was involved in the breaking and entering into the Democratic headquarters either by being personally present or by being somewhere else? Do you know of anybody else, no matter who it might be?"

"No, I don't, Your Honor," Martinez said.

I then asked Gonzalez, "Who paid you for doing that, if anybody?"

"Nobody paid me anything, Your Honor," he said. "I do it because I believe what I did was the right thing to do." He went on to explain his love for Cuba.

"What did Cuba have to do with breaking in and entering the Democratic headquarters?" I asked.

"I don't know, that is what he told me and I believed him." he responded. He said Hunt and Barker had made that assertion.

So I asked Martinez if he had ever worked for the CIA.

"No, Your Honor," he answered, untruthfully.

"Never worked for them?" I asked.

"Not that I know of, Your Honor," he said.

"Who worked for the CIA here among the four of you?" I asked.

"None that I know of," answered Barker, obviously the leader among the group of four. Laughter spread through the courtroom at the absurdity of Barker's answer. Even Gordon Liddy roused himself from a nap at the defense table and joined the laughter. It annoyed me no end. The smart-alecky, cocky Liddy seemed only to be amused by the fact that he might be going to jail for breaking the law.

I then asked the four men if anyone was paying them for pleading guilty, if anyone had promised funds to support them while in jail.

"No one," they answered together, like a well-rehearsed choir.

I turned to Barker, my frustration still growing. I pressed him about the origin of the money, especially the $25,000 check he had cashed for Liddy. This was the check traced by the FBI during its investigation, given to the committee in the name of Kenneth Dahlberg.

"I want to know if you will tell me where did this money come from that was traced to your account—the trust account or your personal account—where did you get this money, these hundred-dollar bills that were floating around like coupons?" And then I asked where he later got the cash to pay his fellow burglars.

"Your Honor, I got that money in the mail in a blank envelope," he said.

"I'm sorry, I don't believe you," I answered.

After a few more attempts to get some answers about promises of clemency and payments, I gave up. Barker's silence had held.

With the number of defendants now reduced to two from the original seven, the attorneys for Liddy and McCord moved for a mistrial, arguing that the jury, which had been absent during the guilty pleas, would assume the missing five defendants had pleaded guilty and would therefore be biased against McCord and Liddy. I denied the motion, since it is quite common when several defendants are on trial for one of them to plead guilty, often even appearing as a prosecution witness against those remaining. Alch pressed the point nonetheless.

"I don't think there is any need to argue the point," I told him. "You have the record protected and if the court of appeals thinks that is error, that is their business, not mine. I am not concerned with what the court of appeals does. I am only concerned with what I do and if I do the right thing. I am not awed by appellate courts. Let's get that straight. All they can do is reverse me but they can't tell me how to try the case. All right, let's proceed."

The trial judge doesn't have the appellate judge's advantage of many days of contemplation before deciding questions of law. He has to more or less shoot from the hip. I like that kind of action, and I was not about to slow up the trial of Liddy and McCord out of fear of a possible reversal in the appellate courts. I followed my instincts, hoping I was right. I

have always been fairly outspoken on the bench, and sometimes I do get into a little trouble. A few minutes after the
exchange with Alch, I noticed that Liddy was talking with his
attorney, Peter Maroulis. As I mentioned earlier, Liddy's attitude annoyed me. I said to Maroulis, sarcastically, "I see
you're getting some good advice from your client, Mr. Liddy,
a former attorney."

Well, Liddy hadn't been found guilty yet and of course
hadn't yet been disbarred. Maroulis objected that Liddy was
still an attorney at law: "He is a lawyer and a member of the
bar of this court."

"I will admit that," I said. Fortunately, the jury wasn't in
the room, so no harm was done.

Through the second week of the trial, the prosecutors gradually developed their case, relying heavily on the testimony of
Thomas J. Gregory, a college student on leave for "off-cam-
pus study." Liddy and Hunt had recruited him to spy on
McGovern's headquarters, where, it turned out, Liddy had intended to put another phone bug. The government also
brought Alfred Baldwin to the stand, to describe his role in
the bugging operation at the Watergate. We took a half day
off on January 19, in observance of a government holiday declared by President Nixon in honor of his second inaugu-
ration. The jury was still sequestered, and I offered them a
room from which to watch Nixon's inaugural parade.

When we resumed for the third week, Baldwin was back
on the stand. One fact that interested me in his testimony was
that at one point he had personally delivered transcripts of
the bugged phone conversations to the headquarters of the
Committee to Re-elect the President. He told the court that
he could not remember to whom he had delivered the transcript, and that aroused my suspicions. I asked the jury to
leave the courtroom and addressed Baldwin: ". . . You
stated that you received a telephone call from Mr. McCord in
Miami in which I think the substance of your testimony was
that as to one particular log he wanted you to put that in a
manila envelope and staple it, and he gave you the name of
the party to whom the material was to be delivered, correct?"

"Yes, Your Honor," Baldwin answered.

"You wrote the name of that party, correct?"

"Yes, I did," he said.

"On the envelope. You personally took that envelope to the
Committee to Re-elect the President, correct?"

"Yes, I did," Baldwin said.

"What is the name of that party?" I asked.

"I do not know, Your Honor," Baldwin said.

"When did you have a lapse of memory as to the name of that party?"

Baldwin said he simply couldn't remember the name even though the FBI had given him several names to test his recollection. He said he handed the envelope to a guard.

"Here you are, a former FBI agent, you knew this log was very important?" I asked.

"That is correct," Baldwin said.

"You want the jury to believe that you gave it to a guard, is that your testimony?" I asked. Every time the path led to the CRP, something happened to memories. We took a recess.

The government finally brought officials of the CRP to the stand to speak for themselves. First was Robert Odle, head of administration for the committee. Then Herbert Porter, and then Jeb Stuart Magruder, deputy director, the highest official of the committee to testify at the trial. Silber certainly asked him the right questions:

"Mr. Magruder, did you ever give Mr. Liddy any assignment concerning the Democratic National Committee?"

"No," Magruder said.

"Did you ever receive any report of any kind from Mr. Liddy concerning the Democratic National Committee offices and headquarters at 2600 Virginia Avenue [the Watergate]?"

"No," Magruder said.

Magruder was as smooth as silk. He did not appear flustered or nervous. He is a handsome man, well dressed, well spoken. If you wanted a model of the respectable, responsible, honest, young executive, Magruder would be perfect. But listening to Magruder, Porter, and Odle, I was not impressed with the logic of their testimony. They simply put everything on Liddy. I still couldn't understand how the CRP officials could turn over that kind of money to someone without any accountability. It didn't make sense.

The next witness was Hugh Sloan, assistant treasurer of the Nixon campaign. He was the very picture of innocence—young, clean-cut, dressed conservatively, and speaking softly. He testified that he had handed Liddy the money personally, after first checking with his boss, Maurice Stans. He explained how he had given checks to Liddy to convert to cash and how that money was kept in safes at CRP headquarters. He, too, said he didn't know what the money he gave Liddy was to be used for.

I just didn't believe these people. The whole case looked more and more like a big cover-up. I was feeling pretty much alone in those days. I really had only my law clerk Todd Christofferson to talk to about the case. As yet, no Senate investigation had been authorized. With Sloan still on the stand, I realized that if I didn't step in fast, this whole parade would go by, right out of the courthouse, laughing at us. Perhaps some other federal judges would have limited themselves to ruling on objections. But one of the reasons I had always wanted to be a federal judge was that, damn it, nobody could stop me from asking the right questions. I didn't have to sit quietly by and watch this procession.

I didn't care how important Sloan or Magruder or Porter was. Liddy had been given a lot of money. Someone must have authorized the payment. Someone had to know what the money was for. Liddy had to be reporting to someone. Now here was Sloan, who had handled the money. I made up my mind very quickly, right there, to ask him some questions myself. I thought, "Listen, Sirica, this is your last chance." I sent the jury out.

"Mr. Sloan, I want to ask you a few questions. I am interested in the checks—Mexican checks. Let's go back there a few minutes. One for $15,000, one of $18,000, one for $24,000, one for $32,000. We call them the Mexican checks, correct?"

"Yes, sir," Sloan answered.

"You turned these over to Mr. Liddy, is that your testimony?"

"Yes, sir."

"What was the purpose for turning them over to him?"

"My concern in this case as with the subsequent Dahlberg check was the fact that under the law and our interpretation on the way we normally handle our affairs, there is a gift tax deduction, but it would raise questions for instance if a $15,000 check were deposited in any particular account. The intent of the donor was for us to handle his donation in such a way we would not incur for him any gift tax liability; therefore the conversion to cash was an administrative method of breaking these checks down into the elements that would fall beneath the contribution limit." This was also the committee's way of getting around the campaign-spending limits and reporting requirements, but I was more interested in Liddy's involvement.

"Did he [Liddy] tell you how he was going to convert them to cash?" I asked.

"No, he just indicated he would convert them."

"What made you believe he could convert these checks to cash?"

". . . I asked him what the best way to handle this would be and we mutually agreed to conversion to cash. And he merely offered at that point and indicated he had some friends who would do it."

"Tell me about the $25,000 check, the Dahlberg check."

"This was presented to me by Secretary Stans in his office sometime the week following April 7. He indicated to me at that time it represented a contribution pre-April 7 from a donor whose name he gave me and the conversion to cashier's check was just one method of transporting it from Florida to our offices."

"You said, I think, and correct me if I am in error, that you turned over a total of about $199,000 in cash?"

"That is the best of my recollection."

"Where did you get that money from?"

"Cash contributions to the president's campaign."

"What was the purpose of turning over $199,000 to Liddy?"

"I have no idea."

"You have no idea?"

"No, sir."

"You can't give us any information on that at all?"

"No, sir. I was merely authorized to do so. I was not told the purpose."

"Who authorized you to turn $199,000 over to Liddy in cash?"

"Jeb Magruder."

"For what purpose?"

"I have no idea."

"This is a pretty sizeable piece of money."

"In and of itself, but not in the context of the campaign."

"You didn't question Mr. Magruder about the purpose of the $199,000?"

"No, sir, I verified with Mr. Stans and Mr. Mitchell he was authorized to make those."

"You verified it with who?"

"Secretary Stans, the finance chairman, and I didn't directly but he verified it with John Mitchell, the campaign chairman."

"This $199,000 could be turned over to Mr. Liddy, is what you are saying?"

"Not the specific amount but Mr. Magruder, his authorization was authorization enough to turn over the sums in question."

"Did anybody indicate to you by their action or by words or deed what this money was to be used for?"

"No, sir."

"You are a college graduate, aren't you?"

"Yes, sir."

"I think you majored in history, is that correct?"

"That is correct."

"What did you know about Mr. Liddy before the time all this cash was turned over to you?"

"I just had known him through hearsay, that he had been an employee with the Treasury Department, a former FBI agent, a former consultant at the White House."

"You said you got some receipts, didn't you, for this money you turned over to him?"

"No, sir, I did not say that."

"Did you ever get any part of the $199,000 back?"

"No, sir."

"You didn't know what Mr. Liddy used it for?"

"No, sir."

"No idea?"

"No, sir."

"He was never questioned by you or anybody else what he did with the $199,000?"

"No, sir."

"You said you saw him coming to headquarters, I suppose near you, on the morning that these five men broke in the Democratic headquarters, is that correct?"

"Yes, sir."

"You knew, did you not, Mr. Liddy was a former FBI agent?"

"Yes, sir, I heard that."

"You know, don't you, it is common knowledge at least before you can be appointed as an FBI agent you must be a member of the bar?"

"Yes, sir."

"Still, you tell the court and the lawyers you saw him passing you, went by you—yes or no?"

"Yes, sir, that is correct."

"And he said something like—repeat what you claim he said."

"To the best of my recollection what he indicated was: 'My boys were caught last night. I made a mistake by using somebody from here, which I told them I would never do. I am afraid I am going to lose my job.'"

"What did you say to that?"

"He was in a hurry and just passed on. I don't believe I responded."

"Here is a man, a former FBI agent, makes a remark to you, . . . which was incriminating, which indicated to any person I think with common sense that he had done something wrong, didn't that flash in your mind when he said, 'My boys got caught last night, I used somebody from here, which I shouldn't have done'? Didn't that occur to you it was mighty strange you knew nothing about this matter, that you didn't see anything wrong with that remark?"

"Not at that point in time, no, sir."

"When did it dawn on you there might be something wrong or improper about this remark, Mr. Sloan?"

"When I read the *Evening Star* that evening."

"What did you think when you read the *Evening Star* that evening?"

"I thought a possibility might exist of involvement in this matter."

"Shortly after that you retained a lawyer?"

"No sir, it was in July, approximately a month later."

"Was this before you were called down to the United States attorney's office?"

"Yes sir."

"When did you resign [from the CRP]?"

"July 14."

"For what reason?"

"Essentially my reasons for resigning involved the Watergate matter and personal considerations, the fact that it was obvious to me at that point that the FBI was making an investigation, that there would probably be others. I had undertaken this job because I felt I could make a significant contribution to the president's campaign and it became abundantly clear to me in that month's period it would be impossible to discharge those duties because of the increasing pressure I knew would be forthcoming, the internal situations that existed in the committee at that time; my wife was pregnant and in view of what I assumed would be adverse publicity, and so forth, I did not want to put her through those additional burdens."

"As a matter of fact, Mr. Sloan, be perfectly frank about the matter, you resigned primarily because you were concerned about the Watergate matter, isn't that the truth of the matter?"

"Yes, sir, I believe that is what I said."

"Did you ever testify before the grand jury?"

"Yes sir, I did."

"Were you granted immunity [from prosecution]?"

"No, sir."

I had asked Sloan forty-two questions. He had changed his testimony slightly by remembering that Liddy on the morning after the break-in had said he used "somebody from here which I told them I would never do. . . ." In Sloan's earlier testimony, "told them" had been omitted. It would have been interesting, at that point, to ask Liddy to identify "them." But, of course, Liddy wasn't about to testify. Sloan had also said that Stans and Mitchell had approved the payment to Liddy. I did feel that my questioning of Sloan had raised questions about his credibility. I decided later that I should read the questions and answers to the jury so they could make their own judgments. Silbert objected mildly, offering to recall Sloan to ask some of the questions I had asked. I was afraid, however, that Sloan would have a lapse of memory.

Despite the little bit that Sloan did add to our understanding of the Watergate break-in, and despite my skepticism at the time, he was essentially telling the truth. He had had no knowledge of the break-in, and as soon as he saw the attempt to keep the committee's involvement secret, he quit. It was really Magruder who was, at least among those in the courtroom, the key to the cover-up. His was the testimony that placed resonsibility directly on Liddy, and that denied any role for him himself or others at the committee in what Liddy planned and did at the Democratic headquarters. I have often wondered what would have happened if I had taken over the questioning of Magruder, instead of Sloan. My instinct, however, was to follow the money.

Liddy's attorney, Peter Maroulis, was naturally unhappy about my plan to read the Sloan testimony to the jury. He felt it would place undue weight behind Sloan's recollection of Liddy's remarks on the morning after the break-in. Maroulis hadn't even cross-examined Sloan, as was his right. He wanted Sloan off the stand as soon as possible. But it was my duty to give as much information to the jury as they needed to understand the case. I told Maroulis: "I exercise my judgment as a federal judge and chief judge of this court and have done it on many occasions and in the presence of the jury examined witnesses where I thought all the facts were not brought out by counsel on either side. As long as I am a federal judge I will continue to do it. As I said, the court of appeals might reverse me in this case, I am not concerned with that. I am concerned with doing what I think is the right thing at the moment and that is the reason I am going to read this testimony to the jury. I couldn't care less what happens to this case on appeal, if there is an appeal. I am not interested in that. I am interested in doing what I think is right."

Of course, I overstated my feelings about the court of appeals. I *was* concerned that the trial be without reversible error. But I had to walk the line between that concern and my duty to get the facts out. I was willing to take the risk.

The exchange with Maroulis seemed to amuse Gordon Liddy.

"Now your client is smiling," I said to Maroulis. "He is not impressed with what I am saying. I don't care what he thinks either. Is that clear to you?" That wasn't an overstatement. I didn't see anything funny about the entire case. It is a most serious matter when an election campaign can't be conducted without bugging and burglary being part of the strategy. Liddy had had all the advantages. He had been to college. He was a lawyer. He had been an FBI agent. He had run for Congress. He wasn't like the poor Miamians who had been sold a bill of goods. Now he was turning himself into the great, silent martyr. I thought, "Let him be the martyr." I have always been amazed that the men around the president tolerated someone like Liddy. I have often thought of Liddy making his bizarre proposals in the meeting with Mitchell. The attorneys general I had known, men like Herbert Brownell, would have locked Liddy up right then and there.

4

Verdict

After the first week of the break-in trial, the crowds that had packed the ceremonial courtroom thinned out. We moved downstairs to my regular courtroom, on the second floor of the courthouse. Because my courtroom is smaller, it is easier for the jury and for me to hear the witnesses and the attorneys. I felt much more comfortable back in my usual surroundings. Beneath the desk top, to the right and left of my high-backed chair, are small stools on which I can prop my feet while listening to the proceedings. On the top of the desk, but hidden from the courtroom by the oak paneling on the front of the bench, is a small white lamp that could be lighted by my clerk, sitting below, to alert me to his messages. With a button next to the lamp I can turn on a small light on the clerk's desk to get his attention. The entire front of the bench is lined with steel to protect me if someone goes berserk in the courtroom and starts shooting. There is also a special switch beneath the bench which lets me sound an alarm in the marshal's headquarters down the hall, should I need a lot of help in a hurry.

The break-in trial itself was relatively short, by some standards. In 1960, I presided over a $90,000,000, treble-damage antitrust suit brought by a large trucking company against all of the major railroads in the country. Those proceedings lasted ten months, accumulated 23,000 pages of trial transcript, and included over 1,800 exhibits, setting a local record for length and complexity. Aside from minor annoyances—I repeatedly asked the marshal to tell a woman reporter to stop chewing gum, a habit that for some reason annoys me—the only trouble in the Watergate trial was the absence of much real information about who was behind the break-in. On January 29, Earl Silbert made his concluding argument to the jury. He laid out the details of the evidence against McCord and Liddy. His theory about the case hadn't changed in the month since his opening statement. Silbert told the jury:

"We heard [from] a number of people from the Committee [to Re-elect the President] that Liddy did have a lot of money, a lot of money had been put into his hands. Where did it come from? He had been authorized to engage in certain intelligence gathering activities, and you heard from Mr. Magruder and Mr. Porter what the purpose was.

"But he [Liddy] wasn't content to follow out what he was supposed to do. He had to divert it. He had to turn it."

Silbert was of course limited to arguing what he had proved. Magruder and Porter had laid full responsibility for the break-in on Liddy. Silbert followed that view. Arguing that McCord was in the scheme for the money, Silbert told the jury, "He and Liddy were off on an enterprise of their own."

I have often thought about Earl Silbert and the way he handled the case. I certainly don't believe he and his colleagues were in any way dishonest. Some have accused Silbert of being part of the cover-up, but I don't believe that. I think Silbert was naïve and somewhat inexperienced. I don't think that it ever occurred to him that people like John Mitchell, Jeb Magruder, and Herbert Porter would lie before a grand jury. Previous to the break-in trial, when Silbert had called Mitchell before the grand jury, Mitchell had testified under oath that the first time he heard of Liddy's bugging scheme was the morning after the arrests at the Watergate. I also think Silbert was too trusting of his superiors in the Justice Department. After the break-in trial, when Silbert was bringing witnesses before the grand jury in his investigation of the cover-up of the break-in, he appeared one day in my office and asked if I would permit the grand jury to leave the courthouse to take a witness's testimony. Without asking why, I said no. "Bring the witness here," I told him. He then said he had hoped that would be my answer. He later told me that the witness in question was John Mitchell, scheduled in the spring of 1973 for his second appearance before the grand jury. Silbert told me the request had come to him from Henry Petersen, head of the criminal division in the Justice Department. Had I been in Silbert's shoes that spring, I'd have said no to Petersen myself.

In the spring of 1974, Silbert was nominated to become United States attorney for the District of Columbia to succeed his boss, Harold Titus, who had resigned. The Senate Judiciary Committee held several days of hearings and received a great many objections to Silbert's nomination. But Special Prosecutor Archibald Cox, who took over the Watergate investigation from Silbert in the spring of 1973, and Cox's successor, Leon Jaworski, both vouched for Silbert's honesty. Senator John Tunney, a Democrat from California, called me one day for my opinion on Silbert. I told him that I would stand on what I said in court, but that perhaps he had made some mistakes in his handling of the case because of inexperience or naïveté. Silbert had often said that his plan was to get convictions in the break-in case, then obtain a grant of immunity from further prosecution and bring all the figures in the case back before the grand jury to give the full story behind the break-in. Had he strongly suspected that some of his witnesses—such as Magruder and Porter—were not telling the whole truth, he could have asked me to take over the questioning to press them further on certain points. Usually, a prosecutor must vouch for the credibility of the witnesses he calls. Silbert obviously didn't want to get tough with his own prosecution witnesses. But he could easily have turned that part of the interrogation over to the court by indicating to me that he had doubts about the credibility of some of the witnesses. Before Silbert's appointment was confirmed, he was named acting U.S. attorney by a unanimous vote of the fifteen active judges on our court. I swore him in then, and I wouldn't have done so if I thought he was dishonest.

Silbert's problems were in some ways, however, fewer than those faced by the lawyers for Liddy and McCord. Silbert could at least put on a convincing case against these two remaining defendants. He had plenty of evidence, plenty of witnesses, and little trouble in getting the basic case against the two men laid out. But Maroulis and Alch couldn't even let their own clients take the stand; there was apparently too much to lose in cross-examination by the government. They couldn't plead with the jury that their clients were being made scapegoats, since their clients were determined at that point to protect the higher-ups who had authorized the Liddy plan. Both Maroulis and Alch were reduced to what I thought were desperation defenses.

Before the end of the trial, Alch submitted a memorandum seeking my approval for an argument to the jury which he hoped would save McCord. Alch had decided to try a "defense of duress" based on the notion that McCord, as director of security for the CRP, was so concerned about the possibility of bodily harm to Republican speakers, to the president, and to CRP officials resulting from bombings and demonstrations by radicals that he broke into the Democratic headquarters to get information on such threats.

"So your argument, in effect, is this," I said to Alch; "he had the right to bug the Democratic National Committee."

"No, it is not, Your Honor," Alch said.

"Wait a minute," I said. "It is all mixed in there, all involved, intertwined, put it that way that he had a right to use an assumed name, he had a right to rent a room or two rooms over at the Howard Johnson's, he had a right to go to Miami, Florida, and hire, or help to finance these four men to come up and break in.

"But you have to consider the background of the defendant, Mr. McCord. He is a former CIA agent. He is a former FBI agent. He is involved in a business that has been operating, probably still is; he is an educated man, he is not unintelligent. . . . If we ever instruct the jury along those lines, particularly in view of the evidence in this case, anybody could come in and put up a defense like that.

"What was there to indicate to Mr. McCord that he had the right, legal right, to take the law in his own hands? All he had to do was to pick up the telephone and call the head of the Secret Service or the FBI or the chief of police and say, 'Now look, I am the head of the security for the Committee to Re-elect the President and we have got certain information the president is in danger.' He knows. Mr. McCord knows as well as anybody else that one of the functions and probably most important things the Secret Service does or one of their functions is to guard the president. . . .

"Now this man is not a youngster or a kid from the ghetto. This man is not in a position where he is standing outside and he sees a fire in a house and he thinks he can go in there and rescue somebody but by doing it he has to break the door down to get in there which would be either unlawful entry or a crime, that isn't the situation here, Mr. Alch. Nowhere near like that. . . . I don't think it takes a whole lot of common sense, frankly, to come to the conclusion that if this kind of defense were permitted in this particular case, well, I just think it would be ridiculous, frankly, to put it bluntly."

In his final argument, Alch nonetheless walked close to the line I had rejected. He argued that McCord's motive was not criminal. "James McCord did not think he was doing anything wrong and he should not be convicted," Alch maintained. "Mr. McCord's intention was completely inconsistent with a criminal motive. He was concerned with violence and he was trying to stop it." Which, of course, may have been true. It would have been easier for Alch to make that contention before the jury if he had been able to say that McCord knew that John Mitchell, the former attorney general of the United States, had approved the Liddy plan to bug the Democrats.

Maroulis, Liddy's attorney, had an even tougher time. I felt sorry for him. His client was more difficult than McCord. He had clowned at the defense table, making a great show of his lack of concern about his future. Maroulis was reduced to picking at the testimony of some of the government's witnesses, arguing that there was a reasonable doubt that their identification of Liddy as the ringleader was correct. He stretched his argument to include the possibility that Liddy didn't really know all that Hunt was up to and that when he was at his observation post during the actual break-in at the Democratic headquarters he was indeed simply observing, not knowing that bugs were being installed on the telephones. Maroulis, I suppose, did as much as he could with the little he had to offer in Liddy's defense.

At 4:32 on the afternoon of January 30, the jury retired to the jury room to consider its verdict. At 6:10 P.M., they returned. The woman chosen by the jury as forelady handed the verdict to the deputy clerk, James Capitano. Cappy had been working with me for years. He made my job easier in hundreds of ways. To my great grief, he died in 1978; he had still been working from time to time at organizing the incredible volume of materials accumulated in the Watergate case. He was a loyal and dedicated public servant and a great courtroom clerk.

Cappy took the verdict, as he had hundreds of times in my court, and read:

"In the case of the United States of America v. George Gordon Liddy and James W. McCord, Jr., Criminal No.

1827-72, members of the jury your Forelady says as to the Defendant George Gordon Liddy, Count One, Guilty; Count Two, Guilty; Count Three, Guilty; Count Four, Guilty; Count Five, Guilty; Count Eight, Guilty.

"As to defendant James W. McCord, Jr., Count One, Guilty; Count Two, Guilty; Count Three, Guilty; Count Four, Guilty; Count Five, Guilty; Count Six, Guilty; Count Seven, Guilty; and Count Eight, Guilty."

There had never been any doubt about that result, at least in my mind. A few days later, I set bail for McCord and Liddy at $100,000 each. I said in court, "I am still not satisfied that all the pertinent facts that might be available—I say might be available—have been produced before an American jury." Looking back, that was quite an understatement.

Who could have guessed just how high up this case would reach? Who could have guessed that the most powerful men in the American government would soon begin a desperate struggle not just to save their own careers but to avoid going to jail? The possibility that the rest of the facts in this case, the very facts I felt were still unknown, could lead to the first resignation of an American president in our country's history, was not even dreamed of at that time. Yet, as the trial ended, those were the very results that were being foreshadowed.

But at that time, all that was left of the Watergate case, as far as I could see, was the sentencing. I scheduled March 23 as the day the defendants would reappear in my court to find out what time they would have to serve for their crimes. I knew right away that I would give all seven men fairly stiff sentences; for the next month and a half, I thought about just how to go about sentencing them, knowing of course that Silbert was planning at some point to bring them back before the grand jury for further questioning.

In early March, my old friend Clark Mollenhoff, of the *Des Moines Register* and *Tribune*, sent me a copy of a column he had written. He had been following the trial on the West Coast of William Wooldridge, an army sergeant major accused of skimming large sums of money from service clubs in Vietnam. Mollenhoff pointed out that after Wooldridge pleaded guilty, the presiding federal judge in that case, Warren J. Ferguson had delayed sentencing and had asked for a presentencing report on the co-operation the sergeant major had given to a Senate subcommittee investigating the scandal. The idea of delaying sentencing further and making the sentences conditional on some show of co-operation appealed to me. None of the defendants had made any move toward telling the full truth about the crime. I began to wonder if, given a bit more time now that all seven had either pleaded guilty or been found guilty, they might reconsider their defiant stance.

I thought about Judge Ferguson's tactic for quite a while. Soon after I received Mollenhoff's column, I called the judge's secretary and asked for a copy of the court proceedings for my own study. The more I thought, the more I liked the idea. But over a month had gone by since the trial, and I felt I couldn't just delay the sentencing further.

One morning in the third week of March I awakened about three o'clock. For some reason, a federal statute I had used years before in a narcotics case had come to my mind. I made a note of its substance, and later that morning I asked Todd to do some research. The exact law I had been thinking of turned out to be Title 18, *United States Code* Subsection 4208(b).* It reads:

> If the court desires more detailed information as a basis for determining the sentence to be imposed, the court may commit the defendant to the custody of the Attorney General, *which commitment shall be deemed to be for the maximum sentence of imprisonment prescribed by law* [my emphasis], for a study as described in subsection (c) hereof. The results of such study, together with any recommendations which the Director of the Bureau of Prisons believes would be helpful in determining the disposition of the case, shall be furnished to the Court within three months unless the Court grants time, not to exceed an additional three months, for further study. After receiving such reports and recommendations the Court may in its descretion (1) Place the prisoner on probation as authorized by Section 3651 of this Title, or (2) affirm the sentence of imprisonment originally imposed, or reduce the sentence of imprisonment and commit the offender under any applicable provision of law. The term of the sentence shall run from the date of the original commitment under this section.

* Subsection 4208(b) of Title 18 of the *United States Code*, was recodified at Title 18, *United States Code* Subsection 4205(c) by the Parole Commission Act of 1976.

That law gave me a legal way to put off final sentencing until I could see just how well the defendants co-operated in the pending investigation. Also, I felt I needed more information than had been furnished to me by the probation officer in his presentencing reports.

5

The McCord Letter

I was far from alone in my skepticism about the facts brought out at the trial. The Senate of the United States had voted to investigate the Republican campaign tactics. The press was full of caustic comment about the trial itself and the government's handling of it. I had been practicing law for thirty years. I had handled cases involving political scandals. I had seen cover-ups in operation before. I had been chief counsel to a congressional committee and had quit when the matter was whitewashed and the investigation stifled. I was often described as an "obscure federal judge," and that was true, but I was not a damn fool. I brought along years of trial experience when I came to the bench back in 1957. I knew the Watergate case was not what the trial in January had made it seem. But by late March, with the trial over, there didn't seem a lot more I could do about it.

There were many things I didn't know at that time. I didn't know that thousands of dollars had been paid to the very defendants who had just appeared before me, to keep their mouths shut. I didn't know that such a pleasant and successful man as Jeb Magruder, the second-ranking official at the Committee to Re-elect the President, had actually committed perjury in my courtroom to protect himself and his boss, the former attorney general of the United States, John Mitchell. I didn't even begin to think that the president of the United States, Richard Nixon, a man for whom I had campaigned twice when he was running for vice-president, had ordered, within days of the break-in in June 1972, the very cover-up that now had me angry and frustrated.

There were people who already thought I had gone too far during the trial in trying to get the truth out. Some believe that a federal judge should sit quietly by, like an umpire at a ball game, and make sure the trial runs smoothly, simply ruling on objections raised by the attorneys. I knew the case would go to the court of appeals in the event of a conviction, because of the way I had handled myself, but I have never believed I should sit through a trial with one eye cocked toward the court of appeals. They can tell you after the fact whether you made a mistake, but they can't tell you how to conduct a fair trial at the moment when you have to make a decision from the bench. I have always wanted trials over which I presided to be above all fair—fair to the defendants, to the government, and to the public. The trial of the original Watergate defendants was fair to the defendants and the government, but it didn't seem to me to have been fair to the public. They were asked to believe a theory about how our election process had been corrupted that made no sense to me whatsoever.

On Tuesday morning, March 20, I was working on what at the time I thought would be one of my last tasks in the Watergate case. I had scheduled the sentencing of the defendants for that Friday and had already decided that in one last attempt to get the truth out, I was going to impose provisional sentences on five defendants who had pleaded guilty. I planned to tell them that one factor in determining their final sentences would be their co-operation with the Senate committee, the grand jury, and the prosecutors. I had given up on Liddy, who had napped and grinned his way through his own trial. I was going to give him a tough sentence. Also, I was prepared to give McCord a substantial sentence. The courthouse press had dubbed me "Maximum John," a nickname Harry Rosenthal of the Associated Press told me had been coined by a lawyer who had never appeared in my court. It was true that, unlike some other judges, I didn't believe in giving white-collar criminals lighter sentences than others. Maybe the chance to avoid some time in jail, I thought, would jog the memories of Hunt and the others. It was the day after my sixty-ninth birthday, and although I was still upset by the way the trial had gone, I was looking forward to the end of the case and to getting a little rest.

At about one thirty that afternoon, I opened the door to the reception room to give a message to my secretary, Mrs. Alease Holley. As I walked through the doorway I saw one of my law clerks, Richard Azzaro, standing in Mrs. Holley's office talking to James McCord. I was shocked. I have a strict policy of not meeting with defendants in criminal cases. Any improper contact between me and a defendant could lead to a mistrial. And here was McCord, whose jail sentence I had just been writing, right in my office.

McCord looked like a modestly successful businessman. He was wearing a conservative suit, white shirt, and dark tie. His demeanor suggested that of a salesman who had come to call on a prospective customer, not a man whose future hung in the balance, who faced the prospect of going to jail, who feared that he was being manipulated by powerful people for their own purposes.

He stood calmly beside Mrs. Holley's desk, his back to the door which opened out to another small anteroom; this in turn opened onto the long corridor that led away from my office. He was not at all surprised to see me or nervous in my presence. I motioned to Azzaro to come into my chambers. "What the hell's going on out there?" I asked. My policy against talking to defendants included the law clerks, and they knew it.

Azzaro explained that McCord had walked into the office alone and unannounced. McCord had said he wanted to talk to me, but Azzaro put him off with a small untruth about my being out to lunch. Azzaro also told him that I never spoke to defendants, especially, he added nervously, to convicted criminals. McCord was calm and under total control, and true to his CIA and FBI training and background, gave away none of his emotions. McCord produced a white envelope and asked that it be given to me. His lawyer, McCord told Azzaro, was not aware that he was trying to see me.

I had come up through the rough-and-tumble police and criminal courts in Washington during the 1920's and 1930's, defending and prosecuting at one time or another gamblers and rum runners. Although it may seem improbable now in the fairly strict and orderly atmosphere of a federal court, the first thing that came to my mind was that I was being set up by McCord. "Suppose," I thought, "he has ten thousand dollars' worth of those famous hundred-dollar bills in that envelope and is trying to make it look as though I were accepting a bribe?" In the light of what we now know was going on to maintain the cover-up, perhaps my instinct wasn't so far off.

I told Azzaro to send McCord to his lawyer or to his probation officer with whatever message he was trying to deliver. I called the U.S. attorney's office to get Earl Silbert, who was prosecuting the Watergate case, and his boss, Harold Titus. I was still worried about protecting myself, and I thought, "Hell, I can't do any better than to call the U.S. attorney."

Within an hour, James D. Morgan, a probation officer, had delivered McCord's envelope to my chambers. Silbert and Titus had come to my chambers. I called in my court reporter, Nicholas Sokal, and my two law clerks, Azzaro and Todd Christofferson, as witnesses. We carefully described McCord's visit, so that Sokal could make an official record of what had happened. Titus and Silbert, however, quickly excused themselves from the proceeding. They felt that since McCord's own attorney wasn't there, it would not be proper for them to stay. I asked them to wait in the reception room outside my chambers. Later, I was glad they had left.

During my years on the bench, I had tried to discipline myself never to display emotion, for fear of letting the jury know how I was reacting to witnesses. My clerks say I kept a poker face as I opened McCord's envelope. But inside, I was anything but calm.

The envelope contained two letters. The first was disappointing. It was a copy of a letter McCord had written to the *New York Times* denying a story they had published the day before linking him to "strong arm tactics." I never figured out whether McCord wanted me to know the story was in error or whether he included it by mistake.

The second letter was addressed to me. It was neatly typed, with only a few errors, on McCord's white stationery. I read it silently to myself first, maintaining my poker face, but I flushed as I realized what McCord was saying. Then I read it aloud:

"Certain questions have been posed to me from Your Honor through the Probation Officer, dealing with details of the case, motivations, intent, mitigating circumstances. In endeavoring to respond to these questions I am whipsawed in a variety of legalities.

"First, I may be called before a Senate Committee investigating this matter.

"Secondly, I may be involved in a civil suit.

"Thirdly, there may be a new trial at some future date.

"Fourthly, the Probation Officer may be called before the Senate Committee to present testimony regarding what may otherwise be a privileged communication between defendant and judge, as I understand it.

"If I answered certain questions to the Probation Officer it is possible such answers could become a matter of record in the Senate and therefore available for use in the other proceedings just described. My answers would, it would seem to me, violate my Fifth Amendment rights and possibly my Sixth Amendment rights to counsel and possibly other rights. On the other hand, to fail to answer your questions may appear to be noncooperation and I can therefore expect a much more severe sentence.

"There are further considerations which are not to be lightly taken. Several members of my family have expressed fear for my life if I disclose knowledge of the facts in this matter either publicly or to any government representatives. Whereas I do not share their concerns to the same degree, nevertheless, I do believe retaliatory measures will be taken against me, my family and my friends should I disclose such facts. Such retaliation could destroy careers, income and reputation of persons who are innocent of any guilt whatever.

"Be that as it may, in the interest of justice and in the interest of restoring faith in the criminal justice system which faith had been severely damaged in this case I will state the following to you at this time which I hope may be of help to you in meting out justice in this case."

It was clear McCord was going to talk, to break the silence that had frustrated me and millions in the country ever since the break-in itself. I began to think, "This is it, this is it, this is the break I've been hoping for." I read on:

"1. There was political pressure applied to the defendants to plead guilty and remain silent.

"2. Perjury occurred during the trial of matters highly material to the very structure, orientation, and impact of the government's case and to the motivation of and intent of the defendants.

"3. Others involved in the Watergate operation were

not identified during the trial when they could have been by those testifying.

"4. The Watergate operation was not a CIA operation. The Cubans may have been misled by others into believing it was a CIA operation. I know for a fact that it was not.

"5. Some statements were unfortunately made by a witness which left the Court with the impression that he was stating untruths or withholding facts of his knowledge when in fact only honest errors were involved.

"6. My motivations were different than those of the others involved but were not limited to or simply those offered in my defense during the trial. This is not the fault of my attorneys but of the circumstances under which we had to prepare my defense.

"I would appreciate the opportunity to talk with you privately in chambers. Since I cannot feel confident in talking with an FBI agent, in testifying before a grand jury whose U.S. Attorneys work for the Department of Justice, or in talking with other government representatives, such a discussion with you would be of assistance to me. I have not discussed the above with my attorneys as a matter of protection for them. I give this statement freely and voluntarily fully realizing that I may be prosecuted for giving a false statement to a judicial official if the statements herein are knowingly untrue. The statements are true and correct to the best of my knowledge and belief."

As I read McCord's signature, I couldn't wait to get Todd Christofferson alone to talk this over. McCord, although he did not name names and was somewhat vague, was indicating not only that he was ready to expose the cover-up but that the cover-up was so extensive that he didn't even trust the FBI or the prosecutors. I ordered the record of the proceeding in my chambers sealed. I decided immediately that no one else was to know about the letter and instructed all present to remain silent about it. I called Titus and Silbert back into my chambers and told them I had decided to seal the proceeding until I could give it further consideration. I thanked them for coming by, and they left. After everyone else was gone, I looked up at Todd, who was to serve as my right arm throughout the Watergate case, and broke into a big grin. The first thing I noticed about the letter was that it was dated the nineteenth, my birthday.

"This is the best damned birthday present I've ever gotten," I said. "I always told you I felt someone would talk. This is going to break this case wide open."

Unlike the other men charged in the break-in case, McCord was not willing to go to jail to protect those who had approved the operation. Despite repeated promises from the White House that he would serve no more than a year in prison, he was refusing to go along with the cover-up. He was devoted to his family and concerned about the effects of the situation on them. The questioning by the probation officer before sentencing had aroused McCord's apprehension even further. In addition, the White House operatives had angered him right from the beginning of the cover-up that followed the break-in. He had seen an attempt to make the CIA the scapegoat for the operation against the Democratic headquarters. McCord had been a CIA employee for nineteen years and was still fiercely loyal to "The Company." In late December, 1972, he had threatened the White House that should the effort to blame the CIA continue, "every tree in the forest will fall. It will be a scorched desert." McCord had even telephoned two foreign embassies in Washington in the fall of 1972, knowing the phones in the buildings were being wiretapped by the FBI. His plan was to ask the government to disclose these wiretaps, taking advantage of the law requiring the prosecutors to reveal any such information involving a defendant. He was betting that rather than disclose the secret taps, the government would drop the case against him. That scheme had failed, and as the time for his sentencing drew close, he decided to come clean.

I was determined to keep his letter secret until it could be read in open court. My instinct was that if handled that way, as a surprise, it would have more impact. That way, I thought, the Justice Department would not dare to ignore it. They would have to get to the bottom of it. It was not that I distrusted Silbert or Titus personally; I just didn't want to take any chances. The first reaction to the letter from the Justice Department, I think, confirmed the wisdom of that judgment.

Late March was a difficult time for those close to Richard Nixon. The day after I received the McCord letter, John

Dean had his famous March 21 meeting with the president, in which he warned of "a cancer on the presidency." At the same meeting, we later discovered, the president approved—or at least seemed to approve—more payments to the defendants to buy their silence. The night of the twenty-first, $75,000 was paid to Howard Hunt, through his lawyer, by an agent of the White House. At about the same time, the president was forcefully asserting his right of executive privilege to prevent the congressional examination of his aides both in the upcoming Watergate hearings and in the difficult confirmation process L. Patrick Gray was facing in his appointment as director of the FBI. The day McCord wrote his letter, Senator Sam Ervin, who was to head the Watergate investigation on the Hill, announced he would put White House aides in jail if they defied committee subpoenas. The next day, White House press secretary Ronald Ziegler denounced Ervin's threat as "sensationalism." On the twenty-first, Attorney General Kleindienst ordered Patrick Gray to refuse to answer any more questions about the FBI handling of the Watergate investigation, but his order was too late, since Gray had already testified that he had sent eighty-two investigative reports from the FBI to John Dean in the White House. On the twenty-second, Gray testified that Dean had lied to the FBI when asked after the break-in whether Howard Hunt had a White House office.

Pressure was mounting on those in the White House who had obstructed justice during the investigation and trial of the seven men I was about to sentence. And I knew that I had in my possession a document that would increase that pressure. For three nights, I barely slept at all, worrying about the letter leaking, worrying about how to handle it in court, and wondering what would happen next.

Sentencing of the break-in defendants had been set for Friday the twenty-third. That occasion was the first opportunity I had to make McCord's letter part of the trial record. That morning, I awoke at three thirty. All of us who knew about the letter were extremely nervous. My law clerk Richard Azzaro was still suspicious of the letter and of McCord. He was a former police officer, trained to take precautions. He ordered Charles Artley, the marshal, to check McCord for weapons and pills prior to the opening of court, fearing that if what occurred in the courtroom didn't please the old CIA man, he would try some dramatic stunt. Artley took McCord into the grim little cell block behind my courtroom and searched him thoroughly.

I tried to be as nonchalant as possible as I entered the courtroom. I said a pleasant good morning and announced that I had a "preliminary matter" to take up. As I stated that I had received a letter from McCord, and asked for the sealed envelope, the courtroom hushed. I've never been in a room so full of people that was so quiet. I began reading the letter in as even a voice as I could manage. Azzaro kept his eyes on McCord, seated in the courtroom. As I read, Azzaro remembers, McCord seemed to slump lower and lower in his chair, as if a great tension had been released. It was clear that I was doing what he wanted; making the matter public. I learned later that McCord hadn't even fully trusted me; he had given Bob Jackson, of the *Los Angeles Times,* a copy of the letter in return for a promise to print it if I didn't take some action.

Four or five minutes passed before I got to McCord's numbered charges about political pressure and perjury. As I worked through them, an excruciating pain began to build directly in the center of my chest. It was nearly more than I could bear, but I couldn't quit before the end of the letter. I finally finished the letter and quickly called for a recess. As I hurried off the bench, the reporters flooded toward the double swinging doors at the back of the courtroom. The dam had broken.

Back in my chambers, I stretched out on a sofa. Harry Kelly, of the *Chicago Tribune,* and Dan Thomasson, of the Scripps-Howard papers, came into the office and urged me to see a doctor. But as I relaxed, the pain subsided. My doctor told me later that I was a victim of fatigue and nervous tension. I felt much better after about twenty minutes and went back to the courtroom to pronounce sentence on Liddy and the other defendants. I put off sentencing McCord at the request of his attorney, who was as surprised as the others by the letter.

I tried to get some rest that weekend. While I was relaxing, others began to pick up important portions of the burden of investigating Watergate. I had told Sam Dash, chief counsel of the Senate Watergate committee, that he would be interested in seeing Friday morning's court proceedings. He was in court that morning, and within hours he was meeting with McCord to find out just what he knew.

Sunday, the *Los Angeles Times* printed a story saying McCord had named White House counsel John Dean and Jeb Magruder as two men close to Nixon who knew about the Watergate break-in in advance. (He was wrong about Dean; Dean only knew that Liddy and Hunt were authorized by Mitchell to gather intelligence information for the Committee to Re-elect the President). The White House quickly issued a denial on Dean's behalf, but remained silent about Magruder, signaling that any attempt to protect him had been abandoned.

Within days after the letter was made public, the U.S. prosecutor, Silbert, reconvened the grand jury and was ready to call McCord, Hunt, and Liddy for further testimony about who had authorized the break-in.

The letter had set off shock waves not just in the press but among the conspirators in the White House. Dean was on the phone all Friday morning giving his evaluation of the letter to various people in the White House. He told the president that it would cause "lots of heat, little foreseeable legal effect." The president remarked to Dean that the young counsel had been right a few days earlier in predicting someone would crack, but he seemed relieved that it was McCord and not Hunt who had come in out of the cold. Apparently Dean and others, immersed in the legalities of their cover-up, discounted McCord's letter because his knowledge of the involvement of higher-ups was mostly secondhand. This, they hoped, made all its assertions hearsay and hence inadmissible in court.

That view was shared, at least in public, by the U.S. attorney general, Richard Kleindienst. In a statement to the press on Monday, March 26, Kleindienst minimized the importance of the McCord letter, declaring that it contained "nothing new so far that was not covered by our investigation. . . . I'm just as certain as I can be that Magruder and Dean didn't know anything about it [the break-in]."

In private, his view was a good bit different. I was in my chambers on the twenty-sixth when a letter from the attorney general was hand-delivered to me. It said:

DEAR JUDGE SIRICA:

The investigation and trial of the case of *United States of America* v. *George Gordon Liddy, et al.,* the so-called Watergate case, has brought into question the credibility and responsibility of the criminal justice system. Perhaps this is unavoidable in a case of such large political connotation; and, as a consequence, the Department of Justice and the United States Attorney's office has been extraordinarily careful to insure that this case was handled in the most competent fashion possible.

Outstanding lawyers of unimpeachable integrity have been assigned to the trial team and I am confident they have performed with the utmost dedication. I am in no position to assure you that every aspect of the case has been unmasked. I can assure you, however, that every defendant against whom sufficient evidence had been developed has been indicted and tried. And as you are well aware, the Department of Justice, through the United States Attorney's office, was prepared to carry on this investigation after the convictions entered in this case. Arrangements had been made to bring those defendants into the grand jury after sentence to attempt to compel additional disclosures under a grant of immunity. In these circumstances I consider it most unfortunate that, when the opportunity presented itself for the development of additional information, the defendant McCord was not immediately referred to the United States Attorney's office so his statement could be taken by the proper authorities.

I am well aware of the statements you have made, both in public and in private, that you consider it your obligation to uphold the credibility of the criminal justice system. We, too, and I speak for the United States Attorney's office and the entire Department of Justice, consider the discharge of our criminal justice responsibilities among the most important entrusted to public servants. I want to assure you that in this case, as in all others, the Department of Justice will make every effort to carry out its responsibilities and to prosecute those involved to the fullest extent of the law.

Sincerely
RICHARD G. KLEIDIENST
Attorney General

The letter infuriated me. I had just been through a month-long trial that had failed to answer the most important questions about the Watergate break-in. Five defendants had pleaded guilty rather than answer these questions. The other two had refused to testify in their own defense. The prosecutors, after what the government said was a thorough investigation, couldn't trace the money paid to the burglars. Now, with McCord's letter we had a break in the case. I had been assuming that the Justice Department would be delighted. I was wrong. The attorney general of the United States was criticizing the release of the McCord letter. He was rapping the judge for making the letter public, for turning up the heat under those who had been unwilling to talk or who had testified falsely in court and before the grand jury. You would think he would congratulate me.

McCord's letter and his distrust of the government had put the prosecutors and the Justice Department in a bad light. Kleindienst must have thought it necessary to defend himself and the department. But at the time I had no idea just how concerned the highest officials of the Nixon administration were about the letter and the case in general. I did not know, for example, that Kleindienst himself had been less than helpful to the investigation. The morning after the break-in, when the police still didn't know of Liddy's and Hunt's involvement, Liddy had cornered Kleindienst at the Burning Tree Country Club and passed along what he claimed was a request from John Mitchell to get the five burglars released from jail. Kleindienst wisely refused, but he did not inform anyone of the Liddy visit or the claim that it was on Mitchell's order. It took several tries by the prosecutors, when they reopened their investigation after the reading of the McCord letter, to get Kleindienst finally to tell the full story of the Liddy visit.

What caused Kleindienst to criticize my handling of the McCord letter? What would he have done with the letter? The reading in open court certainly didn't deprive the prosecutors of McCord's information; it simply made it available to everyone at the same time. We had learned from L. Patrick Gray's Senate testimony that FBI reports had been sent to the White House from the beginning of the Watergate investigation, despite suspicions that men close to the president were involved. We learned later that the FBI investigation itself had been carefully limited by the White House. We also learned later that officials of the Nixon campaign had lied before the grand jury and in my courtroom. Apparently, in March 1973, the men close to President Nixon weren't satisfied with those measures. It seemed from Kleindienst's letter that they wanted to control the judge as well. I am not saying that the prosecutors or the Justice Department would have buried McCord's letter. They couldn't have succeeded anyway; McCord had seen to that by giving a copy to the *Los Angeles Times*. But Kleindienst's public evaluation of the letter was not encouraging. At the least, it is clear that no one close to Richard Nixon in those days liked surprises.

Except for the few people present when I read the McCord letter in my chambers, no one knew what it said until I revealed it in court. But there are indications that something about the letter was known in the White House the very day I received it. The tape of a remark made by Richard Nixon to Haldeman on March 20 gives this hint of what the president knew: "McCord didn't want to go to jail [unintelligible] jail sentence [unintelligible] decided to talk. I said, 'What the hell's he doing?' "

By Wednesday, March 28, the assessment of damage from the McCord letter was still under way. A taped phone conversation that day between Kleindienst and White House aide John Ehrlichman shows that the attorney general had a pretty good idea where McCord's letter might lead:

EHRLICHMAN: O.K. Now the President said for me to say this to you: That the best information he had and has is that neither Dean nor Haldeman nor Colson nor I nor anybody in the White House had any prior knowledge of this burglary. He said that he's counting on you to provide him with any information to the contrary if it ever turns up and you just contact him direct. Now as far as the Committee to Re-elect is concerned, he said that serious questions are being raised with regard to Mitchell and he would likewise want you to communicate to him any evidence or inferences from evidence on that subject.

KLEINDIENST: With respect to them, unless something develops with these seven people who were convicted, all those people testified under oath before a grand jury and their testimony was not contradicted and until something comes along, I think this fellow

McCord, if he has something besides his own testimony, then you'd have to do it. . . . he's facing a long jail sentence and he has all kinds of motives to say all kinds of things, but I also pointed out that most of the people, well, these people who were involved were interviewed by the FBI and they testified under oath before a grand jury to the contrary of what McCord is saying. But I understand the President's direction.

EHRLICHMAN: He's concerned about Mitchell.

KLEINDIENST: So am I.

The two went on to discuss the problem Mitchell's involvement would cause for Kleindienst and other Justice Department officials, most of whom had been appointed by Mitchell. Kleindienst said a special prosecutor might have to be named. Ehrlichman seemed relieved to hear that I wouldn't be the one who would appoint a special prosecutor, but rather the president. Ehrlichman then wondered whether the court or the Justice Department seeks immunity for grand jury witnesses, plainly concerned that McCord or the other defendants might talk more. Kleindienst explained that it was the prosecutors who asked for the immunity and that they now really had no choice.

EHRLICHMAN: What progress are they [the prosecutors] making right now, have you had a reaction on it?

KLEINDIENST: Well, the last time I talked to Henry [presumably Henry Petersen, head of the Justice Department's criminal division and the supervisor of Silbert and Titus] Monday because of Sirica's sentencing procedures it got a little boxed up. Sirica is really lousing this thing up. . . .

Some months later, a transcript of that conversation between Kleindienst and Ehrlichman appeared in the *New York Times.* Kleindienst called to apologize, and we had a cordial conversation. I had known him for years and in fact liked him a great deal; I had attended his swearing-in when he replaced Mitchell as attorney general. But to this day his letter makes me angry. I was so damned mad the day it was delivered that I shouted at my law clerk, "Get him on the phone, get him down here. Let him come into my courtroom and say that in person." It took me three days, even with the patient counsel of my friend Judge Matthew McGuire, to cool off enough to write a restrained response. I wrote that I appreciated his "stated desire to protect our criminal justice system." And I added, "Referring, however, to your apparent disappointment with my decisions concerning information provided to the court by the defendant, James McCord, I must say that I cannot agree with your views. It was, and continues to be, my firm conviction that the letter in question should have been made a part of the record of this case as it was."

Within a month of that exchange of letters, Kleindienst resigned his position as attorney general, when it became clear he had a major conflict of interest in pressing the prosecution of John Mitchell for his role in the Watergate break-in and cover-up. He left the Nixon administration the same day as did Haldeman and Ehrlichman. A year later, Kleindienst was permitted by the Watergate special prosecutor's office to plead guilty to a misdemeanor for falsely testifying before the Senate Judiciary Committee. He had told the committee no political pressure had been put on him to settle the controversial antitrust suit against the International Telephone and Telegraph Corporation. In fact, the president himself had told Kleindienst to halt the case. He was fined $100 and sentenced to thirty days in jail; then both penalties were suspended and he was placed on unsupervised probation for a short time by another judge on our court. But it always seemed to me that Kleindienst's letter was typical of the behavior that got the Nixon White House into so much trouble. They were more interested in protecting their friends than in serving justice.

Within days of the McCord letter, the conspirators in the Watergate cover-up began seeking legal counsel. Each of the conspirators worried about what McCord would tell the grand jury and the Senate committee. Magruder and Dean were soon meeting with the prosecutors, bartering their testimony for favorable treatment.

Before long, Magruder and the government lawyers agreed to an arrangement whereby Magruder would plead guilty to one criminal charge in the case that would involve his role in the planning of the bugging and in the subsequent cover-up. As part of the agreement, he would become one of the government's chief witnesses in any later trials. Fred LaRue, an aide to John Mitchell, was also quick to see the implications of the McCord letter. Without even bothering to hire an attorney, he approached Earl Silbert and told the full story of his part in the case. He eventually pleaded guilty to one count of conspiracy to obstruct justice and, like Magruder, was later a key government witness.

I remember a Herblock cartoon that appeared in the *Washington Post* the week after the McCord letter was made public. It showed President Nixon sitting at a table, a crown on his head, his fingers in his ears. On the table was a pie. Flying around the pie were birds wearing burglars' masks. The caption read, "When the pie was opened the birds began to sing."

Columnist Joseph Kraft wrote that same week, "A sudden flurry of developments has transformed the Watergate affair from a sideshow into a political bomb that could blow the Nixon Administration apart. . . . What all this means is that the issue is obstruction of justice by a systematic cover-up at the highest levels."

In my opinion, this case would never have been broken if McCord had elected to stand pat and had not written the letter to me. That's my conclusion. Once that letter was made public, the parade of people trying to protect themselves began. This was just the beginning of the end. But there was no stopping it.

6
Sentences and Appeals

After reading the McCord letter to a stunned courtroom on the morning of March 23, I began the sentencing.

Liddy came first. His attorney rose to offer a few facts about Liddy's professional history which he thought might be relevant. He pointed out that Liddy had been to Fordham University and Fordham Law School, had been a first lieutenant in the army, and had worked for the FBI from 1957 to 1962. While in the FBI, he had received several commendations from J. Edgar Hoover, and he had once served on a team of agents that captured one of the nation's ten most-wanted men. Liddy was a prosecutor in Dutchess County, New York, for two years and had led the raid on drug guru Timothy Leary's estate. He had run for Congress in 1968, losing narrowly. He had served the secretary of the treasury as a special assistant for organized crime and had been on the Presidential Task Force for Drug Abuse. "Mr. Liddy's life has been one of public service, it has been very deeply involved in the law," his attorney said. All of which seemed only to make more reprehensible what Liddy had done.

"The Court believes knowing and deliberate violation of laws deserves a greater condemnation than a simple careless or uncomprehending violation," I said as I began Liddy's sentencing. ". . . From the evidence presented in the course of these proceedings, the Court has reached the opinion that the crimes committed by these defendants can only be described as sordid, despicable, and thoroughly reprehensible."

I went on to say that given the background of the defendant, rehabilitation wasn't the purpose of the sentence, nor, I said, was a desire for reprisal: "In this matter, the sentences should be imposed with an eye toward a just punishment for the grave offenses committed and toward the deterrent effect the sentences might have on other potential offenders."

I asked Liddy, now for the second time that morning, if he had anything to say.

"Nothing at all, Your Honor," he replied.

For the six counts on which he had been found guilty, I sentenced Liddy to a term of from six years eight months to not more then twenty years in jail, and fined him $40,000.

Howard Hunt's lawyer detailed his client's long career with the CIA, including his assignments abroad, his role in the attempted overthrow of Fidel Castro, his role in the successful coup against the leftist government of Guatemala in 1954. Hunt himself made a moving plea: "Since the Watergate case began I suffered agonies I never believed a man could endure and still survive. I pleaded guilty as charged of my own free will. Humbly with profound contrition I ask Your Honor to look beyond the Howard Hunt of last June 17 to my life as a whole and if it please the Court, to temper justice with mercy. My fate and that of my family and my children is in your hands."

I was touched by Hunt's statement, especially considering the death of his wife and the fate of his four children. But, in fact, Hunt's fate was in his own hands.

I read the statute concerning provisional sentences, and then imposed maximum sentences on Hunt and the four Miamians, as the statute required at this point. For Hunt, the maximum came to thirty-five years. For Barker, Sturgis, Martinez, and Gonzalez, it was forty. I explained that eventually, in imposing the final sentences, I would take a number of factors into consideration. Their voluntary pleas of guilty—I still thought these pleas had been voluntary—were to their benefit. "On the other side of the scale is the fact that none of you have been willing to give the government or other appropriate authorities any substantial help in trying this case or in investigating the activities which were the subject of this case," I pointed out.

"Now I want to speak plainly about this matter. You will no doubt be given an opportunity to provide information to the grand jury which has been, and still is, investigating the Watergate affair and to the Senate Select Committee on Presidential Campaign Activities.

"I sincerely hope that each of you will take full advantage of any such opportunity," I said.

I quoted a section of Judge Ferguson's remarks in the Wooldridge case and then added, "Now I believe that the Watergate affair . . . should not be forgotten. Some good can come from a revelation of sinister conduct whenever and wherever such conduct exists."

The sentences created a great furor immediately. There seemed to be an almost deliberate attempt to misunderstand and to misrepresent what they were. The law, after all, was quite clear. The statute provided that maximum sentences be imposed for the period during which further study was going on. I never had any intention whatsoever of putting those men in jail for thirty to forty years. To be sure, I have always leaned toward stiffer sentences than some of my colleagues on the district court, especially for white-collar crimes, but the outcry about the provisional sentences always ignored two facts: that they were provisional, and that they were required by the statute I had used to put off final sentencing. Even President Nixon, in his memoirs five years later, called the sentences "an outrage." I remember that back on April 30, 1973, President Nixon, then trying to save himself from the Watergate scandal, told the nation I was "a courageous judge." I wonder why he didn't tell the nation then that the sentences I had imposed on March 23, 1973, were outrageous. I guess he "misspoke" himself, as he did frequently during that period. In a radio speech a few days before I set the provisional sentences for the defendants, the president had described his own anticrime program, which included the death penalty for some offenses and mandatory minimum sentences with no bail for others. He condemned "soft-headed" judges who did not impose what he thought to be sufficiently tough sentences. When it came to these seven defendants, however, the president's sense of justice must have been tempered by his own closeness to the crime.

In November 1973, I imposed final sentences on Hunt and the Miamians. Hunt was given a term of thirty months to eight years. Barker received eighteen months to six years. Gonzalez, Martinez, and Sturgis each got a term of one to four years. At the same time, McCord was sentenced to one to five years. I later reduced all the sentences, except Hunt's. He served 31½ months in jail. None of the others served more than 14 months. In 1975, Liddy filed a motion for a sentence reduction. But in the intervening period, Liddy's situation had actually grown worse. Within weeks of the original sentencing, I found him in contempt of court for refusing to answer questions before the Watergate grand jury. He was later tried and convicted in connection with the break-in at the office of Daniel Ellsberg's psychiatrist. After that he was found guilty of contempt of Congress for refusing to testify before a congressional committee. Except for the sentence for contempt in the grand jury proceeding, the sentences in all of these cases were to run concurrently with the one I had originally imposed. Two years later, in considering his plea for a sentence reduction, I concluded that Liddy had shown not the slightest remorse or regret for his actions.* There was no hint of contrition or sorrow, nor had he shown any willingness to assist in the search for the truth behind Watergate. Finally, in 1978, having served about five years in prison, Liddy was released when President Carter commuted his sentence.

I cannot say that the sentences I imposed on these seven defendants helped break the Watergate case. McCord had no idea what sentence I would give him when he wrote his letter. But it was clear that he trusted me, and knew from watching me at his own trial that I was not content simply to sit back and tolerate a half-hearted attempt to get to the bottom of the matter. That had been obvious from my questioning of the Miamians after their guilty pleas and especially from my questioning of Sloan. And it was that intervention in the trial that provoked the strongest criticism. I hadn't had to wait for the trial, however, to begin to hear questions about my fitness to handle this case.

A couple of years before the break-in trial, a Washington lawyer turned "investigative reporter" set out to rate all the judges in our area. He decided I was inadequate because of "carelessness." His article was revived as other reporters began to write about me before the trial. I am told there was also a fair amount of concern that as a conservative and a Republican, I would not be inclined to press too hard in the Watergate case.

After the trial, the criticism was of about the same sort. Some feared that I had been careless in handling the case and that the verdicts would be reversed on appeal. Others felt that I hadn't gone far enough in questioning some of the defend-

---

* The text of the opinion is in the Appendix.

ants and thus had missed a chance to expose the whole cover-up. And some liberals, who before the trial had feared I would be too friendly to the defendants because of their connection to the president's campaign committee, were now outraged by my questioning of the defendants and by the sentencing. Naturally, I was quite sensitive at the time to all this second-guessing. Not many people outside of Washington had ever heard of John Sirica before all this. Now everybody was reading that I was too tough, or too careless, or too conservative. In the end, a trial judge has only himself to rely on.

The criticism outside the court didn't mean much except that it hurt my feelings. I felt it was unjustified. The real test came in the appeal filed after the trial by Peter Maroulis, Liddy's lawyer. He challenged the way we had selected the jury, the reading to the jury of two bench conferences, the admission into evidence of a statement by a witness who heard Liddy say he was fired by the CRP for refusing to cooperate with the FBI, and a few other points. The heart of his appeal, however, was based on my over-all conduct in questioning witnesses and then reading the relevant parts of that questioning to the jury. Maroulis specifically challenged the reading of the Sloan testimony. We had to wait a long time, nearly a year and a half, before the United States Court of Appeals ruled on Liddy's appeal. But the wait was worth it. The District of Columbia Circuit Court of Appeals has the reputation of having some of the finest judicial minds in the country. It is sometimes even referred to as the "mini-Supreme Court." Also, it is a decidedly liberal court, generally very concerned that defendants' rights be protected. When the case got to the court of appeals, Judge Harold Leventhal wrote the opinion for the seven judges, unanimously affirming my judgment and rejecting each of the points made by Liddy's attorney. What has always seemed to me important about the break-in trial is that those in other parts of the government who were trying to push the facts aside—to stop the search for truth at a point where only the seven original defendants had been brought to justice—encountered an active and objective judiciary that was beyond their control. The fact that despite his fears about the Justice Department and even the prosecutors, McCord sensed that he could trust the courts, and would be protected by them, changed the course of the Watergate case. The opinion written by Judge Leventhal seems to me to protect the role of an active *and* fair judicial system.

The precepts of fair trail and judicial objectivity do not require a judge to be inert [Leventhal wrote]. The trial judge is properly governed by the interest of justice and truth, and is not compelled to act as if he were merely presiding at a sporting match. He is not a "mere moderator." As Justice Frankfurter put it, "federal judges are not referees at prize-fights but functionaries of justice." . . . A federal trial judge has inherent authority not only to comment on the evidence adduced by counsel, but also—in appropriate instances—to call or recall and question witnesses. He may do this when he believes the additional testimony will be helpful to the jurors in ascertaining the truth and discharging their fact-finding functions. What is required, however, are reins of restraint, that he not comport himself in such a way as to "tilt" or oversteer the jury or control their deliberations.

Applying these general principles to this particular case, we conclude that, although certain problems are presented by the action of the trial judge in reading to the jury from the testimony first taken from Sloan outside the jury's presence, his overall course was neither an abuse of his judicial function nor a denial of fair trial. . . .

We cannot say that the trial judge abused his discretion either in the questioning of Sloan, or in submitting to the jury the information elicited in its absence. . . .

Liddy's contention of prejudice would have more force if it were predicated on questioning by the judge that had passed outside judicial discretion to an inquisitorial undertaking. While it is ironic that Judge Sirica, concerned as he was with perjury at the trial, did not question Magruder, whose perjury was later developed in the massive, historic inquiry by Congress, this development serves to underline that the judge's questioning of Sloan did not portray a wide-ranging probe of witnesses that transcended the judicial province. We are not here concerned with any indications the judge may have given before or after the trial as to the public need for a broader investigation. So far as the questioning of Sloan is concerned, this was apparently triggered by what seemed to be the improbability of his account as given. It may well be that all that was involved as to Sloan was naivete, and the willingness of an A.B. in history, not versed in law or economics, to follow the instructions of senior officials of the political committee, including a former cabinet member, and to make large disbursements of cash without further inquiry. But the matter must be judged prospectively; there was certainly basis for the trial judge's concern at the time that Sloan was holding back, and that supplemental questioning was needed to prevent pollution by perjury of the trial he was conducting. . . .

Separate problems are raised by the procedure used to present Sloan's testimony to the jury, as distinguished from the fact of its presentation. Sound and accepted doctrine teaches that the trial judge should avoid extensive questioning of the witness and should rely on counsel to develop testimony for the jury's consideration. Here the trial judge not only failed to seek an alternative to personal intervention, he declined the prosecutor's request to elicit the additional testimony by further questioning of Sloan in the jury's presence. A reopening of the record to enhance appraisal of credibility would ordinarily be furthered by presenting the witness, and his demeanor, if available. The problems are certainly not resolved by the trial judge's comment that Sloan "might have a lapse of memory, I don't know."

Nevertheless, we feel that the procedure did not infringe upon the requirement of fair trial. The impact of the extensive questioning by the trial judge was muted. He did not interrupt the direct examination with his inquiries. Reading a record already made tends to have less impact than question and answer by the witness. The judge's editing excised comments that might have been construed as an expression of an opinion regarding the credibility of the testimony given by Sloan.

The case would stand in a different posture if defense counsel had urged the trial judge to recall the witness for additional testimony. But here it was the prosecutor and not the defendant who asked that Sloan testify in person. Appellant's counsel clearly indicated that he did not want any further testimony from Sloan. . . .

We turn to appellant's claim that the reading of Sloan's testimony deprived him of his right to cross-examination. The trial judge afforded appellant an opportunity to cross-examine Sloan and counsel steadfastly declined to exercise this right. He urges that the right to cross-examine includes the right to refuse to cross-examine, and that this right was undercut by the trial judge's action. This is the kind of point that establishes resourcefulness of counsel, but not legal error. Although defense counsel may exercise his discretion regarding cross-examination, he has no absolute right to prevent further testimony by a witness.

In sum, defense counsel has no right to preclude recall of a witness. A judge not only has power of recall, but latitude to use it to remove or dilute the pollution of a trial by testimony he believes to be perjurious or highly questionable. He may supplement the examination by counsel in order to draw out more information from a witness and to enhance the perspective for appraising his testimony. The public interest in safeguarding a record from taint is particularly keen when the case involves the integrity of the nation's political system—as can fairly be said when persons in the campaign of one major political party used clandestine contributions to penetrate the internal process of the other—and is consequently of moment in both the daily press and history. Judge Sirica's palpable search for truth in such a trial was not only permissible, it was in the highest tradition of his office as a federal judge. And although his execution of this objective presented problems, as must be acknowledged, they were not of a kind that deprived defendants of a fair trial. "A defendant is entitled to a fair trial but not a perfect one." *Lutwak v. United States.* . . . Assuming for discussion that the problems already noted reflect error by the trial judge, it must be ranked as harmless rather than prejudicial error.

I'm proud of that decision.

For years, legal scholars have debated the role of the federal judiciary. Much of that controversy has focused on the judicially imposed remedies in the great constitutional controversies over school desegregation, and more recently over other problems like state penal systems and mental hospitals. There has been less attention to the role of the trial judge, especially in criminal cases. Shortly after the break-in trial, Francis J. Larkin, a former associate dean of the Boston College Law School, presiding justice of the Third District Court of Southern Worcester and editor in chief of the *Massachusetts Law Quarterly,* wrote in the *Boston Globe:*

> Taking the long view, the great issue of Watergate may have been the willingness of Judge Sirica to break the fetters which for so long have relegated trial judges to an essentially passive role in the conduct of trials in this country. . . .
>
> The adversary system proceeds on the assumption that the truth will be elicited and justice best served if the lawyers alone do forensic battle in developing the evidence in the case, with the judge remaining essentially aloof from the battle. . . . At the same time it is essential to the functioning of the adversary system and the concept of a fair trial that each side of a controversy be fully presented and carefully considered in order that full weight and value be accorded to competing claims. But before a judge or jury may evaluate the complete impact of an argument, it follows that it must be presented with the full force of the partisan advocate, not by counsel inhibited by the restraints of political office—or otherwise—from developing the complete facts of the case. Neither the judge nor a jury can know the strengths or weaknesses of an argument—the inarticulate major premise of the adversary system—until they have heard it presented by an advocate who has dedicated all of his powers to its development and delivery. The adversary system proceeds on a "no holds barred" basis. Where one or both sides hold back—for whatever reason—then it is entirely appropriate for the trial judge to doff the mantle of the detached bystander and enter the proceedings to develop facts not previously unearthed—in the quest for truth and the search for justice.

The basic strength of our system of government is tied to the continuing independence of the judicial system from political and social pressures. As a trial judge, I found that the greatest pleasure I derived from my work was that very independence. And I offer no apologies or regrets to anyone for the action I took in the break-in trial. I owed it to the court, to our system of justice, and to the country. The more I think about it, the more I believe that it was the proper course to take and in fact the only course to take. If the case were now before me, with the advantages of hindsight, I would do exactly the same thing. Rule 614 of the new Federal Rules of Evidence has incorporated the concept that the court may question witnesses whether called by itself or by one of the parties, because, as the advisory-committee notes say, "the judge is not imprisoned within the case as made by the parties."

Simply stated, I had no intention of sitting on the bench like a nincompoop and watching the parade go by. If the action I took constitutes the action of a so-called "activist judge," I plead guilty to the charge.

In June 1975, I was given an honorary degree by the City University of New York. Two quotations were included in my citation. The first is from Edmund Burke, who said, "It is the duty of the Judge to receive every offer of evidence, apparently material, suggested to him, though the parties themselves through negligence, ignorance, or corrupt collusion, should not bring it forward. A judge is not placed in that high situation merely as a passive instrument of parties. He has a duty of his own, independent of them, and that duty is to investigate the truth." The second is Thomas Aquinas's definition of Justice as "a certain rectitude of mind, whereby a man does what he ought to do in the circumstances confronting him."

7

The Battle for
the Tapes

Every year a group of Washington newspaper reporters known as the Gridiron Club holds a dinner at a downtown hotel. The reporters invite guests, usually the top political figures in town, and the guests themselves are the objects of a satirical revue that is often quite cutting. It is all taken with good humor by everyone. In 1973, just after the break-in trial had ended, I was the guest of the late Eddie Folliard, a *Washington Post* reporter. Columnist Richard Wilson served as master of ceremonies that night. During a break in the proceedings, Wilson turned to one end of the head table and asked President Nixon's chief of staff, H. R. Haldeman, to stand. The room was dark, and as Haldeman rose at his place, a spotlight picked him out of the shadows. Wilson then asked Nixon's appointments secretary, Dwight Chapin, to stand. He, too, was picked out by a spotlight. Wilson then called my name. I was reluctant to stand, but Folliard nudged me pretty hard and I got out of my chair as the spotlight found me. "Gentlemen," Wilson said to Haldeman and Chapin, "since you may be visiting his courtroom soon, I'd like you to meet Judge John Sirica."

Everyone, including Haldeman and Chapin, roared with laughter at Wilson's little joke. Chapin had been named repeatedly as the man who hired Donald Segretti, a young West Coast lawyer, to perform various acts of political espionage against the Democrats. Haldeman, at that time, was suspected of having some involvement in the Watergate scandal, but nothing had been proved against him. I laughed along with everyone else, mostly because the idea that Haldeman, Nixon's most trusted and powerful adviser, would be involved in the Watergate investigation seemed improbable.

But after only a few weeks of testimony before the still-active Watergate grand jury, it was suddenly clear that involvement with the break-in and the attempt to cover up responsibility for the burglary was reaching the highest levels of the Nixon administration. U.S. Attorney Harold Titus and the head of the criminal division in the Justice Department, Henry Petersen, met with Attorney General Kleindienst in April and laid out what they knew about the cover-up and the break-in. Kleindienst, Titus told me, wept as he heard that Mitchell was probably involved and faced indictment. Kleindienst carried word to President Nixon, adding that Haldeman, Ehrlichman, Dean, Colson, and others also faced indictment. On April 30, Nixon announced the resignations of Haldeman and Ehrlichman, whom he called "the finest public servants it has been my privilege to know," as well as of Kleindienst himself. At the same time, Dean's forced resignation was made public. As the prosecutors' efforts went forward, and other conspirators began to talk, resignations took place throughout the Nixon administration. Men like Egil Krogh, who as a White House aide had a hand in the Ellsberg break-in, quit. Magruder left his job in the Commerce Department. Others, among them Chapin and Charles Colson, had resigned earlier.

Nixon himself began to move swiftly but erratically to try to contain the growing scandal and to keep his shaky administration in operation. He replaced Haldeman with General Alexander Haig, a former aide to Henry Kissinger. At the Justice Department, Elliot Richardson, a veteran of two other cabinet jobs under President Nixon, succeeded Kleindienst. L. Patrick Gray was withdrawn as the nominee to head the FBI, and William Ruckelshaus was moved from the Environmental Protection Agency to become acting director of the Bureau. When Richardson appeared before the Senate committee for his confirmation hearing, he was quickly told that a condition of his approval would be that he appoint a special prosecutor to continue the Watergate investigation. The committee had obviously decided that no matter how well Silbert and his team were now doing with the grand jury, the Nixon administration was too tainted by the implication in the case of so many of its key figures to be permitted to handle the job any longer. After two men turned down the job, Richardson finally got Harvard Law School professor Archibald Cox to become the special prosecutor. Richardson promised the Senate that Cox would be totally independent in his investigation.

On April 30, President Nixon made a long public statement about the growing scandal. He told the country that in 1972 he had departed from his usual practice of running his own campaign and had delegated as much responsibility as possible, in order, he said, "that the presidency should come first and politics second." In a characteristic Nixon touch, he blamed those who worked for him while denying that he was doing so: "For the fact that alleged improper actions took place within the White House or within my campaign organization, the easiest course would be for me to blame those to whom I delegated responsibility to run the campaign. But that would be the cowardly thing to do.

"I will not place the blame on subordinates—on people whose zeal exceeds their judgment, and who may have done wrong in a cause they deeply believed to be right."

Now, only a month and a half after the McCord letter, the president of the United States had fired his closest associates and was beginning what would be a year-long struggle for his own survival. I didn't see clearly then just how tough a fight Nixon would have on his hands. There was now even more widespread public suspicion that Nixon himself had known of the break-in beforehand or that, at least, the cover-up which had led to the resignation of his top aides must have gone on with his knowledge. His standing in the opinion polls declined steadily. In a very short period of time, the case had gone far beyond the question of who had authorized the Liddy and Hunt operation. There were now serious, though still very preliminary, inquiries about what the president himself might know about the whole affair. It was, I remember, an amazing time in Washington. We were just entering the difficult and protracted period in which our system of justice was going to have to try to sort out substance from suspicion, to test the truthfulness of all those now trying to save their own necks, to boil down the scandal of Watergate into hard, provable facts that could be tested in a court of law.

In February, the Senate had voted 77–0 to set up the Select Committee on Presidential Campaign Activities to investigate the Watergate case and the large number of other issues growing out of it, including the misuse of campaign finances. On May 17, exactly eleven months after the break-in itself, the committee opened public hearings. The next day, Archibald Cox was named officially as special prosecutor. The Senate investigation and the special prosecutor's office inevitably came into conflict as each tried to proceed with its job. A month after taking office, Cox asked me to prevent the Senate committee from going ahead with its hearings, arguing that the televised proceedings could present insurmountable problems with pretrial publicity in his own prosecutions later on. The committee meanwhile asked me to grant some witnesses limited immunity* from prosecution for their testimony, which would mean that Cox and his team of investigators and lawyers could not use that testimony itself as the basis for charges against those witnesses. The law gave me no choice but to grant the immunity. Cox's efforts to stop the hearings had no merit at that point; he had charged no one with any crime, there was no trial scheduled, there were no defendants, as yet, to protect. I ruled that his request was not "ripe" for judicial action, although I sympathized with his problem and worried about the effect the television spectacle might have on later trials.

At the same time, an intricate game of leaks was being played in Washington. Parts of private interviews with Senate-committee witnesses were finding their way into public print. Some of the suspects in the cover-up case were leaking hints of the testimony they might give later on, apparently to try to convince the prosecutors of the need to make bargains either for immunity from prosecution or for pleas to limited charges. With a great public show, John Dean turned over to me a key to a safe-deposit box which he said held incriminat-

---

* Despite the protection against self-incrimination provided by the Fifth Amendment, a witness may be forced to testify if he is granted protection from prosecution resulting from his testimony. Until 1964, immunity was rarely granted, since the relevant statutes had been interpreted to mean that the witness had to be granted absolute immunity from *any* future prosecution for *any* offense to which the compelled testimony related. In 1964, however, the Supreme Court ruled that immunity only protected a witness from a prosecution resulting *directly* from his testimony. In other words, immunity would only protect the witness from having his testimony used against him. Under the new interpretation, later codified by Congress in the Immunity Act of 1970, prosecution can be brought against such a witness if it is shown that evidence other than the testimony itself is relied upon in bringing the charges.

ing documents. The papers were classified, and since Dean no longer had a security clearance, he could not legally keep them in his possession at this time. We got the papers out of Dean's Alexandria bank and, after reviewing them, turned them over to the prosecutors and the Senate committee.*

Dean was the focus of most of the anxiety inside the White House. He had told his superiors that he was meeting with the U.S. attorney. Furthermore, his appearance before the Senate committee was coming up in late June. President Nixon accordingly made another attempt to blunt growing doubts about his own role in Watergate. While McCord was telling the Senate committee that Mitchell and Dean knew about Liddy's operation, and while he was describing efforts to get him to plead guilty which he claimed came from the White House, Nixon issued a four-thousand-word statement admitting for the first time that his aides in the White House had tried to cover up the facts of the burglary, but denying again that he himself had had any part in the obstruction of justice.

In addition, Nixon explained the origins of the so-called "plumbers" unit under Egil Krogh, which had carried out the burglary attempt at the office of Dr. Lewis Fielding, Daniel Ellsberg's psychiatrist. He admitted ordering an investigation of Ellsberg in reaction to the theft of the Pentagon Papers and their publication in American newspapers, but he denied that he authorized or knew of the break-in at Dr. Fielding's office in Los Angeles. He also admitted ordering the FBI to stay clear of the plumbers and the CIA in their Watergate investigation, but he denied that this was done to cover up anything. His only interest, he claimed, was in protecting the national security. Finally, Nixon said he had no intention of resigning.

This latest explanation from the White House was more complete than any that had preceded it. Nixon, anticipating Dean's testimony, was trying to defuse the charges that he thought would be the most sensational and that could be corroborated by witnesses other than Dean. Left unmentioned were incidents that would impugn Nixon's motives and con-

* The "documents" turned out to be a copy of the so-called "Huston plan" to create a sort of special federal police force aimed at combating radicals. The plan, originated by a young White House aide named Charles Huston, was never implemented, because of objections from FBI director J. Edgar Hoover.

duct during the cover-up period, but that only Dean could allege. Nixon was counting on having his word taken over Dean's.

Along with the rest of the country, I watched with increasing amazement as the cover-up story unfolded on television—McCord, Porter, Magruder, the funny former New York cop named Ulasewicz who dropped pay-off money into phone booths and made so many secret calls from those booths that he wore a metal coin changer on his belt. The sordid facts of the lower-level cover-up came pouring out. The testimony before the Senate committee confirmed my earlier suspicions that many more people than the original break-in defendants were involved, but the intricacy and details of this testimony were well beyond my wildest imaginings. I've often thought that had a writer tried to sell such a script to the movies, he would have been laughed out of Hollywood.

The small fry in the cover-up had been pretty well trapped, mostly by each other's testimony. What remained to be determined was the real guilt or innocence of the men at the top. And it was Dean's testimony that was to be at the heart of that question. On June 25, Dean read a 245-page statement concerning the origins of the break-in, the cover-up, and what he alleged was the president's knowledge of that cover-up. He said his first conversation with Nixon after the break-in came on September 15, the day the indictments were returned, when Nixon congratulated him for limiting the investigation to Liddy and his crew. "I left the meeting with the impression that the President was well aware of what had been going on regarding the success of keeping the White House out of the Watergate scandal, and I also had expressed to him my concern that I was not confident that the coverup could be maintained indefinitely," Dean testified.

Dean said that at their next meeting, on February 27, he told Nixon again that he doubted the cover-up could be maintained. He said that he told Nixon the next day that he, Dean, had been involved in an obstruction of justice in keeping the Watergate investigation contained. Nixon "reassured me not to worry, that I had no legal problems," Dean said. On March 13, Dean said, he told Nixon that the seven Watergate defendants had been demanding money in return for their silence and that as much as a million dollars could be required. Dean said Nixon told him "that is no problem."

And then on March 21, Dean gave Nixon all the details of the cover-up. He warned of "a cancer growing on the Presidency" which if not removed would be fatal to Nixon's chances of holding on to office. Dean said Nixon did not seem particularly concerned with what he had told him. Dean alleged that he told Nixon again that it would take a million dollars to silence the defendants, and Nixon responded that the money could be obtained. No shock, no outrage, no refusals. This was Dean's most sensational charge. He was saying Nixon himself had approved the pay-offs to the defendants.

I must say that I was skeptical of Dean's allegations. He was obviously a key figure himself in the cover-up. He had known of the Liddy plan to gather intelligence even before the break-in. He had a lot to lose and had been dealing carefully with the prosecutors, trying to get immunity for himself. It seemed to me at the time that Dean might well be more interested in protecting himself by involving the president than in telling the truth. On the other hand, Dean's composure on the witness stand was remarkable. For days after he read his statement, the committee members peppered him with hostile questions. But he stuck to his story. He didn't appear upset in any way. His flat, unemotional tone of voice made him believable. But still, his charges against President Nixon were without much support. It was Dean's word against the president's. Dean was not in a strong position: he was admitting his own criminal conduct. That made me suspect his recollections. I had seen too many people in tough spots lying to save themselves.

Colson, Ehrlichman, and others attacked Dean's statements. Stories were leaked to the newspapers suggesting that Dean was so afraid of jail and of homosexual attacks in prison that he was falsely accusing the president. The Senate committee, in an effort to check on Dean's accuracy, sought to get Nixon to appear himself to testify. In early July, Nixon was admitted to Bethesda Naval Hospital suffering from viral pneumonia. At the same time, he refused the Senate committee's invitation, and the committee, treading lightly, declined to subpoena the president, since there was strong disagreement over whether the committee had that power.

But suddenly, in mid-July, there appeared a way to test Dean's veracity. Alexander Butterfield, the head of the Federal Aviation Administration and a former deputy assistant to the president in the White House, revealed to the Senate committee that the president had an extensive tape-recording system operating in his offices at the White House. The fact that such a system existed was itself a shock. The idea of the president secretly taping ostensibly private conversations was repulsive, although such an arrangement apparently was not unprecedented in the White House. The Senate committee quickly wrote a polite letter to the president asking for the tapes of the critical meetings with Dean. The revelation about the tapes had shifted the burden of proof back to the president and his men. Haldeman and Ehrlichman appeared before the committee late in July and directly contradicted Dean's versions of meetings with the president.

Special Prosecutor Cox was of course vitally interested in what the tapes might prove. Like the committee, he sent a letter to the White House requesting tapes of key conversations. On July 23, the president announced that he would not surrender the tapes either to Cox or to the Senate committee. The battle over the tapes had begun.

Cox soon asked me to sign a subpoena for the tapes and other White House records related to the case. Considering the fact that this was thought to be only the second time in our history that a president had been served a subpoena, the procedure was surprisingly routine. The Nixon subpoena was signed by me and then served on Nixon's lawyers in the White House by two young lawyers from the special prosecutor's office. I gave little thought to the fact that the subpoena itself might raise objections, since serving it seemed the natural course to follow in light of the importance of the tapes to the Watergate grand jury investigation. The Senate committee, meanwhile, voted to issue its own subpoena.

At 9:30 on the morning of July 26, a young attorney from the White House named Douglas Parker came to my office. He handed me a personal letter from President Nixon. Later that morning, I read the letter in open court:

DEAR JUDGE SIRICA:

White House counsel have received on my behalf a subpoena duces tecum* issued out of the United States District Court for the District of Columbia on July 23rd

---

* A subpoena *duces tectum* is an order to produce documents or show cause that they need not be produced.

at the request of Archibald Cox. The subpoena calls on me to produce for a Grand Jury certain tape recordings as well as certain specified documents. With the utmost respect for the court of which you are Chief Judge, and for the branch of government of which it is a part, I must decline to obey the command of that subpoena. In doing so I follow the example of a long line of my predecessors as President of the United States who have consistently adhered to the position that the President is not subject to compulsory process from the courts.

The independence of the three branches of our government is at the very heart of our Constitutional system. It would be wholly inadmissible for the President to seek to compel some particular action by the courts. It is equally inadmissible for the courts to seek to compel some particular action from the President.

That the President is not subject to compulsory process from the other branches of government does not mean, of course, that all information in the custody of the President must forever remain unavailable to the courts. Like all of my predecessors, I have always made relevant material available to the courts except in those rare instances when to do so would be inconsistent with the public interest. . . .

In the light of that principle, I am voluntarily transmitting for the use of the Grand Jury the memorandum from W. Richard Howard to Bruce Kehrli in which they are interested as well as the described memoranda from Gordon Strachan to H. R. Haldeman. I have concluded, however, that it would be inconsistent with the public interest and with the Constitutional position of the Presidency to make available recordings of meetings and telephone conversations in which I was a participant and I must respectfully decline to do so.

> Sincerely,
> /s/ RICHARD NIXON

In short, the president asserted that he would turn over to the grand jury only what he wanted to turn over and that the courts had no power to compel him to turn over anything else.

After I read the letter, Cox rose to explain that the tapes he had requested from Nixon "were highly material" to the

investigation and the case before the grand jury. His subpoena had been quite specific, not the kind of catch-all request that lawyers call a "fishing expedition." The subpoena
had requested the tapes of an hour-and-a-half conversation
on June 20, 1972, three days after the break-in, between
Nixon, Haldeman, and Ehrlichman; of a brief phone conversation the same day between the president and Mitchell; of a
conversation on June 30 between Nixon, Haldeman, and
Mitchell; of a meeting of the president, Dean, and Haldeman
on September 15 which Dean had described in his Senate
testimony; of the March 13 meeting of the president, Dean,
and Haldeman; of Dean's March 21 conversation with the
president; of a meeting later on March 21 between the
president, Dean, Haldeman, Ehrlichman, and White House
press secretary Ron Ziegler; of a two-hour March 22 meeting
of Nixon, Haldeman, Ehrlichman, Dean and Mitchell; and of
an April 15 Dean–Nixon meeting.

The special prosecutor said that Nixon's refusal to honor
that subpoena had been reported to the grand jury. "The
grand jury thereupon requested me as special prosecutor, to
seek enforcement of the subpoena by the order to show cause
why the documents should not be produced which I handed
up a moment ago," Cox said. On my desk, at the bench was
a page-and-a-half "order to show cause" which, if I signed it,
would bring the president's lawyers into court to defend his
refusal to comply with the previous court order.

The idea that the president was immune from the subpoena was rejected by the special prosecutor. "It is our view
that the position is not legally sound, that the separation of
power from the beginning of our history has not disabled the
court from issuing orders directed to the executive branch
even when the officers in the executive branch were acting
under the express direction of the president," Cox said. We
were beginning to get into deep legal waters. But for some
reason my mind turned not to the great constitutional issues
that were arising, but rather to the grand jury, which was
present at this proceeding since it was under the grand jury's
legal power that the subpoena had been issued. I asked the
foreman to step forward and state his name.

"Vladimir Pregelj," he said crisply. A graying man with a
goatee, Pregelj worked for the Library of Congress as an
economist and had been serving as the foreman of the Watergate grand jury for nearly a year.

"Mr. Pregelj, you heard the statement of Mr. Cox?" I asked.

"I have, Your Honor," Pregelj said.

"This has been explained to the grand jury I take it?"

"It has," he answered.

"Is it the desire and wish of each grand juror, including yourself, that the court sign this order to show cause?"

"Your Honor, we have not polled the grand jury, but the question was asked informally and no objections have been raised."

"Will you call the names of the grand jurors, Mr. Clerk," I asked Cappy Capitanio. "I will ask each grand juror as your names are called to please stand. . . ."

Cappy began reading the names: "Annie Bell Alford, Lila Bard, Enas Broadway, Ellen Brown, Carolyn Butler, Elayne Edlund, Harold Evans, Clarence Franklin, Maurice Glover, Dorothy Gray, George Gross, Wallace Hawkins, Christopher Hoplins, Ruth Loveridge, Arthur McLean, Ethel Peoples, Susie Robinson, Kathryn Smith, George Stockton, Julie White, Naomi Williams, Priscilla Woodruff."

As he read, each juror stood briefly at his seat in the courtroom. "Now the members of the jury who just stood, each one of you approve of the statement made by your foreman, that the court sign this order to show cause? If there are any objections please state them," I said.

There were none. It was quite a moment. Here was the grand jury made up of ordinary citizens from the District of Columbia, some of them poor people, telling the president of the United States, the most powerful man in the world, to turn over the tapes. If there was ever a moment that gave meaning to the idea that in our democracy the people govern themselves, that was it. It was a moving experience to watch those faces as they challenged the president. I had always been proud of this country and thankful for the life it let me lead. But I was never prouder than that morning in July.

I signed the order to show cause right there at the bench. It said:

> Upon consideration of the verified petition of Archibald Cox, Special Prosecutor, Watergate Special Prosecution Force, on behalf of the Grand Jury in and for the United States District Court for the District of Columbia, for an order directing Richard M. Nixon or any

subordinate officer whom he may designate as having custody and control of certain documents or objects, to show cause why there should not be a full and prompt compliance with a subpoena duces tecum of this court . . . it is hereby ORDERED:

1. That Richard M. Nixon or any subordinate officer whom he may designate as having custody or control of any of the items described in paragraph 1 of the schedule attached to the above mentioned subpoena is ordered to show cause at a hearing on the 7th day of August at 10 A.M., 1973, why the documents and objects described in paragraph 1 of such schedule should not be produced as evidence before the Grand Jury;

2. That at the hearing, and in any affidavits, briefs, or memoranda submitted in connection with this matter, the Special Prosecutor is authorized to disclose matters occurring before the Grand Jury to the extent necessary to show the Grand Jury's entitlement to enforcement of the subpoena;

3. And that the United States Marshal for the District of Columbia is directed to serve forthwith a copy of this order and the above mentioned petition on Richard M. Nixon, J. Fred Buzhardt (as Special Counsel to the President), or any other person of suitable age and discretion at the White House or Old Executive Office Building, Washington, D.C. Such service on or before the 30th day of July, 1973, shall be deemed good and sufficient service.

/s/ JOHN J. SIRICA
Chief Judge

The meaning of the order was that the grand jury was entitled to the best evidence it could obtain in considering the charges being brought by the special prosecutor. The burden was now on the president to show why he should be an exception to that usual rule of law. While Cox had carefully avoided any claim that he was investigating the president, preferring the less sensational view that the tapes were necessary to establish evidence in the cases of Nixon's aides, it was clear to everyone that the tapes might either confirm Dean's allegations about the president's complicity in the cover-up, or exonerate the president. It seemed to me at the time that—legal questions about the president's privileges aside—

Nixon had in his possession evidence that could end the national scandal then threatening him. I still didn't quite believe John Dean, and I hoped the president would take the opportunity to save himself by turning over the recordings.

To be honest, I was more concerned about the job that now faced me than I was about the president's problems. By signing the show cause order, I had for the first time in our history begun a real test of the limits of a president's so-called "executive privilege." Other presidents had invoked the privilege, but no president had ever been challenged in court on its use. Special Prosecutor Cox was, of course, one of the country's pre-eminent constitutional scholars. To argue his case, the president had obtained the services of Charles Alan Wright, from the University of Texas Law School, an outstanding constitutional lawyer. I was going to have to prepare myself to hear these two men argue the constitutional questions involved and then to write an opinion expressing my own views on this challenge to the president. It had been more than forty years since I left law school, and I was rather rusty on constitutional law, to put it mildly. I had a lot of work to do.

I left Washington that weekend for a vacation in Rehoboth Beach, Delaware. I took along some very heavy reading. But within a couple of days, I grew too restless thinking about the case to lounge on the beach. I hurried back to Washington to get ready for the great debate.

8

The Claim of
Executive Privilege

As I waited for Nixon's lawyers to respond to the show cause order, it gradually became clear to me just what I was involved in. Here I was, an obscure judge, facing the president of the United States. The country was in a turmoil over the Watergate case. The president himself had been accused of illegal acts by his former counsel John Dean. Nixon had refused to turn over his tape recordings. He was obviously going to fight this scandal every step of the way, and he had spent a lifetime fighting. I was approaching the most momentous decision of my life, and it made me extremely nervous. My hours of sleep, always minimal, declined further. I was constantly waking up in the middle of the night, worrying about the case and the ruling I'd eventually have to make. Todd Christofferson and I would work all day at the courthouse. I'd take home old casebooks to go over. But by eight or nine o'clock, I'd be too exhausted to read any more. Each night, I'd watch the network news shows. They were filled with stories about the Watergate crisis and only added to the tension I felt. By ten o'clock or so I'd be in bed for some restless sleep. But by three or four in the morning, I'd be up again, reading and worrying.

I had been on the Watergate case for nearly a year, and the strain was beginning to show. I felt tired most of the time. I had always tried to take some exercise every week, even if only a round of golf. But there didn't seem to be any time for anything except Watergate. Nor was it easy for my family. My son, Jack, away at Duke University, was suddenly more famous than he wanted to be. My wife, Lucy, tried to keep things on an even keel at home, but it wasn't easy with me so tired and busy. My daughters, Tricia and Eileen, had to turn to their mother for help with school work and other things, since I was so preoccupied. It was a hard time for all of us.

The more I read, the more I realized how few earlier cases there were to help me make my decision. President Jefferson had been subpoenaed in 1807 to produce a letter involved in the treason trial of Aaron Burr, and I must have read that case five or six times.* I reread the Constitution a half dozen times and pored through sections of *The Federalist Papers*. With two of the most eminent constitutional experts in the country getting ready to argue before me, I felt more than ever before the lack of a college education.

Finally, on August 7, Charles Alan Wright delivered his brief arguing that the president could not be compelled to turn over his tapes. The document was thirty-four legal-sized pages long and was packed full of citations and quotes. His argument was interesting, and I studied it over and over again with Todd.

Wright and the White House lawyers, and presumably the president himself, had pulled no punches. They began by asserting that the effort to secure the tapes represented "a serious threat to the nature of the presidency as it was created by the Constitution, as it has been sustained for 184 years, and as it exists today." They warned that to force the president to turn over the tapes would damage the institution of the presidency severely and irreparably. "The total structure of government . . . will be altered," they stated. That warning would make any judge think twice about disagreeing with their position.

They insisted that if the president were ordered to turn over the recordings of his conversations with his aides, no president in the future could expect candid, unvarnished advice from the people in his administration. Such a breach of presidential privacy would make it impossible, they argued, for Nixon or any president to function. Weakened by the loss of privacy and by an assertion of power from the court, the

---

* Later research showed that President James Monroe had also been served with a subpoena. He was called to testify at a court-martial, declined to appear, but answered written interrogatories from the court.

executive would no longer be an equal and co-ordinate branch of government as provided in the Constitution.

They argued that no precedent existed to justify an order to turn over the tapes. Rather, the doctrine of "executive privilege" empowered the president "to withhold information if he concludes that disclosure would be contrary to the public interest." And, Wright stated, the courts have no power to rule on the president's use of executive privilege. The courts are coequal with but not superior to the president. "The President is answerable to the Nation but not the courts," the brief said.

There is no mention of the idea of executive privilege in the Constitution of the United States or in the statute books. It is a doctrine that has grown up with time, based on the common-sense notion that a president must have some privacy, some protection from inquiries by Congress and the courts, if he is to function effectively. It has most frequently been invoked by presidents to protect themselves and their aides from congressional scrutiny of the policy-making process inside the executive branch. In relation to the courts, the privilege is most often used as a way of preventing military secrets from being revealed during a trial. But the limits of this privilege are vague at best. Whether the privilege is the president's alone, whether other branches of government have the power to decide its limits, is unclear. And Wright, subtly, raised an even more ominous problem. "Whether a decision adverse to the executive could be enforced is a . . . question," he wrote. In other words, precisely how could a court force the president and commander-in-chief to do something he refused, even in good conscience, to do? Congress has the power to impeach and try the president for "high crimes and misdemeanors." But could a court order the arrest of the president? Wright only mentioned the problem in passing, but it troubled me a great deal.

Whatever the limits of executive privilege were, one thing, to borrow a phrase, was perfectly clear, and Wright stated it plainly: "No court has ever attempted to enforce a subpoena directed at the President of the United States. No President—and, for that matter, no department head—has ever been held in contempt for refusing to produce information, either to the courts or to Congress, that the President has determined must be withheld in the public interest. . . . the practice throughout our history shows no exception to the rule that the President cannot be forced to disclose information that he thinks would damage the public interest to disclose." There was no other way to look at the problem that faced me. If I was to do what the special prosecutor wanted, if a subpoena directed at the president was to be enforced, it would be for the first time in our national history. I underlined that part of Wright's brief.

Wright pointed to the privacy of a judge's conversations with his clerk and a congressman's consultations with his aides in trying to show that all branches of the government, not just the executive, were protected by the notion of privilege. He recalled that a Supreme Court justice subpoenaed to appear before the House Un-American Activities Committee had refused on the basis that the fair administration of justice required his independence from congressional inquiry. He noted that one of the first acts of the Constitutional Convention was to vote to keep its deliberations secret.

Arguing that presidential papers are protected from public disclosure by an act of Congress that permits the donors to seal them, Wright insisted this protection was even more necessary with regard to the tapes. "Recordings are the raw material of life. By their very nature they contain spontaneous, informal, tentative and frequently pungent comments on a variety of subjects inextricably intertwined into one conversation," he argued. (Of course, I didn't know until later just how "pungent" the tapes were.) Wright wrote that the parts of the tapes dealing with "sensitive issues of national security" could not be separated from those recording the Watergate conversations.

In normal court proceedings, there are only a few exceptions to the general rule that the court is entitled to everyone's testimony and evidence; conversations between a lawyer and his client, a doctor and his patient, a husband and wife, are privileged. But when such relationships themselves are used to facilitate illegal acts, the privilege generally does not apply. The president's lawyer, however, argued that even if criminal activity were discussed on the tapes, the president had the right to withhold them. And Wright went further yet. He argued that even if the president himself had taken part in the criminal activity, still the court would have no power to command him to produce his tapes. "The President of the United States . . . is not above the law. He is liable to prosecution and punishment in the ordinary course of law for crimes he has committed but only after he has been impeached, convicted and removed from office," the brief stated.

"It may well be that the statements made by other persons to the President at the meeting for which the recordings have been subpoenaed were made by them pursuant to a conspiracy to obstruct justice. Executive privilege cannot be claimed to shield executive officers from prosecution of crime," Wright stated. But, he added, by waiving executive privilege as a shield against *testimony* by his aides, Nixon had effectively permitted the prosecution to continue, despite his own exercise of presidential privilege.

The most amazing assertion in the Wright brief, however, came when the lawyer attempted to distinguish the president's part in the Watergate conversations from the parts played by his aides: "But although remarks made by others in conversations with the President may arguably be part of a criminal plan on their part, the President's participation in these conversations was in accordance with his *Constitutional duty to see that the laws are faithfully executed* [my emphasis]. It is the President, not those who may be subject to indictment by this grand jury, who is claiming executive privilege. He is doing so, not to protect those others but to protect the right of himself and his successors to preserve the confidentiality of discussions in which they participate in the course of their Constitutional duties, and thus ultimately to protect the right of the American people to informed and vigorous leadership from their President. . . ."

I thought it was a clever argument. But, in the end, the attempt to separate the president from his aides in the admittedly criminal discussions under way in the White House was a bit too clever. For months the president had been conceding that his aides were suspect in the cover-up. In the brief, the White House was doing the same thing, and at the same time trying to insulate the president from responsibility and accountability by invoking executive privilege for the president and for "the American people." I thought that Wright's argument on that point was unconvincing.

But it was still a powerful brief. No judge wants to step off into new legal territory if he can avoid it. All lawyers are trained to follow precedent, to read the guideposts established in previous cases and opinions. Wright had effectively focused on the absence of precedent. "There is no case in which the courts have actually compelled the executive to disclose information when the executive thinks it would be detrimental to the public interest," he argued near the end of the brief.

One other point caught my attention. From my own study it was clear that the previous case closest to the situation I faced was the Burr case in 1807. While Charles Alan Wright was correct in stating that no court had ever forced the executive to turn over material, Chief Justice John Marshall had actually issued a subpoena to President Jefferson in the Burr case. The question of enforcement was never reached because Jefferson, despite his initial reluctance to turn over a letter subpoenaed in Burr's defense, finally made most of the letter available to the court voluntarily. Wright in his brief had made little mention of the case. He cited it only twice, and then only to quote the great chief justice's reservations about how a subpoena might be enforced. I was anxious to see how Archibald Cox handled the same question.

Cox's reply brief arrived in my chambers on August 13. It was sixty-seven legal-sized pages long and included an eighty-five page appendix with quotations from Senate-committee testimony showing the disputed versions of the meetings covered by the subpoenaed tapes. Todd and I again began a detailed study. Oral arguments had been scheduled for August 22, and I was anxious to have the strong and weak points in both arguments firmly in mind before the two eminent scholars came to court.

Naturally, Cox attacked the notion that the president has the sole power to decide the limits of his own privilege. "There is no exception for the President from the guiding principle that the public, in the pursuit of justice, has a right to every man's evidence," Cox argued. "Even the highest executive officials are subject to the rule of law, which it is emphatically the province and the duty of the courts to declare." It is the court's role to decide what materials may be withheld by the executive because of particular circumstances, he maintained. And he went beyond even the idea that the recordings should be reviewed by the court before being turned over to the grand jury. He argued that there was no longer any legitimate reason to preserve secrecy, because "the interest in confidentiality is never sufficient to support an official privilege where there is reason to believe that the deliberations may have involved criminal misconduct" and because whatever slight risk existed to the future candor of executive discussions was far outweighed by the need to preserve the integrity of the office of the president from the taint of criminal conduct.

He also argued, I thought persuasively, that Nixon himself had already compromised the secrecy he sought to preserve. In his Senate testimony, H. R. Haldeman had attempted to refute John Dean's account of the March 21 meeting with the president by saying that he had listened to the tapes of the meeting and could say authoritatively that Dean was wrong. "Not even a President can be allowed to select some accounts of a conversation for public disclosure and then to frustrate further grand jury inquiries by withholding the best evidence of what actually took place," the brief stated.

Cox attacked the argument that the executive branch, because of the separation of powers, is immune from the holdings of the court. He focused instead on the interaction between the branches, the fact that Congress makes laws which the president and the courts must enforce, and the executive has power to issue executive orders which the courts must enforce.

He argued that the president himself was in no position to judge the public interest involved in keeping the tapes secret, and came close to saying that the president himself was a suspect. "The evidence on the tapes also may be material to public accusations against respondent himself—a question to which he can hardly be indifferent," Cox wrote.

"For more than a century and a half, all three branches have acknowledged that it is the constitutional function of the courts to interpret the laws . . . and to issue orders directing the cessation of legal wrongs or the performance of legal duties," the brief stated. "From the earliest days of the Republic the courts have issued orders requiring executive officials to comply with the Constitution and laws as judicially interpreted. . . ."

The president's lawyers had conceded that a court has the right to issue a subpoena to the president, but then had argued that the president had an equal right to refuse to honor the subpoena. Cox, on the other hand, said such an argument was inconsistent. "A subpoena is a judicial command. If it is valid, compliance is a legal duty," he wrote. Cox quoted Chief Justice Marshall in the Burr case to show a difference between the situation of the king of England, a hereditary ruler, who does have immunity to judicial process, and that of the president, who gains his position not by birth, but by election, and after serving his term returns to the "mass of the people." And thus, Cox reasoned, if the president was subject to subpoena he had to be subject to enforcement of that subpoena.

Cox, too, seemed a bit alarmed by the implication in the Wright brief that the physical power was lacking to enforce a judicial command on the president. "Happily," Cox argued, "the possession of the naked physical power to frustrate the Court has never led the Executive Branch to disregard a judicial determination of legal rights and obligations. . . . the effect of the President's physical power to disobey a court order is wholly speculative at this juncture, moreover, and undoubtedly will remain so. There is no reason to believe that respondent would disregard a final binding order fixing legal responsibilities. Certainly, the contention that the Court could not force him into prison does not strip the Court, as opposing counsel mistakenly argue, of the jurisdiction to order compliance with a valid subpoena."

Like other privileges offering exemption from judicial process, executive privilege must be balanced against competing needs. In a neat ploy, Cox quoted Charles Alan Wright himself to sustain that point. Wright had achieved a reputation as an expert on federal court procedure and had co-authored a textbook on the subject. Cox quoted Wright's book as saying, ". . . courts in many cases have sustained claims of executive privilege. But in other cases, in which the litigant's need for the information has seemed to outweigh the government's interest in secrecy, the claim of privilege has been overruled and disclosure has been ordered."

The indications of criminal conduct involved in the taped conversations cleary outweighed the necessity for secrecy or confidentiality, Cox argued. "The interest in free discussion by government officials cannot outweigh the interest in the integrity of the government itself," Cox wrote. He supported that argument by citing a case in which the usual right of jury deliberations to be held secret had been overturned because the deliberations in question involved alleged criminal misconduct by a juror.

On a more practical level, Cox denied that the testimony of the accused White House aides would be sufficient for the prosecution of his case. He said that withholding the tapes would frustrate his investigation, would deny him a way to corroborate or refute allegations against the president's aides (he did not mention Dean's charges against the president himself), and could result in the "frustration of the prosecution of a Chief Executive's aides and political associates." This, he said, would cause a loss of confidence in the government that outweighed the slim possibility that future presidents would suffer a loss of privacy because of Nixon's being forced to turn over the tapes.

I felt caught between two conflicting urges. The first was to honor the tradition that no president had been forced to turn over documents he had decided would damage the public interest. In short, I didn't want to be in the position of writing new law. On the other hand, examination of the tapes themselves seemed the only way to settle, once and for all, the questions about Watergate that were gradually destroying the Nixon administration. If I ruled for the president, the idea that he was covering up incriminating evidence might keep alive suspicion and even end public confidence in his administration. If I ruled against him, the revelation of the contents of the tapes could certainly damage his closest aides, and might perhaps hurt the president himself. Either way, I felt, to a large extent I was being asked to decide the fate of the Nixon presidency. Beyond all the legal debate, one question kept nagging at me: If Nixon himself were not involved, why would he stand on such an abstract principle as executive privilege when by voluntarily turning over the tapes he could prove himself innocent and put the Watergate case behind him? After all, there is no legal principle which requires the holder of a privilege to assert it.

A week after Cox's brief was submitted, we returned to the large, austere ceremonial courtroom on the sixth floor of the courthouse to hear oral arguments. I still hadn't made up my mind on the case and was determined to keep an open mind until after the two lawyers had appeared before me. I had studied both briefs several times and was ready with typewritten questions to ask both attorneys. The two men shook hands. The packed courtroom hushed as Wright began his presentation. He stood at the podium at the center of the courtroom, facing me. I was again alone on the bench, in front of the empty chairs on the second tier and still being watched closely by the stone statues of the four lawgivers.

Wright argued that as bad as Watergate was, the need to get to the bottom of that case was not so important as protecting the president's privacy and thus his ability to govern effectively. The courts, he repeated, had no power to compel the president to turn over the tapes. He warned that if I ruled in favor of the special prosecutor, the door would be open to wholesale judicial interference with the president's role.

"There are in the United States today 400 district judgeships authorized by law. A holding that the court has the power to pass on a president's claim of privilege as to his most private papers and to compel him to give up those papers would be a precedent for all 400 of those district judges," Wright said. "This is merely the first installment of many such requests that will be made to be passed on by 400-odd district judges all over the country. . . .

"We must leave it to the good judgment of the president of the United States to determine whether the public interest permits disclosure of his most intimate documents. If we have doubts about the good judgment of any president, there are other forums in which those doubts are to be resolved, not in the United States District Court," Wright concluded. He seemed to be saying that the president was elected by the people, Congress could impeach him, but one unelected federal judge had no right to set himself against the popular will.

Wright in his argument and in his brief had repeatedly said that the president's assessment of the "public interest" was guiding him in withholding the tapes. After Wright finished his argument I asked him to define just how the public interest was being served by this refusal. He answered, as he had in his brief, that the public interest was served by the preservation of the president's right to privacy.

He couldn't escape the possibility that without the tapes the Watergate case might not be resolved. "Does the president believe in this particular case it would be in the public interest to prevent any further prosecution in what we call the Watergate case?" I asked. Wright answered that the president believed the prosecution could go forward on the basis of testimony from the cover-up participants and that the tapes wouldn't make much difference.

Along with the press and the public, I was becoming increasingly suspicious that Nixon was more interested in protecting himself than in advancing the constitutional principles his counsel was arguing. As I said before, the easiest solution was simply to let the tapes speak for themselves; then, if the president's public denials of his own culpability were accurate, he could put Watergate behind him. I asked Wright directly: "Now, is it a correct statement of your position that the only reason these tapes are being withheld by the president is to protect the confidentiality of presidential discussions? Is that the reason they are being withheld?"

"I am certain that is the reason they are being withheld; yes, that the president feels very strongly the principle that confidentiality of conversations with persons who held his office is absolutely essential to the functioning of his office," Wright answered. There was no other answer that Wright could give, of course.

The crew-cut, gray-haired Cox took the podium, looking up over his half-glasses as he addressed me. "This is a grave and dramatic case," he began. "The necessity of seeking a subpoena against the president has not arisen since the trial of Aaron Burr.

"There is strong reason to believe that the integrity of the executive offices has been corrupted, although the extent of the rot is not yet clear," he continued. "Confidence in our institutions is at stake, not only confidence in the executive branch of the government but confidence in the ability and willingness of the courts to administer the same justice when high officials are involved as . . . they would apply normally to other wrongdoers."

The professor also attacked Nixon's argument that he had sufficiently served justice by permitting the testimony of his aides. "What respondent seems to me to be saying is . . . that all testimony of possible criminal conduct can be disclosed so long as it is open to the defects of human recollection, so long as it is open to the charge that a witness is lying, but when it comes to evidence which is not subject to dispute in any way, if we believe Mr. Butterfield's testimony about the quality of the tapes, then he says confidentiality suddenly becomes important," Cox said. He added to the notion that the president was protecting more than constitutional principle by pointing out that in previous cases involving the chief executive, the custom had been to address court orders to a subordinate officer. He cited the fact that the Secret Service once maintained the tapes and that the president's closest aides also had custody and access. "The special prosecutor would have subpoenaed someone other than the president," Cox said, "but we were later told that the president had taken the tapes under his personal control."

Like Wright, Cox was persuasive, eloquent, and thoroughly in command of the supporting cases he cited. He leaned heavily on the idea that no man is above the law, that the courts must interpret the law, and that the president cannot be left to be the sole judge of whatever privileges he claims. Still, there was no precedent for what he asked me to do.

"I take it from your argument . . . that no instance throughout our 184-year history can be cited where a court ever attempted to enforce a subpoena directed to a president?" I asked Cox.

"I know of none," he said simply. "It is a new question."

After a short recess, Wright returned for his rebuttal argument. He surprisingly added a new dimension to his plea that the tapes had to be protected. "The president has told me that in one of the tapes that is the subject of the present subpoena there is national-security material so highly sensitive that he does not feel free even to hint to me what the nature of it is," he said. And this was so, Wright explained, even though he had received a full security clearance before being hired to represent the president. This outrageous assertion proved later to be totally false. There were no such secrets on the subpoenaed tapes. Either Wright was exaggerating or Nixon had lied to him.

I asked Wright how the president felt about having an inspection of the tapes by the court, *in camera*, to excise national-security matters and other irrelevant parts of the taped conversations. The president opposed that course as well, he replied.

Wright also could not resist firing back at Cox for having quoted Wright's own book as support for his opposing argument. "I think this is a matter of much too grave moment for us to attempt to make debater's points by *ad hominem* arguments against opposing counsel," he said, accusing Cox of having misquoted his work. (After the arguments, Cox sent me a letter quoting the full section of Wright's book that did seem to support Cox's position. The incident was more amusing for the sparks it struck between the two experts than for its weight in either argument.)

The oral arguments lasted for two hours. When all was said and done, I was still left with the basic dilemma. My own instinct was to follow Cox's argument that no man is above the law. But my judicial experience told me that I needed the support of previous cases before venturing too far in challenging the president. Both lawyers had agreed that the case in our history closest to the one at hand was the Burr case, so I went back once again to study what Chief Justice Marshall had said. I asked my clerk Richard Azzaro, a student of Marshall's life and work, to research the history surrounding the Burr case.

The legal questions themselves were tough enough; in addition, the atmosphere in the country was growing more and more hostile toward the president. This made careful deliberation that much more difficult for me. Nixon's standing in the polls had dropped lower than that of any president in the two previous decades. The week before the oral arguments, stories appeared in the press saying that the vice-president, Spiro Agnew, was under investigation for accepting bribes while governor of Maryland. The Justice Department then confirmed the fact that they were investigating the vice-president, and asked Agnew to turn over his personal financial records. Echoing the arguments of the president's lawyer, Agnew asserted that he did not "acknowledge the propriety of any grand jury investigation of possible wrongdoing on the part of the vice president so long as he occupies that office." Like the president, the vice-president was claiming that only impeachment can bring a top executive of the land to account for his conduct in office.

Nixon himself had issued another long explanation of the Watergate case in mid-August, but it added nothing to previous denials of any personal participation in the scandal. On the very day of the oral arguments in my court, the president held his first press conference since the case had blown up in March. In an angry and bitter confrontation with the reporters, the president accused Congress and the press of exploiting Watergate as a way to embarrass him politically and frustrate the workings of his administration. My friend Clark Mollenhoff, who had worked briefly in the Nixon administration, asked the question that most interested me: "Where is the check on authoritarianism by the executive if the president is to be the sole judge of what the executive branch makes available and suppresses? And would you obey a Supreme Court order if you are asked and directed to produce the tapes?"

Nixon, barely controlling his rage, answered that the only check was public opinion—backed, he implied, by the possibility of eventual impeachment action by Congress. The president's press secretary had earlier hinted that Nixon would simply refuse to obey an order from my court, that only a "definitive" order from the Supreme Court would be considered binding. Nixon, I believe, was already counting the votes on the high court, knowing that he had appointed four of the nine members. He seemed to me to be thinking that he could at least get a split decision there, and might possibly even win, on the question of releasing the tapes. Nixon told Mollenhoff he wouldn't go beyond the press secretary's ambiguous warning. It appeared to me at the time that I not only had to decide the legal issues, but would also be faced later with a real test of the court's power to enforce its decision.

It's difficult to describe how worried I was about my impending decision. It was the most important one I would ever be called upon to make as a lawyer or as a judge. I was frankly worried that I would miss some part of one argument or another, overlook the language in some previous case, misunderstand the importance of one point or another. What if I was wrong? This wasn't like dealing with the burglars in the break-in trial. Nixon was the president of the United States; he deserved the benefit of the doubt. The court of appeals hadn't yet ruled on my work in the Liddy case, so I still wasn't sure I had been correct in my rulings then. Millions of people had voted for the president. I had voted for him.

Often when Todd and I were working on the case, I'd leave my desk and walk around the courthouse to get some fresh air and to clear my mind. I'd walk outside on the west side of the building, onto a one-block street called John Marshall Place. That always reminded me that Chief Justice Marshall had lived on the very site where our courthouse now stands. Marshall, perhaps the greatest judicial figure in our history, and the only other judge to have dealt with the question of a presidential subpoena. Marshall, who was responsible for many of the early landmark decisions of the Supreme Court, who forged our basic notions of federalism, the separation of powers, and the power of judicial review. John Sirica, a regular trial judge accustomed to trying all kinds of civil and criminal cases, one of hundreds of district-court judges.

"Suppose I'm wrong in my decision," I would think. I could see the criticism that I had overreached my authority. I could hear people saying that I was trying to get publicity by confronting the president, that I had adopted a sensationalist approach and taken advantage of my office as a judge. I felt like hell.

I had promised a decision in a week, and in the end, I had to rely on my own instincts and beliefs. I couldn't get away from the language in Marshall's opinion in the Burr case, in which he said simply that there was nothing in our law that would protect the president from a subpoena. And if he could be subpoenaed, why could that subpoena not be enforced? Marshall had been careful on this point, acknowledging, as Charles Alan Wright had noted in his brief, that the president could not simply be harassed by subpoenas to the point where he couldn't perform his constitutional duties. "The occasion for demanding it [compliance with a subpoena] ought, in such a case, to be very strong, and to be fully shown to the court before its production could be insisted on," Marshal had written.

It seemed to me that the special prosecutor had made a very strong showing. And beyond the courtroom arguments, it was obvious that something needed to be done. The occasion for demanding the tapes seemed to me very strong indeed. Nixon was seen by the public as hiding something by refusing to turn them over. His administration was rapidly failing, his vice-president was in grave legal trouble, the country was in turmoil. I believed that to put presidential privacy ahead of a full disclosure of the available evidence would only subject the judiciary to the same kind of disrespect that now clouded the executive branch. At the same time, I believed that legitimate national-security secrets and personal matters not related to the case deserved some protection. The day after the oral agreements, I made up my mind. We began to draft an opinion that would combine these two goals.

On August 29, after adding a few last-minute refinements, I signed the opinion.* It ordered the president to turn over his tapes for my own private inspection. The point was to walk a sort of middle ground. I felt that the president was entitled to some protection of his privacy and the nation was entitled to some protection from unnecessary publication of national secrets. But I also felt very strongly that no privilege existed for matters of a criminal nature, whether they came from the Oval Office or from anywhere else.

"The Court is willing here to recognize and give effect

* The Text of the opinion is in the Appendix.

to an evidentiary privilege based on the need to protect Presidential privacy," I wrote. "The Court, however, cannot agree with Respondent [the president] that it is the Executive that finally determines whether its privilege is properly invoked. The availability of evidence including the validity and scope of privileges is a judicial decision."

Marshall, again in the Burr case, had said that "the propriety of introducing any paper into a case, as testimony, must depend on the character of the paper, not on the character of the person who holds it." This, in my view, placed the burden on the president to justify in specific terms his withholding of the tapes. My order would require that particular claims of privilege be entered for each section of each tape. The broad claim of privilege would not do. Marshall had said as much in the Burr case. Although he never got to the point of enforcing his subpoena, he clearly planned that he—the court—not the executive, would decide what material had to be withheld. "If it [the letter subpoenaed by Burr] does contain any matter which it would be imprudent to disclose, which it is not the wish of the executive to disclose, such matter, if it be not immediately and essentially applicable to the point, will, of course, be suppressed," he wrote.

I flatly rejected the president's assertion that the court could not infringe upon executive functions. There was simply too much history running the opposite way. In the famous case in which President Truman, through his secretary of commerce, was ordered to turn back the steel mills he had seized, the Supreme Court had noted that the Constitution "enjoins upon its branches separateness but interdependence, autonomy but reciprocity."

I also took note of the implied threat in Wright's brief about the absence of power to enforce a court ruling against the president. I noted, "That the court has not the physical power to enforce its order to the President is immaterial to a resolution of the issues. Regardless of its physical power to enforce them, the Court has a duty to issue appropriate orders. The Court cannot say that the Executive's persistence in withholding the tape recordings would 'tarnish its reputation,' but must admit that it would tarnish the Court's reputation to fail to do what it could in pursuit of justice."

I ended the opinion with a paraphrase from Marshall. It was as if his presence had never left the place where I was working: ". . . if it be apparent that the tapes are irrelevant to the investigation, or that for state reasons they cannot be introduced into the case, the subpoena *duces tecum* would be useless. But if this be not apparent, if they *may* be important in the investigation, if they *may* be safely heard by the grand jury, if only in part, would it not be a blot on the page which records the judicial proceedings of this country, if, in a case of such serious import as this, the Court did not at least call for an inspection of the evidence in chambers?"

The reaction from the president, from his home in San Clemente, California, was troubling. He had his press spokesman announce that he would not comply with the order. The spokesman said the White House was considering an appeal, which was their right of course, but added that they were looking "how otherwise to sustain" the president's legal position. I had no idea how they could "otherwise" sustain the position. But it wasn't too long before we found out.

9

Saturday-Night Massacre

I certainly wasn't surprised that the president was upset with my decision calling for him to turn over the tapes for my inspection. But I was a bit surprised that the special prosecutor was not satisfied either. In early September, the president's lawyers filed an appeal with the United States Court of Appeals asking that my opinion be overturned. Cox appealed, too, arguing that instead of being reviewed by me *in camera* for a determination of whether any materials were irrelevant or covered by privilege, the tapes themselves should be turned over directly to the special prosecutor and the grand jury. But even as the appeals process was getting under way, the president was still saying that only a "definitive" ruling by the Supreme Court would cause him to relinquish the tapes. At a press conference on September 5, the president was asked again to define what he would regard as a "definitive" decision. He refused, saying absurdly that it was inappropriate to discuss such matters until the appeals process was complete. I was concerned that whatever the outcome of the tapes case in the courts, the president would simply refuse to obey the law. I hoped, naturally, that the court of appeals would sustain my ruling. I felt I needed all the support I could get.

Charles Alan Wright's argument on the appeal was about the same as the one he had made in my court. Cox argued that there was no executive privilege attached to the tapes and therefore I should not have to review them at all. He further argued that I had set no guidelines for my own review. Of course I had deliberately set no guidelines, preferring instead that the president's lawyers make particular claims of privilege based on the specific content of each section of the tapes. Cox would then have the right to oppose each particular claim. With that procedure, I felt, my decisions would be based on the actual content of the tapes, not on the president's vague assertions of privilege. Since I was named in the suit by Cox, I had to have attorneys representing me in the court of appeals. George D. Horning, Jr., and Anthony C. Morella, professors at the Washington College of Law of American University, filed a brief defending my decision but inviting the court of appeals to add any guidelines they felt were appropriate for my review of the tapes.

Seven judges on the nine-man court heard the case. When they first ruled on September 13, it was clear I wasn't the only judge in town who was worried about confronting the president. The judges issued a unanimous memorandum urging the president and Special Prosecutor Cox to try to reach an out-of-court compromise on the tapes issue, saving the court the burden of ruling directly on the case. It seemed to me at the time that there was little chance that the two sides could settle their differences, since their views were so diametrically opposed. Three days of meetings between the president's lawyers and the special prosecutor proved I was right. They went back to the court of appeals saying no agreement was possible.

A month later, the court of appeals, in an opinion joined by five of the seven judges, upheld my ruling.* They stated that the president's claim to executive privilege does have some validity, but agreed with me that this privilege cannot be invoked to protect his subordinates from prosecution for crimes. The court also ruled that the president has no absolute privilege against a subpoena. While agreeing with Chief Justice Marshall that a careful screening of subpoenas directed at the president is necessary to protect him from harassment, they added that it is decidedly the role of the courts, not of the president himself, to set the limits of executive privilege. They required the president to turn over the subpoenaed tapes for my inspection and subsequent rulings on specific claims of privilege.

I assumed that the president would appeal that decision to the Supreme Court. Under normal circumstances, that would have been the next logical step for him to take. But October 1973 presented nothing that could be called normal circum-

* The text of the opinion is in the Appendix.

stances. On October 6, war broke out in the Middle East, and for a time, America's traditional ally Israel seemed to be on the defensive against Egypt and Syria. On October 10, Vice-president Agnew walked into the federal courthouse in Baltimore and pleaded *nolo contendere*—no contest—to a one-felony count accompanied by a forty-page bill of particulars charging him with accepting pay-offs and bribes while he was a county executive in suburban Baltimore, while he was governor of the state, and even while he was vice-president. Nixon quickly selected Congressman Gerald R. Ford to replace Agnew, and Congress began to prepare for the first vice-presidential confirmation hearings ever.

With the Soviet Union heavily rearming the Arab side in the Middle East war, the president and the country were increasingly concerned about a confrontation between the United States and Russia. Under pressure on the foreign front, recently embarrassed by the Agnew scandal, and now facing the necessity either to appeal the tapes ruling in the Supreme Court or to turn over the tapes, the president decided to take a big gamble. Instead of appealing the decision or turning over the tapes, Nixon began to plan what he called a "compromise" solution. The tapes would be given for review to a third-party "verifier," who would compare a White House–prepared transcript to them. Then the verified transcript would be given to the investigators in place of the tapes themselves. For the job as "verifier," Nixon chose Mississippi senator John Stennis, a Democrat, a conservative, and an old ally of the president's, especially on defense policy, and this proposal was therefore referred to as the "Stennis compromise." The second provision of the plan was that, after the compromise had been worked out, Archibald Cox would be fired and the Watergate investigation would be returned to the Justice Department, where it would be under tighter control. Nixon had been horrified when Attorney General Richardson had picked Cox as the special prosecutor. Cox had been solicitor general in the Kennedy administration, was a close friend of the Kennedys', and looked to Nixon like the same kind of political enemy he had fought for years. With Cox successfully pursuing the tapes in court, Nixon had plenty of reason to fear the special prosecutor.

There were two major problems with the president's plan. First, he would have to get Cox himself to agree to the Stennis compromise. This would be difficult, since Cox would have to be asked to give up access to the tapes which he had already won in two courts. Cox would have to be convinced that the "verified" transcripts would be as solid evidence in court as the tapes themselves would have been. Second, the attorney general, during his own confirmation hearings in the Senate, had promised that he would not fire Cox except for gross improprieties. To fire Cox under the Nixon scheme would compromise Attorney General Richardson's integrity, possibly to the point of forcing his resignation, thus adding to the public perception that Nixon was concealing his own role in the Watergate cover-up.

In an effort to solve this second problem, the president's men told Richardson that, after all, Cox would not necessarily be fired. Eventually, they did get the attorney general to agree to the Stennis compromise. Through the week of October 14, Alexander Haig, Nixon's new chief of staff, met off and on with Richardson and then Richardson met with Cox, attempting to work out details of the plan that would deprive Cox of the tapes and substitute transcripts verified by Stennis. From all accounts, Cox took the offer seriously and attempted to introduce provisions to insure that the transcripts would hold up in court. Cox proposed that Stennis be made a "special master" by court designation and that the special prosecutor's office have a role in aiding the senator, thus removing suspicion that the White House might alter the transcripts and that Stennis would either agree to the alterations or miss some important point in the tapes. Cox argued, and correctly so, that only the prosecutors knew the case well enough to understand the importance of the conversations on the tapes.

However, Cox's proposals were ignored, and the White House developed the plan in such a way that he could not possibly accept it. By the end of that week, Richardson had exhausted his efforts to convince Cox of the merits of the plan. Charles Alan Wright was called into the game, and he presented Cox with several ultimatums. Cox said later that Wright told him he would have to agree to seek no more evidence from the White House. To accept such a stipulation would have required Cox to give up the very independence he had insisted on before taking the job. And it was that independence that made Cox a trustworthy figure in Washington at the time. By Friday, the White House had Cox backed into a corner. Having constructed a "compromise" they knew

Cox couldn't accept, they decided that instead of having Cox fired after agreement on the plan had been reached, they would get him fired now for not accepting the compromise. There was still concern that if Richardson resigned in consequence, the public too would support Cox, not the president. But apparently Nixon and his men believed Richardson fully accepted the Stennis plan and would therefore agree to fire Cox for his refusal to accept it.

That Friday morning, John Dean appeared in my courtroom to enter his guilty plea. He looked even younger than he had on television. He was dressed neatly in suit and tie, his round, shell-rimmed glasses giving him a prep-school air. I asked him the usual questions—whether his plea was entered voluntarily, whether he understood his right to trial by jury, and so on. He did understand, since the plea was the result of months of bargaining with the special prosecutor. That bargaining had begun as an attempt by Dean to get total immunity from prosecution in exchange for his damning testimony about the others in the cover-up conspiracy. But young Dean was too heavily involved himself to be let go completely. He had agreed to plead guilty to a one-count felony charge, for conspiracy to obstruct justice and defraud the United States. In the plea-bargaining arrangement, the prosecutor had agreed that this charge would cover all of Dean's offenses in the Watergate case, but had wisely reserved the right to charge him with perjury should his allegations later be proven false, especially if the White House tapes showed he had lied.

I put off Dean's sentencing until later. As he left the courtroom, Dean's lawyer, Charles Shaffer, one of the shrewdest criminal lawyers in town, released a statement explaining that Dean had given up his search for total immunity because he no longer feared becoming "the Watergate scapegoat." The statement also said that Dean hoped "others involved will also come forward and accept responsibility for their complicity." Dean was the third member of the cover-up conspiracy to plead guilty and agree to testify at the later trials. Magruder, who had committed perjury in my courtroom during the break-in trial, and Fred C. LaRue, who had assisted in the pay-off arrangements for the break-in defendants, had pleaded guilty earlier. With Dean a government witness, the men in the White House must have become even more intent upon stopping Cox as quickly as possible.

Shortly after Dean's plea, I left town with my daughter

Tricia for Fairfield, Connecticut, to keep an appointment with the president of Fairfield University, Father Fitzgerald. Tricia wanted to look into Fairfield as a possible college to attend the next fall. By the time we arrived, on Friday evening, I already regretted having left Washington.

That evening the White House released a statement saying that Nixon would neither appeal the court of appeals order on the tapes nor turn them over to me. Rather, he would provide a summary of their contents, and Senator Stennis, after listening to the tapes, would report on whether or not that summary was correct. The statement also explained that Nixon had ordered Cox, "as an employee of the executive branch to make no further attempts by judicial process to obtain tapes, notes, or memoranda of presidential conversations." The president was trying to slam the door on the Watergate scandal. But he had made the worst blunder of his entire political life.

Cox announced that night that he would not follow the directive since it did not agree with the conditions under which he had agreed to serve. At a Saturday press conference, which I saw on television along with almost everyone else, Cox explained his refusal in reasonable, patient tones. If the White House had been gambling that Cox would seem arrogant in not accepting the Stennis plan, they had lost. Cox's performance turned the tables on the White House and added further to the impression that Nixon was covering up the Watergate scandal.

Since the president's ploy was already public, he could not turn back. Later Saturday afternoon, Nixon's chief of staff, Alexander Haig, ordered Richardson to fire Cox for refusing the Stennis arrangement. Rather than betray his promise to the Senate, Richardson resigned. Haig then called the deputy attorney general, William Ruckelshaus, who similarly refused, and said he would quit his post in protest. Solicitor General Robert Bork, a brilliant and very conservative law professor from Yale, became acting attorney general and, finally, issued the notice that Cox was dismissed. Bork later explained that he felt the president had the authority to fire Cox and that someone had to carry out that order. The White House then announced the results of what was soon called the "Saturday-Night Massacre": Cox had been fired, Richardson had resigned. Ruckelshaus had been fired before his letter of resignation reached the White House, and the office of special prosecutor had been abolished.

Of all the incredible events during the Watergate affair, that Saturday's were the most unbelievable. As I watched the story unfold on television, I couldn't get away from the feeling that the president had lost his grip on reality. My secretary told me later that reporters had been ringing my phone off the hook, but she had refused to tell them where I was. That was lucky, because by Saturday evening I was seething. Tricia and I had dinner together, and I couldn't relax for thinking about what was going on in Washington.

In the first place, the Stennis plan had been silly. What the hell did Senator Stennis know about the case anyway? And how could the president and his lawyers conclude that I would ever have let into evidence a version of the tapes prepared by the White House, no matter what a single senator said about that version? The plan was, to my mind, an open defiance of my court order and of the order from the court of appeals. President Nixon had let the deadline for an appeal to the Supreme Court pass and was now plainly going to ignore the courts.

On television, I saw FBI agents taking charge of the special prosecutor's office. It began to look as if some colonels in a Latin-American country had staged a coup. "What the hell is this crowd doing?" I thought. I cheered the resignations of Richardson and Ruckelshaus. I had been impressed by Cox, thinking that if the Watergate case was to be disposed of without further suspicion, the White House needed someone like him to carry out the investigation. I thought his firing was brutal, contemptible, unjustified, and arrogant.

As far as I was concerned, the president was breaking the law. And I was in no way alone in that opinion. After the weekend, as I was returning to Washington, eighty-four members of the House of Representatives introduced the legislation calling for impeachment of the president of the United States. Ninety-eight members introduced the legislation to create a new special prosecutor's office independent of the administration. Western Union had to add special facilities to handle the flood of telegrams flowing to the Capitol protesting Nixon's action.

On Saturday night, Archibald Cox issued a statement in which he said, "Whether we shall continue to be a government of laws and not of men is now for Congress and ultimately the American people to decide." He was clearly implying that impeachment was the only course of action available to bring the Watergate scandal to a close. I had set Tuesday, October 23, as the date on which the White House had to produce the tapes. That date still stood; the president's lawyers were due in court on that day. As I traveled back from Connecticut I was determined that the president was not going to fool around with the courts the way he had with Cox. The awe of the presidency that I had felt when considering how to frame the opinion about the tapes had diminished. I was just plain damned angry. I had the deep feeling that something I had spent my life serving—the rule of law—was in terrible danger. I didn't know quite what I was going to do when the president's lawyers showed up in court on Tuesday, but I knew I was going to do something.

In a normal case, someone who defied court orders as Nixon had would be inviting, at least in my court, a stretch in jail for contempt. I knew I couldn't order the president arrested, although I must admit the thought occurred to me more than once that weekend. I didn't know what Congress would do. But I knew I had to act. This sort of defiance could not be tolerated if the role of the courts in our system of government was to continue to mean anything. I had a couple of long talks with Todd as we began considering and rejecting various plans. Finally, we settled on a course of action to deal with the president's defiance. I asked Todd to start the paper work. I began actually to look forward to the confrontation that was coming on Tuesday.

10
Confrontation

On Monday, October 22, a White House messenger delivered Charles Alan Wright's motion proposing the Stennis
compromise. I reviewed the proposal carefully to make sure
it was the same as the plan released by the White House the
previous Friday night. It was the same, and it didn't change
my mind about what steps to take. Todd and I continued to
work on our own plan to deal with the president's refusal to
turn over the tapes.

Like nearly everyone else in Washington, I wasn't certain
what would happen next. As things stood, the office of the
special prosecutor apparently had been abolished and the
Watergate investigation returned to the Justice Department
and Henry Petersen, head of the criminal division there. The
feeling was very strong, however, that the investigation had
come to an end. That left two grand juries, one of which had
been hearing evidence in the case for more than a year, without any leadership. So my first concern was that the grand
juries be protected. Even if the firing of Cox and the aboli-
tion of the special prosecutor's office was within the president's authority, the grand juries were clearly within my
authority. So I arranged to have both juries called into open
court Tuesday morning.

Todd and I discussed the possibility of my naming a
special, court-appointed prosecutor to take up where Cox had
left off. But the authority for such an appointment seemed to
be lacking. I decided to move carefully, within the clear limits the law allowed. I felt that two things needed doing. First,

the grand juries had to be reassured about their role. Second, the president's contempt of my order had to be dealt with.

I slept hardly at all Monday night, even though I was tired from my trip to Connecticut and emotionally exhausted by the anxiety the president's defiant attitude was causing me. I was worried, but as I said before, I knew I had to act and I knew it was time to face the issue with the president directly.

Just before ten o'clock Tuesday morning, I finished writing a statement I wanted to read to the two grand juries. The courtroom was again jammed. Ten lawyers from the special prosecutor's office were crowded around the government's table in front of the bench. All the members of both grand juries were present. My old friend John J. Wilson and his associate Frank Strickler were in court representing H. R. Haldeman, who had been scheduled to testify before one of the grand juries that day. They wanted to find out if those proceedings were still scheduled. Reporters, law students, and other lawyers filled the rest of the room, all gathered to see how I would react to the events of the weekend.

I asked Cappy Capitanio to read the names of the members of the two grand juries. He began with the first jury, which had been sworn in June, 1972, and had gotten the Watergate case right after the break-in. Then he read the names of the August, 1973, grand jury, which had been impaneled to handle the growing number of associated investigations stemming from the Watergate affair—investigations, for example, into illegal corporate campaign contributions, into improper influence on the government setting of milk-price supports, and into the relationship between the International Telephone and Telegraph Corporation, the Nixon administration, and the disposition of an antitrust suit against that company.

Members of the jury [I began], I thought it prudent to call you here this morning to explain, in so far as possible, your present status.

I imagine that in view of events that have recently transpired many, or perhaps all, of you may be experiencing some anxiety regarding your role as grand jurors and the role of the grand juries themselves. My brief remarks perhaps may alleviate some of that anxiety. Such, at least, is my intent this morning.

"You are advised first, that the grand juries on which

you serve remain operative and intact. You are still
grand jurors and the grand juries you constitute still
function. In this regard you should be aware that the
oath you took upon entering this service remains binding on each one of you. You must all be especially
careful at this time to fully and strictly adhere to that
oath. . . .

To impress upon each member of the two juries that they
could not be interfered with, I read the oath that pledges
each member to treat the business of the grand jury "as absolutely sacred and secret." And I repeated the charge I had
given the juries when they started their work, in which I said,
"[You] must permit no one on the outside to talk to you
concerning any matter relating to the discharge of your duties." Then I continued:

To my knowledge, each of you has been true to your
oath and the trust reposed in you as grand jurors. You
are to be commended for the orderly, efficient, and honorable manner in which you have conducted your affairs. I implore you to carry your work forward in the
future as you have in the past.

This brings me to my second point; these two grand
juries will continue to function and pursue their work.
You are not dismissed and will not be dismissed except
by this court as provided by law upon the completion of
your work or the conclusion of your terms. Your service
to date, I realize, has occasioned personal sacrifices for
many of you and inconvenience for all of you. You did
not choose this assignment; it is an obligation of citizenship which it fell your lot to bear at this time, and you
have borne it well. The court and the country are grateful to you. Nevertheless, you must be prepared to press
forward. We rely on your continued integrity and perse-
verance.

Finally, I urge you to be patient while the various and
immediate problems surrounding your investigations are
resolved by the court. I understand that the August,
1973, grand jury will be meeting this morning to hear
testimony, and that the June, 1972, grand jury will similarly convene tomorrow. I hope you will proceed in your
regular fashion. In due course, the questions which now

plague us will be answered, and you may rely on the court to safeguard your rights and to preserve the integrity of these judicial proceedings. Meanwhile, you must steadily and deliberately pursue your investigations.

I felt that by that statement I had at least served notice that the courts and their official investigative bodies, the grand juries, were still on course in the Watergate investigation. I again looked in the direction of the table where the young members of the Special Prosecution Force were gathered, with Archibald Cox conspicuously absent. At that point, I really didn't know what their status was. They had obviously come to court for some reassurance. Richard Ben-Veniste, one of the young lawyers concentrating on the cover-up case, told me later that they had all hoped for some sign from the bench indicating support from the court. I should have injected a personal commendation for their work and their courage right there in open court. The day was so tense, and the prospect of the afternoon session concerning the tapes so preoccupying, that it slipped my mind. I only thought of it later.

John Wilson stood before the bench to say that he had been informed that members of the special prosecutor's office still wanted to question his client before the grand jury that day. My charge to the juries had answered his questions. It was a strange time. I was reassuring the grand juries that, unlike the Special Prosecution Force, they were still in existence. And yet here were the junior members of the special prosecutor's office preparing to question one of the chief suspects in the cover-up case. Despite his announcement Saturday night, the president and his men had apparently been so shocked by the public outrage at their actions that they had never actually disbanded the rest of the prosecutor's staff. Although the status of these men was unclear that morning—had they been fired, were they working for Henry Petersen at the Justice Department, or what?—they had bravely decided to plow ahead until someone stopped them.

Next a law professor from George Washington University addressed the court. His name was John F. Banshaf III, and he had achieved a local reputation as a public-interest lawyer. He had decided to try to intervene in the case by asking that I appoint a special counsel to the grand jury and that I issue an injunction stopping the firing of Cox and the Special

Prosecution Force. I resented his appearance. I'm sure he was well-intentioned, but I didn't feel I needed other lawyers stomping around in what was already a touchy and difficult situation.

"If the court decides it is necessary to appoint special counsel, the court doesn't feel it needs guidance or service from outside organizations. If this time comes the court will select someone to represent the grand jury," I said rather gruffly, and adjourned the session until 2 P.M.

Actually, the idea that the grand juries themselves and thus the court had the right to have a counsel presenting evidence in the Watergate investigation had been raised with me before the court session. Archibald Cox had written to me on Monday, and had stated:

> The dismissal clearly terminates any authority I may have had under the Attorney General. I am anxious not to involve your court or any other in avoidable controversy; and such proceedings as may be required ought not to be colored by my involvement or personal concerns.
>
> At the same time I am genuinely doubtful concerning my professional duty. The grand jury unanimously voted that I should seek to have the subpoena enforced, and the grand jury is, of course, wholly independent of the Executive Branch. Both the Court of Appeals and this Court explicitly recognized that I appeared on behalf of the grand jury as well as an officer in the Executive Branch. In addition, as an attorney I am an officer of the Court. It seems quite possible that my dismissal does not terminate my duties to the Court in these capacities; and although I am reluctant to intrude myself, I wish not to shrink from any obligations.
>
> I write this letter, therefore, to ask guidance from the Court. . . .

Cox seemed to be volunteering to serve as counsel to the grand jury, despite his firing by the president. It was an interesting idea. But I also wondered what the reaction would be should Cox, fired as special prosecutor, be reinstated by the court. I decided to let the matter rest for a few days while I saw what other developments took place. Besides, I was still too concerned about the president's refusal to turn over the tapes to think much about appointing my own prosecutor, even if a thorough study proved I had the power to do so.

After court, I asked Todd to bring Henry Ruth, the senior member of the Special Prosecution Force, and a group of his assistants, to my chambers. I had admired how calm they had been, at least in public, during the past few difficult days. I told them, "The law can take care of this situation." And I praised them for not issuing inflammatory statements that could only make the situation worse. I urged them to proceed with their work while I considered what more I could do. They seemed relieved to have that reassurance, and I still wish I had given it to them in public.

We worked through the luncheon recess to get ready for the afternoon confrontation with the president's lawyer. There was no doubt in anyone's mind that Charles Alan Wright would attempt to argue for the Stennis plan. And there was no doubt in my mind that I would reject it. I prepared a nine-page set of questions to ask Wright. The questions would be preceded by a reading of my own order to produce the tapes, and the court of appeals order affirming my decision. Just as I left my chambers, I took out of Mrs. Holley's typewriter a one-page court order that I would sign and serve on Wright following the arguments.

Again, my courtroom was full. The young special prosecutors were again crowded around the government's table, without their leader. Charles Alan Wright was accompanied by Leonard Garment and Douglas Parker from the White House. I felt a little as I had when I fought Tommy Thompson in Miami. Only this time the test of strength was between two branches of government. The courts and the executive had been sparring since summer over the question of the president's tapes. Nixon had attempted to end the struggle the previous Friday. Now, it seemed, the crowd had gathered to see how the bout would end.

I read aloud my own order to produce the tapes, and the court of appeals order. My nervousness caught up with me then. Having read the order, and intending to ask Wright for the president's response, I said instead, "The court will now read the order." Then I mumbled that I had already read the order, annoyed with myself for stumbling at that tense moment.

"Now are counsel for the president prepared at this time to

file with the court the response of the president to the modified order of the court?" I finally asked Wright.

"Mr. Chief Judge, may it please the court," Wright began. "I am not prepared at this time to file a response. I am, however, authorized to say that the president of the United States would comply in all respects with the order of August 29 as modified by the court of appeals. It will require some time, as Your Honor realizes, to put those materials together, to do the indexing, itemizing [that] the court of appeals calls for."

I couldn't believe what I had heard.

"As I understand your statement, that will be delivered to this court?"

"To the court *in camera*," Wright answered.

"You will follow the decisions or statements delineated by me?" I asked, still not sure that I understood.

"[He] will comply in all respects with what Your Honor has just read," Wright replied quickly. "As the court is aware, the president yesterday filed with the clerk of the court a response along different lines, along the lines indicated in the statement to the country on Friday. That statement, if it was ever officially filed with the court, is now withdrawn.

"The response that was made yesterday, the president's statement on Friday, was what we hoped would be a satisfactory method of accommodating the needs that led Your Honor and the court of appeals to rule as they did, while minimizing the danger to confidentiality. We had hoped that that kind of a solution would end a constitutional crisis. The events of the weekend, I think, have made it very apparent that, even if I had been successful as I hoped I would be in persuading you, Mr. Chief Judge, that this did adequately satisfy the spirit of the court of appeals ruling, there would have been those who would have said the president is defying the law. This president does not defy the law, and he has authorized me to say he will comply in full with the orders of the court."

I was overwhelmed with relief. The president had backed down from the confrontation. He had stepped away from perhaps the worst clash between two branches of government in our history. I had been prepared to deal harshly with Nixon's defiance, but I was delighted to be relieved of that burden.

"Mr. Wright, the court is very happy the president has reached this decision. I appreciate the efforts in that," I told the president's lawyer. I felt a smile creeping across my face. Less than twenty minutes after we had begun, I adjourned the court. I took my nine pages of questions and the court order with me. I laid them, unused, on my desk and stretched out on my couch to unwind a bit.

The series of questions had been drawn up to determine the president's precise intentions for each of the nine subpoenaed tapes. For example, I was going to ask Wright, "Will the president at any time produce to this court for its inspection *in camera* the tapes and other electronic and/or mechanical recordings or reproductions of the meeting of June 20, 1972, in the president's Executive Office Building office involving the president, John Ehrlichman, and H. R. Haldeman from 10:30 A.M. to noon (time approximate) excepting any segments relating to national defense or foreign relations?" For each subpoenaed tape, the question spelled out the time, place, and participants in the conversation. After each of those questions, I had planned to ask whether such tape existed, whether the president planned to produce memoranda, papers, transcripts, or other writings relating to the tape, and whether such papers existed.

I was prepared to hear Wright say, in each case, that the tape would not be turned over. "Based on these responses," my prepared statement went on, "the court concludes that the president has not and apparently will not comply with the grand jury subpoena *duces tecum* as ordered by this court and the court of appeals. The court will, therefore, file at this time and serve counsel in open court with an order directed to the president to show cause why he should not be held in contempt of court and be subjected to a fine for such contempt." The order I had drawn up required the president to appear the next morning in my court to explain why a contempt citation should not be issued and fines not be imposed. And should he elect simply to send his lawyers, I required that he personally sign a waiver of his right to appear.

There was no doubt in my mind that when the president's lawyers appeared pursuant to that order, I would find Nixon in contempt. And I had decided that after he was found in contempt, I would levy a stiff fine to try to force compliance. As I said, I had thought a few times about imposing a jail sentence, but that was absurd. The country couldn't stand it; there wasn't even a vice-president. And what would I have done to enforce the sentence? Send the United States marshals over to confront the Secret Service?

But a fine was possible. I knew the president loved money. I knew he had expensive homes in Florida and California. So I decided to hit him in his pocketbook; I would fine him between $25,000 and $50,000 for each day the tapes weren't turned over. I think that would have brought him around in a short time. And since the court of appeals had supported the subpoena in the first place, I didn't doubt that they would uphold the fines. Wouldn't that have been a hell of a situation? The president of the United States being fined thousands of dollars a day for being in contempt of court.

Though a president of the United States had never been fined for contempt of court, or indeed even been held in contempt, there were ample legal precedents to justify the fines. The first to come to mind were two cases in the 1940's involving the United Mine Workers. In 1946, the United States government had taken control of the coal mines under a special war labor act. The mines were operated under an agreement between the secretary of the interior and the United Mine Workers and their president, John L. Lewis. At one point, the union wanted to renegotiate that agreement, and when that effort failed, Lewis notified the workers, who immediately went on strike. The government sought a temporary restraining order, and the court ordered the union and Lewis to stop the strike. When Lewis took no action, the union was fined $3.5 million and Lewis himself was fined $10,000. The Supreme Court upheld that ruling, which had come from Judge T. Alan Goldsborough, of our federal district court in Washington. Later, the union again refused to instruct its members to return to work, this time while under a Taft-Hartley Act back-to-work order. Judge Goldsborough again found Lewis and the union in contempt, and fined the union president $20,000 and the union $1.4 million. That ruling was upheld by the United States Court of Appeals.

What had caused President Nixon's change of mind? I can only guess, but surely his lawyers warned him that unless he complied with the court order on the tapes, he took the risk of being found in contempt. Perhaps they even anticipated that the logical course for me to follow, after a finding of contempt, would be to impose a large fine. There couldn't have been much doubt in their minds that I would not permit the orders of two courts to be defied.

The president had plainly been taken by surprise by the scope and intensity of the reaction against his firing of Cox. He had failed to see that Cox, and the courts as well, stood higher in the estimation of most Americans than did his administration. With impeachment resolutions being introduced wholesale in Congress, the risk of facing a contempt citation and a fine was too much for the president's shattered political strength to bear. I had felt that in the end I had been left no choice but to try, as dramatically as possible, to enforce the law. And in the end, the president's gross miscalculation in firing Cox had left him no choice but to comply with the rule of law. Looking back on those days now, I think that had the president not capitulated on the tapes in October, he would have been impeached within months.

Throughout that week, there was still a great deal of confusion about the status of the special prosecutor's office. Henry Petersen, in the Justice Department, had formally taken control of the investigation, and that raised some questions in my mind. I had seen Petersen in operation as Earl Silbert's boss during the break-in case, and I wasn't at all sure how he would handle the case now.

Two days after Wright announced in court that the tapes would be turned over, the special prosecutor's office petitioned me to issue an order protecting their files and prohibiting anyone except the prosecutors and Petersen from having access to them. I signed that order the next day, with visions of the FBI "seizure" of the prosecutor's office the previous week still fresh in my mind.

One thing wasn't confusing, though. We were finally going to get those nine White House tapes. At least I thought so. Exactly one week after Wright had assured me that the tapes were forthcoming, we had a private meeting in my chambers, attended by White House counsel, J. Fred Buzhardt, a mild-mannered Mississippian who had taken up the thankless job of representing the president, and three attorneys from the special prosecutor's office—Richard Ben-Veniste, Henry Ruth, and Philip Lacovara. We had been discussing the procedures to be followed in making the tapes available for my review when, in the middle of the conversation, Buzhardt quietly announced that two of the tapes could not be turned over—one for June 20, 1972, that recorded the first telephone conversation between the president and John Mitchell after the break-in, and one for the evening of April 15, 1973, that covered a meeting in which John Dean informed the president that he had been meeting with the prosecutors. Buzhardt said, it seemed to me with some embarrassment, that they didn't exist.

Incredible! Every time I thought this case was on track, something happened to derail it. The subpoena for the tapes had originally been issued in July. Here it was the end of October, and the White House was making the first public admission that two critical tapes didn't exist. My immediate reaction was to get the matter into the public view as soon as possible. I told the lawyers to appear in open court the next afternoon to begin a hearing on the missing tapes.

On October 31, we began the inquiry into the missing tapes. Hearings on the tapes were to drag on into the next year. And it seemed that with each passing day some new problem was brought to light, casting even more doubt on the credibility of the White House and on the integrity and safety of the tapes.

The first problem Fred Buzhardt faced in trying to explain why the tapes were missing was to get his story straight. On the opening day of the hearing, Buzhardt said there was no tape of the president's April 15 meeting with Dean because a timer on the elaborate White House taping system had failed to function. The timer was designed, a Secret Service technician explained in court, to change tape reels automatically when a reel was full. But before long, Buzhardt revised his first explanation. He now said that the April 15 meeting with Dean, in the president's office in the Executive Office Building, hadn't been recorded because both of the available tapes had been filled up during a busy day of meetings in that office. April 15 was a Sunday, and the Secret Service only checked the tapes on weekdays, he said. Under this explanation, there had been nothing wrong with the timing device. Buzhardt also explained that the June 20 Nixon–Mitchell conversation hadn't been recorded because the tape system was attached to only three of the White House telephone extensions and the president had apparently been using another extension, not linked to the recorders.

It was really the first time the younger members of the Special Prosecution Force had faced the president's lawyers in a trial-like atmosphere. I was most impressed with them. Richard Ben-Veniste was a real tiger. In the painstaking examination of the Secret Service experts and other White

House personnel, Ben-Veniste, despite his youth, showed a lot of courtroom savvy. He managed over the weeks of that hearing to reveal the sloppiness and carelessness with which the tapes had been handled; he even brought out the fact that part of the Secret Service log listing who had borrowed the tapes, and for what periods, was written on a piece of brown paper that looked like a fragment of a grocery bag.

Under Ben-Veniste's questioning, the details of the taping system were laid out for the first time. In the president's main office in the White House—the Oval Office—microphones had been concealed in small holes drilled in the wood of his mahogany desk. That system, along with the one in the Executive Office Building office and one in the Lincoln Room, was sound activated: when someone in the office spoke, recording began automatically. But it also began, as I was to discover myself a month later, when a vacuum cleaner was run, a band played outside the office, or the president coughed or whistled or set his coffee cup down in its saucer. There was also a tape system in the cabinet room, but that one was manually operated. The switches, at the president's place at the large, oval cabinet table, were marked "Haldeman" and "Butterfield."

Ben-Veniste also developed the information that H. R. Haldeman had taken twenty-two separate tapes out of the White House the previous spring before his testimony before the Senate Watergate committee. Haldeman was subpoenaed to testify at our hearing, his first courtroom appearance in the case. It seemed strange to see the president's most powerful adviser on the witness stand. He had let his severe crew cut grow out to a slightly more fashionable length, but he was as reserved and careful in court as he must have been playing politics inside the White House. He admitted listening to only one of the tapes and said he then had returned all of them to the White House. But for a man of his reputation and responsibility, he was awfully vague on details. He laced his testimony with "no recollection" and "it's conceivable" and "I couldn't confirm that." He testified for two days, and shed very little light on the problem of the two tapes.

White House aide Stephen Bull was also called. He was a model Nixonite, clean-cut, an American-flag pin in his lapel, his speech so burdened with corporate jargon as nearly to defy understanding. His testimony that Nixon himself had reviewed the tapes for twelve hours in June, 1973, prompted a request from Ben-Veniste that the tape of the president reviewing the other tapes be produced, since Nixon had listened to the tapes in his bugged Executive Office Building office. I agreed with Ben-Veniste and suggested that Buzhardt look for the so-called "tape of the tapes." But Buzhardt was shocked by the request and announced he had no authority to produce any more tapes. The tape was eventually brought in and proved to have no record of the missing April 15 conversation. The testimony from Bull also showed that he had told the president on September 29 that one tape was missing, yet at that very time the president's aides had been assuring the prosecutors that all the tapes were intact.

Jill Wine Volner, an attorney from the special prosecutor's office, shared the cross-examination duties with Ben-Veniste. On November 8, she brought the president's personal secretary, Rose Mary Woods, to the stand to try to find out how she had handled the tapes. The two clashed almost immediately, and their confrontation that day only foreshadowed a long-running battle to come later. By this time, the prosecutor's office was concerned not just with the two missing tapes but with the integrity of all the tapes. Under Mrs. Volner's questioning, Miss Woods admitted that some White House tapes were still locked in her office safe, even though Buzhardt had said in court that all the tapes were in the White House vault.

Rose Mary Woods obviously regarded having to testify in court as a major indignity to someone so close to the president. She told how she had taken twenty-nine hours to transcribe the first White House tape she had been given. When Mrs. Volner asked, "What precautions specifically did you take to avoid . . . recording over it, thereby getting rid of what was already there?" Miss Woods snapped back, "What precautions? I used my head. It is the only one I had to use."

The final witness in this sequence was the president's counsel, Fred Buzhardt. I could see that this was a difficult time for him. I had the feeling that he was doing the best he could, but that the president and others in the White House had kept him in the dark on a number of issues. He spoke so quietly from the witness stand that I had to remind him repeatedly to speak up so he could be heard.

The April 15 tape had been sought originally by Archibald Cox because the president himself, in a conversation with

Henry Petersen, had said he had taped the meeting with John Dean. Cox had written to Buzhardt requesting the tape. Buzhardt had written back saying that there was no actual tape; rather, the president was referring to a Dictabelt on which he had recorded his recollections of the meeting. This exchange of letters had taken place in June, before Alexander Butterfield had revealed the existence of the White House taping system. Now Ben-Veniste grilled Buzhardt about whether he had been instructed by the president to deliberately mislead the prosecutors about the existence of the taping system. But Buzhardt became even more vague than Haldeman had been. He said repeatedly, "I can't recall."

Finally Buzhardt had to admit that even the Dictabelt for April 15 did not exist. And he testified that he, the president, and Alexander Haig had discovered that the Dictabelt was missing on November 5, the day the White House press office was telling reporters that it would be supplied to the court in lieu of the tape.

The whole episode was a sad one for the White House. It seemed that every explanation they offered had to be revised a few days later. The lawyers on both sides had agreed that a panel of experts should be appointed to check the tapes to make sure no one had tampered with them. And the sloppy way in which the tapes had been handled led me to grant a request from the special prosecutors that the originals be turned over to me for safekeeping. The White House lawyers said they had already begun making copies for that purpose.

The last two weeks of October and the first two of November marked, I think now, the beginning of the end of Nixon's presidency. The Cox firing and the public reaction against it made it nearly impossible for the president to recover his credibility with the American public. The report of the missing tapes only added to the sense of disbelief that began to surround every statement he made about Watergate. Impeachment talk began and grew on Capitol Hill. After the disclosure that the April 15 and June 20 tapes did not exist and that the promised Dictabelt was missing, the calls for the president's resignation grew louder and more frequent. The *New York Times* on November 4 editorialized that "the one last great service that Mr. Nixon can now perform for his country is to resign." *Time Magazine* broke a fifty-year tradition by running an editorial November 12 calling for the president's resignation, saying he had "irredeemably lost his moral authority, the confidence of most of the country and therefore his ability to govern effectively." The Gallup poll showed that less than a third of the people surveyed approved of the way Nixon was handling his job as president.

The president, however, was not in a mood to leave office without a fight. He began what was soon mockingly nick-named "Operation Candor," a sort of public-relations blitz to get his side of the story over to the American people. On October 26, a few days before the disclosure that two of the sub-poenaed tapes didn't exist, the president attacked television reporting of the "Saturday-Night Massacre" as "outrageous, vicious, distorted." In early November, he issued a long ex-planation of why the tapes and Dictabelt were missing, and offered to send me a series of other tapes and personally record-ed Dictabelts to "shed light on" the missing conversations. I rejected the offer, and indicated in a memorandum that if there was additional evidence the president wanted the grand jury to have, he should send it to the jury through the special prosecutors. White House spokesmen had also indicated that they wanted to make some portions of the subpoenaed tapes public but felt it inappropriate to do so while I was getting ready to review them. That seemed like a nice way to protect themselves from discussing the tapes, so I added a note to my memorandum saying I thought the president had the right to make such information public any time he wanted to.

His most important move to retrieve his plunging political position was the announcement in late October that a new special prosecutor would be appointed. A few days later, Leon Jaworski, a prominent Texas lawyer and former presi-dent of the American Bar Association, who had been close to former President Lyndon Johnson, was picked for the job. Despite announcements that the courtly, soft-spoken Jaworski would have as much independence as his predeces-sor Archibald Cox had, there was great doubt that, having gone through the political agony of getting rid of Cox, Nixon would accept a truly tough and independent new prosecutor. That doubt would dissipate after a few weeks, however, as Jaworski turned out to be as much of a threat to the president as Cox had been. In Congress, there was still a good deal of sentiment for legislation giving the courts—and that meant my court and me—the right to appoint their own special prosecutor. Once it was clear that Jaworski was more than competent to do the job, I announced publicly that we didn't want that right, and the legislation was allowed to die.

Nixon then made a series of public appearances, still trying to rebuild his political popularity. In Orlando, Florida, he told a group of newspaper editors who were interrogating him about his tax returns, "I am not a crook." Questions had been raised previously about government spending to improve Nixon's two homes and about a large tax deduction he had taken when he turned his vice-presidential papers over to the National Archives. He was not under attack just for Watergate; his personal financial integrity was also being examined.

Nixon repeatedly asserted that he would not resign, and in one press conference, he bragged about his handling of the Middle East war even while the worst of the Watergate problems were plaguing him. "I have a quality," he told reporters, "which is—I guess I must have inherited it from my Midwestern mother and father—which is that the tougher it gets the cooler I get." He was to have plenty of chances in the coming months to get cooler.

On November 20, Nixon met with a group of Republican governors in Memphis. They asked if they should brace themselves for any "other bombs" that might be about to explode in the Watergate case. He said, according to the governors, that if there were any, he was not aware of them. The next day in my chambers, Fred Buzhardt dropped another of those bombs.

11

The Eighteen-Minute
Gap

Fred Buzhardt was as pale as a ghost. He was obviously extremely nervous and very troubled. His colleague on the White House legal staff, Leonard Garment, didn't look much better as the two came into my chambers to join Special Prosecutor Jaworski and three of Jaworski's staff members. It was the day before Thanksgiving, 1973, and I had been looking forward to a long weekend before resuming hearings on the two nonexistent tapes. But Leon Jaworski had called late that morning, saying it was urgent that he and the White House lawyers have a meeting with me that day.

Buzhardt got right to the point.

"Judge, we have a problem," he said.

He told me that in the process of preparing their own analysis of the subpoenaed tapes before submitting them to me for review, they had discovered an eighteen-minute gap on a tape of a conversation between the president and his two top aides, Haldeman and Ehrlichman. Strangely, he called the gap an "obliteration of the intelligence," and, he added quickly, "it doesn't appear from what we know at this point that it could have been accidental."

The harried lawyer was right. He did have a problem. The White House was to some extent recovering from the revelation that two of the subpoenaed tapes didn't exist. Now they were faced with explaining what Buzhardt was describing as the deliberate erasure of a part of another tape. From the very beginning of the Watergate case, the president's problem had been that he appeared to be helping to cover up the facts. That was what John Dean had charged in his Senate testimony. The president's long battle to avoid turning over the tapes, and his firing of Archibald Cox, had been seen as further attempts to frustrate the investigation. Now charges of obstruction of justice and contempt of court were clearly a possibility.

"So there is a lapse?" I asked Buzhardt.

"Yes. And the circumstance is even a little worse than that, Your Honor," he answered.

"I don't know how it could get much worse," I said.

"Just wait," Garment added grimly.

Buzhardt explained that the gap appeared on the June 20 tape, made three days after the break-in at the Democratic headquarters, during the president's first day back in the White House after a vacation in Florida. Archibald Cox had subpoenaed that tape believing that it might include a discussion by the president and his aides on how to handle the embarrassing incident. On the morning of June 20, Nixon had had two separate meetings, one with Ehrlichman and one with Haldeman. The gap occurred about three minutes into the discussion with Haldeman. Buzhardt said he had timed the gap at eighteen minutes fifteen seconds.

Worse than that, the lawyers had found Haldeman's own notes of this meeting with the president. They covered two pages of yellow legal-sized paper. Notes on the second page indicated that the two men talked about Watergate. This, Buzhardt said, proved that the erased portion of the tape was related to the break-in. After the gap, the conversation was about some unrelated matter. Apparently, someone had picked out the Watergate section and erased it to protect President Nixon.

Buzhardt explained that he had actually known there was a gap on the tape some weeks before. While trying to make a transcript of the tape, Rose Mary Woods had made what Buzhardt was told was a "slight erasure." But, the lawyer said, he had thought this had affected a portion of the tape that was not covered by the subpoena, and he had given it no more thought until he realized the length of the gap and the fact that the erased portion was indeed included in the court order. Miss Woods, according to the White House lawyers, was the last person to have listened to the altered tape. In their view, she was the person most likely to blame for the eighteen-minute gap.

Buzhardt pleaded for a few more days to investigate the question before having to make the gap public. "Announcement of this type of thing could have a devastating effect, he said. Jaworski, pointing out the potential criminal charges that could result from the gap, urged that the matter be disclosed quickly.

My own instinct was to make the problem public as soon as possible. Obviously, something was very wrong, and I didn't want to give the White House a lot of time to dream up explanations before I took the matter into open court. I was concerned too since there had already been a week's delay in reporting the gap—Buzhardt claimed he had discovered its length and importance the previous Wednesday—and I didn't want to authorize any more delay. In a way, I was reminded of the McCord letter. Something was being concealed again. They didn't want it out in the open. "I always find it better to bring these things out as fast as you can," I told Buzhardt. "I am for disclosure as soon as possible. I just can't help it. It is a sad thing to have to report." I asked the lawyers to be in my courtroom at 4 P.M.

Buzhardt was stunned. He protested that he couldn't get Rose Mary Woods into court by that time. But all I planned was to make the gap public and schedule a hearing to investigate the cause. Buzhardt protested further that Rose Mary Woods would need her own attorney, signaling that the White House team was letting her fight her own battle. Buzhardt was also worried about just what he'd say in court.

"I would like a little bit of time to write this out. In fact, I would like to take a while to write it out because I want to be very careful what I say here," he said.

I gave him an hour and a half to compose his thoughts, and at four o'clock, in open court, he announced the tape gap. I then asked the White House to turn over voluntarily the original versions of the subpoenaed tapes, for safekeeping by the court. Buzhardt had initially opposed turning over the full reels of tape, mainly because they contained more than the subpoenaed conversations. He had apparently thought he would cut them to eliminate all but the requested material. But the prosecutors objected strenuously, arguing that with a panel of experts ready to examine all the tapes to determine whether there had been tampering—and now to determine what had happened to the eighteen minutes of "obliterated intelligence"—only full reels would do. I agreed and asked for the full reels.

By the following Monday, the White House had turned over the seven reels of tape for June 20. We took elaborate precautions to make sure this precious evidence was well protected. We had obtained an especially strong file cabinet-safe from the supersecret National Security Agency. It was installed in a corner of my chambers, right under my framed judicial commission signed by President Eisenhower. I chose three numbers from Lucy's birthdate, December 27, 1923, and then reversed them to form the combination 23-27-12. Todd and I both memorized the numbers, and we told them to no one else, not even Lucy. United States marshals were put on twenty-four-hour duty outside my offices, and the security forces in the courthouse were told to be especially alert. Eventually, we added a closed-circuit-television system to monitor the outside door to my chambers from a security post on the first floor of the courthouse. It was tempting to think about listening to the tapes now that they were in my office, but I could not rightfully do so until the White House had prepared an index of their contents and had submitted a detailed listing of sections to be exempted, either for national-security reasons or because they dealt with matters irrelevant to Watergate. It would be several weeks before I would get my first hearing of the president and his aides at work on Watergate.

When Rose Mary Woods returned to my courtroom on the Monday after Thanksgiving, her manner was quite different than it had been in her previous appearance, when she testified about the two nonexistent tapes. Before she had been self-assured, often indignant; now the president's secretary was subdued and appeared quite worried. During her first appearance, she had apparently been represented by the White House lawyers. Now they had abandoned her. She had hired Charles S. Rhyne, another former president of the American Bar Association and an old friend of mine from my days as an active member of the District of Columbia Bar Association. The questioning of Miss Woods was handled by Jill Wine Volner, whose youth and innocent-looking face were in sharp contrast to Miss Woods's age and her heavy make-up. Mrs. Volner set the tone of the confrontation with her first remarks to Miss Woods:

"Miss Woods, I would like to advise you of your constitutional rights. You have a right not to answer any questions, the answers to which may tend to incriminate you, do you understand that?"

"Yes, ma'am," said Rose Mary Woods quietly.

The president's closest associate over many years of his public life, Rose Mary Woods was in an awkward position. She was above all, a Nixon loyalist. She had even been referred to over the years as "the fifth Nixon," the first four being the president and his wife and two daughters. She obviously wanted to protect Nixon from any further Watergate problems. But at the same time, she would face a criminal charge herself if it could be proved that she had deliberately destroyed evidence critical to the Watergate case. She wanted to take responsibility for the gap, so that Nixon would not be blamed, yet she also wanted to avoid any criminal liability for obstructing justice. It was a difficult line to draw.

Rose Mary Woods explained that she had been instructed by the president to make a typewritten transcript of the tapes so that he and his lawyers could determine just what evidence they contained. On the weekend of September 29, she testified, she had gone with Nixon to the presidential retreat at Camp David, Maryland, and had begun work on the June 20 tape. She worked for twenty-nine hours on that tape, she said, using a Sony tape recorder like those in the White House taping system. Many recorders have a foot pedal, so that the secretary's hands are left free to type, but this machine did not. In addition to the inconvenience of hand operation, she had trouble understanding the words on the tape. Speakers often interrupted one another, and there were loud noises from coffee cups being moved, doors opening and closing, and the like. At one point during the Camp David weekend, she said, the president himself stopped by her office to check on her progress. He listened to some of the tape, pushing buttons on the machine to move the tape forward and backward, and offered his sympathy about the difficult job.

After that weekend, Miss Woods testified, she returned to the White House on Monday, October 1, and began work on the tape again, this time with a new recorder, a Uher 5000 machine made in West Germany. This one had a foot pedal, which made her work easier. That morning she finished the portion of the tape in which the meeting between Nixon and Ehrlichman was recorded. Miss Woods read in court a note to her from Alexander Haig, the president's top aide, who had taken Haldeman's place the previous spring. The note said that only the Ehrlichman portion of the tape was under subpoena. Having finished that section, she continued to listen to the tape to make sure that Ehrlichman had left the president's office and that only Haldeman was now present.

She listened for a few minutes, until her phone rang, she testified. At that point, she made a critical mistake. The easiest way to stop the machine was simply to remove her foot from the pedal. But instead, she testified, she reached for the control buttons. By accident, she pushed the button marked "Recording" rather than the one marked "Stop." And even though her phone was five feet away, she left her foot on the pedal, thus keeping the machine operating and erasing the conversation on the tape.

"I must say after I turned around from the telephone, being someone who has tried to do a good job, I practically panicked," Miss Woods testified. "I pushed back the button, the 'Return' button—and then heard the noise."

She realized her mistake immediately and went into the president's office to inform him. She told the court that he was reassuring, saying that the part of the tape she had erased was not subject to the subpoena.

Most important, she testified that the phone conversation during which she kept her foot on the pedal lasted only four or five minutes. She was willing to accept responsibility for that much of the eighteen-minute gap and no more. She could offer no explanation for the rest of the erasure.

What most annoyed me about Rose Mary Woods's testimony was the fact that she had mentioned none of this during her previous appearance about three weeks earlier. The subject of that hearing had been the integrity of the tapes, and she had been specifically asked what precautions she had taken to avoid altering them during transcription. ("I used my head," she had snapped.) Now, with the gap discovered and made public, she was discussing it for the first time. I interrupted to ask her why she had omitted the subject the first time she was questioned.

"My question to you, Miss Woods, is did you at any time during your testimony last time you were in this court mention what you have mentioned on the stand today?"

"No sir, I didn't," she answered. "I am sorry. I may have been wrong, but I thought it was not relevant because it was not a subpoenaed tape."

"Didn't you think it was important on November 8 to tell everything you knew about what happened while you were making a transcript of these tapes?" I asked a few minutes later. "You were questioned very carefully and thoroughly. Didn't you think that was important?"

"I would say, Your Honor, that I would today but I didn't then. I think, if you may remember, that I was petrified, it was my first time ever in a courtroom, and I understood that we were talking only about the subpoenaed tapes. And I think all I can say is that I am just dreadfully sorry."

She was sorry, but there was still not a satisfactory explanation of the full gap. Jill Volner was not even satisfied with her explanation of the first four or five minutes of the gap. During the next few days, Mrs. Volner kept picking at her version of the story. At one point, with the Uher recorder in front of her at the witness stand, Rose Mary Woods was asked to go through the motions she had made when she erased the tape. She put on the earphones and went through the steps necessary to operate the recorder.

"The telephone rings," said Mrs. Volner. "Would you show us what you did?"

Rose Mary Woods demonstrated that she pushed the recording button after she had taken off the earphones plugged into the recorder.

"Right," interrupted Jill Volner, "and you also just picked your foot up off the pedal."

"That is because I don't happen to be doing anything," Mary Woods said defensively.

But the point had been made. The description that she had offered of the series of awkward actions that led to the accidental erasure was hard to believe. Attempting to bolster that explanation, Rose Mary Woods and her lawyer the next day had the White House photographer take a picture of her at her White House desk in the stretched-out position necessary for her to have kept a foot on the recorder pedal and a hand on the telephone. The photograph only made things worse for her. It appeared on the cover of *Newsweek* the following week under the caption "Rosemary's Boo Boo." One newspaper columnist called the pose a "sliding-into-third-base" stretch. The national joke was at her expense, but beneath that laughter the White House position was eroding further. It got to the point where no one believed anything offered to explain the gap.

We played the tape itself in court, and for the first time I heard the poor quality of the recording. There was some mumbled conversation between the president and Haldeman and then a high-pitched hum that sounded, someone said, like a television set turned on after the station has signed off. That sound continued for about five minutes; then the hum grew noticeably softer, and during the next thirteen minutes it was interrupted by sporadic clicks.

Fred Buzhardt was cross-examined by Richard Ben-Veniste and offered an explanation for the part of the gap that Miss Woods couldn't explain. He said that after learning of the gap, he had found by experimentation that on tape the sound of Miss Woods's electric typewriter and her high-intensity desk lamp closely resembled the hum on the erased tape. His implication was that although Miss Woods said her mistake accounted for only four or five minutes, she might well be responsible for the entire gap.

Charles Rhyne felt his client had been taken advantage of. Under his questioning she testified that during her first appearance in court she believed that the White House lawyers, Buzhardt and Garment, were representing her. Rhyne also objected because these lawyers had "rehearsed" her; this accusation brought an angry objection from the White House lawyers, though they did admit discussing her testimony with her at length before her first court appearance. From time to time, in the courtroom, Rhyne would curse under his breath at Buzhardt and Garment. Outside the courtroom, he told friends that he could blow the roof off the White House with what he knew about the tapes mess, but apparently he never felt that he could prove anything definite about the erasure. Once, in a conference in my chambers, he seemed about to explode at the White House, and I felt that perhaps he was ready to prove who had erased the tape. But when I suggested we move into open court, all the lawyers present agreed that the matter was not ripe for a public confrontation. My patience with the White House was long since exhausted. I was concerned about the integrity of the tapes, and I wasn't at all satisfied either with Rose Mary Woods's explanation of the gap or with the attempts of other witnesses to explain it.

In early December, the prosecutors called the chief presidential aide, Alexander Haig, to testify about his own involvement in the tapes controversy. Richard Ben-Veniste seemed especially interested in trying to show that perhaps the Stennis compromise had been devised as a way to cover up the fact that part of the June 20 tape had been erased, but Haig firmly denied that. Finally, Ben-Veniste asked Haig what theories he could offer to explain the portion of the gap not accounted for by Miss Woods's admitted five-minute erasure. His first suggestion pinned responsibility for all of it on Rose Mary Woods.

"One is that perhaps Miss Woods was very tired and did not realize how long she was away from the machine. That is conceivable," Haig said. Later, leaving the courthouse, Haig embellished this theory by saying he knew women who thought they had talked for only a few minutes when in fact they had talked longer.

In court, Haig went on to offer what he called a "devil theory." "Perhaps there had been one tone [i.e., hum heard on the tape] applied by Miss Woods in accordance with her description to the president of four and a half to five minutes' gap, and then perhaps some sinister force had come in and applied the other energy source and taken care of the information on that tape," he testified.

I interrupted to ask the obvious question. "Has anyone ever suggested who that sinister force might be?" I inquired.

Haig, of course, didn't want to speculate. But his unhappy choice of words made headlines around the world. Quite by accident, Nixon's closest aide had supplied a description that many people all over the country thought probably fitted the president of the United States as well as anyone.

A panel of experts picked jointly by the prosecutors and the White House lawyers took the tapes in special antimagnetic boxes to New York to test them and to try to shed some light on the eighteen-minute erasure. In mid-December, they issued a preliminary report rejecting as impossible Buzhardt's contention that the hum heard during the rest of the gap could have been produced by Miss Woods's electric typewriter and desk lamp. Finally, in January, the panel of experts reported back to the court. They had concluded that the gap could not possibly have been caused accidentally in the way Rose Mary Woods had described. "The erasures and buzz recordings were done in at least five, and perhaps as many as nine, separate and contiguous segments," their summary stated. "Erasure and recording of each segment required *hand* operation of keyboard controls on the Uher 5000 machine."

"In other words," I asked the experts, "it had to be deliberately done?" They would never use the word "deliberate," but they testified that "it would have to be an accident that was repeated at least five separate times." Finally, I recommended that the problem be presented to the grand jury for possible indictments.

In the end, the prosecutors could not produce enough evidence, in Leon Jaworski's judgment, to justify recommending an indictment from the grand jury. Despite the efforts in court to bring out the truth, and despite the government's spending $100,000 for the experts' investigation, we never did find out precisely who was responsible for the erasure. But the experts' report did convince me that it was not an accident. I never quite believed that Rose Mary Woods caused the first part of the gap, at least in the way she described it. Her story about the foot pedal being depressed as she reached over her shoulder to answer her phone appeared to me as ridiculous as the pictures of her re-enacting the scene. That story seemed to have resulted more from her talks with the White House lawyers before her testimony than from her independent recollection. Yet, she may somehow have been responsible for part of the erasure. I believed her when she said she had had nothing to do with the remaining thirteen minutes.

Was the president himself responsible? Leon Jaworski has said he thinks Nixon did erase the tape. Nixon, in his memoirs, declares, "I know I did not do it." He says he has wondered whether Buzhardt may have done it, accidentally. He also criticizes the experts' report and conclusions. In the end, I really don't know who caused the gap. I do believe that, as the panel of experts implied, there was a deliberate attempt to obstruct justice. I regret that the guilty party was never found.

12
Listening to the Tapes

In retrospect, the problem of the tape gap appears to have been a fairly minor episode in the whole Watergate case. Its importance was more symbolic than substantive. There turned out to be plenty of evidence left, despite the crude attempt to obliterate the June 20 recordings. Haldeman's notes of that meeting include an instruction from Nixon to launch some sort of public-relations offensive to deal with the problem of the break-in. It is interesting that the erasure of that conversation led to one of the most damaging public-relations beatings Nixon took during the Watergate scandal.

While the White House was trying to make Rose Mary Woods the scapegoat during much of the controversy over the eighteen-minute gap, Fred Buzhardt also came in for his share of public humiliation from his bosses there. In late November, Press Secretary Ron Ziegler, speaking for the president, criticized Buzhardt's handling of the tapes matter and then announced a shake-up in the legal department at the White House. The next day, several new lawyers were assigned to the office of the White House counsel, but within a few days they were gone, leaving Buzhardt to wrestle with the insoluble legal problems of the Nixon White House. The criticism of Buzhardt seemed designed to take the heat off the president. I was always amazed to see how readily the White House staff cannibalized their own people in attempting to save the president.

In January, the White House announced that James St. Clair, an experienced trial lawyer from Boston was taking over from Buzhardt. His job was to launch a new legal offensive to end the Watergate crisis for Nixon. In a way, it was like the public-relations offensive the president had ordered to divert attention from the break-in a year and a half earlier.

Before the end of the hearings on the tape gap, I had begun to make preparations to review the White House tapes that had been turned over to me for safekeeping. Once it was clear that the hearings were not likely to produce a quick solution to the gap problem, there seemed no reason to delay any further my rulings on the White House claims of privilege with respect to the existing tapes.

We didn't even have a tape recorder in the office, so the White House obliged by sending over one of their seemingly endless supply of Sony machines, like the one used in the president's secret recording system. For good measure, they sent along a Uher machine, like the one Rose Mary Woods had used to transcribe the president's conversations. By this time no precaution seemed excessive, so I had Todd send the machines over to the United States marshal's office to be checked for bugs. Representatives of the Defense Department came over to the courthouse and checked both my office and the small jury room behind my courtroom for bugs. They found nothing, but advised that I move my desk to take it out of a possible line of fire from an adjacent building. I figured that if someone wanted me that badly, he'd get me sooner or later anyway. The desk stayed where it was.

The White House had sent over the original tapes and the copies that had been made. But the copies were worse than the originals. Carl Feldbaum, the Special Prosecution Force specialist on tapes, informed Todd that one member of the panel of experts had invented a machine that could significantly enhance the quality of tape recordings. There was only one such machine, however, and it was owned by the CIA. A few days later the agency delivered the machine and installed it in the small jury room. Starting in the late afternoon of December 6 and working through the night, Mark Weiss, the machine's inventor, along with his assistant Ernest Aschkenasy, Todd, and representatives from the White House and the Special Prosecution Force, copied and improved the tapes. The next morning, I got to the courthouse before seven, just as the "tape cleaning," as we called it, was finishing up. I remember that Aschkenasy, a very devout member of the Jewish faith, needed a private place for his morning devotions. I was happy to offer him my office for that purpose.

After his prayers, Aschkenasy rigged up a strange-looking device for the White House Sony machine. He cut a small piece of cardboard, and somehow, using cellophane tape, made a double plug so that Todd and I could listen to the tapes simultaneously, through separate earphones. Later, as we sat listening to the tapes, I looked at the strange jury-rigged plug and noticed that its creator had autographed it "Compliments of E. Aschkenasy—NYC." That night, the CIA machine was taken back to Langley, Virginia, the same way it had been brought in—under a big gray blanket.

On Saturday, December 8, Todd and I began listening to the tapes. At first, it was a stunning experience. We had sequestered ourselves in the small jury room off my courtroom. This was the very room in which the jurors, after discussing the case around the large, oak conference table that occupies most of the floor space, had found the break-in defendants guilty. Painted government green, this room has no distractions at all—no windows and only one door. It is virtually soundproof, and we were shut away from the rest of the world. The recorder was set up on a scarred wooden table next to one wall. Paper was stuffed under the record key to prevent accidental erasure. As we sat there alone, headphones on, the sounds of the president and his lieutenants seemed to put them in the same little room with us. It was the first time in history that someone other than the president and his aides themselves had had so intimate a view of the innermost workings of an American executive and his staff.

At first, we were shocked by the frequent profanity. I came up the hard way, and the language was far from unfamiliar to me. But the shock, for me at least, was the contrast between the coarse, private Nixon speech and the utterly correct public Nixon speech I had heard so often. Public figures often present this contrast, I know, but Nixon's swearing was somehow more surprising than that of other men I had heard relax their speaking standards in private. As I first realized the barnyard quality of his conversations, I couldn't help remembering the rather self-righteous attack Nixon had made, during the 1960 television debates with John F. Kennedy, on Harry Truman's salty language.

That Saturday, Todd and I worked our way through two tapes—one of a conversation on March 13, 1973, between the president, John Dean, and H. R. Haldeman, in the Oval Office, and one of a meeting on March 22, 1973, involving the president, Dean, Ehrlichman, Haldeman, and Mitchell, in the president's office in the Executive Office Building. The March 13 tape included a very blunt discussion of Senator Lowell Weicker of Connecticut (a Republican who had charged Haldeman with some responsibility for the Watergate mess), the president's advice to Haldeman to sue Weicker, some talk about a scheme to hire Charles Colson as an unpaid consultant so that he would have the protection of executive privilege if called to testify before the Senate Watergate committee, and a discussion of dumping L. Patrick Gray as the nominee to head the FBI.

The March 22 meeting focused on a plan to have Dean write a report that would give the appearance of being a thorough explanation of the White House role in the Watergate affair, but would in fact omit damaging information. This meeting was held the day before the letter from James McCord was read in court. The president suggested to Dean that he go to Camp David to write his report. Near the end of the meeting, the president asked his aides, "Do you think we want to go this route now? Let it all hang out, so to speak?"

Dean said, "Well, it really isn't that—"

Haldeman chimed in, "It is a limited hang-out."

"It's a limited hang-out. It's not an absolute hang-out," Dean concluded.

What was most striking about these tapes was the total absence of any desire by the president to clean up the mess. His public statements for nearly a year had emphasized his own insistence, once Dean had informed him of the facts on March 21, on rooting out the wrongdoers in the White House. By the time I heard the tapes, I was not surprised that Nixon was more intent on maintaining the cover-up than on getting to the bottom of the case. But as I actually listened to him coaching his aides on the cover-up, and realized that he was displaying no outrage, not even the normal anger that one would expect from a politician whose aides have gotten him into trouble, I found the whole thing disgusting. A lifetime of dealing with the criminal law, of watching a parade of people who had robbed, stolen, killed, raped, and deceived others, had not hardened me enough to hear with equanimity the low political scheming that was being played back to me from the White House offices. I had given lectures on the virtues and privileges of American citizenship to thousands of people during naturalization proceedings. I had praised our form of government to these new citizens. It was one of the most disillusioning experiences of my life to have to listen now to what had gone on at the highest levels of the government of the United States of America. I'll never forget hearing the president tell his aides on the March 22 tape, "And, uh, for that reason, I am perfectly willing to—I don't give a shit what happens. I want you all to stonewall it, let them plead the Fifth Amendment, cover-up or anything else, if it'll save it—save the plan."

From that moment on, there was no longer any doubt in my mind that there had been a conspiracy to obstruct justice operating inside the White House. I thought back over the months of legal arguments over the tapes, the high-sounding claims of executive privilege, the pleas to protect the ability of the president to function in private, and thanked God that I had ruled as I did. It all seemed so hollow after hearing the president calling for a stone wall, a cover-up, to protect himself and his highest aides from criminal prosecution and from political disaster. I had taken the arguments about executive privilege very seriously indeed. Now they seemed just another stage of the cover-up. Nixon, it was clear from his own words, was deeply involved in the whole rotten mess. It was impossible to say, right then, just what this tape would mean for Nixon himself. But added to the testimony of Dean, Magruder, and others, these tapes, it seemed to me, would clinch the indictment of Haldeman, Mitchell, and Ehrlichman. I left the office that weekend more depressed than ever.

But I really hadn't heard the worst of it. On Monday, Todd again went to the big, gray file-safe. He took out the March 21 tape and set it up on the recorder in the jury room. Again, he stuffed paper under the record key to prevent any accidental erasures. The two of us again closed the door, put on our earphones, and began listening to the president of the United States and his private responses to the Watergate problem. This was the tape of the critical meeting with John Dean, the meeting about which Dean had testified so thoroughly before the Senate committee the previous summer. It was over Dean's account of this meeting that the White House had challenged his allegations of Nixon's complicity in the cover-up.

Whatever Nixon had known before March 21 (his public statements had stressed that he first learned of the cover-up at this meeting with Dean, but this position was of course destroyed by the other tapes), he certainly knew everything after the meeting, which took nearly two hours. Dean, frightened that the whole scheme was falling apart, had come to Nixon to lay out all the facts and seek the president's advice on what to do next. The most critical problem that Dean laid before Nixon was the difficulty in raising money to keep the defendants in the break-in case quiet. Dean's recitation of the facts of the Watergate cover-up was almost as complete as that of a prosecutor laying out the theory of his case before a jury. Again, I noticed the absence of shock or surprise or anger in Nixon's responses as the details of the conspiracy were presented by Dean.

Dean mentioned that Nixon's personal attorney, Herbert Kalmbach, had been raising money to pay attorneys' fees for the defendants. Nixon sounded as if he already knew about this. His response was, "They put that under the cover of a Cuban committee. . . ."

Dean told the president that Howard Hunt's wife, killed in a plane crash in Chicago, had been carrying money to pay off the Miamians. ". . . I would certainly keep that cover for whatever it's worth—Keep the committee," Nixon responded, endorsing the idea of continued payments to the defendants.

Dean told the president directly that his top White House aides were probably guilty of obstructing justice: "The most trouble post-thing [post-break-in], uh, because (1) Bob is involved in that; John is involved in that; I am involved in that; Mitchell is involved in that. And that's an obstruction of justice."

The president wanted to know just how Haldeman was involved. Dean explained that Haldeman controlled $350,000 in cash in a secret White House fund that was used to make the pay-offs to the break-in defendants.

Dean went on to estimate that it might cost a million dollars to keep up payments to insure silence from Hunt, Liddy, and the Miamians. Again, there was no outrage that the White House was being blackmailed; rather, there was a calm discussion of how to handle that amount of money.

"Yeah. Well, what do you need, then? You need, uh, you don't need a million right away, but you need a million. Is that right?" the president asked.

"That's right," Dean said.

"You need a million in cash, don't you? If you want to put that through, would you put that through, uh—this is thinking out loud here for a moment—would you put that through the Cuban committee?" Nixon asked.

The more immediate problem, however, was what to do with E. Howard Hunt. Dean explained that Hunt was asking for $120,000 and was threatening to start talking to the prosecutors, not just about Watergate, but about other White House adventures, like the Ellsberg case, unless he was paid off quickly.

"Well, your, your major, your major guy to keep under control is Hunt," observed Nixon, with the same calm that might prevail in a discussion of the budget for the Commerce Department.

"That's right," Dean agreed.

"I think, because he knows," the president said.

"He knows so much," Dean said.

"About a lot of other things," Nixon continued.

"He knows so much. Right, uh, he could sink Chuck Colson. Apparently, apparently, he is quite distressed with Colson. He thinks Colson has abandoned him—"

"Don't you, just looking at the immediate problem, don't you have to have—handle Hunt's financial situation?" the president asked.

"I, I think that's—"

"Damn soon," Nixon ordered. "Either that, or let it all blow right now."

The two continued to discuss the pay-offs, then Nixon returned to Hunt: "But at the moment, don't you agree that you'd better get the Hunt thing? I mean that's worth it, at the moment."

"That, that's worth buying time on, right," Dean agreed.

Later, the president said to Dean, "That's why you, for your immediate thing, you've got no choice with Hunt but the hundred and twenty or whatever it is. Right?"

"That's right," Dean agreed.

"Would you agree that that's a buy-time thing, you better damned well get that done, but fast? Well, for Christ's sake get it in a, in a way that, uh—who's going to talk to him? Colson? He's the one who's supposed to know him."

The tape not only gave the lie to the president's public contention that after the March 21 meeting with Dean he had begun to try to root out the conspirators in the White House, it put Nixon at the head of the conspiracy to obstruct justice, as far as I was concerned. I had heard for myself the president of the United States order a pay-off to a criminal defendant to buy his silence.

On a piece of white, lined paper I scribbled a note to Todd: "Would it not be advisable to hear the complete tape again?" We did, still locked in the jury room. We listened all the way through, for nearly two hours. Neither Todd nor I said much afterward. I did note to Todd that the tape certainly provided corroboration for Dean's testimony. But it did much more. It provided indisputable evidence, as far as I could tell, of the president's engaging in a criminal act.

I had really hoped the president himself would not be so involved, that he would survive this scandal. After all, I had campaigned for him twice when he ran with President Eisenhower, in 1952 and 1956. I remembered the speeches I had made in 1952, shouting from the hilltops about the scandals in the Truman administration, urging the election of Ike and Nixon to clean up the government. Not that I had had a big role in their election, but I had believed in them. I had spoken out for them. After listening to Nixon on tape, I felt foolish. I am a Republican. As angry as I had been at Nixon over the past months, as much as I had thought he was following the wrong course in opposing the release of the tapes, I still, in my heart, didn't want to hear what Todd and I had just listened to. We had voted for him in 1968 and again in 1972.

Todd and I left the courthouse that evening tired and dispirited. I remembered Nixon saying earlier in the fall, "I am not a crook." Well, I felt we did have a dishonest man in the White House, a president who had violated the law, who had conspired to obstruct the very laws he was sworn to uphold. It was a frightening thing to know.

In April, 1975, I denied a motion filed by the television networks and other commercial organizations which had sought the right to copy and broadcast the contents of the Nixon tapes. At that time, the cover-up case was still in progress. I felt that more publicity would only make the judicial process much more difficult. Since written transcripts of the tapes were then available, I decided there was no rush about releasing the tapes themselves.

Later, the court of appeals reversed my ruling and ordered the tapes released. But Nixon's lawyers appealed to the Supreme Court, where they won the right, for a time, to keep the tapes from being played to the public. The Supreme Court also ruled that future access to the tapes should be determined by decisions of the legislative and executive branches.

The struggle over access to the tapes still goes on. Nixon's lawyers are now fighting the General Services Administration, which has taken possession of the tapes, over the same question. The case has gone back to the district court for resolution.

I have to ask: Why is Nixon fighting so hard to keep people from hearing the actual words which were eventually played for the jury in the cover-up trial? The answer is obvious. Reading the transcripts is bad enough. But to hear the tapes, as Todd and I and eventually the jury did, is quite another thing. There is no explaining away what is said on those tapes. In my opinion the hearing of those tapes would eliminate any chance that Nixon might have of explaining away his role in Watergate. I regret that I had to rule against release of the tapes because of the pending case. I feel that they should be released now, especially those that are part of the official record of the court case. Everyone should have a chance to listen to these recordings and to judge for himself what they mean.

13

The Countdown Begins

Looking back now on the last seven months of the Nixon presidency, we see what appears to have been an inevitable progression of events, leading to his resignation in early August. Once the tapes had been turned over to me and to the special prosecutor, each step, in retrospect, seems to have followed logically, closing the circle around the president ever tighter. In many ways, however, that impression is wrong. At the time, the outcome appeared anything but inevitable. Although I had heard the incriminating March 21 tape and felt strongly that Nixon was guilty of complicity in the cover-up, it was certainly not for me to take any action on that information. That was up to Leon Jaworski and the special prosecutor's office. And their precise course with regard to the president was at best a difficult one.

Jaworski faced a number of problems, and I had no idea just how he would deal with them. First, he had to make his own judgment about the evidence on the tapes. While I had reached the conclusion that the March 21 tape totally corroborated John Dean's accusations against Nixon, and even went beyond what Dean had said about the president's role in the cover-up, I couldn't know just how Jaworski would view that evidence.

Even if he decided, as I had, that the tapes incriminated the president, just what would he do about it? During the Agnew affair the previous fall, the argument had been made that the vice-president, like the president, was beyond the reach of the courts on criminal matters. The argument had been rejected in relation to Agnew. But it seemed fairly clear that the Constitution prescribed that Congress, through the impeachment process, should have the primary jurisdiction over a president who committed criminal acts. Thus, even if Jaworski and his staff thought the evidence against Nixon strong enough to merit an indictment, it was questionable whether such a course would lead to anything other than a long legal and constitutional struggle over the power of the courts to punish a sitting president.

The House Judiciary Committee, by late January, 1974, had begun to get itself organized for a full-scale impeachment inquiry. But that body too faced what seemed at the time nearly insurmountable problems. First, almost by definition, impeachment was a political process rather than a strictly legal one. In the end, politics would have to play a major role in the votes both of the committee itself and—if the committee should vote articles of impeachment—of the full House. A trial in the Senate, though observing legal formalities, would still culminate in a vote of the members, and that vote too would heavily reflect the political climate of the country.

The politics of early 1974 were complicated indeed. The president's standing in public opinion was extremely low. Politicians in both parties no longer trusted him. Yet the political risk of trying to make Nixon the second president in United States history to face impeachment seemed still to make such action by Congress unlikely. In late January, the Gallup poll found that only 27 percent of those polled approved of Nixon's performance as president; 63 percent disapproved. Despite the low rating, there was no consensus on whether he should leave office. The country was split 46 percent to 46 percent over whether he should resign. And opinion was nearly 2 to 1 against impeaching President Nixon, in spite of the fact that, according to the Lou Harris poll, 3 out of 4 believed Nixon knew about the Watergate cover-up attempt. Correspondingly, 3 out of 4 of the people questioned by the Harris organization felt the tape erasure was not caused by accident by Rose Mary Woods, but was instead a deliberate attempt to protect Nixon. In view of these results, it seemed to me that Congress would be most reluctant to move against the president, yet at the same time the president was nearly crippled by the lack of public confidence. It was this contradiction that I found most troubling; we seemed to have a president who was trusted or believed by very few, yet could not be removed from office.

The Harris poll also asked what struck me as an odd question, inquiring whether Nixon "should be impeached if Judge Sirica were to decide that the President was negligent in the care he took of the Watergate tapes." Forty-eight percent of the respondents said that under those circumstances, Nixon should be impeached; 40 percent said that he should not. The question was strange because it was not my job to evaluate Nixon's handling of the tapes, beyond recommending further investigation by the grand jury, which I had done. What the responses seemed to indicate, however, was that the public, though no longer believing in Nixon, was still waiting for final proof. Although the White House knew, and now the prosecutors and I knew, what was on the tapes, the evidence still was not before the American people. They had made a negative judgment about Nixon's character, but they were waiting, like a responsible jury, to see the evidence that would support an action so drastic as impeachment.

The late winter and early spring of 1974 were consumed with the problem of accumulating and organizing that evidence. But even that process was filled with difficulties. In his State of the Union speech at the end of January, Nixon repeated what had now become a common promise—that he would not resign. And, he announced, "One year of Watergate is enough." By that he meant he had given all the tapes and other evidence to the special prosecutor that he intended to give. He said he would co-operate with the House Judiciary Committee's investigation, but only in ways "I consider consistent with my responsibilities to the office of the presidency of the United States." He would do nothing that "weakens the office . . . or impairs the ability of the presidents of the future to make the great decisions that are so essential to this nation and to the world." The words sounded much like those he had used months earlier in arguing against the release of the tapes to the special prosecutor. Many guessed at the time that he would give up little or nothing in the way of evidence to the committee.

And they were right. Several weeks after that speech, Leon Jaworski sent a letter to the Senate Judiciary Committee, which had requested, when they confirmed Jaworski's nomination, that it be kept informed about White House co-operation with the prosecutor. Jaworski explained that on January 27 he had asked the White House for more tapes and documents that he felt were critical for the trial of those he

expected to indict for Watergate cover-up activities, and
Nixon had refused to produce them. Jaworski told the committee the absence of the new evidence would not stop indictments, but would hinder effective prosecution of his cases.
The letter was in effect a notification that the White House
was breaching the promise that Jaworski would be independent and free to pursue the Watergate investigation as he saw
fit. It was this White House promise that had saved the
president from the worst of the reaction that could have followed his firing of the first prosecutor, Archibald Cox. Clearly,
another confrontation between the prosecutor and the
president was brewing. But this time, it seemed, the fight
would be much rougher. The president did not bother to
couch his refusal in any particular legal language, any reference to executive privilege. He simply announced that releasing more tapes and documents was not in "the public
interest."

Although Jaworski was being stonewalled, he still had in
his possession the most valuable evidence in the case. The
House Judiciary Committee recognized this and wanted
Jaworski to share what he knew, thus making the committee's
job easier. Although the committee had been given subpoena
power, their problem in enforcing subpoenas directed at the
president was in many ways worse than the problem I had
faced earlier with respect to enforcing court subpoenas. If
Nixon simply defied the congressional subpoenas, what could
the committee do? They could find him in contempt of
Congress, but then what? Apparently their only recourse
would be to make Nixon's refusal to comply with the subpoenas a basis for impeachment. They were trapped, at least
with regard to forcing compliance with their subpoenas, in an
all-or-nothing situation. Jaworski himself announced that he
thought it would be improper to share any evidence with the
committee, since under the Federal Rules of Criminal Procedure, grand jury matters are to be kept secret. As far as I
could see, Jaworski had the evidence, but not the power to do
much about the president. The committee, and Congress, did
have ultimate power, but in early 1974, they lacked the evidence.

On March 1, the grand jury that had been hearing Watergate evidence since the summer of 1972 returned indictments
against seven members of the White House staff and the staff
of the Committee to Re-elect the President. The three most

powerful Nixon associates, former Attorney General John Mitchell and White House aides H. R. Haldeman and John Ehrlichman, were all charged with obstruction of justice and conspiracy to impede the Watergate investigation. Mitchell and Haldeman were also charged with giving false testimony to the Senate Watergate committee, and Mitchell and Ehrlichman were charged with lying to the FBI and to the grand jury. Charles W. Colson, formerly the president's special counsel for domestic affairs, was charged with obstruction of justice and conspiracy to impede the Watergate investigation, as were Kenneth W. Parkinson, the attorney for the CRP, and Gordon Strachan, a former assistant to Haldeman. Strachan was also charged with lying to the grand jury. Robert C. Mardian, a former assistant attorney general, under Mitchell, and a former consultant to the CRP, was indicted for conspiracy to impede the Watergate investigation. These were the last of the big fish to be caught in the White House scandal. They joined such others as John Dean and Jeb Magruder who had pleaded guilty rather than face trial. Herbert Kalmbach, Nixon's personal attorney from California, who had helped raise pay-off money for the break-in defendants, entered a guilty plea before me a few days before the indictments. He had negotiated a plea of guilty to having raised money illegally for Republican campaigns in the 1970 general elections and to having promised an ambassadorship to one Republican donor that year in exchange for a $100,-000 contribution. In return for this plea, the prosecutors had agreed to drop the Watergate charges against Kalmbach. The net had finally closed around the Nixon people. Mitchell was already on trial in New York in the so-called Vesco case, as was former Commerce Secretary Maurice Stans, who had been Nixon's chief fund raiser for the 1972 campaign. Both were charged with hampering a Securities and Exchange Commission investigation into Vesco's financial affairs in return for a large contribution by Vesco to the 1972 Nixon campaign. (Both were later acquitted of those charges.) Dwight Chapin, a young man who had been the president's appointments secretary, had earlier been charged with perjury as a result of his false grand jury testimony about the activities of Donald Segretti, the young West Coast lawyer whom Chapin had authorized to perform "dirty tricks" like distributing phony campaign literature to harass Democratic candidates. (Chapin was later found guilty of two counts of perjury.) And John Ehrlichman was also facing a trial on the West Coast for his role in the break-in by Hunt and Liddy at the office of Daniel Ellsberg's psychiatrist; later, he and Charles Colson were also charged by the special prosecutor's office for that incident. Egil Krogh, the young man who had headed the "plumbers" unit in the White House and who had dispatched Liddy and Hunt to burglarize Ellsberg's psychiatrist's office, had pleaded guilty the previous fall to charges of conspiracy against the rights of citizens.

The list of indicted and guilty Nixon aides was truly remarkable. There had never been such wholesale criminal proceedings against the top men in the administration of an American president. Those closest to Richard Nixon were the ones most involved. Even those who were close to the men closest to Nixon got caught up in the incredible scandal.

Still, there was the problem of the president himself. The indictments had eliminated part of that problem. Since the grand jury was no longer actively considering evidence against the principals in the Watergate case, Jaworski and his staff reasoned, the need for total grand jury secrecy had diminished. Along with the indictments presented on March 1, the grand jury returned a sealed report listing the major facts it had discovered that tied the president of the United States directly to the Watergate cover-up. The jury requested that I send the report, along with an overstuffed brown briefcase—the "bulging briefcase" the press called it—filled with tapes and other evidence, directly to the House Judiciary Committee. Jaworski had chosen to give assistance to the impeachment inquiry not by sharing his own evidence directly, but rather by having the grand jury issue this special report. I read the first page of the report, resealed the envelope, and locked it and the briefcase in the safe in my office that contained the president's tapes. I had not studied the question of whether the grand jury's evidence could properly be sent to Congress, and I expected that the president's lawyers would object strenuously. It seemed to me that his only hope was to keep that evidence out of the hands of the impeachment committee.

On March 6, I heard arguments on the disposition of the grand jury report. To my surprise, the White House lawyers announced they had no objection to my sending the report to the Judiciary Committee. I didn't know why they had taken that course, but I guessed that the president must have felt that any opposition to the report would only increase public suspicions about his role in the investigation. Although the White House made no objection, the seven men indicted by the grand jury argued that release of the report to the committee would jeopardize their chances for a fair trial, since the committee staff might leak it to the press. I couldn't tell whether their objections were serious or whether they were simply still trying to protect the president.

Todd and I reviewed the legal precedents, and it was clear to me that grand juries have the right to issue reports—sometimes called presentments—focused on wrongdoing but not indicting guilty parties. The Federal Rules of Criminal Procedure do specify that matters occurring before a grand jury shall be held secret and may be disclosed "only when so directed by the court preliminarily to or in connection with a judicial proceeding." One of the defendants' lawyers argued that release to the House committee was not covered by that provision.

On March 18, I ruled that the report should go to the committee.* I wrote that it seemed incredible that grand jury matters should lawfully be available to groups like "disbarment committees and police disciplinary investigations and yet be unavailable to the House of Representatives in a proceeding of so great import as an impeachment investigation." I also noted that I could not justify keeping the report from the House "on the basis of speculation that leaks will occur, added to the further speculation that resultant publicity would prejudice the rights of defendants" in the cover-up trial. Three days later, the court of appeals upheld my ruling, agreeing that the time to deal with that problem was after leaks of the report actually took place, with possible damage to the defendants' rights, not beforehand. A cynical lawyer would guess that lacking any better defense, the cover-up defendants should have prayed for some damaging pretrial publicity on which to base a plea for a change of venue or even the dropping of the charges. Of course, the report itself had to do only with the president, not with the defendants. That the White House lawyers had raised no objection left me little choice but to rule for turning the report over to the committee, and the defendants' objections seemed a bit silly.

On March 26, Judiciary Committee counsel John Doar,

* The Text of the opinion is in the Appendix.

and his Republican counterpart Albert Jenner, came to my office to pick up the grand jury report and the briefcase filled with evidence. A lawyer from the special prosecutor's office showed up too; he went over each item in the briefcase and checked it against a list of the evidence supplied. Under a heavy police guard, Doar and Jenner carried their new evidence back to the Capitol Hill offices, where it was added to the computerized summary of testimony and evidence they were preparing. When finally presented for a vote by the House committee members, the charges were in the same format the prosecutors had used in preparing the grand jury report. Without that assist from the grand jury, I believe the House committee would have taken months more to reach a decision. Perhaps, without that evidence, the decision would never have been reached.

The seven Nixon men indicted on March 1 appeared in my courtroom on Saturday, March 9, for their arraignment. The unusual Saturday session had been scheduled because Mitchell had to be in New York during the week for his trial on the Vesco charges. That morning, a large crowd assembled outside the courthouse to watch the president's former high command being brought to book. The courtroom itself was again jammed, as reporters, lawyers, and the curious gathered to watch the strange spectacle of the most powerful men in the Nixon administration hear the charges against them. They all entered pleas of not guilty. Their lawyers asked that the usual mug shot and fingerprint procedure be waived for these once-powerful people, but I ordered them treated like all the other felony defendants who come into my courtroom. They were taken to the basement of the old post office building on Pennsylvania Avenue, where the FBI took their pictures and their fingerprints. The whole arraignment procedure lasted only fifteen minutes. It was the first time this group had been in my courtroom together. I must say I was not a bit awed to see them assembled at the defendants' table, even though a year earlier, they had been helping run the United States government. Now they were as meek as lambs, and beginning a long and bitter struggle to stay out of prison.

Jaworski, as he prepared for the trial of the seven cover-up defendants, persisted throughout the spring in his requests to the White House for more tapes and other documents. But Jaworski, and the House committee, met nothing but resistance from the White House. St. Clair, now apparently

Left: With my law clerk
Todd Christofferson.
WIDE WORLD PHOTOS

Below, left: G. Gordon Liddy.
WIDE WORLD PHOTOS

Right: James McCord arriving
for the break-in trial.
WIDE WORLD PHOTOS

Right: E. Howard Hunt.
UPI

Below: Frank A. Sturgis
(left) and Virgilio Gonzalez
on inaugural-parade bleachers
near the courthouse.
WIDE WORLD PHOTOS

Opposite, top, left:
Eugenio Martinez *(left)* and
Bernard L. Barker after
their guilty pleas in the
break-in case. UPI

Top, right: Jeb Stuart Magruder.
STEVE NORTHUP. CAMERA 5

Bottom, left: Hugh Sloan.
STEVE NORTHUP. CAMERA 5

Bottom, right: L. Patrick Gray,
for a time acting FBI director.
STEVE NORTHUP. CAMERA 5

John Dean.
STEVE NORTHUP,
CAMERA 5

Earl Silbert.
GEORGE TAMES,
NEW YORK TIMES

Left: Henry Petersen, head of the criminal division of the Justice Department.
WIDE WORLD PHOTOS

Below: Richard Kleindienst announcing his resignation as attorney general.
STEVE NORTHUP, CAMERA 5

Opposite, top, left:
My mother, Rose, at the age
of eighteen or nineteen.

Top, right: My father,
Ferdinand, at the age of
twenty-one.

Bottom, left: My brother,
Andy.

Bottom, right: Andy (*right*)
and I as youngsters.

This page, left:
Sparring with Jack Britton
in Miami in 1927.

Below: Dempsey almost
lands a jab.

Above: With Peter Rodino, chairman of the House Judiciary Committee. NATIONAL ITALIAN AMERICAN FOUNDATION

Right: With my wife, Lucy, and the poodle, Coco. EVELYN HOFER

Above, left: Eileen.
Right: Tricia.
Left: Jack.

Top: The first special prosecutor, Archibald Cox (*left*), with Attorney General Elliot Richardson. WIDE WORLD PHOTOS

Bottom, left: Charles Alan Wright. WIDE WORLD PHOTOS

Right: Rose Mary Woods in her White House office, demonstrating how she may have caused part of the eighteen-minute tape gap. WHITE HOUSE PHOTO

Top: Former New York cop Tony Ulasewicz, with a photograph showing how hush money was passed to the break-in defendants. UPI

Bottom, left: John Mitchell. STEVE NORTHUP, CAMERA 5

Right: Herbert Kalmbach. STEVE NORTHUP, CAMERA 5

Top: H. R. Haldeman (*left*) and John Ehrlichman.
STEVE NORTHUP. CAMERA 5

Bottom, left: Charles Colson arriving at the courthouse. UPI

Right: Kenneth Parkinson on his way out of the courthouse. UPI

Top: Robert Mardian (*right*) with his attorney
David Bress. STEVE NORTHUP, CAMERA 5

Bottom, left: William Frates, Ehrlichman's attorney.
WIDE WORLD PHOTOS

Right: John Wilson, Haldeman's attorney.
STEVE NORTHUP, CAMERA 5

Right: Parkinson's attorney, Jacob Stein (*left*), with Mitchell's attorney, William Hundley, at curbside outside the courthouse. WIDE WORLD PHOTOS

Left: James Neal, chief prosecutor in the cover-up trial. UPI

Right: Special Prosecutor Leon Jaworski (*left*) with his successor, Henry Ruth. WIDE WORLD PHOTOS

Top, left: Richard Ben-Veniste and Jill Wine Volner.
WIDE WORLD PHOTOS

Right: J. Fred Buzhardt. WIDE WORLD PHOTOS

Bottom: White House chief of staff Alexander Haig (*left*)
with White House counsel Leonard Garment. UPI

Top: James St. Clair. WIDE WORLD PHOTOS

Bottom: Richard Nixon after his resignation.
WIDE WORLD PHOTOS

running the White House legal operation, would first promise co-operation, and then, after delaying days or weeks, would retract that offer. The special prosecutor finally moved in mid-April to subpoena sixty-four tape recordings, all of which he said were needed to complete the evidence for the trial. Included in that group were tapes from June 23, 1972, recording three conversations between Nixon and Haldeman in which they discussed the use of the CIA to short-circuit the FBI investigation of Watergate. According to Richard Ben-Veniste and his associate George Frampton, the three tapes were asked for almost as an afterthought by the prosecutors, mainly to help rebut any claim the cover-up defendants might make at their trial that they were protecting security secrets involving the CIA.

We had been over the subpoena question thoroughly the previous fall and had been sustained by the court of appeals, so I approved Jaworski's subpoena request. I wrote a short opinion in the press room on Saturday morning, since the electricity had failed in my office. A few days before, the House Judiciary Committee had issued its own subpoena for forty-two White House tapes. This was the first time a congressional subpoena had ever been issued in an impeachment inquiry.

As I've said, I felt that the March 21 tape was as incriminating a piece of evidence as could be imagined in determining Nixon's role in the cover-up. But obviously, Nixon knew better. There were worse things on his other tapes. He began a two-front stalling operation, aimed at both Jaworski and the House Judiciary Committee. Jaworski's subpoena had a return date of May 2, and the committee subpoena required delivery of the White House tapes by April 25.

14

Last Desperate Ploy

As spring gradually edged toward the hot, muggy summer that afflicts the capital, Nixon concocted his last desperate ploy to avoid giving up any further evidence. With warnings coming from Capitol Hill that failure to comply with the House committee subpoenas would lead to impeachment, and with Jaworski waiting for the deadline to seek enforcement of his subpoena against the president, Nixon on April 30 published 1,308 pages of transcripts of the White House tapes. Compared to the tapes I had heard, the transcripts were mild indeed. In places where the president had used one vulgarity or another, the transcripts noted "expletive deleted." That phrase was repeated so often in the texts that it became a national joke. Filling in the blanks required little imagination. More important than the deletion of curses, however, was the editing out of long and critical sections of the conversations. I checked the printed transcripts against my own memory of the March 22 tapes and found the stunning "I don't give a shit . . ." quote missing. The transcript of the March 21 tape bore little resemblance to the original, with the most incriminating statements by the president either fuzzed over or missing altogether, so that the real impact of that tape was gone.

But as incomplete as the transcripts were, they caused a great tide of disgust to rise against the president. Even in their mild form, people found them as low and demeaning to the office of the presidency as Todd and I had five months earlier. Newspapers all over the country ran the full text of the released transcripts. Paperback book companies packaged the transcripts and within days had a million copies in stores all across the country. Television and radio stations staged dramatic readings, with actors taking the parts of the president and his aides. Nixon, now apparently cornered, was betting that even having the revulsion of the public directed at him because of the transcripts was better than losing office. If he could get away with releasing just the transcripts, he must have reasoned, the issue of his guilt would be blurred enough to avoid impeachment. It was Nixon's last big lie in the years of lying about Watergate. He was apparently willing to humiliate himself to save himself. I was puzzled by this ploy, since I knew what was actually on the tapes that had been turned over to the prosecutor and were now also in the hands of the House committee. Surely Nixon knew that at some point the true versions of those first tapes would be published and compared to the edited transcripts. But Nixon also knew what was on the remaining tapes, and even the fact that his transcripts would certainly be found to be bogus must have seemed to involve less of a risk than did direct release of the new tapes.

The House committee quickly concluded that the transcripts were no substitute for the actual tapes. The White House then came into court to attempt to quash Jaworski's trial subpoena. In the argument this time the old executive-privilege claim that had been offered by Charles Alan Wright was abandoned, for two reasons. First, that issue had already been decided by me and by the court of appeals in favor of the prosecutor. Second, by publishing the tape transcripts himself, the president had obviously forfeited any claim to confidentiality. This time, St. Clair argued that since the tapes were of the president's conversations and since the president was not indicted in the cover-up, the tapes were "inadmissible hearsay."

In preparing to meet this argument, Jaworski asked me for permission to disclose in his own brief some evidence from the grand jury investigation that had not been included in the indictments. He didn't specify just what that evidence was, and to continue to protect the grand jury's secrecy, I suggested he submit his brief to me *in camera* before making it public. He agreed.

In early May, the prosecutors, the lawyers for the cover-up defendants, and the president's lawyers gathered in my office to review the briefs filed by Jaworski and the White House. Jaworski had already informed the White House counsel, but the defense lawyers and I were surprised when we saw that when indicting the seven defendants in the cover-up, the grand jury had also named the president of the United States as an unindicted co-conspirator. That meant the jurors had concluded that he was part of the conspiracy to obstruct justice in the Watergate investigation. But they had decided not to indict him because of the constitutional problems and because of the pending impeachment proceeding in the House of Representatives. Incredibly, this piece of information had been kept absolutely secret. I had not been told, nor, until a few days before this meeting, had the president's lawyers. St. Clair's argument that the tapes were hearsay was now useless. And sooner or later, the grand jury's judgment on Nixon's role was sure to be made public. That seemed to be only just and also seemed to add one more straw to the camel's back. I figured the president was doomed.

I wanted to hold the arguments about the tapes in public. My preference from the beginning of the case had been that whenever the proceedings didn't damage the rights of the defendants, they should be open to public view. I felt that the grand jury's action should now be a matter of public record, since it was the basis for Jaworski's request for the tapes. The grand jury's vote to name Nixon an unindicted co-conspirator tied the president to the cover-up and made the tapes germane to the proceedings. But Jaworski and his staff, the White House lawyers, and the defense lawyers all wanted the arguments held in secret. Jaworski was still unwilling to make public the grand jury's action, for fear—I suppose—of getting too far ahead of the Judiciary Committee's proceedings. The White House simply didn't want this damaging fact known, and the defense lawyers figured their clients certainly would not be helped when the public found out that their clients' boss had been named as a co-conspirator.

I went along with the lawyers and heard arguments on the new subpoena *in camera*. St. Clair had wisely shifted away from the hearsay argument. But he hadn't come up with anything much better. This time he claimed that since Jaworski was an employee of the executive branch and Nixon was his boss, there was no real legal controversy; Jaworski was simply supposed to follow his boss's instructions. This was an old technical argument that had been talked about the previous fall. It unfortunately ignored the fact that Jaworski had something of a congressional charter and that the president himself had promised him real independence of the executive branch when he appointed him months before. The argument was absurd and insulting, since any fool could see that a more genuine controversy couldn't be imagined. A few days later I ruled that the subpoena should be enforced. And thus the last chapter in the sad story of Richard Nixon's presidency began.

I think Leon Jaworski deserves a lot of credit for the way he handled this case. The strategy of having the grand jury issue a report on the president, of asking that it be sent to the House committee, of encouraging the grand jury to name the president as an unindicted co-conspirator, and then playing that card when it counted most, all these were the mark of a careful and experienced lawyer. He avoided overreaching himself by bringing charges directly against a sitting president. That course could have produced a great constitutional crisis and could have totally obscured the issue of the president's conduct.

After my ruling that his subpoena for the president's tapes should be enforced, Jaworski and his assistants made another very smart move. Instead of letting the appeals process run its normal course, through the court of appeals and then, eventually, to the Supreme Court, Jaworski jumped ahead of the White House lawyers and asked for a direct review of the case by the Supreme Court. The law provides for such a direct appeal when especially important issues are involved and when a quick review is necessary. In this instance, speed was important. The Supreme Court normally adjourns for the summer in June, and had Jaworski not gone directly to the high court, the appeals would have dragged on into the fall. The absence of a Supreme Court decision would have delayed the cover-up trial perhaps into 1975 and would certainly have left the crippled president in office well beyond the time when he was able to govern effectively.

Despite White House opposition the Supreme Court agreed to take the case directly and even scheduled an unusual July session to hear argument. The White House, again probably counting votes on the high court as if this were an election rather than a legal question of paramount national importance, still hoped that the Nixon appointees on the court would support the man who had put them there. Again, the White House hinted that anything short of a "definitive" ruling might not be obeyed.

As the oppressively humid July days passed, we waited. The Judiciary Committee was moving slowly through its massive evidence. The White House was regularly attacking the committee for permitting leaks. One White House aide, Patrick Buchanan, even attacked the grand jury for having been drawn from a city that voted heavily against Nixon and was predominantly black. The suggestion that the people of Washington, black or white, couldn't do their legal duty because of their political preferences was deeply offensive to me. There seemed to be no limit to the contempt in which the White House men held the legal process. It was shameful the way the question of guilt or innocence kept getting turned into a question of politics. They seemed always concerned about politics, never about whether their actions were right or wrong.

On July 24, the Supreme Court upheld my ruling on the subpoenas.* The vote was 8–0, with one of the nine justices, William Rehnquist, a Nixon appointee and former associate of John Mitchell's in the Justice Department, disqualifying himself because of his closeness to a principal in the case. The remaining Nixon appointees, and five others, voted against the president, overruling, as I had nearly a year earlier, the president's assertion of his sole right to decide the limits of executive privilege. I had expected that result, but I still felt vindicated by the decision and especially by the unanimity of the vote. The Supreme Court's ruling was the final demonstration that the judiciary was in fact a truly independent branch of our government.

James St. Clair appeared in my courtroom two days later to begin discussions on when the tapes would be delivered. Todd and I had considered just how we could assure that the tapes were brought to me and then transmitted to the prosecutors quickly, and, we hoped this time, without erasures. Fred Buzhardt, though replaced by St. Clair as the lawyer arguing the president's case in court and before the Judiciary Committee, was still deeply involved in the screening and transcribing of the tapes, and he had had a good deal to do with the preparation of the misleading transcripts the president had released in April. After Buzhardt's performance during the hearings on the two missing tapes and on the eighteen-minute gap, I felt I should make St. Clair personally

---

* The text of this opinion is in the Appendix.

responsible for delivery of the tapes and for their integrity. As an "officer of the court," as all lawyers are, he had that legal responsibility already, but I felt that if I made a point of it in court, we could at least avoid chasing around later trying to find out who was in charge of the tapes at the White House. In addition, I wanted St. Clair to be able to argue from his own knowledge when it came time to decide on questions of privilege in the new batch of tapes. The trial date for the cover-up case had already been set for September 9. I was determined that we would begin as close to that date as possible, and I was not in a mood to tolerate any further delay. But St. Clair and the president were not in any hurry. The president and Buzhardt already knew what was on the tapes and must have realized that every day they delayed relinquishing them gave Nixon another day in office.

St. Clair hemmed and hawed about delivery dates. "It is hard for me to say to Your Honor right now that we can do this in x days," he said. While promising expeditious delivery, he resisted fixed deadlines. He suggested that he would simply report to me every week on how the work of copying and indexing the tapes was going.

I felt St. Clair was simply dragging his feet. Transcripts of twenty of the subpoenaed tapes had already been published by the White House in April, and I couldn't see why these tapes shouldn't be turned over immediately. The appeal to the Supreme Court had eaten up two months more. I told St. Clair I thought he was making the whole business more complicated than necessary. "I don't think it's going to take the time you think it's going to take," I said.

Trying to get St. Clair to name a specific delivery date, I began to question him about the twenty tapes already published: "Let us assume that somebody has listened to these tapes, including the president, I take it, right? And including yourself, probably?"

"No, I wouldn't say that," St. Clair said.

"Well do you mean to say you would go before the Judiciary Committee up there and make the statements you made up there and the arguments without being fully acquainted with all of the material in these tapes that we are talking about?" I asked.

St. Clair tried to dodge the question.

"Wait a minute," I interrupted, "would you answer my question. Do you mean to say that you could have gotten up

there and argued this case the way you did before the committee with the great legal ability that you have, without
knowing all the background of this matter?"

St. Clair objected that he was not "a good listener" and
said he had neither the time nor the expertise to listen to the
tapes. I found this unbelievable. St. Clair had argued the case
for the president without himself having heard any of the
tapes involved. He said the president would have permitted
him to hear the tapes, but he never had bothered. I couldn't
imagine a lawyer defending a client without knowing every
possible detail of the case. To this day, I haven't figured out
whether St. Clair simply trusted President Nixon totally, or
whether he had some fear of finding out the truth that the
tapes contained.

Finally, I instructed St. Clair to take personal charge of the
copying and indexing process. I had decided on that course
before court convened, and now that I had discovered that
St. Clair himself didn't know what was on the tapes, I was
doubly glad to make him come to grips with the evidence
from the White House. He was in for a big surprise.

On July 27, the House Judiciary Committee voted 27–11
to approve the first Article of Impeachment, charging that the
president of the United States had "prevented, obstructed and
impeded the administration of Justice. . . ." Six Republicans
on the committee joined the majority. It was clear now that
unless he resigned, President Nixon would eventually have to
stand trial before the Senate of the United States for his role
in the Watergate scandal. The political process of impeachment had finally caught up with the judicial investigation.
The congressmen on the committee were saying, in effect,
that the people of the country had had quite enough of
Richard Nixon and Watergate. Two more articles of impeachment were approved later, one of which directly condemned the president for his continuing refusal to honor the
subpoenas issued by the committee for his tape recordings.
The impeachment vote had come without those subpoenas
ever being honored; the grand jury's evidence had been more
than convincing to the House committee members.

Throughout the next week, the final assessments of damage
were taking place inside the White House. Acting on my
directions, St. Clair at last began to listen to the tapes. Nixon
himself, it turned out, had picked the June 23 tapes for
special review back in May, when considering whether to

fight it out with Jaworski over his new tapes subpoenas.
Nixon had warned Buzhardt of problems involving those
tapes after the Supreme Court's unanimous ruling. And now
St. Clair and Alexander Haig reviewed them as well. I believe
this was the first time that Nixon's closest aides all finally
knew the full story of Watergate.

During his general review of the subpoenaed recordings,
St. Clair discovered more gaps and missing tapes and reported them sheepishly to me in court. But what would have been
a major news story some months before was now hardly noticed. And St. Clair himself knew that the gaps and missing
tapes he had found were of little significance compared to
what he had heard on the June 23 tape.

Except for the June 20 conversation with Haldeman that
had been erased, the June 23 discussions were the closest to
the June 17 break-in. Through the months and months of
public defense of the president, Nixon's lawyers and Nixon
himself had said time and again that he knew nothing of any
involvement by his aides until Dean briefed him on March
21, 1973. There had been testimony that he had tried to get
the CIA to intervene with the FBI to limit its Watergate investigation in the name of national security. Nixon had admitted
having the CIA warn off the FBI, but had described that as a
legitimate attempt to prevent the bureau from discovering a
sensitive CIA operation unrelated to Watergate. Just three
months earlier, in May 1974, Nixon had told the nation that
in no way had he intended to use the CIA to shut down the
Watergate investigation. And up to this time, there had been
no way to prove the contrary. The June 23 tapes, however,
directly contradicted the president's defense. Those tapes so
frightened his lawyers, who themselves had made those arguments and who probably now feared being implicated in the
conspiracy, that they insisted he release them to the public.
On Monday, August 5, the transcripts were released. In an
accompanying statement Nixon apologized for not informing
his lawyers of the damaging tape and expressed the now for-
lorn belief that the full record of his conduct in the Watergate affair did not justify impeachment.

The tapes themselves had been delivered to my office the
previous week. I had not listened to them or the others because, as usual, I was waiting to see the White House
briefs arguing executive privilege for particular segments before starting my review. But the explosive reaction to the

June 23 tapes led Todd and me to lock ourselves in the jury room again on Tuesday, August 6, and listen to them.

The most significant conversation* began with Haldeman telling Nixon that "we're back in the problem area," implying that the two had discussed "the problem area" before, perhaps during the erased portion of the June 20 conversation. The problem was that "the FBI is not under control," Haldeman said, adding that the bureau had begun to trace to the burglars the money that came from the CRP. He suggested that the CIA be told to order the FBI to "stay the hell out of this." The idea of involving the CIA, Haldeman said, came from Mitchell. After some discussion of the Dahlberg check, Haldeman continued: "And the proposal would be that Ehrlichman and I call them [the CIA officials] in."

"All right, fine," Nixon said, approving the cover up plan.

Here was the "smoking pistol" the investigators had been looking for—the direct, undeniable evidence that from the very beginning Nixon had been in on, had approved, had condoned and supported the attempt to bury the Watergate mess out of sight of the prosecutors, the courts, Congress, and the public.

As I have said, the March 21 tape had convinced me of Nixon's guilt. The June 23 tapes confirmed it and proved his involvement from the beginning. I don't remember saying much to Todd, except to note that the game was over for Richard Nixon.

Now seven of the Republican members of the House Judiciary Committee who had supported the president announced they would vote for the Articles of Impeachment when they came to the House floor. Republican leaders in the Senate and House urged the president to resign. Even the loyalist core of the staff in the White House agreed. And on August 8, after a tearful farewell to his staff, Richard Nixon left the White House for the last time. I watched that departure on television. I had been disgusted by the evidence of his role in the cover-up. I was appalled by his lying. But I couldn't help feeling sorry for him as he left, having lost the very thing he had spent most of his life trying to win, the presidency of the United States. I felt sorry for him, but I was also relieved to see him go.

* The text of this segment is in the Appendix.

The Pardon

With a last wave and a brave smile, Nixon boarded his helicopter on the south lawn of the White House for the first leg of his flight to San Clemente. His presidency had ended. But his legal problems were not over. No longer shielded against prosecution by the power of the office, the former president faced the possibility that he would be indicted for his actions in the cover-up. Some congressmen introduced resolutions urging that he be left alone, reasoning that his disgrace was complete and that the loss of his office was punishment enough. I don't remember any public officials calling for an indictment, although there may have been a few. In general, official Washington seemed glad that the worst of Watergate was over, and had little appetite or energy to pursue Nixon further.

Exactly one month after his resignation, Nixon received a full pardon from his successor, Gerald R. Ford. Before the pardon, Leon Jaworski had been considering asking the grand jury to indict the former president; he had been waiting until we selected a jury for the cover-up trial so that the publicity surrounding such an indictment would not prejudice potential jurors. The problem of whether to indict Nixon, once he was out of office, was a question not of law, but of judgment—of balancing considerations arising from compassion and even forgiveness against those based on the notion that fairness required everyone associated with Watergate to be treated the same. The idea of equal justice under law that had been fought over so hard during the tapes struggle weighed on the side of indictment and trial of the former president. Exhaustion, and sadness for Nixon's suffering, weighed against that course. President Ford's pardon, however, was not at all popular. He explained that one reason for the pardon was his fear, supported by Leon Jaworski's own estimate, that nearly a year would have to go by before public passions had cooled sufficiently to permit a fair trial of the former president. This delay, Ford said, would be unfair to Nixon and to the country. However, though publicity surrounding the case would indeed have been a problem, it would not have been an insurmountable one.

Some commentators, editorial writers, and legislators, and ultimately President Ford, also argued that Nixon could not be brought to justice because the proceedings would cause an uproar that would unsettle the country for months, if not years. But who would have been responsible for the uproar and delays and unsettling? The defendant himself, Richard M. Nixon. If either impeachment proceedings before Nixon's resignation or a criminal trial afterward had been dragged on and on, the slowness, confusion, and frustration would all have originated with the defendant and the defendant's supporters, as did the on-again-off-again business about the tapes and the road blocks thrown in the path of the Judiciary Committee. The prosecution's charges would have been straightforward and the evidence uncomplicated. In fact, very little evidence was required beyond the tapes that had already been made public. The argument came to this: Nixon couldn't be properly tried because he wouldn't allow anyone to try him properly.

Nixon's tactic was really the same as the tactic behind the behavior of the Black Panthers and others who in those years disrupted their trials by yelling and throwing things and screaming insults at the judge. Nixon's threatened uproar would have taken the more genteel form of legalistic objections and emotional appeals for sympathy, but that made him no different from the others. The only difference between them was that Nixon got away with it. He almost made it appear that he was doing the nation a favor by not standing trial. Thus, as he had so many times in his career, Nixon was able to make his own shortcomings and misbehavior work for him.

The fact that seven men who had served Nixon were still facing trial and possible jail sentences added to the public's sense of outrage. Those men, like Nixon, had lost their high offices and had been humiliated. Yet they were still subject to final legal accountability for their actions.

I have thought a lot about the pardon over the years. My first reaction was that President Ford's decision had been tough to make, and that perhaps he was right, perhaps both Nixon and the country had had enough. By accepting the pardon, I felt then, Nixon did at least imply that he was guilty of something, even though no formal charges had been brought.

I can't say, however, that even at the time I was totally neutral about the pardon. As I will explain later, the pardon caused a considerable problem in the selection of a jury for the trial of the seven cover-up defendants, a process that started only a few weeks after the pardon was announced. I felt then that President Ford should have waited until we had a jury selected and sequestered, so that the pardon question would not get involved in this trial.

When Nixon accepted the pardon, he admitted mistakes and misjudgments in his handling of Watergate. In his television interviews with David Frost, he went somewhat further, admitting that he had let down the country in the way he performed his duties at the time. And in his memoirs, the same themes were played again: too busy to notice what was going on around him, he misjudged the seriousness of his actions; he should have moved quickly to expose the wrongdoing and not permit the cover-up to continue. He has also made it seem that he was thrown out of office by some sort of political conspiracy, that only the failure to muster sufficient political support in the House and Senate led to his resignation.

Frankly, this explanation bothers me, not because Nixon believes it (I don't expect any more from him), but because eventually others may believe it too. The truth is that Richard Nixon left office because he was on the verge of impeachment. He was on the verge of impeachment because there was overwhelmingly convincing evidence, mostly from the grand jury sitting in the Watergate case, that he had committed criminal acts. The weight of that evidence overcame the natural political reluctance to attempt so radical a solution to a national problem as impeachment. In other words, Nixon has it exactly backward. It wasn't politics that drove him from office. It was the evidence against him, the proof of his own acts, that cost him his office.

Looking back now, I think the problem is that Nixon left office with the process for his removal incomplete. Impeachment had not been voted by the full House of Representatives, although it was certainly going to be. The Senate did not conduct a trial, though it was undoubtedly going to. And I have no doubt that the verdict in the Senate would have been to convict Richard Nixon—not because of the politics of the time but because regardless of political risk, no self-respecting politician could ignore the hard evidence.

From my point of view, the fact that the judicial process did not run its course has had additional unfortunate consequences. The initial evidence presented was compelling enough to cause the grand jury to name the president as an unindicted co-conspirator in March 1974. The prosecutors in the position to know best, because they worked with the grand jury nearly every day, have since reported that the jury was prepared then to return an indictment against Nixon. Only the arguments of Leon Jaworski persuaded them that the impeachment process provided the better forum for bringing the president to account. Once Nixon had left office, the grand jury was again ready to indict him, but was waiting for the jury to be selected in the cover-up case so that that trial would not be delayed by the publicity. Jaworski, as he has since told me, was prepared to approve an indictment.

I now feel that Nixon should have been indicted after he left office and after the cover-up jury was sequestered. And then, no matter how long it took, he should have stood trial. Of course, that was made impossible by the pardon. I take this view not because I would wish any more suffering on Nixon or his family, but because I feel it would have been better for the country if the legal process had been allowed to run its course—either to acquit the former president or to find him guilty. As it was, only one committee of the House and a grand jury ever took any official action against the president. After a trial, after the best prosecution case possible had been presented, after the best defense had been offered, after testimony and cross-examination *under oath* had been completed, a final verdict would have put the president's guilt or innocence beyond dispute. No one then could wonder whether or not he had done wrong. No one, not even Nixon himself, could any longer argue that his fate was the product of politics rather than the result of justice being served. This may not seem a problem now. After all, not many people take his explanations and evasions all that seriously. Yet the question may, some day, be a matter of historical debate. I would feel better knowing that the final processes of our system of justice had been permitted to function.

I still have the lingering feeling that no matter how great his personal loss, Nixon did manage to keep himself above the law. He was forced to give up his office, but he was not treated the same way as the other defendants. His associates served time in jail. He received a large government pension, and retired to his lovely home in San Clemente. I think people still wonder whether the concept of equal justice under law really applies if one climbs high enough in terms of wealth, power, or influence. All of my life as a lawyer and judge, I have tried to make the idea of equal justice mean something. I have always tried to treat white-collar criminals like other criminals. It still bothers me that Richard Nixon escaped that equal treatment. I feel that if he had been convicted in my court, I would have sent him to jail.

Most depressing is my feeling that Nixon could have been one of the great presidents of this century. I say that, of course, as a long-time Republican and as one who campaigned on behalf of the Republican National Committee for the Eisenhower-Nixon ticket twice and voted for Nixon for president twice.* We shared a good many political beliefs. I still think his accomplishments in foreign policy will be praised in years to come. I think the course he set in domestic policy was in many ways the proper one. He recognized a growing national demand for less interference in our lives and for more efficiency and less waste in the operation of the government. But because of Watergate, he will be remembered for his failings, not his accomplishments.

And it was so unnecessary. I have thought often how easy it would have been for him to prevent the entire mess from ever threatening his presidency. Haldeman's notes of the June 20 meeting—the conversation erased from the tape—tell us that Nixon ordered "a PR offensive to top this" (that is, the embarrassment of the Watergate break-in). Instead, all Nixon needed to do was to say to Haldeman: "I want to know who was responsible. I want their resignations by the end of the day. And I don't care who those individuals are, they must

---

* In 1960, I couldn't vote for anyone, since the District of Columbia did not get voting rights until 1964.

go. Now!" Any honest president would have done exactly that. Essentially President Eisenhower reacted in this way when his chief of staff, Sherman Adams, was discovered to have taken gifts from New England industrialist Bernard Goldfine. Eisenhower trusted Adams, valued his service immensely, but when Adams's conduct cast doubt on the level of honesty in the Eisenhower administration, he was asked to resign. And Nixon claimed to have played an active role in getting Adams out, largely because the president couldn't stand the idea of firing Adams himself.

Nixon often mentioned during the Watergate crisis, and in his reflections on it, that his reluctance to clean house after the break-in was based on his loyalty to his staff, a loyalty he thought was stronger than Ike's toward Adams. This humane instinct, he has said, prevented him from firing the aides responsible for Watergate. The tapes paint quite a different picture, showing not a president worried about the welfare of his aides, but rather a president worried about *his own political skin*. And in the end, of course, the very aides Nixon said he wanted to protect were the men who suffered most, serving jail terms while their chief escaped that fate.

Why didn't Nixon take the proper course in June 1972? What prevented him from reacting honestly, from carrying out his constitutional duty to see that the laws were enforced? I can only speculate, but it seems to me that one of two things—or maybe both of them—kept Nixon from doing what he should have done. The first possibility is that he knew about the break-in beforehand and had, in some way or another, approved of it. There is no proof of that, of course, although perhaps the answer is preserved on tapes recorded in the spring of 1972 and never made public. If he had approved the break-in, he would have had strong reason to be reluctant to fire those who had carried out his orders. The second possibility is that the Watergate break-in simply didn't strike Nixon as unusual, given the kinds of demands for political "intelligence" he had been making. It was so similar to the Ellsberg break-in, the work of the "plumbers," the wiretaps ordered on newsmen and on members of Henry Kissinger's National Security Council staff, and the attempt to develop the "Huston plan" for a co-ordinated national intelligence and spying program that the operation may have seemed routine to Nixon. By then, so many other illegal things had been done that there was no reason for great excitement after the Watergate incident. Either way, Nixon clearly shared the ruthless attitude characteristic of the White House staff. He couldn't really change and begin playing the prosecutor or the outraged executive whose aides had broken the law. In short, Nixon was personally responsible for the break-in, either because he knew about it and had participated in the planning, or because he had created the climate in which the break-in and other illegal actions were taken for granted.

We may never know whether Nixon was aware of the break-in plan ahead of time. But because of the White House taping system, we do know a lot about his part in the cover-up. Without those tapes, Nixon's role would never have been established beyond doubt. If some of his top aides had come to trial—and I'm sure they would have even without the tapes—I doubt that sufficient proof could ever have been elicited from their own self-protective testimony to force the president to resign. So why, people ask me all the time, didn't Nixon destroy the tapes?

Before the taping system was revealed to the public by his aide Alexander Butterfield, Nixon, I think, must have recognized that its existance would eventually be made public. Too many people inside the White House knew about it. He may have thought he could use selected portions of the tapes to rebut the testimony of John Dean. Once the existence of the tapes was known, Nixon must have felt certain that no court would have the courage to try to force him to turn them over. He took the notion of executive privilege to mean that he himself was the final judge of the law. As the legal arguments over the release of the tapes proceeded, and it became clear that he would lose his argument in my court and in the court of appeals, he probably counted on his four appointees to the Supreme Court (Chief Justice Warren Burger and Justices Harry Blackmun, Lewis Powell, and William Rehnquist) to sustain his position out of personal and political loyalty. Apparently he was prepared to argue that the split vote he hoped for was not a "definitive" decision, even though there would be a majority against him, and on that basis was going to ignore the ruling. With these notions of his own power in mind, I doubt that it ever occurred to Nixon that the destruction of the tapes would be necessary to save himself. And, of course, after my own ruling ordering the tapes produced for the special prosecutor, their destruction would have been so patently illegal as to cause Nixon's immediate impeachment.

Nixon's argument on the tapes and his view that the president is above the law fitted closely with the attitudes in the White House that bred the Watergate break-in, that condoned the looting of Ellsberg's psychiatrist's office, that gave rise to the "Huston plan." In his memoirs, Nixon compares these actions to Franklin Roosevelt's incarceration of Japanese-Americans during World War II and to President Lincoln's suspension of the writ of habeas corpus during the Civil War. But his reasoning is flawed. Since Roosevelt's action was regrettable and unnecessary in every sense, comparison with it can provide no justification for Nixon's operations. And the domestic situation during Nixon's presidency hardly compared to the problems faced by the nation in the 1860's.

Nixon has several times quoted this passage from Jefferson to support his own illegal acts as president: "A strict observance of the written laws is doubtless one of the high duties of a good citizen, but it is not the highest. The laws of necessity, of self-preservation, of saving our country when in danger, are of a higher obligation. . . . To lose our country by a scrupulous adherence to written law, would be to lose the law itself, with life, liberty, property and all those who are enjoying them with us; thus absurdly sacrificing the end to the means." Jefferson's proposition might arguably be correct in times of dire national emergency. But Nixon's appropriation of that view to cover his own situation is false, arrogant, and nearsighted. Throughout the Watergate crisis, Nixon confused preservation of himself in office with preservation of the office. The only emergency Nixon perceived was his personal one—the threat that he would lose his office. The real national emergency was that our president had set himself above the law and had threatened our constitutional form of government. And, I might point out, only a strict adherence to the letter of the law, enforced by the three courts of our federal system, resolved that emergency.

If Nixon had had the character of President Eisenhower, or any other honest president, this scandal would never have happened. He had been through his "six crises," and he should have known better. I regret that I supported him in his national campaigns. I hope no political party will ever stoop so low as to embrace the likes of Richard Nixon again.

16

Lawyers, Defendants, and Jurors

The resignation and pardon of Richard Nixon relieved much of the national tension surrounding the Watergate crisis. Even though there was widespread opposition to the pardon itself—which I believe caused President Ford to lose his bid for election two years later—the feeling that the government was paralyzed by and preoccupied with the scandal ended when Nixon left office. But I still had to conduct the trial of the president's men.

In a way, the fact that Nixon had escaped the ultimate judgment of the law only made the cover-up trial itself more important. Any final accounting for those charged with crimes in connection with Watergate would have to come in the approaching trial. It was obvious, and had been for months, that no matter how strong the evidence against these defendants seemed, there was going to be a tough legal defense. Most of the defendants had hired top-notch attorneys with long experience in criminal procedures. The thing that concerned me most was whether I could get through a tense, difficult trial, with a battery of defense lawyers lying in wait for any legal errors I might commit, without making some technical mistake. I thought beforehand, and I believe even more strongly now, that this was probably the most important criminal trial ever conducted in this country. That meant that not only were the president's lieutenants on trial, but so were the courts themselves. The nation was watching to see if justice would be done, if a fair and final verdict would be reached. In a sense, I felt I faced almost as much of a trial as did Mitchell, Haldeman, Ehrlichman, and the others.

On March 19, 1974, I celebrated my seventieth birthday. According to a federal statute, the chief judge must step down when he reaches seventy, although he doesn't have to retire altogether. He simply gives up the title of chief judge and the responsibility for assigning cases and handling administrative duties for the court. In the months before my birthday, I had thought a great deal about whether I would assign myself to the cover-up trial if indictments were returned while I was still chief judge. I was of two minds about that question. I was tired of the pressures of the case, but I also felt that having seen the thing through since the beginning, I should not quit in the middle. Furthermore, I felt that because I had supervised virtually every aspect of the case, I was the judge best qualified to try it. Several days before the indictments were returned, I was talking with Judge Sherman Christensen, a federal judge from Utah who was sitting by designation—that is, filling in—on our court of appeals. His opinion was that if I didn't take the case, it would be said that I tried the little people but then ran out when the big names came to trial. Several other friends were of the same opinion.

When the indictments came in on March 1, I immediately assigned myself to the cover-up case. Had the indictments come just two and a half weeks later, after I had to step down as chief judge, the case probably would have gone to someone else. When I finally finished the last of the Watergate business, in the fall of 1977, I had spent fifty years of my life with the law.

As soon as I assigned myself to the case the defendants' lawyers began bombarding me with motions of all sorts. Just listing the motions and petitions filed between March and the beginning of the trial in October takes up more than forty pages in the court's docket. That I was going to hear the case was obviously not pleasing to the defendants. They argued that I should be disqualified because of my involvement in the break-in trial and my active attempt then to get beyond the cover stories fabricated by those defendants. Because McCord had sought me out when he began his withdrawal from the cover-up conspiracy, and because of my role in the year-long controversy over the presidential tapes, they argued, I had a personal stake in the outcome of the final trial. My view was quite the opposite. I felt that my experience with the case made me better qualified than any other judge on our court to handle the trial. I also felt that my only interest was in seeing that the trial was fair. Looking back now, I think I was more concerned with protecting the rights of the defendants than with any other aspect of the proceedings. I had learned the hard way as a young lawyer what it means to have a defendant's rights trampled on by the court and the prosecution.* Whatever the verdict was going to be, I didn't want the Watergate case tainted by legal errors. In the end, I think I gave the defendants more latitude than most other judges would have permitted.

I'm sure the defense lawyers were sincere in their efforts to get me off the case, but I think that for most of them, at least part of their motivation was the fact that they expected their clients to be found guilty and didn't want me to be the judge doing the sentencing. This view is supported by two incidents that occurred before the trial even got underway. In the early summer, Charles Colson's lawyers informed me that their client was ready to plead guilty in return for the dropping of some of the charges against him, but that he would do so only if another judge was assigned to hear the plea and pronounce sentence. I had no particular feeling that I should keep Colson in my court for sentencing. I also felt that the guilty plea would perhaps simplify the coming trial. Besides, the prosecutors had endorsed the arrangement, so I felt I shouldn't stand in the way. I assigned him to Judge Gerhard Gesell, and Colson pleaded guilty. He was sentenced—no less severely than he would have been by me—and dropped from the cover-up case.

The second incident occurred while the trial was in its preliminary stage. My old friend John J. Wilson, who was representing H. R. Haldeman, came to my chambers along with Jaworski and others from the prosecutor's office. He wanted some idea of what sort of sentence I would give Haldeman should he decide to plead guilty rather than stand trial. I have made it a long-standing practice never to get involved in plea bargaining. My policy has been that I often accept plea bargains worked out between prosecutors and de-

* In 1935 in Washington, I had defended a man charged with running a large gambling operation. He was found guilty, but I felt that the jury had been tainted by exposure to newspaper stories which suggested that one member of the jury was a "plant" determined to vote for acquittal. Both the trial judge and the court of appeals rejected—unfairly, I thought—my attempts to get my client a new trial.

fendants, but I will not play any part in arriving at those arrangements, especially by agreeing beforehand to a specific sentence. So I refused to make any commitments whatsoever to Haldeman. Without any promises about the sentence, Haldeman decided to take his chances with the jury.

With all the legal maneuvering that was going on, it took seven months to get the cover-up case to trial. Much of my time during those months was of course taken up with the efforts to enforce the subpoena filed by Leon Jaworski for the Nixon tapes. But there were a variety of other problems as well. Gordon Strachan, Haldeman's deputy in the White House, had been charged with obstruction of justice for having received reports gathered from the wiretaps on the Democratic National Committee and then, after the arrests of the burglars, having destroyed those records. But Strachan had been given immunity from prosecution in exchange for his testimony before the Senate Watergate committee. His lawyers argued successfully that the charges by the prosecutors in this case violated his immunity. As a result, Strachan's case was severed from the main case. Ultimately, the complications involving the use of immunized testimony became overwhelming and the case against him was dropped altogether.

After President Nixon's resignation in early August, the defendants renewed their motions for a delay in the trial and for a change in venue, to get the trial out of Washington. I felt then—and I still think I was correct—that the defendant could get as fair a trial in Washington as anywhere else. Attention to the case was, naturally, extremely heavy in Washington, but then it was heavy everywhere else too. I didn't see any useful purpose being served by moving the trial to another city. The question of delay was a little different. For months I had been determined that the trial would begin in early September, and I refused requests for delays based on the publicity surrounding Nixon's resignation. But the court of appeals felt differently. They issued an advisory opinion suggesting a delay of three or four weeks so that the public attention focused on Nixon's resignation could subside. I granted a three-week delay and set a new trial date, October 1. That still didn't satisfy friends of the accused. In mid-September, someone bought full-page newspaper advertisements saying in bold headlines:

YOU ARE CORDIALLY INVITED TO
A PUBLIC LYNCHING

The ads complained that I was making some sort of bid for immortality by trying to keep the trial on schedule. They overlooked the part of the law that guarantees defendants not just a fair trial, but also a speedy one. The ads went on to repeat the despicable argument fostered in the White House that because the District of Columbia had voted for George McGovern for president in 1972, Nixon's aides couldn't possibly get a fair trial. I suppose that for the people who bought those advertisements, political loyalty was the only thing, and they just couldn't understand how the citizens who serve on our juries could put politics aside and return a verdict based on the facts of a case.

For every person who thought I was crucifying the Nixon people, there were at least ten who thought I was trying to do the right thing; at least, that was the way my mail made it seem. Just a few days before the advertisements criticizing me appeared, I got a note from a family in Philadelphia announcing the birth of a son. Mr. and Mrs. Robert Colbert told me they had named their son John Sirica Colbert in my honor. Of the thousands of letters I got during those years, that was the one that touched me the most. The Colberts asked me to write a few words of advice to be given to their son when he was old enough to understand. I wrote to the Colberts, "The first thing I'd tell him when he gets old enough is that he should always obey his mother and father; that he should try to get a wonderful education; that he should be a good and honest American, and above all that he must always strive to do what he thinks is right."

From the time the Supreme Court ruled against President Nixon, and St. Clair began processing the tapes and delivering them to me, I spent hours and hours listening to the rest of the subpoenaed recordings. For each tape, I had to rule on claims by the White House lawyers that certain sections were irrelevant or were subject to the narrow rules of executive privilege endorsed by the Supreme Court. And there were other problems with the tapes as well. The defense attorneys debated endlessly the accuracy of the transcripts that the prosecutors planned to give to the jurors as an aid to listening

to the hours of tapes that were to be played at the trial. Near
the end of September, we met in my chambers to resolve
some of those questions of accuracy. We got under way at
nine thirty in the morning, and by late afternoon, the lawyers
were still arguing about this word and that word in the transcripts, each lawyer trying to get the interpretation of each
passage that would be most advantageous to his own client.
Much of the debate was meaningless and tedious, so I warned
the lawyers that unless we could wrap up the discussion soon
after our dinner break, I was prepared to go on until mid-
night. It was a Monday and the Washington Redskins were
playing at home that night. Several of the attorneys had tick-
ets for the game and, suddenly, we began making progress.
We managed to finish twenty minutes before game time,
without a dinner break.

Finally, on October 1, 1974, two years three and a half
months after the break-in at the Democratic national headquarters at the Watergate office building, we began the trial
of five men accused of trying to conceal the facts of that
case. They were charged with various counts, including conspiracy to obstruct justice, and lying to the grand jury, to the
Senate, and to the FBI. With Strachan separated from the
main case and Colson having pleaded guilty, we were left
with Haldeman, Ehrlichman, and Mitchell, the president's
high command; with Robert Mardian, Mitchell's deputy at
the Justice Department; and with Kenneth Parkinson, the
lawyer who had for a time represented the Committee to Re-
elect the President. That there were only five men on trial
was in itself remarkable, since the actors in this sordid drama
actually numbered a couple of dozen. But many, like Dean,
Magruder, and Herbert Kalmbach, Nixon's personal attorney
who had helped raise the money to keep the burglars quiet,
had already pleaded guilty, as had Colson (who was also
charged in the Ellsberg case) and Fred LaRue, an aide to
Mitchell who also had a hand in the hush-money pay-offs.
Still other had been left out of the case by the prosecutors,
who—faced with the enormous task of trying the principal
figures—chose not to prosecute those against whom their evidence was weaker. Many of these minor figures had been
named as unindicted co-conspirators and would appear at the
trial as witnesses. And as we began the trial, it was impossible
to forget that the most important unindicted co-conspirator of

all, Richard M. Nixon, was safely sheltered in his home in San Clemente.

We were again in the large, ceremonial courtroom on the sixth floor of the courthouse. Part of the room was packed with spectators and some of the more than three hundred reporters from around the world who would at one time or another cover the trial. The rest of the room was filled with the first of the 315 potential jurors from whom we were eventually to select twelve jurors and six alternates to sit through what I knew was going to be a long and difficult trial. I also knew that the jurors would be sequestered for at least two months, perhaps longer, and that this would impose substantial hardship on them and their families.

Clustered around the defense tables to my right, in the front of the courtroom, were four of the five defendants and their battery of lawyers. None of the defendants any longer held a government job. John Mitchell had left the Justice Department to take over the CRP and then had left that job because of domestic problems. Haldeman and Ehrlichman had both been forced to resign more than a year and a half before, as Nixon tried to save himself from the Watergate crisis. Mardian had quit the CRP shortly after Mitchell. Parkinson had served only a few months as the committee's lawyer. Yet the aura of power still surrounded these men, especially Mitchell, Haldeman, and Ehrlichman. It was impossible for me not to feel some pity for them, thinking of how successful they had been, how far they had risen in their careers, and how demeaning it must be for them to sit there ready to face trial.

Mitchell was, as always, well dressed. He had made a small fortune in private law practice in New York before joining the Nixon administration. He had never been anxious to leave that practice, and he must by then have doubly regretted ever coming to Washington. He had been at the pinnacle of his profession. Now he was the first man who had held the office of attorney general of the United States ever to face trial for criminal acts.* After Mitchell left the Justice Department to run the Nixon campaign, I attended the swearing-in of his successor, Richard Kleindienst. Mitchell introduced me to a friend there as "the best judge on the district court," ap-

---

* President Harding's attorney general, Harry M. Daugherty, was forced to resign as a result of the Teapot Dome scandal, but he was never indicted or tried.

parently feeling I was his kind of "law and order" judge. Naturally, I felt flattered; I appreciated the compliment, although I didn't agree with his assessment.

I had met Robert Mardian only once, at a luncheon given some time before by the District of Columbia Bar Association, at which Mitchell was the guest speaker. Mardian and I sat next to each other talking Republican politics. I had felt honored to sit next to him, since he was an assistant attorney general and was highly regarded. He had been one of the masterminds behind Barry Goldwater's presidential nomination in 1964 and was one of the Nixon administration's leading advocates of a tougher approach to crime. While in the Justice Department he had expanded the use of the conspiracy statutes to prosecute antiwar activists. Now he was being tried for violating the same conspiracy laws.

Aside from the president, Haldeman and Ehrlichman had been more responsible for conducting the affairs of this country during their years in the White House than anyone else in the government. They had been called Nixon's "German shepherds" by press and government workers whose access to the president they controlled. Now Ehrlichman sat at the defense table, sketching pictures of the four statues on the marble wall behind me. This was his second trial of the year. He had been found guilty during the summer in the Ellsberg case, tried in our court by Judge Gesell. Mitchell, too, had been through an earlier trial that year, having been acquitted in the Vesco case in New York.

Haldeman was probably even closer to Nixon than Ehrlichman. Formerly an advertising executive on the West Coast, he had been with Nixon through several campaigns, including Nixon's disastrous run for the governorship of California in 1962, two years after his defeat by John F. Kennedy. He had devoted most of his professional life to Nixon and was the only one of the defendants who was not a lawyer. With his newly acquired longer hair his appearance was softer than in the days when he wore a bristling crew cut, but it was soon clear that he hadn't yet accepted his fall from power. As we began the jury selection, he and one of his lawyers could just barely be heard making unkind remarks about some of the prospective jurors. At one point, when I made a ruling on a prospective juror that Haldeman didn't like, he couldn't resist shaking his head in disagreement. The gesture angered me. I turned to Haldeman and said, "You may not like it, but I'm the judge and you're the defendant."

I felt especially sorry for Kenneth Parkinson. I had known his late father very well when we were both practicing law. I couldn't help wondering what his father would have thought if he had been alive to see his son in my courtroom, not representing a client as he had done before, but as a defendant himself. I think it would have broken his heart. Parkinson was a young lawyer on his way up. He had apparently developed a fine practice with a good firm. He and his lawyer, Jacob Stein, one of the finest attorneys in Washington, deliberately sat separately from the other defendants, symbolizing later attempts to disassociate Parkinson from the rest.

Without the trappings of power, the defendants were now in the hands of their lawyers. Most of the defense teams had at least two members in court each day. The special prosecutor's office usually sent seven lawyers, who shared the duties involved in direct and cross-examination, the preparation of the evidence to be introduced, and the choice and arrangement of the lengthy sequences from the White House tapes that would be played for the jury. There were times, when the lawyers approached the bench, that I felt terribly outnumbered. I sometimes felt like an overworked school teacher trying to keep order in a classroom crowded with bright, ambitious, and quarrelsome students.

Although each defendant was offering his own defense, John Wilson was regarded as the dean on that side of the courtroom. The other defense attorneys seemed to defer to him from time to time, and it was obvious from the very beginning of the trial that as Haldeman's counsel, Wilson was prepared to lead the charge—not so much against the government's case as against me. Wilson, an extremely able lawyer, was seventy-three years old when the trial started, and was more experienced in the law than anyone else in the courtroom, including me. Everyone recognized from the outset that the government would be able to offer an extremely powerful case. Wilson and the others, I believe, hoped that if they couldn't beat the government they might at least lay the groundwork for a mistrial by provoking me into a legal error of some sort.

Wilson was the perfect one to lead this attempt. We had known each other for more than forty years, and he knew as much about me as a lawyer and a judge as anyone in Washington. When I first entered the United States attorney's office as an assistant to Leo Rover, John Wilson was already working there. His office was right next to mine. From his memory of those days, Wilson knew that my Italian temper was one of my main weaknesses. From the start of the cover-up trial, he tried to use that weakness to his client's advantage. I remembered very well the day Wilson had first heard me lose my temper. I had prosecuted a sensational arson case in which two young men were accused of setting fire to a local fraternity house. After the two had been found guilty, an attorney for one of the boys came to my office. He asked permission to interview the jurors in the case in the hope of finding some error that could serve as the basis for a motion for a new trial. I was being co-operative and raised no objection to the jury's being interviewed. But soon, the lawyer became very abusive and started berating me and the jurors for having convicted his client. I got so angry with the man that I finally invited him outside to settle the matter. From his office next door, John Wilson heard the fracas and stepped in. He personally escorted the offensive lawyer out of my office, preventing, I'm sure, an unpleasant incident. Because he knew me so well, Wilson always called me Johnny. He didn't use that nickname during the trial, but it seemed that our long friendship made him willing to push me further than did the other defense lawyers. Wilson never knew just how close he came to succeeding in his attempts to make me lose control, nor did he know how close he came to paying the price for that tactic with a citation for contempt.

John Mitchell's sour demeanor, I thought during the trial, presented a real problem in terms of building sympathy from the jury. But almost as if aware of that liability, Mitchell had chosen the affable, humorous William Hundley as his attorney. Hundley could always be counted on to get off a wisecrack that would break the tension and relax everyone in the courtroom. He also happened to be a first-rate lawyer. When we were playing the White House tapes, it was not uncommon for someone in the courtroom to break into a sort of perverse laughter as the ugly and damaging details of the cover-up were heard at first hand. I repeatedly had to remind those present that no laughter would be tolerated. After one of those warnings, Hundley joked, "How do you feel about crying, Judge?" All of us, including the jury, had a good laugh.

Mardian had hired David Bress as his chief defense counsel. Like Wilson, I had known Dave Bress for years. He had been the Democrat recommended along with George Hart and me for the seat on the district Court which I got in 1957, and was one of our best trial lawyers. He had served as the United States attorney during the 1960's and had been nominated by Lyndon Johnson to serve on our court. But that nomination was made in the last days of Johnson's presidency and was blocked by Senator Strom Thurmond. I know it was one of Dave's major disappointments. In my opinion, he would have made a fine judge. He was quite an expert on criminal law and was teaching a course on the rules of evidence at a local law school. He used that expertise effectively during the early weeks of the trial when he raised objections to the conduct of the government attorneys. At about the midpoint of the trial, Bress became seriously ill and was forced to leave the defense of Mardian in the hands of his assistant Thomas Green. Bress entered the hospital for a major operation and was not able to return until late in the trial. He died a short time later, much to my sorrow. His long absence from the case became the principal point of a post-trial appeal by Mardian, which I will discuss later.

The only one of the principal defense attorneys I didn't know before the trial was William Frates, from Florida. Frates, who was Ehrlichman's counsel, seemed the least experienced of the group, at least in terms of his familiarity with the rules of federal procedure. But what he lacked in experience in the federal courts, he more than made up for with his rugged good looks and his deep, resonant voice that absolutely dominated the courtroom every time he spoke. In fact, his voice had such power that during private bench conferences, which the jury was not supposed to hear, I continually had to remind him to try to speak softly. He was obviously a great orator, and must have impressed juries in Florida, where he usually practiced. He had to be kept in check, since he tended to deliver long speeches instead of presenting concise arguments during various parts of the trial.

All in all, the defense lawyers were a most impressive group. They all had tough cases to defend, and I didn't envy them their jobs one bit. Part of their problem was that they faced a prosecution team of extremely high quality. Shortly after the trial began, Leon Jaworski resigned as special prosecutor. Although some people felt he was running out on the toughest part of his case—the trial itself—I could understand his reasons. He had brought the case to trial. Nixon had left office and had been pardoned, so there was nothing more to do on that front. Jaworski was anxious to return to Houston, and more important, he left Henry Ruth in charge. Ruth, who had been deputy to both Jaworski and Archibald Cox, was a man of obvious competence and experience. There was nothing left in the investigative part of the prosecutor's job that Ruth could not handle very capably. The trial team was headed by James Neal, and I daresay even Leon Jaworski couldn't have done any better than Jim Neal did in the trial itself.

Neal is from Tennessee. When I first heard him speak in the courtroom, his soft southern accent reminded me of the way I talked when we first moved to Washington from Richmond. Neal's accent gave the impression that he was most relaxed and easygoing. But within days of the beginning of the trial it was apparent that nothing in the courtroom escaped his attention. He seemed prepared for every turn of events. Not a single legal question arose that Neal hadn't apparently anticipated and had ordered researched by his staff. He seemed determined to do anything necessary to make sure that I would never be forced to make a ruling on the law without having been thoroughly briefed by his side. More than any other lawyer in the case, it was Neal who dominated the courtroom. He had the ability to be both intense and graceful at the same time. He could be tough when it was necessary, sympathetic when it was appropriate, and even humorous at the right moment.

Neal's job was made easier by the quality of his assistants. Young Richard Ben-Veniste, who had led the Watergate task force in the prosecutor's office, handled a substantial portion of the examination and cross-examination for the government. For a time, I was sure Ben-Veniste was, like me, of Italian ancestry, but I finally found out that he descended from Sephardic Jews. Ben-Veniste had been a federal prosecutor in the tough Southern District of New York, and for a man his age, he certainly handled himself with great self-assurance in the courtroom. Despite the difference in their ages, he showed my friend John Wilson no deference whatsoever. He was able to trade verbal jabs with Wilson on an equal basis. Ben-Veniste had a quick wit and a fine sense of humor. I was amused once when, in an argument over what documents he could show a witness, he snapped, "With respect to what he can be shown, he can be shown anything in the world, he can be shown a cheese sandwich if it is going to refresh his recollection." After a bit more than a month of the trial had passed, when I had begun to feel overwhelmed by the avalanche of legal memoranda the government was giving me, I complained one day at the bench, "You are memo-ing me to death." Ben-Veniste responded, "That is a good title for a tune, Judge."

Jill Volner, who had done such a fine job questioning Rose Mary Woods the year before during the hearings on the tape gap, was handling a large amount of the work in the courtroom for the special prosecutors. She was quietly competent, and her appearance fooled some of the other lawyers into trying to soft-soap her. Once, during the jury-selection process, there was a discussion of a prospective woman juror who happened to be quite attractive. John Wilson joked that the woman was "Jill's competition in the courtroom." Mrs. Volner put Wilson in his place and on notice that he was to treat her as a lawyer, not a woman lawyer. "Mr. Wilson," she said firmly, "I'd appreciate your not making that kind of remark." And Wilson never did again.

With the defendants at their places and with one of the most impressive batteries of lawyers that had ever been in my courtroom ready to begin, we started jury selection. Choosing a jury under the circumstances of the Watergate case obviously presented a great problem. So much publicity had been generated by the case that we needed to take extreme care that the jury was in no way tainted. I felt that only the most rigorous *voir dire*—that is, screening of the jury panel—could prevent a later appeal based on a finding that some jurors had already made up their minds about the case before trial. An additional problem, I knew, was that the jury would be sequestered for a long period and many prospective jurors thus could not serve because of economic, family, or health considerations. I was especially worried that someone would be selected for the jury, only to be discovered later to have kept secret some connection with the case, or the lawyers, or one of the defendants. As we began the long process of picking the jury, with the ceremonial courtroom filled with the panel members, I issued a stern warning:

"Now, the following admonition, of course, is not given for

the purpose of intimidating, coercing or frightening this jury panel or any member of the panel. Its purpose, rather, is to advise you of the solemnity of your duty. I want each prospective juror to understand that should it develop after this case has been tried and the jury dismissed, or at any other time during the trial of this case, for example, that any juror has knowingly, intentionally, or deliberately failed to answer truthfully any of the questions I am about to propound or that may be propounded by the attorneys for the parties in this case to the prospective jurors, that juror could be cited for contempt of court and he or she might receive a jail sentence as a consequence. . . ."

We began the questioning of the jurors in the ceremonial courtroom, but soon moved downstairs to my regular courtroom, which we sealed off from the press, even covering the windows with paper to guarantee our privacy. Although many reporters were angered by the secrecy, I felt very strongly that this unusual step was necessary to make it easier for the potential jurors to answer my questions candidly and truthfully. We initially excused 170 people from service because of problems connected with a long period away from homes and jobs. My warning seemed to have had some effect. Memories suddenly improved. Members of the panel lined up to divulge to me events in their lives which they had previously failed to disclose and which in some cases led to their being excused from jury duty.

For another seven days, we continued to question the prospective jurors. I decided that the process could be speeded up by asking certain questions, more or less routine inquiries about prior jury service and the like, of people assembled in groups of twelve to eighteen. After the group sessions, I questioned each one of the veniremen individually in the presence of lawyers for both sides, with special attention to their views about the case. In these private sessions I attempted to find out whether all the publicity about the case had caused any of the prospective jurors to come to some conclusions about the guilt or innocence of the defendants. I made a special attempt to see if the jurors were aware that Ehrlichman had been convicted that summer in the Ellsberg case. The record of this whole process, to give some idea of its length and intensity, fills about two thousand printed pages. I felt that every conceivable protection was being given to the defendants, lest they be judged by a biased jury.

By the time we finished this stage of the questioning, it seemed to me that if the remaining veniremen could be said to be leaning one way or another, it was toward acquitting the defendants rather than convicting them. I say this because many of the prospective jurors had indicated that they felt the Nixon pardon made it unfair to try the former president's aides. They reasoned that if the top man went free, so too should those around him. But most of those who felt that way also said, in answer to my questions, that they could set that opinion aside and decide the case on the basis of the evidence presented at trial and of the law applicable. In the end, several people who believed that the Nixon pardon left the defendants unfairly exposed to jail actually served on the jury.

As we got down to the final selection of the twelve jurors and six alternates, I made one more decision that I thought helped protect the rights of the defendants. I gave the defense lawyers the right to excuse fifteen jurors without specific cause, while the government could challenge only six. The last stage of the selection became like a poker game, with the lawyers for one side or the other challenging a juror in hopes of getting a better one in his or her place. The selection process was, I believe, fair, and led to the choice of a fair jury. After the trial, the defendants appealed the case, and one of the points in that appeal was that the jury had been unfairly biased against them and that the jury-selection process had been to blame. The court of appeals disagreed. "On the basis of our own review," the majority of the appeals court ruled, "we have no doubt that the jury was impartial. Accordingly, we find no reversible error associated with the impaneling of the jury."

17

Trials and Judgments

The cover-up trial was not my first experience with a case in which defendants had helped to protect higher-ups in a crime. In 1940, I had assisted in the defense of the executive vice-president of the Union Electric Company of Missouri, who was charged with perjury in connection with a Securities and Exchange Commission investigation of company kick-backs and political pay-offs.

The defendant was a feisty little man named Frank J. Boehm. He was charged with accumulating a slush fund of more than a half million dollars and then giving that money to politicians who did favors for Union Electric. During the SEC investigation, he had denied any wrongdoing, and as a result, he faced the perjury charge.

There was little we could do to help Boehm; the evidence was overwhelmingly against him. He was convicted in the summer of 1940, sentenced to five years in prison, and fined four thousand dollars.

Boehm was an incredible man. He lived in a fancy house and always traveled in a chauffeured limousine. He had a very bad heart condition and once during the trial had to be excused from the courtroom because of a mild attack. After he had been revived by his nitroglycerin pill, we jokingly suggested that he should have stayed in the courtroom to win some sympathy. Even his legal difficulties hadn't humbled Frank Boehm. "To hell with them," he answered. "I don't want any sympathy."

He always managed to stay in high spirits, even when he was facing jail. After the trial, he announced that he wanted to settle up his legal fees with the firm I was assisting. He didn't have a personal check with him at the time, so he carefully tore from a brown bag a piece of paper of the appropriate size. He printed on it the name of his bank, and then wrote out a check for ten thousand dollars. It cleared the bank with no trouble at all.

Boehm had many friends in high places. After he had spent two years in jail, President Roosevelt commuted his sentence. Boehm promptly sued Union Electric and its holding company, North American Company of New York, for $3.5 million, charging that the higher-ups in both companies had engineered the pay-off scheme. According to Boehm's son, Frederick J. Boehm, A Florida insurance company vice-president, his father won an out-of-court settlement.

On October 14, the prosecutors opened their case. Richard Ben-Veniste spent the entire day, except for a short lunch break and a few conferences at my bench, outlining and then detailing the government's charges against the five defendants. Standing at the lectern in the center of the courtroom, he described the origins of the outrageous Gemstone plan, G. Gordon Liddy's attempts to get the secret intelligence-gathering scheme approved and paid for by the Committee to Re-elect the President, and Jeb Magruder's report that at a meeting on March 30, 1972, former Attorney General John Mitchell finally approved a $250,000 budget for the Liddy operation.

Once the break-in had occurred, Ben-Veniste told the jury, and McCord and the men from Miami were arrested, the conspiracy to obstruct justice began. The five men who were arrested began by giving the police false names. "In the hours following the arrest at Watergate," Ben-Veniste said, "the word went out across the United States notifying high White House officials and Nixon campaign officials that McCord and the others had been caught in the Democratic Headquarters." Liddy himself, who had escaped the initial arrest inside the Watergate, called Magruder in California. Magruder told Mitchell, Mardian, and Fred LaRue of the arrests. Magruder also advised Haldeman, in Florida with President Nixon, of the arrests, and then told John Dean, who was returning from a trip to the Philippines.

The conspirators first tried to get the five men out of jail so that their real names wouldn't be discovered. Liddy went to the Burning Tree Country Club, an exclusive men's golf club in suburban Bethesda, Maryland, to locate Attorney General Richard Kleindienst. Liddy told Kleindienst that John Mitchell wanted the five men out of jail. Kleindienst refused to take any action, telling Liddy that if Mitchell had something to say, he should contact him personally.

Since they couldn't conceal the names of the burglars for long, the next step was the preparation of false statements, Ben-Veniste explained. The officials at the CRP simply denied they knew anything at all about McCord's operation. Although they admitted they were embarrassed by the fact that McCord happened to be the security director for the committee, they claimed that he also worked for other employers and that, in this instance, he was off on some bizarre lark of his own.

The pattern of the entire conspiracy had already emerged. One lie would lead to another. As one story or one action failed, a more elaborate story would be developed or a more extreme step taken to protect the committee and then the White House from two threats: from the burglars themselves, whose silence was essential; and from the government investigators, who constantly threatened to pull down the whole conspiracy by finding out the truth.

When the denials of any knowledge of Liddy's operation became unbelievable, the conspirators invented their next story. To explain the already completed transfer of nearly $200,000 to Liddy, the claim was made that Liddy had been paid to provide security for the committee headquarters and for so-called "surrogate" candidates. The "surrogates" were cabinet officers and others who had been sent around the country to campaign on President Nixon's behalf. Nixon was avoiding the campaign so that he would be perceived as above the political battle and totally preoccupied with his official duties. As part of this strategy, "Campaign Director Mitchell and White House Assistant Ehrlichman also helped perpetuate this false cover story by making false statements to FBI agents who interviewed them in July, 1972," Ben-Veniste told the jury.

The results of the Watergate bugging had been reported to the CRP and to the White House. Liddy even had his own stationery with the Gemstone code name printed on the top. If the story that the burglars were off on their own was to be maintained, this evidence and other incriminating documents had to be destroyed. Liddy went back to his office right after the break-in and put his secret papers through a shredder. At a meeting with Mitchell, Mardian, and LaRue, Magruder was ordered to burn his Gemstone file. He followed those orders, using the fireplace at his home in a Washington suburb. Haldeman ordered his assistant, Gordon Strachan, to clean out their files and destroy documents that dealt with the Watergate operation. Howard Hunt had put his own secret papers, including some records of his and Liddy's break-in at the office of Daniel Ellsberg's psychiatrist, in his safe in the Executive Office Building. Now John Ehrlichman urged John Dean to "deep-six" (i.e., dump into the river) the contents of Hunt's safe. Dean thought better of that plan and instead turned over the most incriminating documents to acting FBI director L. Patrick Gray with the instruction that Gray could not disclose them to his own investigators at the bureau. Gray admitted that he himself later destroyed that evidence.

The FBI was important to the conspirators in other ways as well. To make sure that the cover-up story held, the White House and committee officials needed to know precisely what the investigators were turning up. Through White House counsel Dean, and at the urging of Dean's superiors, including Nixon, the bureau was providing up-to-the-minute reports on the status of the investigation. The White House was not just getting reports of interviews by the FBI agents, but was also being told what leads the bureau planned to pursue. With that sort of information the conspirators were able to alter their cover-up plan to stay one jump ahead of the investigators.

Even so, the White House and the committee leaders couldn't afford to let the FBI move freely on the case. There were too many loose ends, too many clues that would connect the burglars with the committee and with those close to President Nixon who knew about the secret operation. Ben-Veniste also described to the jury how, with Nixon himself approving Haldeman's and Mitchell's suggestion, Haldeman and Ehrlichman met with the top leaders of the Central Intelligence Agency. The two presidential aides told CIA director Richard Helms and his deputy, General Vernon Walters, that they should instruct the FBI to curtail its investigation into the laundered money that had gone through Mexico on its way to the CRP and then to Liddy and the burglars, because such an investigation could compromise CIA activities in

Mexico. That was, of course, totally untrue. But Walters met with FBI director Gray and told him to limit the investigation. Gray agreed, but when his own agents objected, Gray asked for a written instruction from the CIA. Walters, now smelling a rat, refused, and the earnest Gray went to warn Nixon that his aides were misusing the two agencies, never knowing that Nixon himself had approved that misuse.

All the denials, phony stories, manipulation of the investigators, even the destruction of evidence, were not enough to hide the facts of the case, to cover up the role the president's aides had played in the bugging and the break-in. The trouble was that the burglars themselves knew the truth. Should these men begin to talk freely, all the rest of the efforts to suppress the truth would be to no avail. "The government's proof will show," Ben-Veniste said, "that within two weeks after the arrest on June 17, 1972, a massive covert, secret operation was set into motion by the conspirators to accumulate and deliver cash funds, which over an eight-month period totaled more than $400,000 to the Watergate burglars, to the very people who they were saying at the same time were off on a lark of their own. We will show that this money—all in cash—was collected by the conspirators from the coffers of the Committee to Re-elect the President, from additional campaign contributions, and from a secret White House cash fund under defendant Haldeman's personal control."

The existence of "hush money" was, naturally, the keystone of the government's case. Jim Neal and his staff were ready for all sorts of explanations from the defense, including the argument that the CIA had been invoked to protect some national-security interest, that the bugging plan hadn't really been approved by Mitchell, and so on. But it was the payment of the money that clinched the case, in the prosecutor's view.

"That is the question, ladies and gentlemen, that we ask you to keep in mind as you hear the evidence during this trial. Why were these payments made?" Ben-Veniste said.

The answer was obvious to everyone. The money had been paid in return for the silence of those arrested at the Watergate, the men who were going to jail, whose families would be alone, whose financial situation would be desperate without those pay-offs, whose reputations would be ruined. The Nixon men were asking the burglars to take the rap, to serve their time quietly, in order to protect those in high places who had paid for, approved, and gotten the results of the illegal operation at the Democratic headquarters. Finally, to ease the burden of the prison terms, some of the burglars and even some of the officials at the CRP who were being investigated were assured by men in the White House that their stays in jail would be reduced by the president of the United States if they aided the cover-up. Hunt and McCord were given those promises; later Jeb Magruder was told the same thing. And as the cover-up began to fail, and John Mitchell was being asked to step forward and take the blame to protect those others in the White House, the former attorney general of the United States of America was told that he wouldn't have to stay in jail for long.

The prosecutors had a very strong case and had obviously prepared it well. And they also had John Dean.

During the summer, I had sentenced Dean to jail for his confessed part in the cover-up conspiracy. I had been reading about Dean's testimony in the trial of John Mitchell and Maurice Stans for their alleged roles in attempting to halt the SEC investigation of Robert Vesco. When Dean was on the stand in the New York case, the defense attorneys had suggested from time to time that he was testifying against Mitchell and Stans in order to get a lighter sentence from the court in Washington. It was a legitimate way for those attorneys to try to discredit Dean, given the fact that he hadn't yet been sentenced by me. But I didn't want the defense to use the same tactic in the cover-up case. Dean had already made his plea bargain with the prosecutors. As long as he appeared to testify fully and truthfully, I knew that what he said on the witness stand was not going to make any difference in the sentence I handed down. So to prevent the suggestion that he was testifying in the hope that I would reduce his sentence, I decided to give Dean that sentence well before the trial. He had come forward voluntarily, but not until after the McCord letter had been made public. He had been of enormous help in making the case against the other White House aides, but he had also been perhaps the most central character in the cover-up, from the days immediately after the arrest of the burglars until April 1973, when he finally told his story to his lawyer and then to the U.S. attorney. I sentenced him to one to four years. I remember that years before the Watergate mess, my wife's sister had called to inquire about how I selected my law clerks. She explained that a friend of hers,

Mrs. Thomas Hennings, the wife of the late senator from Missouri, had a son-in-law about to graduate from Georgetown Law School who was interested in working for me. I told my sister-in-law that my clerks are usually screened by the law school clerkship committee and advised her to tell her friend that her son-in-law should first apply to that committee. I never heard any more about the young man until 1973, when John Dean was implicated in the scandal.*

Dean spent nine days on the witness stand. Seemingly without error or lapse of memory, he recounted the details of the whole case just as he had presented them the summer before during the Senate Watergate hearings. The defense lawyers, when it came their turn to cross-examine Dean, were extremely cautious with him and didn't really discredit any part of his testimony. However, the procedural arguments among the lawyers kept getting more and more emotional. I was reminded of an old legal axiom: "If the law is against you, argue the facts. And if the facts are against you, argue the law. If the law and the facts are against you, then abuse the prosecutor." At one point, I warned the lawyers, "I am not going to have this bickering back and forth. We are not before a Senate committee where they have television and cameras and everything else. We are in a federal courtroom."

With Dean's testimony damaging their clients badly, the defense lawyers, led by John Wilson, seemed to step up their attempts to get me so angry that I would make a critical mistake. If they couldn't hope for an acquittal, they could at least play for a mistrial. Much of the argument between Wilson and me was over the White House tapes which were going to be used to support Dean's testimony. Wilson especially objected to the written transcripts of the tapes prepared by the prosecutors, which were intended to help the jurors understand the conversations they heard but which were not to be treated as evidence themselves. In fact, after the tapes were played, the transcripts were to be taken away from the jurors.

Wilson thought that some of the transcripts were misleading and would push the jurors toward negative conclusions about the participants, especially his own client, Haldeman. He had good reason to be worried; the tapes were terribly in-

* Dean divorced Mrs. Henning's daughter and later married Maureen Dean, who was his wife while he was working in the White House.

criminating, and when added to the testimony of Dean and other witnesses, pretty much sealed Haldeman's fate.

But Wilson probably had more in mind when objecting to these transcripts than simply raising his legal points. I felt he was trying to annoy me as much as possible by objecting and objecting and arguing and arguing. Any lawyer can make any objection he sees fit. The judge rules on the objection. The lawyer has then made his record clear and can use that record to fashion an appeal after the trial is over. But Wilson never quit.

The exchanges between us got increasingly bitter. When I ruled for the prosecutors on one point, Wilson responded, "Now if the prosecutor wants to lead you into error, that is his business. I want a fair trial here. I want to try to save you from error, although it may be to our advantage for you to commit error." This of course irritated me because Wilson seemed to be doing exactly what he was saying he didn't want to do. He wanted me to commit error, not through my rulings on the tapes transcripts, but rather through some loss of control.

He frequently implied that I was making legal mistake after legal mistake. He was attempting, I assumed, to shake my confidence. In discussing the question of the transcripts, Wilson said, "All I can do is to call it to your attention that it is error and put it in my error bag, which is getting bigger and bigger."

I wanted Wilson to know that I would follow my own instincts and not be shaken by his tactics. "If this case gets to the court of appeals and if I commit error, I am sure the court of appeals will correct it at the proper time. I do what I think is right. I don't have one eye on the court of appeals when I make a decision," I said.

The issue really was one of control over the proceedings. Wilson was edging ever closer to an open disrespect for the court. One reason for his behavior, I feel sure, was the long friendship we've had and the number of times he had appeared in my courtroom. There was a kind of familiarity that made him a bit careless in his remarks. The combination of familiarity and deliberate provocation really began to get under my skin. I can remember exploding in the privacy of my office more than once, with Todd as the only witness. I would blow off some steam and go back into court feeling much better.

Wilson referred over and over to his "error bag." Finally one day I snapped at him, "The point is that if you think that frightens this court—"

Wilson shot back, "I couldn't frighten you any more than you can frighten me."

"I am not overawed by your ability," I told Wilson.

"And I'm not overawed by you either," he said.

Of course, these exchanges occurred out of the presence of the jurors and had no effect on them. But they took their emotional toll on me. Wilson was also quite provocative, I thought, with the government attorneys. He and Jim Neal got into an argument once about the relevance of one of the presidential tapes. Neal, exasperated by Wilson, concluded his bench argument by saying that if the tape wasn't relevant, "I'm a monkey's uncle." "You're a monkey's uncle," Wilson said.

Wilson and Ben-Vensite got into quite a few tiffs too. Ben-Veniste was every bit as fast with his tongue as Wilson, and the two men, separated by years of age and experience, had an almost instinctive wariness of each other. Ben-Veniste once described a point raised by Wilson as "bogus." Wilson fired back, "Let me answer this youngster, Your Honor. You tell me what is bogus. Son, I have tried more cases in my life than you are ever going to try. Don't tell me what is bogus. I could start criticizing you until doomsday."

On several occasions I had to warn the lawyers that their conduct was getting out of hand. Even the spectators in the courtroom were from time to time acting out their emotions. One day, when William Frates and his client Ehrlichman were entering the courtroom, they were greeted, they complained, with "visible hissing," which I suppose meant that they could actually see the hissers as well as hear them. I warned that I would clear the room if there were any further outbursts.

But the problems with the lawyers—their increasingly bitter arguments with one another and their ever louder arguments with me—kept getting worse. My temper was near the breaking point, so I decided to get tougher. One morning, after thinking about the problem overnight, I called the lawyers to the bench. In an off-the-record conversation, I told them that I felt they were trying to make me lose my temper. But, I told them, their tactics would not work; there would be no mistrial, and if they continued to conduct themselves in the

same fashion I would take appropriate action after the trial
was over. They knew exactly what I meant. I had in mind the
sensational trial in New York in 1949 of eleven men charged
with Communist activities. In that case, federal judge Harold
Medina took enormous abuse from the defense attorneys during the trial and then, afterward, put several of them in jail
for contempt of court. That is exactly what I intended to do
if things didn't calm down during the Watergate trial.

After that tempers began to cool off. Even Wilson's "error
bag" became the object of some humor. Just before Thanksgiving, Wilson asked if he could make a constitutional point.

"I can't stop you from that," I told him.

"I know it won't have an effect on you,"he said.

"Why do you want to make it then?" I asked.

"I am in need of my error bag," Wilson said. "It burst a
seam already."

Jim Neal jumped in at this point. "Your Honor, may I respond to the error bag thing?" he asked with a straight face.
"I've heard a lot about that. There is an old expression in
Tennessee, a term 'fertie bag,' and it is two pounds of ma-
nure in a one-pound bag." Everyone in the court broke into
laughter. Neal went on. "I would like to believe rather than
an error bag, Mr. Wilson is carrying around a fertie bag."

There was more laughter, mostly at John Wilson's expense.
"We have had eight weeks of this product of the moonshine
district in Tennessee and I'm getting tired of it," Wilson replied, to more laughter.

I couldn't resist the chance to kid Wilson myself, since the
jury was out of the room during this exchange. "We might
give the bag another name which I have heard it described
as," I said. "It is not only your error bag, but also your wind
bag."

Much of the conflict in the early stages of the trial had
been between Wilson and myself. But I felt that, if anything,
I was bending over backward to make sure the defendants
could not claim later, on appeal, that I had in any way deprived them of a fair trial. I had given them an unusually
large number of challenges during the jury-selection process,
and I felt that I had given them a large amount of latitude in
cross-examining the government's witnesses. During Dean's
testimony, for example, I announced in the presence of the
jury that, despite the government's objections on a point of
law, "I am not trying to try this case quickly, according to

the strict rules of evidence." I meant that I did not intend to cut off the defense questioning of government witnesses in order to save time, even though an extremely literal reading of the evidentiary rules would have justified that course.

"What we are trying to get, members of the jury, is the truth of what happened," I said. "You can sum up the case in one little word at the proper time—an objective finding by the jury of the truth, T-R-U-T-H. That is what we are trying to find out about the whole picture."

This remark caused a great furor in the press. Liberals and civil libertarians misread it as indicating that I was trying to push forward the government's case, which to most observers seemed already nearly airtight. In fact, I had meant exactly the opposite—that I would not jeopardize the defendants' rights in order to expedite the trial. It was an interesting reaction. Many of the people now jumping up and down over that remark—and not bothering to find out exactly what I had meant—were the ones who months earlier had been screaming for Richard Nixon's head. To be truthful, the reaction made me angry.

Of course, in trying a widely publicized case you have to expect one and all to have something to say about it, no matter how much they know and no matter which side they are on. I did get myself into a little trouble one day—although the civil liberties people never said anything about it that I remember—when I couldn't resist making an observation about the sadness of the whole case. It was late October, and Frates was cross-examining John Dean about his account of how Mitchell had first met with Liddy to discuss the Gemstone plan. The jury was out of the courtroom, and as I looked down at Mitchell I felt some sympathy for the man who so recently had commanded so much power and respect. I knew I should have kept my mouth shut. "I suppose a judge shouldn't say anything because every time I say something people put the wrong interpretation on it. Maybe I shouldn't say what is on my mind—" I observed. Frates urged me on, suggesting I say what I was thinking.

"I will tell you what is on my mind," I ventured. "It is too bad that Mr. Mitchell didn't say, 'Throw them out of here, get them out fast,' and you wouldn't be in this courtroom today. It is too bad it didn't happen that way. Anyway, it is not for me to say what should have been done. The jury hasn't heard that and no harm can be done—I have got to say I used a very mild expression at that."

As long as I live, I will never quite understand what kept Mitchell from throwing Liddy out of his office when Liddy came in with the preposterous plan to spend a million dollars bugging the Democrats and the rest of it. I had respected Mitchell, and I couldn't quite comprehend how he could have acquiesced in the plan. I suppose he was worried about the other people around Nixon, such as Haldeman and Colson who he felt might be encouraging the Gemstone project and might have the president's ear on such matters. But still, the idea of Mitchell's even listening to such a plan was a bit beyond my understanding.

Of course, Mitchell himself had said just about the same thing in his testimony the year before during the Senate committee hearings. But William Hundley, Mitchell's attorney, moved for a mistrial anyway, on the grounds that my remark showed I was prejudging the case. I denied that motion, but worried a bit that I might have gone too far. However since the jury was out, I did feel no damage had been done. Nothing more was ever made of the incident. Even today it seems to me really tragic in many ways that Mitchell didn't follow what he said were his instincts at the time. Had he done so, we probably would not have had the Watergate scandal.

As the trial went on, the case against the defendants seemed to grow stronger and stronger. But the special prosecutors had their troubles too. Much of their case was built upon the testimony of people who had admitted that they themselves had been involved in the conspiracy. Dean was the first, but there were others as well. Jeb Magruder testified, and was subjected to a grueling cross-examination about his confessed crimes. While the testimony from these already convicted conspirators was in most cases quite believable, the defense pounded away at the past lies and evasions that the witnesses had already admitted. E. Howard Hunt was called by the prosecutors as a key witness, but by the time he appeared in the cover-up trial Hunt had given so many different versions of the Watergate affair—he had even written a book in which he repeated much of the original cover-up story and charged incorrectly that the prosecutors had attempted to coerce him into giving false testimony to aid the government's case—that the prosecutors asked that I call Hunt as a court witness so they would not have to vouch for his complete credibility.

There were some funny moments in the trial, despite the awful, depressing picture that was being painted by the prosecutors and their witnesses. In mid-November, Ben-Veniste brought to the stand Tony Ulasewicz, the former New York City cop who had been the deliveryman for the hush-money payments. Ulasewicz was as amusing as he had been on television during the Senate hearings. He told the same story about secret drops of big cash payments in phone booths all over Washington. And he repeated the tale of how he was making so many calls from public phone booths to avoid being traced that he began wearing a busman's metal coin changer on his belt. I had to struggle hard to suppress a smile when Ben-Veniste, with a totally straight face, put the coin changer engraved with Ulasewicz's initials into evidence.

There were terribly sad moments too. Herbert Kalmbach, who was serving his prison sentence in Baltimore, testified about how he had been recruited by the White House to help raise the money to pay off the original Watergate defendants. He told how he had plunged into the job, confident that if the people around President Nixon, whom Kalmbach had served as a personal attorney, wanted him to raise money, that job must be legitimate.

Kalmbach testified that at one point during the scramble to find hush money, he had approached the president of the Northrop Aircraft Company, who had pledged $50,000 to support President Nixon. Kalmbach explained that Northrop president Thomas Jones had no idea his money was to be given to the Watergate burglars. Kalmbach picked up the money from Jones one day, and took it to his home in Newport Beach, California, to count. Kalmbach testified that his wife, who was at home with him while he was counting the money, had no idea what was going on. He discovered that instead of $50,000, Jones had actually given him $75,000. When informed of the error, Jones told Kalmbach to keep the extra money.

When Jim Neal asked about Jones's knowledge of the payoffs, Kalmbach again started to explain that Jones was in the dark about the Watergate cover-up. "I'm glad you asked this question," Kalmbach said, "because when I met with Mr. Jones, who is a fine man, I—well, I said, 'Tom, this is confidential.' "

Kalmbach paused, and Neal observed, "You feel like you betrayed Mr. Jones, I am sure."

Kalmbach was nearly in tears. He was obviously ashamed that he had deceived Jones and had now dragged his name into the Watergate proceedings. He was even more embarrassed that his family now had to endure his stay in prison. I feared Kalmbach would break down completely, so I called a recess to let him rest awhile, after which he returned to the stand and completed his testimony.

Just after Thanksgiving, James Neal rose in the courtroom to announce, "Your Honor, the prosecution rests." Some thirty witnesses had appeared. More than 130 separate documents and pieces of physical evidence had been introduced. But perhaps most important, the jury and the press and spectators had heard more than twenty hours of the White House tapes. I doubt that there has ever been anything quite like those tape sessions in a federal courtroom. Small terminals had been installed in the jury box and throughout the room. Every person seated there had been handed a set of earphones like those given to airline passengers about to watch an in-flight movie. The earplugs were colored—blue for the left ear, red for the right. The prosecutors turned on the machine, and the room fell silent as more than a hundred people sat transfixed, often for over an hour at a time, listening in on the most intimate and most damning conversations conducted in the Nixon White House.

The jury and court heard the whole thing—the profanity, the scheming, the plotting, the development of false stories as one layer after another of the cover-up began to disintegrate. Over strenuous defense objections, the jury heard Dean and Nixon puzzling over my handling of the break-in case, with Dean observing that I was "a peculiar animal." And they heard Nixon complaining about the provisional sentences given after the break-in trial. Said Nixon, "That son-of-a-bitch of a judge gave him thirty-five years. . . ."

It was a solid case, a case so difficult to defend that I really couldn't imagine what the defendants' lawyers would or could do. At the end of the government's presentation, I dismissed the counts against Ehrlichman and Mitchell for lying to the FBI, largely for technical reasons, and the trial moved on, as Nixon's aides attempted to save themselves from prison.

18
Justice Is Done

It was what I call a "dog-eat-dog" defense. Each defendant was quite naturally most interested in saving his own neck, although the lawyers for the five men did take as much care as possible to avoid directly hurting each other's cases as they examined or cross-examined witnesses. Still, there was an irreconcilable conflict, especially between Mitchell, Mardian, and Parkinson, who had worked at the CRP, on the one hand, and Ehrlichman and Haldeman, who were White House men, on the other. The committee men wanted to throw as much blame as possible on the White House, while Ehrlichman and Haldeman wanted to attach the guilt to the CRP operation.

Indeed, during a cross-examination of Dean by Ehrlichman's counsel, William Frates, a motion for a mistrail was made by Mitchell's counsel, William Hundley, who was not given to frivolous motions. "I think it is now just crystal clear," he said, "that the defenses here are so antagonistic that we are faced with the situation . . . where we have two prosecutors." Frates agreed, knowing that they were all being tarred by one another's brushes. Yet the law is clear that defendants accused of committing the same crime can be tried together. It would have been an impossible burden to try each one separately.

Most of the defendants felt that John Dean was their chief tormentor. Each defendant's lawyer did as much as possible, especially in the closing argument, to show Dean to have been the real culprit behind Watergate.

Hundley began his defense of Mitchell in late November by making another motion for severance from the case. The White House tapes contained several sections recording attempts by Nixon, Haldeman, and Ehrlichman to paint Mitchell as the person chiefly responsible for the Liddy plan, and Hundley contended that these passage were damaging to Mitchell. I denied the motion.

But those same passages were also Hundley's major weapon in defending Mitchell. He argued that the top men in the White House were the chief culprits in Watergate and that rather than being a conspirator in the effort to cover up the truth, Mitchell was actually a victim of that conspiracy. He was referring to the long rehearsals during which Nixon, Haldeman, and Ehrlichman planned even the words they would use to get Mitchell to take all the blame. For example, at a meeting on April 14, 1973, Nixon advised his two top aides on the way to approach Mitchell: " 'The president's asked me to see you,' " Nixon instructed them to say. Then they were to tell Mitchell that they had "come in today with this report; these are the cold facts. . . ." Nixon went on to describe what he wanted them to get Mitchell to say. " 'I am responsible, I did not know it. But I assume the responsibility. Nobody in the White House is involved,' and so forth." Ehrlichman was chosen for the job of getting Mitchell to take the rap. In that same meeting, Nixon explained how he would approach Mitchell: "I'd say, 'The jig, you know, basically, the jig is up, John, and uh, I've listened to, uh, Magruder and, and uh, uh, uh, he's gonna, he's in my opinion he's about to blow—It, its time I think, to rethink what best serves the president and also what best serves you.' "

When he took the stand in his own defense, Mitchell, often speaking so quietly that I had to urge him to get closer to the microphone in the witness box, denied that he had ever seen any of the results from the first break-in and bugging at the Watergate, thus also denying that it was his dissatisfaction with the preliminary results of the eavesdropping that caused the Hunt-Liddy team to organize a second entry into the Democratic headquarters. Despite testimony by Magruder to the contrary, Mitchell also denied that he had ordered Magruder to burn the Gemstone documents in his fireplace at home.

It was always Mitchell's contention that he did not approve the Liddy intelligence-gathering plan at the meeting in

Florida at which Magruder presented it for the third time. Hundley used this denial to argue that since Mitchell hadn't approved the plan, he had no motive in trying to cover it up.

The former attorney general also denied that he had in any way approved pay-offs to Hunt to buy his silence after the Watergate arrests, and his lawyer offered a tortured explanation of why he didn't tell the full truth to the FBI and at the original sessions of the Watergate grand jury. "Since at that time," Hundley argued, "John Mitchell was sincerely convinced that President Nixon had no knowledge [of] or connection with any of these reprehensible White House activities, and out of a complete sense of loyalty and belief in his president and former law partner, John Mitchell unquestionably made a conscious decision not to volunteer his very strong suspicions about Colson, Magruder, and these White House activities to law-enforcement authorities, to Nixon, or anyone else. But he did not perjure himself. He did not obstruct justice."

Under a tough cross-examination by James Neal, Mitchell was reduced to building highly legalistic explanations of his actions. Mitchell was asked, for example why as attorney general he would even listen to a proposal that included kidnapping:

NEAL: Mr. Mitchell, did the Liddy plan include kidnapping?

MITCHELL: Mr. Neal, I have to go back to what the plan encompassed and if you want to place the legal definition of kidnapping on it—

NEAL:—did it include getting people without their will and taking them across to Mexico?

MITCHELL: I don't know if it was Mexico but it was segregating out radical leaders and keeping them from the activities they were proposing to carry on or would be carrying on in connection with the Republican convention.

NEAL: Was it contemplated these radical leaders would agree to this segregation?

MITCHELL: I wouldn't presume so.

Jim Neal finished his cross-examination of Mitchell by referring him to the tape of Mitchell's meeting with Nixon on

March 22, 1973. "Do you remember him [Nixon] telling you to 'stonewall it'?"

"I remember that very well, Mr. Neal," Mitchell said.

"And you have stonewalled it, haven't you Mr. Mitchell?" Neal concluded.

Hundley and Mitchell made a special target of Charles Colson, who had, as I've said, pleaded guilty to reduced charges and was not on trial. Most of the defense attorneys seemed to regard Colson as a very dangerous witness and decided not to call him. But Frates plunged ahead and put him on the stand in early December. Hundley had previously argued that Colson was the "trigger man" behind the Liddy plan, that Colson had pressured Magruder into giving Liddy money.

So when Colson appeared, Hundley, no longer the affable, good-natured lawyer he seemed during most of the trial, tore into Colson. "Mr. Colson," he began abruptly, "my name is Hundley and I represent Mr. Mitchell." He then played a tape of the January 8, 1973, meeting between Colson and Nixon in which the two talked about Hunt and the possibility of offering him some hope of clemency. Colson infuriated Hundley by saying that, yes, the voices on the tape were his and the former president's, but that, no, even hearing the tape brought back no recollection of the conversation. Colson simply stonewalled Hundley.

Colson did manage to insinuate that he had always thought Mitchell was responsible for the break-in, and this led the angry Hundley into making the classic lawyer's error: He asked a question to which he did not know the answer.

"Well, what evidence did you have?" Hundley nearly shouted. "You are a lawyer. What evidence did you have that you could pin on Mr. Mitchell?"

Colson, who had never liked or been liked by Mitchell, must have been delighted. A few days before the break-in, Colson explained, he had been talking with Mitchell about a meeting Hubert Humphrey was having in a New York City hotel. "Tell me what room they are in and I will tell you everything that is said in the room," Colson quoted Mitchell as saying, implying, of course that Mitchell was bugging everybody on the Democratic side.

Colson didn't stop there. He said that a few days after the break-in, before Hunt's arrest, he had asked Mitchell whether Hunt was involved. "Up to his ears," Colson quoted Mitchell as saying. Hundley maintained his composure, but my feeling was that it was not easy.

Hundley argued in his closing statement that Mitchell was more a victim of the conspiracy than a participant in it, that Colson was the one who had launched the whole bugging operation, and that to the extent that Mitchell had misled the Senate committee and the grand jury, he had done so out of personal and political loyalty to President Nixon, not in an attempt to obstruct justice.

Haldeman's defense seemed to be based mostly on the notion that he was so important and so busy with affairs of state that he didn't notice what was going on around him. When the content of the tapes and other evidence and testimony showed him to have been in the middle of something that looked criminal, he would explain that John Dean had misled him or that the special prosecutors were putting the wrong interpretation on what happened. It also seemed that Haldeman had an incredibly bad memory for a man as bright as he obviously was, who had kept notes on nearly every meeting he attended, and who had been testifying about those crucial days of his life for more than a year.

On the stand, Haldeman said he couldn't remember ever getting any reports from his assistant, Gordon Strachan, about the CRP's political-intelligence program and that he also couldn't remember ever ordering Strachan to "clean out" such reports from the files. Nor could he remember ever giving John Dean approval for the use of Kalmbach to raise funds to pay off the burglars.

He did admit that the $350,000 secret White House fund was under his control, that it did get turned over to the CRP, and that it might have been used as hush money, once Kalmbach quit as special fund raiser. But he said that to the extent that he knew about money going to the burglars, he was convinced that it was paid only for "legal fees and family support," in effect asking the jury to believe that the White House would approve large outlays simply for humanitarian reasons.

Ben-Veniste handled the cross-examination of Haldeman well. At one point, he caught Haldeman in an inconsistency in his testimony. Haldeman tried to explain away the mistake as "an error in overamplification." Ben-Veniste bore down hard on Haldeman with respect to a taped discussion with

Nixon in which the president seemed to be coaching Haldeman on how to testify safely before the grand jury, in order to avoid a perjury "rap."

"That's right," Nixon had said, agreeing with a suggestion by Haldeman, "Just be damned sure you say, 'I don't remember: I can't recall, I can't give any honest, an answer that I can recall.' But that's it."

". . . That discussion was not a discussion of evading telling the truth," Haldeman testified; "it was a discussion on my part of finding out what the operating procedures were in terms of testifying before various forums, the grand jury and the Senate committee."

The most incriminating incident of all, the ordering of Walters of the CIA to call the FBI off its investigation of the money trail to the Miamians, Haldeman tried to explain as stemming from a political concern about the origins of that contribution.

The testimony of Dean and Magruder had been terribly damaging to Haldeman. John Wilson spared nothing in his closing argument assaulting his client's two accusers. "They are two men who have dealt with untruth, who have lived with a callousness of ignoring the truth, of distorting the truth," Wilson asserted. "He [Dean] is a liar. He is a perjurer, he has a kaleidoscope of criminal activity which seems to me to be almost beyond the pale of an ordinary human being." To hear Wilson tell it, Haldeman was an innocent bystander who just happened to be there when a lot of illegal things took place.

Dean was the bad guy in Ehrlichman's presentation as well. But Nixon too was heavily blamed by William Frates for Ehrlichman's actions. The president and Dean, Frates claimed, had used Ehrlichman as "a pawn." In his opening argument, Frates said, "President Nixon, who knew the full story, withheld it from Ehrlichman and prevented Ehrlichman's recommended disclosure of the facts known to Ehrlichman at that time over and over again." Of course, Ehrlichman could have walked out of the White House, down Pennsylvania Avenue, and into the office of the U.S. attorney any time he chose, but Frates did not address that point.

Like Haldeman, Ehrlichman was portrayed as an innocent bystander. At the meeting at which Haldeman told Walters to have Gray limit the FBI investigation, Ehrlichman was simply the host, Frates argued. "All Ehrlichman knew," Frates said, "was that the meeting was in his office. When the president of the United States tells you to go to a meeting, you go to a meeting."

Ehrlichman was the most active of the defendants in seeking Nixon's appearance as a witness at the trial, presumably so Frates could reveal just how much Nixon knew and how he had misled Ehrlichman. I would have loved to have Nixon in court. I had a few questions I wanted to ask him myself. But he became seriously ill and his lawyers appeared in court to say he couldn't travel. I sent a team of three very fine physicians—Charles A. Hufnagel, Richard A. Ross, and John A. Spittell—to California to check on Nixon's condition. They served at my request, voluntarily taking time out of their busy schedules and charging the court only minimal expenses. In December they reported that Nixon couldn't possibly travel until well into the following year. I ruled, over Frates's objection, that the trial could not be delayed until the former president was well enough to testify. I ruled reluctantly, since I would have had Nixon testify if that had been possible. But I did feel that no matter how anxious many of us were to see Nixon face the lawyers and testify under oath, having him in court was not really critical to Ehrlichman's defense. I feel I was right in that judgment, but I am disappointed that Nixon wasn't in court.

The special prosecutors had argued that Ehrlichman joined the cover-up conspiracy to prevent Hunt from telling the authorities about his raid on the office of Ellsberg's psychiatrist. As has been mentioned, Ehrlichman had already been tried for his role in that raid. Frates, at an earlier stage of the trial had gotten into an argument with me in the attempt to show that Ehrlichman had no criminal intent in approving the "covert" operation.

"What is a covert operation?" I asked Frates.

"Your Honor, a covert operation is if I walk back into your office . . . secretly, without you knowing it. That would be a covert operation."

"It would also be housebreaking, wouldn't it?" I asked.

"No sir, I think this courthouse belongs to the people," Frates answered without a pause.

"I don't think it gives you a right to go into my office if I don't consent to it," I said.

"Your Honor," Frates said, "I don't want to get off on

that. Judge, I am trying to get back to Florida. That is my main problem."

Throughout the trial, Frates's real problem, like that of Wilson and Hundley, was that there was simply too much evidence, especially on the White House tapes, against his client. But that was not quite as true for Mardian and for Parkinson. Even Neal admitted that these two had played smaller roles than the others.

Mardian was accused of having made the call to Liddy the day after the initial arrests urging him to arrange through Kleindienst to get McCord and the Miamians out of jail. On the stand, Mardian denied making the call.

Mardian had heard the full story of the Watergate operation from Liddy a few days after the break-in, but never divulged it, except to Mitchell. Mardian contended that because he had a lawyer-client relationship with Liddy, he was required by the canons of ethics to keep the story secret. The government hammered away about why he went so far as to mislead Parkinson, whom he brought into the CRP to help defend against the Democrats' civil suit. Within a month of the break-in, Mardian had quit the CRP and left Washington, for his own reasons. I felt right along that he had a chance for acquittal. But his conduct on the stand diminished that chance.

I have rarely seen a more hostile witness than Mardian during his cross-examination by Jill Volner. He argued with her incessantly, prolonging the cross-examination for what seemed an eternity. He was sneering and contentious all the time. Mrs. Volner handled the situation very nicely, I thought. She was firm and polite and let Neal and Ben-Veniste do most of the objecting to Mardian's conduct on the stand. She was winning her case before the jury simply by letting Mardian lose his.

Parkinson, on the other hand, was the perfect witness. His lawyer, Jacob Stein, painted him as a political innocent, suddenly employed by a group of real sharpies. He argued that Parkinson had been misled by Mitchell and Mardian and by Howard Hunt's lawyer, William Bittman, who apparently used Parkinson to transmit Hunt's requests for money to the White House. Parkinson hadn't stayed at the CRP very long. The testimony showed that shortly after he arrived, Magruder told him the full story of the break-in and its origins. But Mitchell and Mardian denied that this version, which implicated Mitchell in approving the plan, was correct. Magruder then told Parkinson that this first (i.e., true) account was in fact false, and fed him the approved cover story, and Parkinson thereupon shredded the notes of his first meeting with Magruder. Stein did a fine job of defending Parkinson. As I've said, he carefully kept Parkinson physically apart from the other defendants. He delivered a terrific closing argument, working himself nearly into tears in pleading for Parkinson's acquittal. He also produced seventeen character witnesses, including five judges, on Parkinson's behalf.

A key point in the case against Parkinson was testimony from Howard Hunt that his lawyer, William Bittman, had said that a memo written by Hunt detailing his demands for payment and containing his threat to divulge other "seamy" things he had done for the White House had actually been read to Parkinson. After Hunt testified, much to everyone's surprise, that the memo had been given to Bittman, a partner in my old firm of Hogan and Hartson, Bittman suddenly produced it for the prosecutors, about midway through the trial.

Bittman, called as a witness, claimed that he had never read the memo to Parkinson. That testimony apparently helped Parkinson, but Bittman had more explaining to do.

Neal, who had been close to Bittman when they had worked in the Justice Department years before, was, I think, heartbroken that his old friend had not told him the full truth.

Neal asked him, "Bill, didn't you tell me during the summer of 1973, 'Jim, I have no knowledge or information that Mr. Hunt contends he was doing anything or maintaining silence in exchange for funds.' Didn't you tell me that?"

Bittman agreed that he had said that "in substance."

"At the same time, Bill, you had the memorandum and were aware of the memorandum which you did not divulge to me."

Bittman tried to explain that the lawyer-client privilege kept him from admitting knowledge of the memo, but by that time Neal was so disappointed and disgusted that he simply left the courtroom, not wanting to confront Bittman any longer. Ben-Veniste took over the questioning and asked Bittman why he hadn't told Neal that summer that privilege kept him from answering the question. Bittman said it was because there were things in the memo that he didn't believe. This part of the testimony involving Parkinson, Hunt, and Bittman was given with the jury not present.

The whole incident was unpleasant for me, too. I called in other partners from my old firm to be questioned about the memo and its existence. They said that when the memo was first mentioned in court, they conducted a search of their files, and while not finding the memo itself, they did find a reference to it in their index of files. They had quickly supplied that information to the prosecutors. The testimony showed that Bittman had been getting large sums of cash as payments from Hunt, delivered during the night to his mailbox at home by some unidentified person. Also, a large amount of cash had been left for him in a telephone booth in the lobby of his office building. Most lawyers I know refuse large cash payments and insist on bank checks, for their records and for their own protection. Bittman was never charged with any criminal act.

Shortly before Christmas, presentation of the closing arguments began. James Neal summed up the case for the special prosecutor's office in what I think was one of the best arguments I have ever heard in a courtroom. Before discussing the specific facts of his case, Neal put the crime of obstruction of justice into proper perspective.

"Justice and its pursuit is an elusive goal," he said. "Our court system is a delicate institution. It can work only if it is not impeded or tampered with and only if it gets to the facts and the evidence. Justice requires access to documentary evidence and true testimony from people with information. If people can be improperly induced to remain silent an injustice will be done in one trial, then in another, and then there will be no justice for any of us."

Neal then addressed the heart of his case against the defendants. "Now let us put one thing straight in the beginning," he said. "There has been an effort to beguile you by stating over and over again that this nearly half million dollars paid for the original Watergate defendants was attorney fees, family support, income replacement, and bail. And so what is the big problem now?

"The government agrees that the use to which this money was put was attorney fees, income replacement, family support, and bail; but we say most emphatically, and the court will so charge, that that does not answer the question. That simply poses it.

"The question is," Neal continued, "what was the motive or intent behind the payment of these things? One billion dollars, or one trillion dollars paid for family support, income replacement, attorney fees, bail, is not an offense. It is fine if it is motivated purely by charitable or humanitarian purposes and nothing else. But one red cent paid to keep somebody from talking and divulging information to the appropriate authorities, whether it is a red cent for attorney fees or a red cent for a haircut, it is obstruction of justice. . . .

"If you will pardon the expression a moment, the gut issue in this case is why documents were destroyed, why was the CIA used to obstruct the FBI investigation in the Watergate, why was a cover story developed to explain the money given to Liddy prior to the break-in, why were veiled, camouflaged offers of clemency made without using the word and why finally was nearly a half million dollars paid for seven people caught wiretapping and burglarizing the Democratic National Committee headquarters? Why?"

It was exactly the right question. Why were these things done by the White House and the Committee to Re-elect the President? What was their stake in these burglars? And could there possibly be an innocent explanation?

We took Christmas Day off. Earlier in the month, I had offered the jury the option of sitting later each day and having Saturday sessions, in order to try to complete the entire trial before the holidays. They had sent a note to me indicating that we should not try to rush the case, that although they would like to be home by Christmas, they preferred to sacrifice their holidays to make sure the case was handled carefully.

After Christmas, the final arguments were presented and I charged the jury on the relevant laws. Deliberations began on Monday, December 30. I was relieved that the heavy work of the entire case was over. For two and a half years, I had done nothing but worry about one aspect or another of the Watergate case. For three months, every day had been taken up with the difficult trial and the endless wrangling. While we waited, just to make sure nothing went wrong I again instructed my marshal and my clerk on the correct procedures to be followed in receiving the verdict.

At 4:55 on New Year's Day, 1975, the verdict was

reached. We all filed back into the courtroom, where the foreman, a member of the United States Park Police named John Hoffar, who incidentally happened to be a Republican, handed Cappy the verdict. I read it to myself: Mitchell, guilty on five counts. Haldeman, guilty on five counts. Ehrlichman, guilty on four counts. Mardian, guilty on one count. Parkinson, *not guilty*.

It took Cappy only about a minute to read the verdict to the silent courtroom. His voice quavered as he read. Mitchell, Haldeman, and Ehrlichman showed no emotion. Mardian slumped into his chair, gray and stunned. Parkinson was overjoyed. I must say the verdict seemed to me fair to all the defendants. I felt that, finally, justice had been done.

About a week later, I happened to be watching television and saw NBC's Carl Stern inverviewing the head of the United States Parole Board. Stern was inquiring about the possibilities of parole for Dean, Kalmbach, and Magruder, since all had been in jail for some time and had co-operated with the government. It suddenly struck me that this was not really the Parole Board's problem; it was mine. Motions by all three defendants for reduction of sentence were pending before me. I had given these men fairly tough sentences, but each of them, it seemed to me, had admitted his guilt, had testified fully and truthfully, had co-operated with the government, and was obviously deeply sorry for what he had done. I feared that the Parole Board might get mixed up in political considerations, and anticipating public reaction one way or another, might have difficulty considering the cases of these three men.

The next morning I signed an order granting the motions to reduce the three sentences to time served. The men were quickly released and returned to their families.

For more than a month, I wrestled with the problem of sentencing Mitchell, Haldeman, Ehrlichman, and Mardian. On February 21, we gathered for the last time in my courtroom. William Hundley, asked if he wanted to say anything on behalf of Mitchell, said he preferred not to prolong the unpleasant occasion. John Wilson reminded me that Haldeman's boss, Nixon, was free, and that whatever Haldeman had done "he did for the president of the United States." John Ehrlichman had hired a young, local lawyer to plead for a sort of alternative service instead of jail. He asked that Ehrlichman be sentenced to serve time at an institution in the southwestern part of the country, where he could give free legal advice to Indians. Mardian and his counsel chose to remain silent.

I sentenced Mitchell, Haldeman, and Ehrlichman to terms of not less than thirty months and not more than eight years in prison. Mardian was sentenced to serve not less than ten months and not more than three years.

Subsequently, appeals by Haldeman, Ehrlichman, and Mitchell were denied. Mardian's appeal, however, was upheld. The court of appeals ruled that once David Bress became ill, I was in error in refusing to sever Mardian from the main case. They ruled that while the three principal defendants had been charged with substantive counts in the cover-up, Mardian was charged only with conspiracy and therefore needed protection against the more damaging evidence being brought against the three major defendants. He had this protection, the court decided, while Bress was active in the case. I felt he was just as well protected by the counsel of Thomas Green, Bress' fine young assistant. However, the court ruled that with the principal attorney replaced, Mardian was in some jeopardy. They sent the case back for a new trial, but the government prosecutors decided not to try Mardian a second time. He went free.

Some people, of course, felt that the sentences imposed on Mitchell, Haldeman, and Ehrlichman were too severe. Some of their friends in the administration, for example, were anxious to see the sentences reduced. I remember one such plea quite well. It took place in January 1977, on the evening President Ford delivered his third—and last—State of the Union message to Congress. It had been a cold day, one of the worst of the winter, and the street in front of our house was almost impassable because of its steep grade and the amount of ice and snow that had accumulated. I had received a call from Treasury Secretary William Simon, who asked if he and Henry Kissinger could stop by the house for a chat after the State of the Union address. I agreed to see them. When I had returned home that afternoon, I had to leave my car at the foot of our street because of the ice. But within a few hours, I noticed that, miraculously, our street had been salted, and much of the ice and snow had been removed.

The two arrived in a big black limousine about ten-thirty. Simon said the purpose of their visit was to speak up for his old friend John Mitchell. I replied that I could not discuss the matter with them at all and advised them to contact Mitchell's lawyer and to write a letter to the probation officer, who would see that I received it, if and when an appropriate motion to reduce the sentence was filed. They stayed a little while, chatting about President Ford and politics, and about Nixon, who—Kissinger claimed—had never spoken as profanely in front of him as he had on the tapes.

My feeling was that the sentences were appropriate in view of the offenses committed. But I also felt, as time passed, that the main objective of the sentencing—that is, to deter future offenders and to make the point that no one, not even the highest government official, is beyond the reach of the law and its penalties—had been accomplished. It was also very much on my mind that the three defendants were in jail while their boss was free. After the appellate courts affirmed the convictions, the respective attorneys filed motions for reduction of the sentences. I sent a probation officer to record on tape the defendants' own feelings about their crimes and punishment, and each expressed sorrow and regret. In the fall of 1977, I reduced the sentences of the three men to the same term I had given John Dean—one to four years—and within a short time they were all eligible for parole.

My feelings about the sentences were best expressed by *New York Times* columnist Anthony Lewis. He wrote: "The ceremony of sentencing, if such it was, celebrated the relearning of an old piece of wisdom. Those who manage the delicate institutions of government have a special responsibility to represent the law. Justice Louis D. Brandeis put it in classic words in 1928: 'In a government of laws, existence of the government will be imperiled if it fails to observe the law scrupulously . . . if the government becomes a law-breaker, it breeds contempt for law; it invites every man to become a law unto himself; it invites anarchy.'"

Epilogue

There were times during the five years I was involved in the Watergate proceedings that I thought the case would never come to an end. On more nights than I now care to remember, I would wake up after only a few hours of sleep, my heart racing, wondering what new stumbling block President Nixon and his associates would throw in front of me the next day.

I have been asked on many occasions why I didn't just quit after the trial of the original Watergate burglars, and how I made the decisions I did at crucial junctures in the case. I've really never had any easy answers for those questions, and now, looking back on the whole ordeal almost seven years after the original burglary, about all I can say is that my instincts wouldn't let me walk away until I had completed the job.

Those who know me well sometimes remark that I keep my worries to myself. That is exactly what I had to do during Watergate. Unfortunately, as the case dragged on, my thoughts became increasingly painful to conceal.

As I have mentioned before, if it had not been for the Republican party, I might never have done much better than my father, who died at sixty of a heart attack after years of trying desperately to build a secure life for my mother, my brother, and me. I traveled to various parts of the country in 1940 and 1948 for Republican presidential candidates like Wendell Willkie and Thomas E. Dewey; I was never willing to admit that Willkie didn't stand much of a chance.

I had no money to speak of, and one of the best ways that I knew to make something of myself was through politics. I stuck with the party long enough to see Dwight Eisenhower and his running mate, Richard Nixon, elected in 1952. Without the backing of President Eisenhower and his attorney general, Herbert Brownell, I would never have realized my dream of becoming a federal judge.

But day after day, from 1972 on, I was confronted with new evidence which showed that the Republican party had fallen into less trustworthy hands since the days when I had been active in politics. And though it saddened me to watch the party being hurt as I sent some of its leading figures off to jail, this was obviously something I had to do.

And now, although I still sometimes marvel that we came through that awful mess with our government intact, Watergate is finally over. My initial suspicions that no one but top party leaders could have authorized the burglary were proved true by President Nixon's own tapes. And although our nation went through a trauma which could easily have led to a severe constitutional crisis, I believe that the United States is stronger for having successfully weathered that storm.

Had there been no Watergate, wealthy contributors might still be pumping undisclosed millions into political campaigns in hopes of buying favor with elected officials. Now we have an independent Federal Election Commission and a stronger campaign law, which demands that all candidates for national offices disclose their sources of funding in writing.

Had there been no Watergate, it is unlikely that we would have seen the tremendous increase in the public scrutiny of federal officials' conduct, a scrutiny which has led to investigations and indictments such as those involving the General Services Administration.

And had there been no Watergate, Congress would probably not even be discussing public financing of federal election campaigns. Although there are a great number of unanswered questions about the issue, I believe some type of legislation to reduce politicians' reliance on contributions from special interests would in the long run benefit the entire nation.

Most important, Watergate, unlike any previous scandal in our political history, was both a crisis and a reaffirmation of our constitutional form of government. Unlike past episodes of dishonesty in Washington, it was a product not of greed in the usual sense, but of greed for power.

The bugging itself obviously resulted from an attempt to guard against political surprise and electoral defeat. The stupidity of that endeavor was fully revealed in November 1972, when Nixon rolled up one of the biggest victories any presidential candidate in our history had ever won. Yet, before the election, his staff members were worried that defeat would come, so worried that to guard against that remote possibility, they violated the law.

Nixon and his aides did not view their tenure in the White House as a period of stewardship, a trust granted for a fixed term that could be revoked by the popular will. Rather, Nixon and his people were arrogant enough to believe that they should substitute their own judgments for those of the electorate. Some of them believed it was permissible to short-circuit the electoral process by eavesdropping on their opponents. Their lust for power, their arrogance, their raw disregard of the law, of fairness, and of the very constitutional processes that they had sworn to enforce and protect, led them to break the law in order to keep themselves in office. After the arrests at the Watergate, they knew that if the truth were revealed, they would lose their coveted power. They broke the law in the spring and summer of 1972 to hold onto power. And then they broke the law again and again in the fall of 1972 and the spring of 1973 to protect their offices.

The country should take great pride that this naked attempt to thwart the Constitution of the United States—to substitute the will of a few powerful men for the rule of law which we have struggled so long and hard to win and to protect—was in the end defeated, with the perpetrators driven from office and brought to justice. Yet I can never forget Senator Sam Ervin's observation that "they almost got away with it." I think it's worth asking, Why didn't they get away with it?

Everyone has a tendency to find heroes, to claim that individual acts of decency or bravery or devotion bring about great historical events. But I think the lesson of Watergate is quite the opposite. I firmly believe it was our system of government and our system of law that ended that crisis and saved the very constitutional form of government that gave us that system and those laws.

Take the role of the press, for example. The two young reporters at the *Washington Post*, Carl Bernstein and Bob Woodward, became popular heroes for a time after their work helped keep the pressure of public scrutiny on the unanswered questions in the Watergate case. They deserve the attention and the acclaim, of course. And so does the owner of the *Post*, Mrs. Katharine Graham, for having the courage to let those two young men pursue the Watergate story even when other news organizations were ignoring it. But as important as the *Post* and its officers and reporters were, what is more important is that the *Post* is part of a free press, protected by the Constitution. *Who* emerged in the press to expose Watergate is less important than the fact that our system allows reporters the freedom to do so.

And consider the role of Congress. Sam Ervin, to my mind, represented in his conduct of the Watergate hearings the best traditions of American political leadership. But I believe that had there been no Sam Ervin from North Carolina, there would have been someone on Capitol Hill capable of and willing to lead the kind of fair-minded investigation Senator Ervin did manage. It is more important that we have an independent legislative branch than that a particular senator or group of senators be seen as heroes.

In the difficult days of 1974, as the Watergate crisis was reaching some sort of breaking point, many in Washington doubted that the often unruly politicians in the House of Representatives could manage an impeachment inquiry that would be seen as nonpartisan and fair. Peter Rodino and other members of the House Judiciary Committee did just that, despite all the efforts by the White House and other defenders of Nixon to provoke the committee into a partisan fight. Peter Rodino deserves enormous credit for his role. But I think the fact that our constitution gives Congress the remedy of impeachment to use against a chief executive who breaks the law is ultimately more important than any one legislator's role.

I feel the same way about the courts. It is more important that we had a totally independent judiciary than that I, or any other judge or group of judges, happened to be presiding over the case.

Naturally, I have a special feeling about the role of the courts in the whole crisis. I feel that without the courts, without their ability to get to the facts, to compel testimony and the production of evidence, the Watergate case might never have been cracked. The press played a critical role, of course, but the press cannot subpoena witnesses, it cannot demand the truth under any penalty other than temporary embarrassment, it can only help force further public attention and investigation.

Not even Congress, standing as a coequal branch of the government, had the ability in its investigative role to resolve conflicting testimony, to force out the whole truth, to render final and enforceable judgments. The congressmen conducting the impeachment inquiry found themselves nearly powerless to demand the kinds of evidence needed to reach a final decision. It was the courts that demanded and got the evidence on which the Judiciary Committee finally acted. Without this evidence, I do not believe the impeachment inquiry would have gotten off the ground.

The judiciary, standing above politics as the enforcer and arbiter of our laws, was the critical branch of government in the resolution of the Watergate crisis. And it is our faith and trust in the law, our devotion to the notion that ours should be a government of laws and not men, that saved us from this scandal.

It was the courts and the law that throughout this crisis could compel that the truth be told. Despite efforts in our executive branch to distort the truth, to fabricate a set of facts that looked innocent, *the court system served to set the record straight*. When the people involved in Watergate lied to the public, nothing could be done. But when they lied to the grand jury, and I should say the *courageous* grand jury that sat for months and months looking into the matter, they were sent to jail. When the president and his aides lied about their own activities, it was our courts and our law that compelled them to produce the best evidence in the case—the presidential tapes—to test their versions of what happened. And when the most powerful men in our government tried to obstruct the law, to ignore it, to frustrate the process of justice, the law itself penalized them. The law and our faith in that law was too powerful for even those powerful men.

I don't mean to suggest that our system guarantees that misuses of power such as were engineered by the Nixon White House will always be found out, always be punished and cleaned up. There were, without doubt, some amazing accidents, some incidents of pure good fortune, that helped save us. Had Frank Wills, the night guard at the Watergate complex, not found the telltale tape on the door, the whole business might have gone undetected. The greatest accident of all, of course, was that Nixon had chosen to tape his conversations in the White House. Without this evidence, and of course without the court's power to compel that it be made public, I wonder whether the real truth of Watergate would ever have come out.

I have always felt that no matter how bitter the experience one endures, and surely Watergate was a bitter experience, there are some beneficial lessons to be learned. Watergate taught us that our system is not invulnerable to the arrogance of power, to misdeeds by power-hungry individuals, and that we must always be on guard against selecting such people as our leaders. It taught us that our system of law is the most valuable asset in this land and that it must be nurtured, protected, and respected. The misuse of campaign funds was exposed during the Watergate investigations, and we have moved, though not perfectly to be sure, to make our presidential elections more fair by preventing single, large contributors from having too great an influence on the outcome of those elections. Likewise, we have strengthened the laws that force public officials (including judges) to disclose their financial assets and income, so the public can be reassured that those officials have not been bought and paid for by some special interest.

Most important, I hope we have learned the value of citizens who do their duty, who do the work set out for them by our laws and our system of government. Like the scores of common citizens who served unselfishly on the grand juries and trial juries in the Watergate cases, or the lawyers who prosecuted and defended in those cases to the very best of their ability, or members of Congress who put politics aside to do their unpleasant jobs, or the news reporters who wouldn't drop a story when they were under pressure to do so, the so-called heroes of Watergate were no more than people doing what was right, doing their jobs whether they were scared or exhausted or being criticized, or were all alone.

After my sudden heart attack in February 1976, I awoke from a long period of unconsciousness. One of my doctors, Stephen Nealon, was with me in the hospital as I began to realize how close to death I had come and in how much danger I remained. He told me later that I said to him, "If I go out, I'd like to think that I did something for my country."

I think I did do something for my country. I think I did my job as best I could. I think I did my duty as a citizen and as someone fortunate enough to hold a position of public responsibility in our system of government.

Notes on Sources

PROLOGUE

The details of this chapter are of course drawn mostly from my own recollection of events and from accounts passed on to me by other members of my family. In 1976, as I was recovering from my heart attack, I dictated onto tape hours of these recollections, which were subsequently transcribed; they have proved invaluable in writing this account. Over the years, I have filled scrapbook after scrapbook with newspaper clippings about events in my life, and they too have helped enormously in reconstructing these early years.

CHAPTER 1

Throughout this book, I have made extensive use of the official transcripts of the trials and proceedings before me in the United States District Court for the District of Columbia. Those transcripts are on the public record. In no case have I used records that remain sealed. I should point out that I deliberately waited until every aspect of this case was completed in all its phases before attempting this history.

The most complete accounts of the planning and execution of the Watergate break-in are contained in the opening statement at the break-in trial by Earl Silbert, the principal assistant U.S. attorney; in the Senate testimony; and in the cover-up trial testimony of John Dean and Jeb Magruder. Dean's book about Watergate, *Blind Ambition* (New York, Simon and Schuster, 1976), and Magruder's book, *An American Life* (New York, Atheneum, 1974) are also helpful.

Analysis of the converging political and national-security fears in the White House that produced the attempt at political-intelligence gathering is presented in J. Anthony Lukas's *Nightmare: The Underside of the Nixon Years* (New York, Viking, 1976) and Jonathan Schell's *Time of Illusion* (New York, Knopf, 1976).

My own records and correspondence provide the background for the discussion of Wright Patman's reaction to the gag order. John Dean's version of the attempt to stop the Patman investigation, in *Blind Ambition*, is relied upon for the White House view of Patman's situation.

Pretrial activities in my courtroom are reported in full in the official transcript of the proceedings, *United States v. George Gordon Liddy, et al.*, Criminal No. 1827-72.

As noted, the book by Bob Woodward and Carl Bernstein, *All the President's Men* (New York, Simon and Schuster, 1974), provides an account of their reaction to my lecture on their attempt to gain information from the grand jury.

Throughout, descriptions of events outside my courtroom are based upon articles appearing in the *Washington Post* and *Congressional Quarterly*. The weekly reports on Watergate in *Congressional Quarterly* were subsequently collected and published as *Watergate: Chronology of a Crisis*, 2 vols. (Washington, D.C., Congressional Quarterly, 1973–74).

The full transcript of the FCC proceeding in 1944 is contained in five volumes of the records of the House Select Committee to Investigate the Federal Communications Commission, Seventy-eighth Congress. The investigation was well covered in newspapers and magazines. See especially the *Washington Post*, the *Washington Daily News*, the *Washington Times-Herald*, the *Louisville Courier-Journal*, and *Broadcasting Magazine*.

CHAPTERS 2 and 3

These chapters are based entirely on my own recollections of the trial and on the official transcript of the proceedings, *United States v. George Gordon Liddy, et al.*, Criminal No. 1827-72.

CHAPTER 4

Final arguments and summations for the government and the defense are contained in the official transcript of the break-in trial, *United States v. George Gordon Liddy, et al.*, Criminal No. 1827-72.

For a detailed discussion of Earl Silbert's conduct of the prosecution, see the transcript of the Senate Judiciary Committee hearings on the nomination of Earl J. Silbert to be United States attorney, 93rd Congress, 2nd Session, Parts 1 and 2.

Clark Mollenhoff's column discussing Judge Ferguson's sentencing in the Wooldridge case was dated for release on March 10–11, 1973, by the Register and Tribune Syndicate.

CHAPTER 5

For the description of the McCord visit and its aftermath I relied on my own recollections, on those of my clerks, and on the now unsealed transcripts of the proceedings in my chambers. Discussion of the pressure on McCord is based on his own testimony before the Senate Watergate committee and on J. Anthony Lukas's account in his book *Nightmare: The Underside of the Nixon Years* (New York, Viking, 1976).

John Dean's book on his Watergate involvement, *Blind Ambition* (New York, Simon and Schuster, 1976), recounts his comment to the president regarding the impact of McCord's letter, and the president's response.

The account of the Kleindienst letter is based on my own records and correspondence and, as noted, the *New York Times* version of the transcript of the Ehrlichman-Kleindienst conversation. Parts of that conversation were inserted into the record in the Senate Watergate hearings by Senator Lowell Weicker of Connecticut.

CHAPTER 6

The full text of my sentencing statement, including the reference to a section of Judge Ferguson's opinion, is reported at

United States v. *Liddy*, 397 F.Supp. 947 (D.D.C. 1975). My own thinking regarding Liddy's sentence and my decision on his motion for a reduction of sentence is also reported at 397 F.Supp. 947 (D.D.C. 1975). The text of my decision on this motion is reprinted in the Appendix.

Judge Leventhal's full opinion and the court of appeals summary of the break-in trail is cited as *United States of America* v. *George Gordon Liddy, a/k/a George F. Leonard*, 509 F.2d 428, 438–442 (D.C.Cir. 1974).

CHAPTER 7

The best available summary of the proceedings of the Senate select committee is contained in the *Congressional Quarterly* compilation of their weekly reports, *Watergate: Chronology of a Crisis*. This account is drawn largely from volume 1 (Washington, D.C., Congressional Quarterly, 1973) of the two-volume publication. Reports from the *Washington Post* and the *New York Times* of the period have also been used.

Special Prosecutor Cox's motion for a subpoena and the polling of the grand jury for the order to show cause is contained in the transcript of the proceedings, *In Re: Post-Trial Watergate Grand Jury Proceedings*, Misc. No. 47–73, Thursday, July 26.

CHAPTER 8

The brief submitted in defense of the president's position is titled *In re Grand Jury Subpoena Duces Tecum Issued to Richard M. Nixon, or any Subordinate Officer, Official, or Employee with Custody or Control of Certain Documents or Objects*, Misc. No 47–73. It was filed, as noted, on August 7, 1973. Joining Charles Alan Wright on the brief were White House lawyers Leonard Garment, J. Fred Buzhardt, Douglas M. Parker, Robert T. Andrews, and Thomas P. Marinis, Jr.

The special prosecutor's reply carries the same title and case number and is captioned "Memorandum in Support of an Order to Produce Documents or Objects in Response to the Subpoena." It was filed on August 13. Joining Cox on the brief were Philip A. Lacovara, Peter M. Kreindler, and

James F. Neal, all of the Watergate Special Prosecution Force.

Although both briefs invoked scores of legal precedents, the critical case in my view was the Burr case, *United States v. Burr*, 25 F. Cas. 187 (Case No. 14,695) (1807). For a full history of the case, see Raoul Berger's *Executive Privilege: A Constitutional Myth* (Cambridge, Mass., Harvard University Press, 1974) and Leonard Baker's *John Marshall: A Life in Law* (New York, Macmillan, 1974).

The account of the oral argument of August 22, 1973 is from the official court transcript of that day, "In the Matter of a Grand Jury Subpoena Issued to Richard M. Nixon," Misc. No. 47–73. My order requiring submission of the tapes, *In re Grand Jury Subpoena Duces Tecum . . .*, Misc. No. 47–73, is dated August 29, 1973. The order, with the accompanying opinion, is reprinted in the Appendix.

The White House reaction to my order is reported in *Watergate: Chronology of a Crisis*, vol. 2 (Washington, D.C., Congressional Quarterly, 1974), p. 16.

CHAPTER 9

For the full court of appeals opinion, including dissents by Judges MacKinnon and Wilkey, see *Nixon v. Sirica*, 487 F.2d 700 (D.C.Cir. 1973). The majority opinion of the court is reprinted in the Appendix.

Again, *Watergate: Chronology of a Crisis*, vol. 2 (Washington, D.C., Congressional quarterly, 1974) has provided an invaluable day-by-day summation of the Watergate events.

The best discussion of the events leading up to and including the firing of Special Prosecutor Cox is provided in James Doyle's *Not Above the Law* (New York, Morrow, 1977), especially chapters 4–9. *RN: The Memoirs of Richard Nixon* (New York, Grosset and Dunlap, 1978), pp. 923–935, presents the former president's view of the necessity for firing Cox.

CHAPTER 10

The proceedings on the morning of October 23, during which I reassured the grand juries, are reported as *In Re: Post-Trial*

Watergate Grand Jury Proceedings, Misc. No. 47–73 and Misc. No. 108–73. The afternoon session, in which Charles Alan Wright delivered the president's decision to turn over the tapes, is reported as *In Re: Post-Trial Watergate Grand Jury Proceedings*, Misc. No. 47–73.

The quotations from my prepared questions for Charles Alan Wright are from my own files, as is the instruction to Wright for the president to show cause why he should not be held in contempt. Obviously, they were never made a part of the official record, nor was the actual order I had prepared but not signed.

Judge T. Alan Goldsborough's decision in the United Mine Workers case is reported at 70 F. Supp. 42 (1946). His second decision is reported at 77 F. Supp. 563 (1948). The Supreme Court's affirmation of his first ruling is contained in *United States v. UMW*, 330 U.S. 258 (1947). The court of appeals ruling in the second case, *United States v. International Union, UMW*, is reported at 177 F.2d 29 (1949).

As noted, the editorials calling for the President's resignation appeared in the *New York Times* for November 4, 1973, and in *Time Magazine* for November 12, 1973. The two are cited only as examples. Other newspapers joined the call for the president's resignation.

And again, for events outside my courtroom I have relied on *Watergate: Chronology of a Crisis*, vol. 2 (Washington, D.C., Congressional Quarterly, 1974)—in this case especially for the reporting and verbatim transcripts of presidential press conferences.

CHAPTERS 11 and 12

The records of proceedings held *in camera*, such as the meeting of November 21 at which the eighteen-minute gap was revealed, are often sealed and not made a part of the public record of a trial or hearing. But at the request of Rose Mary Woods's lawyers, the transcript of the November 21 session was unsealed on January 18, 1974, and read into the record of the tapes hearings. The request was made because at that meeting the White House lawyers had suggested that Miss Woods was responsible for the tape gap. I have relied upon the unsealed transcript of that meeting to reconstruct it here.

The full transcript of the tapes hearings is titled *In Re:*

Subpoenas Duces Tecum Issued to President Richard M. Nixon for Production of Tapes, Misc. No. 47-73.

Quotations from the tapes present something of a problem. Because former President Nixon has opposed the public release of the tapes used in the cover-up trial, it has not been possible to listen again to the tapes to refresh my own recollection. I have therefore had to rely on written transcripts. When Todd and I first heard the tapes, there were no transcripts available. The transcripts later released by the White House were quickly shown to be incomplete and in many instances very inaccurate and misleading. Both the special prosecutor's office and the House Judiciary Committee continually improved their own transcripts. In this chapter, I have quoted from the transcripts prepared for the cover-up trial by the Watergate Special Prosecution Force.

CHAPTER 13

The results of the Harris and Gallup polls taken in January 1974 are reported in *Watergate: Chronology of a Crisis,* vol. 2 (Washington, D.C., Congressional Quarterly, 1974).

The indictment of the seven Nixon aides in the cover-up case was returned, as noted, on March 1. It is titled *United States v. John N. Mitchell, Harry R. Haldeman, John D. Ehrlichman, Charles W. Colson, Robert C. Mardian, Kenneth W. Parkinson and Gordon Strachan.* The accompanying description of Nixon's role is titled *Report and Recommendation of the June 5, 1972 Grand Jury Concerning Transmission of Evidence to the House of Representatives.* My opinion releasing the report to the Judiciary Committee was filed March 18, 1974, under Misc. No. 74-21. It is reprinted in the Appendix.

CHAPTER 14

The Supreme Court's opinion in the tapes case is titled, awesomely enough, *United States v. Nixon,* 94 S. Ct. 3090 (1974). This opinion is reprinted in the Appendix.

The court proceeding in which I ordered St. Clair to listen to the tapes himself is contained in the transcript of *United*

States v. John Mitchell, et al., C.C. No. 74-110, July 26, 1974.

Quotations from the June 23 tape are from the special prosecutor's transcript. The transcripts of two of the June 23 tapes are reprinted in the Appendix.

CHAPTER 15

This chapter is, of course, based on my own views and analysis of Richard Nixon's role in the Watergate scandal, and upon my own notions, based on the former president's written and televised comments about Watergate, of how he views his own responsibility for those events. The quotation from Thomas Jefferson is contained in *RN: The Memoirs of Richard Nixon* (New York, Grosset and Dunlap, 1978), p. 476.

CHAPTERS 16 and 17

The printed transcript of the cover-up trial has proved invaluable for refreshing my own recollections of the proceedings. The case is titled *United States of America v. John N. Mitchell, et al.*, Criminal No. 74-110.

The appeal of the case is reported at 559 F.2d 31. The appeal was argued in the United States Court of Appeals, District of Columbia Circuit, on January 6, 1976, and decided October 12, 1976. A rehearing was denied by the court of appeals on two parts of the appeal on December 8, 1976. The Supreme Court of the United States declined to hear any further appeal on May 23, 1977. That refusal is reported at 97 S. Ct. 2641.

The full record of the Union Electric of Missouri case is reported in the appeals record captioned *Boehm v. United States*, 123 F.2d 791 (8th Cir. 1941). I have also relied on newspaper accounts from the time, especially those in the *St. Louis Post-Dispatch*, the *St. Louis Daily Globe Democrat*, and the *St. Louis Star-Times*. I have also relied on the recollections of Boehm's son, Frederick J. Boehm, of Miami, Florida.

CHAPTER 18

The account of the defenses offered in the Watergate trial is based on the court transcript, as cited in the notes for the previous chapter.

Anthony Lewis's column in the *New York Times* appeared on Sunday, February 23, 1975.

EPILOGUE

The revelation during the Watergate affair of the serious inadequacies and abuses of the then current election campaign funding process provided a direct stimulus to Congress, which in 1974 set about changing the process. The result was the Federal Election Campaign Act Amendments of 1974, Public Law No. 93–443, 88 Stat. 1263, which toughened and expanded the existing regulation of federal campaign funding.

This legislation established the Federal Election Commission to supervise the enforcement of the regulations, provided for public financing of the presidential election campaigns, renewed and re-emphasized the disclosure provisions of the original act, and took other measures to insure that the purpose of the original act would be effectuated.

Congress also passed the Ethics in Government Act of 1978, which required detailed financial disclosures by high-ranking officials in all three branches of government. In addition, the law institutionalized the concept, which worked so well during the Watergate investigation, of having a special prosecutor to look into the possibility of criminal violations in the top ranks of the executive branch; it established a formal process for the appointment of a temporary special prosecutor when one is needed. See Public Law No. 95-521, 92 Stat. 1824.

Appendix

TRANSCRIPTS

What follows is a transcript of two of the tapes made in the
White House on June 23, 1972. Under court order, the original tapes were turned over to my court. The White House
lawyers then filed requests that certain portions of the uned-
ited tapes be deleted because they contained matters protected by executive privilege. In some cases, I agreed, and, when
the tapes were re-recorded for delivery to the special prosecutors, those portions were omitted. The special prosecutors
then prepared a written transcript for use during the cover-up
trial. At that point, defense counsel and their clients were
permitted to review both the tapes and the transcripts, and in
some cases they objected on evidentiary grounds to certain
passages. More deletions were made, to meet these objections.
Finally, the tapes were played as evidence in the trial, and
the transcripts, exactly as reproduced here, were used as a
"listening aid" and became exhibits, not direct evidence, in
the trial. In these texts, ". . ." indicates a pause or a break in
thought.

*Transcript of a Recording of a Meeting
between the President and H. R. Haldeman,
the Oval Office, June 23, 1972, from 10:04 to
11:39 A.M.*

HALDEMAN: Okay—that's fine. Now, on the investigation, you
know, the Democratic break-in thing, we're back to
the—in the, the problem area because the FBI is not un-

der control, because Gray doesn't exactly know how to control them, and they have, their investigation is now leading into some productive areas, because they've been able to trace the money, not through the money itself, but through the bank, you know, sources—the banker himself. And, and it goes in some directions we don't want it to go. Ah, also there have been some things, like an informant came in off the street to the FBI in Miami, who was a photographer or has a friend who is a photographer who developed some films through this guy, Barker, and the films had pictures of Democratic National Committee letter head documents and things. So I guess, so it's things like that that are gonna, that are filtering in. Mitchell came up with yesterday, and John Dean analyzed very carefully last night and concludes, concurs now with Mitchell's recommendation that the only way to solve this, and we're set up beautifully to do it, ah, in that and that . . . the only network that paid any attention to it last night was NBC . . . they did a massive story on the Cuban . . .

PRESIDENT: That's right.

HALDEMAN: . . . thing.

PRESIDENT: Right.

HALDEMAN: That the way to handle this now is for us to have Walters call Pat Gray and just say, "Stay the hell out of this . . . this is ah, business here we don't want you to go any further on it." That's not an unusual development, . . .

PRESIDENT: Um huh.

HALDEMAN: . . . and, uh, that would take care of it.

PRESIDENT: What about Pat Gray, ah, you mean he doesn't want to?

HALDEMAN: Pat does want to. He doesn't know how to, and he doesn't have, he doesn't have any basis for doing it. Given this, he will then have the basis. He'll call Mark Felt in, and the two of them . . . and Mark Felt wants to cooperate because . . .

PRESIDENT: Yeah.

HALDEMAN: . . . he's ambitious . . .

PRESIDENT: Yeah.

HALDEMAN: Ah, he'll call him in and say, "We've got the signal from across the river to, to put the hold on this." And that will fit rather well because the FBI agents who are working the case, at this point, feel that's what it is. This is CIA.

PRESIDENT: But they've traced the money to 'em.

HALDEMAN: Well they have, they've traced to a name, but they haven't gotten to the guy yet.

PRESIDENT: Would it be somebody here?

HALDEMAN: Ken Dahlberg.

PRESIDENT: Who the hell is Ken Dahlberg?

HALDEMAN: He's ah, he gave $25,000 in Minnesota and ah, the check went directly in to this, to the guy Barker.

PRESIDENT: Maybe he's a . . . bum.

* * *

PRESIDENT: He didn't get this from the committee though, from Stans.

HALDEMAN: Yeah. It is. It is. It's directly traceable and there's some more through some Texas people in—that went to the Mexican bank which they can also trace to the Mexican bank . . . they'll get their names today. And [pause].

PRESIDENT: Well, I mean, ah, there's no way . . . I'm just thinking if they don't cooperate, what do they say? They they, they were approached by the Cubans. That's what Dahlberg has to say, the Texans too. Is that the idea?

HALDEMAN: Well, if they will. But then we're relying on more and more people all the time. That's the problem. And ah, they'll stop if we could, if we take this other step.

PRESIDENT: All right. Fine.

HALDEMAN: And, and they seem to feel the thing to do is get them to stop?

PRESIDENT: Right, fine.

HALDEMAN: They say the only way to do that is from White House instructions. And it's got to be to Helms and, ah, what's his name . . . ? Walters.

PRESIDENT: Walters.

HALDEMAN: And the proposal would be that Ehrlichman [coughs] and I call them in . . .

PRESIDENT: All right, fine.

HALDEMAN: . . . and say, ah . . .

PRESIDENT: How do you call him in, I mean you just, well, we protected Helms from one hell of a lot of things.

HALDEMAN: That's what Ehrlichman says.

PRESIDENT: Of course, this is a, this is a Hunt, you will—that will uncover a lot of things. You open that scab there's a hell of a lot of things and that we just feel that it would be very detrimental to have this thing go any further. This involves these Cubans, Hunt, and a lot of hanky-panky that we have nothing to do with ourselves. Well what the hell, did Mitchell know about this thing to any much of a degree?

HALDEMAN: I think so. I don't think he knew the details, but I think he knew.

PRESIDENT: He didn't know how it was going to be handled though, with Dahlberg and the Texans and so forth? Well who was the asshole that did? [*Unintelligible*] Is it Liddy? Is that the fellow? He must be a little nuts.

HALDEMAN: He is.

PRESIDENT: I mean he just isn't well screwed on is he? Isn't that the problem?

HALDEMAN: No, but he was under pressure, apparently, to get more information, and as he got more pressure, he pushed the people harder to move harder on . . .

PRESIDENT: Pressure from Mitchell?

HALDEMAN: Apparently.

PRESIDENT: Oh, Mitchell, Mitchell was at the point that you made on this, that exactly what I need from you is on the—

HALDEMAN: Gemstone, yeah.

PRESIDENT: All right, fine, I understand it all. We won't second-guess Mitchell and the rest. Thank God it wasn't Colson.

HALDEMAN: The FBI interviewed Colson yesterday. They determined that would be a good thing to do.

PRESIDENT: Um hum.

HALDEMAN: Ah, to have him take a . . .

PRESIDENT: Um hum.

HALDEMAN: An interrogation, which he did, and that, the FBI guys working the case had concluded that there were one or two possibilities, one, that this was a White House, they don't think that there is anything at the Election Committee, they think it was either a White House operation and they had some obscure reasons for it, nonpolitical. . . .

PRESIDENT: Uh huh.

HALDEMAN: . . . or it was a . . .

PRESIDENT: Cuban thing—

HALDEMAN: Cubans and the CIA. And after their interrogation of, of . . .

PRESIDENT: . . . Colson.

HALDEMAN: Colson, yesterday, they concluded it was not the White House, but are now convinced it is a CIA thing, so the CIA turnoff would . . .

PRESIDENT: Well, not sure of their analysis, I'm not going to get that involved. I'm [*unintelligible*].

HALDEMAN: No sir. We don't want you to.

PRESIDENT: You call them in.

* * *

PRESIDENT: Good. Good deal. Play it tough. That's the way they play it and that's the way we are going to play it.

HALDEMAN: O.K. We'll do it.

PRESIDENT: Yeah, when I saw that news summary item, I of course knew it was a bunch of crap, but I thought, ah, well it's good to have them off on this wild hair thing because when they start bugging us, which they have, we'll know our little boys will not know how to handle it. I hope they will though. You never know. Maybe, you think about it. Good!

* * *

PRESIDENT: When you get in these people . . . when you get these people in, say: "Look, the problem is that this will open the whole, the whole Bay of Pigs thing, and the President just feels that" ah, without going into the details . . . don't, don't lie to them to the extent to say there is no involvement, but just say this is sort of a comedy of errors, bizarre, without getting into it, "the President believes that it is going to open the whole Bay of Pigs thing up again. And, ah because these people are plugging for, for keeps and that they should call the FBI in and say that we wish for the country, don't go any further into this case," period!

HALDEMAN: OK.

PRESIDENT: That's the way to put it, do it straight. [*Unintelligible*]

HALDEMAN: Get more done for our cause by the opposition than by us at this point.

PRESIDENT: You think so?

HALDEMAN: I think so, yeah.

Transcript of a Recording of a Meeting between the President and H. R. Haldeman, the Oval Office, June 23, 1972, from 1:04 to 1:13 P.M.

[*Background noise, sound of writing and some unintelligible conversation*]

HALDEMAN: [*On the phone*] [*Unintelligible*] Where are they? Okay. I'll be up in just a minute.

[*40-second pause, with sounds of writing*]

HALDEMAN: I see a time way back [*unintelligible*] might find out about that report before we do anything.

PRESIDENT: [*Unintelligible*]

[*35-second pause*]

PRESIDENT: *Okay* [*unintelligible*] and, ah, just, just postpone the [*unintelligible, with noises*] hearings [*15-second unintelligible, with noises*] and all that garbage. Just say that I have to take a look at the primaries [*unintelligible*] recover [*unintelligible*] I just don't [*unintelligible*] very bad, to have this fellow Hunt, ah, you know, ah, it's, he, he knows too damn much and he was involved, we happen to know that. And that it gets out that the whole, this is all involved in the Cuban thing, that it's a fiasco, and it's going to make the FB, ah CIA look bad, it's going to make Hunt look bad, and it's likely to blow the whole, uh, Bay of Pigs thing which we think would be very unfortunate for CIA and for the country at this time, and for American foreign policy, and he just better tough it and lay it on them. Isn't that what you . . .

HALDEMAN: Yeah, that's, that's the basis we'll do it on and just leave it at that.

PRESIDENT: I don't want them to get any ideas we're doing it because our concern is political.

HALDEMAN: Right.

PRESIDENT: And at the same time, I wouldn't tell them it is not political . . .

HALDEMAN: Right.

PRESIDENT: I would just say "Look, it's because of the Hunt involvement," just say [*unintelligible, with noise*] sort of thing, the whole cover is, uh, basically this [*unintelligible*].

HALDEMAN: [*Unintelligible*] Well they've got some pretty good ideas on this need thing.

PRESIDENT: George Schultz did a good paper on that, I read it . . . [*Unintelligible voices heard leaving the room*]

Opinion Sustaining Subpoena
Issued to Richard Nixon,
August 29, 1973, by Judge Sirica

In re Grand Jury SUBPOENA Duces Tecum Issued TO Richard M. NIXON, or any Subordinate Officer, Official, or Employee with Custody or Control of Certain Documents or Objects.

Misc. No. 47–73.

United States District Court,
District of Columbia.

Aug. 29, 1973

ORDER

SIRICA, Chief Judge.

This matter having come before the Court on motion of the Watergate Special Prosecutor made on behalf of the June 1972 grand jury of this district for an order to show cause, and the Court being advised in the premises, it is by the Court this 29th day of August, 1973, for the reasons stated in the attached opinion.

Ordered that respondent, President Richard M. Nixon, or any subordinate officer, official or employee with custody or control of the documents or objects listed in the grand jury subpoena *duces tecum* of July 23, 1973, served on respondent in this district, is hereby commanded to produce forthwith for the Court's examination *in camera,* the subpoenaed documents or objects which have not heretofore been produced to the grand jury; and it is

Further ordered that the ruling herein be stayed for a period of five days in which time respondent may perfect an appeal from the ruling; and it is

Further ordered that should respondent appeal from the ruling herein, the above stay will be extended indefinitely pending the completion of such appeal or appeals.

OPINION

On July 23, 1973, Watergate Special Prosecutor Archibald Cox acting on behalf of the June 1972 grand jury empanelled by this court, caused to be issued a subpoena duces tecum to the President of the United States, Richard M. Nixon.[1] The subpoena required the President, or any appropriate subordinate official, to produce for the grand jury certain tape recordings and documents enumerated in an attached schedule. The President complied with the subpoena insofar as it related to memoranda of Gordon Strachan and W. Richard Howard, but otherwise declined to follow the subpoena's directives. In a letter to the Court dated July 25, 1973, the President advised that the tape recordings sought would not be provided, and by way of explanation wrote:

> . . . I follow the example of a long line of my predecessors as President of the United States who have consistently adhered to the position that the President is not subject to compulsory process from the courts.

Thereafter, the grand jury instructed Special Prosecutor Cox to apply for an order requiring production of the recordings. On July 26, the Special Prosecutor petitioned this Court[2] for a show cause order directed to the President. At the time of this application a quorum of the grand jury was polled in open court, and each juror expressed his or her desire that the Court order compliance. Subsequently, the Court ordered that the President or any appropriate subordinate official show cause "why the documents and objects described in [the subpoena] should not be produced as evidence before the grand jury."

In response to the show cause order, the President, by his attorneys, filed a special appearance contesting the Court's jurisdiction to order the President's compliance with the grand jury subpoena.[3] The Court allowed for the filing of a response by the Special Prosecutor and reply by the President, and the matter came on for hearing on August 22nd.

The parties to the controversy have briefed and argued several issues including the Court's jurisdiction in the matter of compulsory process, the existence and scope of "executive privilege" generally, applicability of "executive privilege" to the tape recordings subpoenaed, and waiver of privilege. The Court has found it necessary to adjudicate but two questions for the present: (1) whether the Court has jurisdiction to decide the issue of privilege, and (2) whether the Court has authority to enforce the subpoena *duces tecum* by way of an order requiring production for inspection *in camera*. A third question, whether the materials are in fact privileged as against the grand jury, either in whole or in part, is left for subsequent adjudication. For the reasons outlined below, the Court concludes that both of the questions considered must be answered in the affirmative.

I

A search of the Constitution and the history of its creation reveals a general disfavor of government privileges, or at least uncontrolled privileges. Early in the Convention of 1787, the delegates cautioned each other concerning the dangers of lodging immoderate power in the executive department.[4] This attitude persisted throughout the Convention, and executive powers became a major topic in the subsequent ratification debates.[5] The Framers regarded the legislative department superior in power and importance to the other two and felt the necessity of investing it with some privileges and immunities, but even here an attitude of restraint, as expressed by James Madison, prevailed:

> Mr. Pinkney moved a clause declaring "that each House should be the judge of the privilege of its own members."

> *   *   *   *   *   *

> Mr. Madison distinguished between the power of Judging of privileges previously & duly established, and the effect of the motion which would give a discretion to each House as to the extent of its own privileges. He suggested that it would be better to make provision for ascertaining by *law*, the privileges of each House, than to allow each House to decide for itself. He suggested also the necessity of considering what privileges ought to be allowed to the Executive.[6] (Emphasis in original)

The upshot of Madison's final suggestion regarding a definition of executive privileges was that none were deemed necessary, or at least that the Constitution need not record any. As Charles Pinckney, the South Carolina delegate, later explained in a Senate speech:

> I assert, that it was the design of the Constitution, and that not only its spirit, but letter, warrant me in the assertion, that it never was intended to give Congress, or either branch, any but specified, and those very limited, privileges indeed. They well knew how oppressively the power of undefined privileges had been exercised in Great Britain, and were determined no such authority should ever be exercised here. They knew that in free countries very few privileges were necessary to the undisturbed exercise of legislative duties, and those few only they determined that Congress should possess; they never meant that the body who ought to be the purest, and the least in want of shelter from the operation of laws equally affecting all their fel-

low citizens, should be able to avoid them; they therefore not only intended, but did confine their privileges within the narrow limits mentioned in the Constitution.

. . . Let us inquire, why the Constitution should have been so attentive to each branch of Congress, so jealous of their privileges, and have shewn [sic] so little to the President of the United States in this respect. . . . No privilege of this kind was intended for your Executive, nor any except that which I have mentioned for your Legislature. The Convention which formed the Constitution well knew that this was an important point, and no subject had been more abused than privilege. They therefore determined to set the example, in merely limiting privilege to what was necessary and no more.[7] (Ellipsis in original)

Pinckney's words just quoted, "They therefore determined to set the example, in merely limiting privilege to what was necessary and no more," constitute an apt description of the Convention's purpose and outlook. Are there, then, any rights or privileges consistent with, though not mentioned in, the Constitution which are necessary to the Executive? One answer may be found in the Supreme Court decision, United States v. Reynolds, 345 U.S. 1, 73 S.Ct. 528, 97 L.Ed. 727 (1953). The Court recognized an executive privilege, evidentiary in nature, for military secrets. *Reynolds* held that when a court finds the privilege is properly invoked under the appropriate circumstances, it will, in a civil case at least, suppress the evidence. Thus, it must be recognized that there can be executive privileges that will bar the production of evidence. The Court is willing here to recognize and give effect to an evidentiary privilege based on the need to protect Presidential privacy.[8]

The Court, however, cannot agree with Respondent that it is the Executive that finally determines whether its privilege is properly invoked. The availability of evidence including the validity and scope of privileges, is a judicial decision.

Judicial control over the evidence in a case cannot be abdicated to the caprice of executive officers.[9]

It is emphatically the province and duty of the judicial department to say what the law is. Those who apply the rule, to particular cases must of necessity expand and interpret that rule. If two laws conflict with each other, the courts must decide on the operation of each.[10]

In all the numerous litigations where claims of executive privilege have been interposed, the courts have not hesitated to pass judgment.[11] Executive fiat is not the mode of resolution.[12] As has been stated most recently in this Circuit:

> [N]o executive official or agency can be given absolute authority to determine what documents in his possession may be considered by the court in its task. Otherwise the head of an executive department would have the power on his own say so to cover up all evidence of fraud and corruption when a federal court or grand jury was investigating malfeasance in office, and this is not the law.[13]

The measures a court should adopt in ruling on claims of executive privilege are discussed under Part III herein.

II

If after judicial examination *in camera*, any portion of the tapes is ruled not subject to privilege, that portion will be forwarded to the grand jury at the appropriate time. To call for the tapes *in camera* is thus tantamount to fully enforcing the subpoena as to any unprivileged matter. Therefore, before the Court can call for production *in camera*, it must have concluded that it has authority to order a President to obey the command of a grand jury subpoena as it relates to unprivileged evidence in his possession. The Court has concluded that it possesses such authority.

Analysis of the question must begin on the well established premises that the grand jury has a right to every man's evidence and that for purposes of gathering evidence, process may issue to anyone.

> The court can perceive no legal objection to issuing a subpoena *duces tecum* to any person whatever, provided the case be such as to justify the process.[14]

The important factors are the relevance and materiality of the evidence.

> The propriety of introducing any paper into a case, as testimony, must depend on the character of the paper, not on the character of the person who holds it.[15]

The burden here then, is on the President to define exactly what it is about his office[16] that court process commanding the production of evidence cannot reach there. To be accurate, court process in the form of a subpoena *duces tecum* has already issued to the President, and he acknowledges that pursuant to *Burr*, courts possess authority to direct such subpoenas to him. A distinction is drawn, however, between authority to issue a subpoena and authority to command obedience to it. It is this second compulsory process that the President contends may not reach him.[17] The burden yet remains with the President, however, to explain why this must be so. What distinctive quality of the Presidency permits its incumbent to withhold evidence? To argue that the need for Presidential privacy justifies it, is not persuasive. On the occasions when such need justifies suppression, the courts will sustain a privilege. The fact that this is a judicial decision has already been discussed at length, but the opinion of Chief Justice Marshall on the topic deserves notice here. When deciding that a subpoena should issue to the President, the Chief Justice made it clear that if certain portions should be excised, it being appropriate to sustain a privilege, the Court would make such a decision upon return of the subpoena.

There is certainly nothing before the court which shows that the letter in question contains any matter the disclosure of which would endanger the public safety. If it does contain such matter, the fact may appear before the disclosure is made. If it does contain any matter which it would be imprudent to disclose, which it is not the wish of the executive to disclose, such matter, *if it be not immediately and essentially applicable to the point, will, of course, be suppressed.* It is not easy to conceive that so much of the letter as relates to the conduct of the accused can be a subject of delicacy with the president. *Everything of this kind, however, will have its due consideration on the return of the subpoena.*[18]

And again:

The propriety of requiring the answer to this letter is more questionable. It is alleged that it most probably communicates orders showing the situation of this country with Spain, which will be important on the misdemeanor. *If it contain matter not essential to the defence, and the disclosure be unpleasant to the executive, it certainly ought not to be disclosed. This is a point which will appear on the return.*[19]

To argue that it is the constitutional separation of powers that bars compulsory court process from the White House, is also unpersuasive. Such a contention overlooks history. Although courts generally, and this Court in particular,[20] have avoided any interference with the discretionary acts of coordinate branches, they have not hesitated to rule on non-discretionary acts when necessary.[21] Respondent points out that these and other precedents refer to officials other than the President, and that this distinction renders the precedents inapplicable. Such an argument tends to set the White House apart as a fourth branch of government. It is true that Mississippi v. Johnson, 4 Wall. 475, 18 L. Ed. 437 (1866) left open the question whether the President can be required by court process to perform a purely ministerial act, but to persist in the opinion, after 1952, that he cannot would seem to exalt the form of the *Youngstown Sheet & Tube Co.* case over its substance.[22] Though the Court's order there went to the Secretary of Commerce, it was the direct order of President Truman that was reversed.

The Special Prosecutor has correctly noted that the Framers' intention to lodge the powers of government in separate bodies also included a plan for interaction between departments. A "watertight" division of different functions was never their design. The legislative branch may organize the judiciary[23] and dictate the procedures by which it transacts business.[24] The judiciary may pass upon the constitutionality of legislative enactments[25] and in some instances define the bounds of Congressional investigations.[26] The executive may veto legislative enactments,[27] and the legislature may override the veto.[28] The executive appoints judges and justices[29] and may bind judicial decisions by lawful executive orders.[30] The judiciary may pass on the constitutionality of executive acts.[31]

> While the Constitution diffuses power the better to secure liberty, it also contemplates that practice will integrate the dispersed powers into a workable government. It enjoins upon its branches separateness but interdependence, autonomy but reciprocity.[32]

That the Court has not the physical power to enforce its order to the President is immaterial to a resolution of the issues. Regardless of its physical power to enforce them, the Court has a duty to issue appropriate orders.[33] The Court cannot say that the Executive's persistence in withholding the tape recordings would "tarnish its reputation," but must admit that it would tarnish the Court's reputation to fail to do what it could in pursuit of justice.[34] In any case, the courts have always enjoyed the good faith of the Executive Branch, even in such dire circumstances as those presented by Youngstown Sheet & Tube Co. v. Sawyer, 343 U.S. 579, 72 S.Ct. 863, 96 L.Ed. 1153 (1952), and there is no reason to suppose that the courts in this instance cannot again rely on that same good faith. Indeed, the President himself has publicly so stated.

It is important also to note here the role of the grand jury. Chief Justice Marshall, in considering whether a subpoena might issue to the President of the United States observed:

In the provisions of the constitution, and of the statute, which give to the accused a right to the compulsory process of the court, there is no exception whatever.[85]

Aaron Burr, it will be remembered, stood before the court accused though not yet indicted. The Chief Justice's statement regarding the accused is equally true with regard to a grand jury: "there is no exception whatever" in its right to the compulsory process of the courts. The Court, while in a position to lend its process in assistance to the grand jury, is thereby in a position to assist justice.

The grand jury is well known to Anglo-American criminal justice as the people's guardian of fairness. Ever since the Earl of Shaftesbury relied upon its integrity, the grand jury has been promoted as a shield for the innocent and a sword against the guilty.[86] Among the Bill of Rights enacted by the First Congress was the Fifth Amendment which reads in part: "No person shall be held to answer for a capital, or otherwise infamous crime, unless on a presentment or indictment of a Grand Jury." The grand jury derives its authority directly from the people,[87] and when that group, independent in its sphere, acts according to its mandate, the court cannot justifiably withhold its assistance, nor can anyone, regardless of his station, withhold from it evidence not privileged.[88] Marshall concluded that, contrary to the English practice regarding the King, the laws of evidence do not excuse anyone because of the office he holds.[89]

. . . the single reservation alluded to is the case of the king. Although he may, perhaps, give testimony, it is said to be incompatible with his dignity to appear under the process of the court. Of the many points of difference which exist between the first magistrate in England and the first magistrate of the United States, in respect to the personal dignity conferred on them by the constitutions of their respective nations, the court will only select and mention two. It is a principle of the English constitution that the king can do no wrong, that no blame can be imputed to him, that he cannot be named in debate. By the constitution of the United States, the president, as well as any other officer of the government, may be impeached, and may be removed from office on high crimes and misdemeanors. By the constitution of Great Britain, the crown is hereditary, and the monarch can never be a subject. By that of the United States, the president is elected from the mass of the people, and, on the expiration of the time for which he is elected, returns to the mass of the people again. How essentially this difference of circumstances must vary the policy of the laws of the two countries, in reference to the personal dignity of the executive chief, will be perceived by every person.[40]

In all candor, the Court fails to perceive any reason for suspending the power of courts to get evidence and rule on questions of privilege in criminal matters simply because it is the President of the United States who holds the evidence. The *Burr* decision left for another occasion a ruling on whether compulsory process might issue to the President in situations such as this. In the words of counsel, "this is a new question," with little in the way of precedent to guide the Court. But Chief Justice Marshall clearly distinguished the amenability of the King to appear and give testimony under court process and that of this nation's chief magistrate.[41] The conclusion reached here cannot be inconsistent with the view of that great Chief Justice nor with the spirit of the Constitution.

III

In deciding whether these tape recordings or portions thereof are properly the objects of a privilege, the Court must accommodate two competing policies. On the one hand, as has been noted earlier, is the need to disfavor privileges and narrow their application as far as possible. On the other hand, lies a need to favor the privacy of Presidential deliberations; to indulge a presumption in favor of the President. To the Court, respect for the President, the Presidency, and the duties of the office, gives the advantage to this second policy. This respect, however, does not decide the controversy. Such a resolution on the Court's part, as Chief Justice Marshall observed, "would deserve some other appellation than the term respect."[42] Nevertheless, it does not hurt for the courts to remind themselves often that the authority vested in them to delimit the scope and application of privileges, particularly the privileges and immunities of government, is a trust. And as with every trust, an abuse can reap the most dire consequences. This Court, then, enters upon its present task with care and with a determination to exercise the restraint that characterizes the conduct of courts.

The teaching of *Reynolds* is that a court should attempt to satisfy itself whether or not a privilege is properly invoked without unnecessarily probing into the material claimed to be privileged.[43] A decision on how far to go will be dictated in part by need for the evidence.

In each case, the showing of necessity which is made will determine how far the court should probe in satisfying itself that the occasion for invoking the privilege is appropriate. Where there is a strong showing of necessity, the claim of privilege should not be lightly accepted, but even the most compelling necessity cannot overcome the claim of privilege if the court is ultimately satisfied that military secrets are at stake. A fortiori, where necessity is dubious, a formal claim of privilege, made under the circumstances of this case, will have to prevail.[44]

The grand jury's showing of need here is well documented and imposing. The Special Prosecutor has specifically identified by date, time and place each of the eight meetings and the one telephone call involved. Due to the unusual circumstances of having access to sworn public testimony of participants to these conversations, the Special Prosecutor has been able to provide the Court with the conflicting accounts of what transpired. He thus identifies the topics discussed in each instance, the areas of critical conflict in the testimony, and the resolution it is anticipated the tape recordings may render possible.[45] The relative importance of the issues in doubt is revealed. One example, quoted from the Special Prosecutor will suffice:

> *Meeting of September 15, 1972.* On September 15, 1972, the grand jury returned an indictment charging seven individuals with conspiracy and other offenses relating to the break-in. Respondent met the same day with Dean and Haldeman in his Oval Office from 5:37 to 6:17 p.m. Both Dean and Haldeman have given lengthy but contradictory accounts of what was said (S. Tr. 2229–33, 6900–93).
>
> According to Dean, the purpose of the meeting was to brief respondent on the status of the investigation and related matters. Dean said that respondent then congratulated him on the "good job" he had done and was pleased that the case had "stopped with Liddy." Dean said that he then told respondent that all he had been able to do was "contain" the case and "assist in keeping it out of the White House." (S.Tr. 2230.) If this testimony is corroborated, it will tend to establish that a conspiracy to obstruct justice reached the highest level of government.
>
> Haldeman, after reviewing a tape recording of the meeting, has agreed that there was discussion of the Watergate indictments, of the civil cases arising out of the break-in, of the possibility of a continuing grand jury investigation, of internal politics at the Committee for the Re-Election of the President, and of other matters. He denies, however, that respondent congratulated Dean on Dean's efforts to thwart the investigation. (S. Tr. 6090–93, 6456.).
>
> If Haldeman's innocuous version of the meeting can be sustained, it is because the meeting only involved an innocent discussion of political interests. The question of Dean's perjury would then arise. Resolution of this conflict between two of the three persons present and an accurate knowledge of plans or

admissions made on this occasion would be of obvious aid to the grand jury's investigation.[46]

The point is raised that, as in *Reynolds,* the sworn statements of witnesses should suffice and remove the need for access to documents deemed privileged. Though this might often be the case, here, unfortunately, the witnesses differ, sometimes completely, on the precise matters likely to be of greatest moment to the grand jury. Ironically, need for the taped evidence derives in part from the fact that witnesses *have* testified regarding the subject matter, creating important issues of fact for the grand jury to resolve. It will be noted as well in contradistinction to *Reynolds,* that this is a criminal investigation. Rather than money damages at stake, we deal here in matters of reputation and liberty. Based on this indisputably forceful showing of necessity by the grand jury, the claim of privilege cannot be accepted lightly.

In his Brief in Support, the Special Prosecutor outlines the grand jury's view regarding the validity of the Respondent's claim of privilege. Its opinion is that the right of confidentiality is improperly asserted here. Principally, the Special Prosecutor cites a substantial possibility, based on the sworn testimony of participants, that the privilege is improperly invoked as a cloak for serious criminal wrongdoing.

According to the testimony of John W. Dean, many of the conversations in which he participated were part and parcel of a criminal conspiracy to obstruct justice by preventing the truth from coming out about the additional participants in the original conspiracy to break into and wiretap the offices of the Democratic National Committee. He has testified that in the presence of H. R. Haldeman he told respondent on September 15, 1972, that "all [Dean] had been able to do was to contain the case and assist in keeping it out of the White House." Dean also told respondent that he "could make no assurances that the day would not come when this matter would start to unravel." Respondent allegedly congratulated him on the "good job" he was doing on that task. (S.Tr. 2229–30). Dean also has testified that on March 13, 1973, respondent told him that respondent had approved executive clemency for Hunt and that there would be no problem in raising $1 million to buy the Watergate defendants' silence (S.Tr. 2324). In addition, there is uncontradicted testimony that respondent was briefed on Watergate on June 20, 1972, three days after the arrests, by Haldeman, Ehrlichman and Mitchell, his closest political advisors (S.Tr. 5924, 3407–08). If these three told respondent all they allegedly knew, respondent would have been aware of details of the nascent cover-up.

It is true, of course that other testimony indicates that the conversations did not include direct evidence of criminal misconduct. While this is not the time or place to judge credibility, Dean's testimony cannot be dismissed out of hand. In fact, Haldeman has confirmed many of the details of the meetings at which both he and Dean were present. The opposite conclusions he draws are based upon a different interpretation and different recollection of some of the details.[47]

If the interest served by a privilege is abused or subverted, the claim of privilege fails. Such a case is well described in Clark v. United States, 289 U.S. 1, 53 S.Ct. 465, 77 L.Ed. 993 (1933), a decision involving the privilege of secrecy enjoyed by jurors.

The privilege takes as its postulate a genuine relation, honestly created and honestly maintained. If that condition is not satisfied, if the relation is merely a sham and a pretense, the juror may not invoke a relation dishonestly assumed as a cover and cloak for the concealment of the truth.

* * * * * * * * * * *

With the aid of this analogy [to the attorney-client privilege] we recur to the social policies competing for supremacy. A privilege surviving until the relation is abused and vanishing when abuse is shown to the satisfaction of the judge has been found to be a workable technique for the protection of the confidences of client and attorney. Is there sufficient reason to believe that it will be found to be inadequate for the protection of a juror? No doubt the need is weighty that conduct in the jury room shall be untrammeled by the fear of embarrassing publicity. The need is no less weighty that it shall be pure and undefiled. A juror of integrity and reasonable firmness will not fear to speak his mind if the confidences of debate are barred to the ears of mere impertinence or malice. He will not expect to be shielded against the disclosure of his conduct in the event that there is evidence reflecting upon his honor.[48]

These principles are, of course, fully applicable throughout government.[49] A court would expect that if the privacy of its deliberations, for example, were ever used to foster criminal conduct or to develop evidence of criminal wrongdoing, any privilege might be barred and privacy breached. So it is that evidentiary privileges asserted against the grand jury may be ruled inapplicable if the interest served by the privilege is subverted.

Nevertheless, without discrediting the strength of the grand jury's position, the Court cannot, as matters now stand, rule that the present claim of privilege is invalid. The President contends that the recorded conversations occurred pursuant to an exercise of his duty to "take care that the laws be faithfully executed."[50] Although the Court is not bound by that conclusion, it is extremely reluctant to finally stand against a declaration of the President of the United States on any but the strongest possible evidence. Need for the evidence requires that a claim not be accepted lightly, but the vitality of Presidential deliberations in like manner requires that the claim not be rejected lightly. The Court is simply unable to decide the question of privilege without inspecting the tapes.

It is true that if material produced is properly the subject of privilege, even an inspection *in camera* may constitute a compromise of privilege. Nevertheless, it would be an extremely limited infraction and in this case an unavoidable one. If privileged and unprivileged evidence are intermingled, privileged portions may be excised so that only unprivileged matter goes before the grand jury (which also meets in secret proceedings). If privileged and unprivileged evidence are so inextricably connected that separation becomes impossible, the whole must be privileged and no disclosure made to the grand jury.

It should be observed as well that given the circumstances in this case, there is every reason to suppose an *in camera* examination will materially aid the Court in its decision. The fact that extensive accounts of the recorded conversations given under oath by participants are available, will enable the Court to make an intelligent and informed analysis of the evidence.

The Court is unable to design a more cautious approach consistent with both the demonstrated critical need for the evidence and the serious questions raised concerning the applicability of the privilege asserted. The Court has attempted to walk the middle ground between a failure to decide the question of privilege at one extreme, and a wholesale delivery of tapes to the grand jury at the other. The one would be a breach of duty; the other an inexcusable course of conduct. The approach comports with precedent in this district,[51] and honors the injunction of *Reynolds* and *Burr* to pursue fairness and protect essential privacy.[52]

To paraphrase Chief Justice Marshall,[53] if it be apparent that the tapes are irrelevant to the investigation, or that for state reasons they cannot be introduced into the case, the subpoena *duces tecum* would be useless. But if this be not apparent, if they *may* be important in the investigation, if they *may* be safely heard by the grand jury, if only in part, would it not be a blot on the page which records the judicial proceedings of this country, if, in a case of such serious import as this, the Court did not at least call for an inspection of the evidence in chambers?

1. The Special Prosecutor has been designated as the attorney

for the Government to conduct proceedings before the grand jury investigating the unauthorized entry into the Democratic National Committee Headquarters and related offenses. Order of the Attorney General No. 517–73, 38 Fed. Reg. 14688 (June 4, 1973). A grand jury subpoena *duces tecum* was issued by the clerk under seal of the court. F.R. Crim.P. 17(a), (c). The Special Prosecutor appears before the Court on behalf of and under the specific authorization of the grand jury, seeking compliance with the subpoena (Transcript of Hearing of July 26, 1973, on Petition for Order to Show Cause 8–12). In this capacity he appears as an officer of the Court and counsel for the grand jury, in addition to being the attorney for the United States.

2. Local Rule 3–6 provides:

> In addition to the trial of such cases as he may undertake and other duties provided by these rules, the Chief Judge shall:
>
> (3) empanel the grand jury and hear and determine all matters relating to proceedings before the grand jury.

3. No objections to the technical adequacy of the subpoena or service of process have been raised.

4. See *e.g.*, 1 Farrand. The Records of the Federal Convention of 1787, 64–69 (1967).

5. The Federalist Nos. 67–77, J. E. Cooke, ed., The Federalist, 452–521 (1961).

6. 2 Farrand. The Records of the Federal Convention of 1787, 502, 503 (1967).

7. 3 Farrand. The Records of the Federal Convention of 1787, 384, 385 (1967). See also, 2 Elliot's Debates, 480 (1836).

8. The Court agrees with Respondent that Presidential privacy, in and of itself, has no merit. Its importance and need of protection arise from "the paramount need for frank expression and discussion among the President and those consulted by him in the making of Presidential decisions." Brief in Opposition at 3. This comports with the court's statement in Kaiser Aluminum & Chemical Corp. v. United States, 157 F.Supp. 939, 944, 141 Ct.Cl. 38 (1958) that the executive privilege is granted "for the benefit of the public, not of executives who may happen to then hold office."

9. United States v. Reynolds, 345 U.S. 1, 10, 11, 73 S.Ct. 528, 533, 97 L.Ed. 727 (1953). For the courts to abdicate this role to Presidents or anyone else, to make each officer the judge of his own privilege, would dishonor the genius of our constitutional system and breed unbearable abuse. Respondent maintains that an adequate remedy for abuse is provided in the impeachment power. Impeachment may be the final remedy, but it is not so designed that it can function as a deterrent in any but the most excessive cases. The argument

overlooks the many possible situations in which only a few may suffer the consequences of abuse: situations where impeachment is not a reasonable solution. The Court intends no suggestion that Respondent could not be trusted as his own judge in matters of privilege, but it would hesitate to set a precedent, in contravention of basic constitutional principles, that might permit or encourage some future high executive officer to become a despot.

10. Marbury v. Madison, 1 Cranch 137, 177, 2 L.Ed. 60 (1803).

11. See *e.g.*, the cases and authorities cited at 8 Wright & Miller, Federal Practice and Procedure, 167–173 (1970).
    These statements are not represented as necessarily accurate where an executive privilege is asserted in opposition to Congressional demands for information.

12. While it is true that Attorneys General have never hesitated to claim an uncontrolled executive discretion in this area, such opinions usually come in response to Congressional demands for information, and therefore have little relevance to the present issue. Insofar as they may have any bearing here, however, assertions that the courts have stamped their approval on this doctrine of absolutism should not be left unchallenged. Such claims rest on unsteady foundations. See *e. g.*, Bishop, The Executive's Right of Privacy: An Unresolved Constitutional Question, 66 Yale L.J., 477, 478, n. 5 (1957).

13. Committee for Nuclear Responsibility, Inc. v. Seaborg, 149 U.S.App.D.C. 385, 463 F.2d 788 (1971).

14. United States v. Burr, 25 Fed.Cas. pp. 30, 35, (Case No. 14,692d) (1807).

15. *Id.* at 34.

16. No claim is made for the President, nor can it be, that apart from his office, he is immune from the obligations of subpoenas and court orders.

17. In oral argument, the Court put a hypothetical situation to the President's counsel regarding the production of unprivileged evidence. Counsel responded as follows:

    MR. WRIGHT: On the set of facts that Your Honor puts, the President would have no privilege, since you have hypothesized the President obtained the evidence wholly independent of any official duties. I must say that in my submission a court would lack power, nevertheless, to compel the President to produce the evidence so long as he remains President. I cannot concede that a court has power to issue compulsory process to an incumbent President of the United States. (Misc. 47–73, Transcript of Proceedings, August 22, 1973, at 16, 17.)

It is certainly arguable that a subpoena is compulsory process as well as any subsequent order mandating production either *in camera* or to a grand jury. Be that as it may, the Court recognizes a distinction between issuing a subpoena to the President and commanding that he honor it.

18. United States v. Burr, *supra*, n. 14, at 37. President Jefferson, upon forwarding the subpoenaed letter to Mr. Hay, counsel for the United States, authorized Hay to excise those portions of the letter "not material for the purposes of justice." Mr. Hay was willing to refer the "accuracy" of his opinion on that matter "to the judgment of the court, by submitting the original letter to its inspection." United States v. Burr, 25 Fed.Cas. pp. 187, 190 (Case No. 14,694) (1807).

19. *Id.*

20. See In Re Application of Senate Select Committee (DCDC 1973), Misc. No. 70–73 (June 12, 1973).

21. See *e.g.*, United States v. United States Dist. Ct., 407 U.S. 297, 92 S.Ct. 2125, 32 L.Ed.2d 752 (1972); Powell v. McCormack 395 U.S. 486, 89 S.Ct. 1944, 23 L.Ed.2d 491 (1969); Youngstown Sheet & Tube Co. v. Sawyer, 343 U.S. 579, 72 S.Ct. 863, 96 L.Ed. 1153 (1952); D.C. Federation of Civic Assn's v. Volpe, 316 F.Supp. 754, 760, n. 12 (DCDC 1970).

Discretionary duties and acts are not at issue here. The grand jury does not ask that the Court command or forbid the performance of any discretionary functions. The President is not asked to account in any way for the conduct of his office. The questions here concern the obligation of the President to provide evidence, something more akin to a ministerial duty if indeed it concerns official duties at all.

Nor is this a case, as Respondent suggests, where the Court in deciding the applicability of privilege, substitutes its judgment for that of the President on a matter committed to Presidential discretion, the public interest. Where a court, for example, determines whether probable cause existed for an arrest, it does not substitute its judgment for that of the arresting officer. A judge simply decides whether the condition is met, whether there were reasonable grounds. He does not decide whether he would have arrived at the same conclusion as the officer did on the need to arrest. Here, the Court must determine whether the conditions for privilege exist. Should it so find, it does not then judge the wisdom of withholding evidence in the public interest.

An attempt to dictate or to require an account of the President in the discretionary matters committed to him under Article II would truly be an instance of one branch pitting itself against another. Such is not the case here.

22. Youngstown Sheet & Tube Co. v. Sawyer, 343 U.S. 579, 72 S.Ct. 863, 96 L.Ed. 1153 (1952).

23. United States Constitution, Article III, Section 1.
24. See *e.g.*, 28 U.S.C. §§ 2, 44(c), 144, 1731–1745, 2403; 18 U.S.C. §§ 2519, 3331(a), 6003(a).
25. Marbury v. Madison, 1 Cranch 137, 2 L.Ed. 60 (1803).
26. See *e.g.*, Barenblatt v. United States, 360 U.S. 109, 79 S.Ct. 1081, 3 L.Ed.2d 1115 (1959); United States v. Rumely, 345 U.S. 41, 73 S.Ct. 543, 97 L.Ed. 770 (1953); Sinclair v. United States, 279 U.S. 263, 49 S.Ct. 268, 73 L.Ed. 692 (1929).
27. United States Constitution, Article I, Section 7.
28. *Id.*
29. United States Constitution, Article II, Section 2.
30. See *e.g.*, Environmental Protection Agency v. Mink, 410 U.S. 73, 93 S.Ct. 827, 35 L.Ed.2d 119 (1973).
31. See *e.g.*, United States v. United States Dist. Ct., 407 U.S. 297, 92, S.Ct. 2125, 32 L.Ed.2d 752 (1972).
32. Youngstown Sheet & Tube Co. v. Sawyer, *supra*, n. 22.
33. See Baker v. Carr. 369 U.S. 186, 82 S.Ct. 691, 7 L.Ed.2d 663 (1962).
34. See United States v. Burr, *supra*, n. 14, at 37. In the words of the Chief Justice:

> It cannot be denied that to issue a subpoena to a person filling the exalted position of the chief magistrate is a duty which would be dispensed with more cheerfully than it would be performed; but, if it be a duty, the court can have no choice in the case. United States v. Burr, 25 Fed.Cas. pp. 30, 34 (Case No. 14,692d) (1807).

35. United States v. Burr, *supra*, n. 14, at 34.
36. For a full exposition of the purpose and role of grand juries see Branzburg v. Hayes, 408 U.S. 665, 92 S.Ct. 2646, 33 L.Ed.2d 626 (1972).
37. Hale v. Henkel, 201 U.S. 43, 61, 26 S.Ct. 370, 50 L.Ed. 652 (1906); In Re April 1956 Term Grand Jury, 239 F.2d 263, 269 (7th Cir. 1956).
38. Sullivan v. United States, 348 U.S. 170, 75 S.Ct. 182, 99 L.Ed. 210 (1954); United States v. United States Dist. Ct., 238 F.2d 713 (4th Cir. 1956), cert. denied, 352 U.S. 981, 77 S.Ct. 382, 1 L.Ed.2d 365 (1957); In Re Miller, 17 Fed.Cas. p. 295 (Case No. 9,552) (1878); In Re Times Mirror Company, 354 F.Supp. 208 (DCDC 1972).
39. The practical obstacles to compliance alluded to by Chief Justice Marshall in the Burr case are not a factor here. At page 34 the Chief Justice wrote:

> If, upon any principle, the president could be construed to stand exempt from the general provisions of the constitution, it would be, because his duties as chief magistrate demand his whole time for national objects. United States

     v. Burr, 25 Fed.Cas. pp. 30, 34 (Case No. 14,692d)
     (1807).
    The President here need not respond in person to the subpoena
inasmuch as it is directed to "Richard M. Nixon, *or* Any Subordinate Officer, Official, or Employee with Custody or Control of Certain Documents or Objects." The Court is advised
that the tape recordings have previously been entrusted to the
custody of others and no reason appears why they could not
again be held in the possession of a subordinate official for
purposes of answering the Court's order.

40. United States v. Burr, *supra*, n. 14 at 34.

41. *Id.*

42. *Id.*

43. United States v. Reynolds, 345 U.S. 1, 10, 73, S.Ct. 528, 97
    L.Ed. 727 (1953).

44. *Id.* at 11, 73 S.Ct. at 533.
    Occasionally when the executive privilege question comes be-
fore a court, need for the evidence cannot be termed great because it is possible to indirectly satisfy the need without
breaching the privilege claimed. This is accomplished in criminal cases, for example, by requiring the government to choose
between foregoing its prosecution or coming forward with the
information claimed to be privileged. Whichever choice the
government makes does justice to the defendant. In addition
the situation creates an incentive for the government to criti-
cally evaluate its claim of privilege. Compare Vaughn v.
Rosen, 484 F.2d 820 at 825, 826 (D.C.Cir.1973). This case,
however, is more akin to those arising under the Freedom of
Information Act, 5 U.S.C. § 552. There, as here, the party pe-
titioning access to information gains absolutely nothing from
dismissal of the action. The question of need must be directly
confronted.

45. See Brief in Support at 10, 11.

46. See Brief in Support at 6, 7.

47. See Brief in Support at 48, 49.

48. Clark v. United States, 289 U.S. 1, 14, 16, 53 S.Ct. 465,
    469, 470, 77 L.Ed. 993 (1933).

49. See *e.g.*, Gravel v. United States, 408 U.S. 606, 92 S.Ct.
    2614, 33 L.Ed.2d 583 (1972); United States v. Brewster, 408
    U.S. 501, 92 S.Ct. 2531, 33 L.Ed.2d 507 (1972); Spalding v.
    Vilas, 161 U.S. 483, 498, 16 S.Ct. 631, 40 L.Ed. 780 (1896);
    Bivens v. Six Unknown Narcotics Agents, 456 F.2d 1339
    (2nd Cir. 1972).

50. United States Constitution, Article II, Section 3.

51. Nader v. Butz, C.A.No.148–72 (DCDC August 20, 1973).

52. The President urges that a production order from the Court
    would open the floodgates to innumerable subpoenas. The
    above procedure is designed to prevent such a result. It should

be noted as well that this is apparently the first time since the *Burr* decision in 1807 that a subpoena of this sort has been directed to the President. If we may rely on history, there is little indication that the President will be subjected to the "parade of horrors" he describes.

Chief Justice Marshall was sensitive to the need to protect the President against abuse that would employ judicial process to gain its end:

> The guard, furnished to this high officer, to protect him from being harassed by vexatious and unnecessary subpoenas, is to be looked for in the conduct of a court after those subpoenas have issued; not in any circumstance which is to precede their being issued. United States v. Burr, *supra*, n. 14 at 34.

Later in the pretrial proceedings, the Chief Justice had occasion to elaborate on the judicial procedures that might be useful as presidential "guards." The passage is too lengthy for an exposition here, but interested persons are referred to United States v. Burr, 25 Fed.Cas. pp. 187, 191, 192 (Case No. 14, 694) (1807). The Court has here attempted to implement the Chief Justice's guidelines.

53. United States v. Burr, *supra*, n. 14 at 35.

Opinion on Nixon's Appeal to the United States Court of Appeals, October 12, 1973

Richard M. NIXON, President of the United States, Petitioner

v.

The Honorable John J. SIRICA, United States District Judge, Respondent

and

Archibald Cox, Special Prosecutor, Watergate Special Prosecution Force, Party in Interest.

UNITED STATES of America, Petitioner

v.

The Honorable John J. SIRICA, Chief Judge, United States District Court for the District of Columbia,

Respondent

and
Richard M. Nixon, President of the United States,
Party in Interest.

In re GRAND JURY PROCEEDINGS.
Nos. 73–1962, 73–1967 and 73–1989.

United States Court of Appeals,
District of Columbia Circuit.

Argued Sept. 11, 1973.

Decided Oct. 12, 1973.

As amended Oct. 12 and Oct. 25, 1973.

I.

We deem it essential to emphasize the narrow contours of the problem that compels the Court to address the issues raised by this case. The central question before us is, in essence, whether the President may, in his sole discretion, withhold from a grand jury evidence in his possession that is relevant to the grand jury's investigations. It is our duty to respond to this question, but we limit our decision strictly to that required by the precise and entirely unique circumstances of the case.*

II.

In their petitions for relief, both the President and the Special Prosecutor invoke this court's statutory authority to issue "all writs necessary or appropriate in aid of" its jurisdiction.[12] As the Supreme Court has noted, the peremptory writ of mandamus, one of the group authorized by the All Writs Act, "has traditionally been used in the federal courts only 'to confine an inferior court to a lawful exercise of its prescribed jurisdiction or to compel it to exercise its authority when it is its duty to do so.' "[13] And although jurisdiction, for purposes of the writ, need not be defined in its narrow, technical sense, "it is clear that only exceptional circumstances amounting to a judicial 'usurpation of power' will

---

* The remainder of this section, with its accompanying notes, has been omitted.

justify the invocation of this extraordinary remedy."[14] Beyond these considerations, the writ may not be used as a substitute for an appeal, nor to subvert the general congressional policy against appeals from interlocutory orders,[15] a policy that is particularly strong in criminal cases.[16]

With these general parameters in mind, we turn first to the President's petition, which seeks to accommodate a well settled limitation on direct appeals challenging subpoenas. As recently restated by the Supreme Court, ordinarily "one to whom a sub-poena is directed may not appeal the denial of a motion to quash that subpoena but must either obey its commands or refuse to do so and contest the validity of the subpoena if he is subsequently cited for contempt on account of his failure to obey."[17] Contrary to the argument of the respondent Chief Judge, we see no basis for broadly differentiating an order to produce evidence for an *in camera* inspection to determine whether it is privileged from dis-closure to a grand jury.

From the viewpoint of mandamus, however, the central question that the President raises—whether the District Court exceeded its authority in ordering an *in camera* inspection of the tapes—is essentially jurisdictional.[18] It is, too, a jurisdictional problem of "first impression" involving a "basic, undecided ques-tion."[19] And if indeed the only avenue of direct appellate review open to the President requires that he first disobey the court's or-der, appeal seems to be "a clearly inadequate remedy."[20] These circumstances, we think, warrant the exercise, at the instance of the President, of our review power under the All Writs Act,[21] par-ticularly in light of the great public interest in prompt resolution of the issues that his petition presents.[22]

We find the Special Prosecutor's petition much more problematic.[23] The Supreme Court "has never approved the use of the writ to review"—at the instance of the Government—"an in-terlocutory procedural order in a criminal case which did not have the effect of a dismissal."[24] And while the Court has not de-cided "under what circumstances, if any, such a use of mandamus would be appropriate,"[25] we have grave doubt that it would be ap-propriate in this case. It is by no means clear that a writ directing the District Court to dispense with *in camera* inspection and or-der immediate production to the grand jury could fairly be char-acterized as aiding this court's jurisdiction, however non-technically jurisdiction might be defined.

Moreover, any resolution of the President's petition necessitates consideration of the validity of the projected *in camera* in-spection—the object of the Special Prosecutor's sole objection—and of the need for instructions governing any such inspection—the subject of his sole request in the alternative. In Schlagenhauf v. Holder,[26] the Supreme Court sustained the inher-ent power of the courts of appeals in special circumstances to re-

view by mandamus a "basic, undecided question,"[27] and "to settle
new and important problems."[28] Although one of the problems
raised in that case would not normally have justified an exercise
of mandamus authority, the Court recognized the propriety of
avoiding piecemeal litigation by resolving all issues arising out of
the same set of operative facts.[29] Surely the extraordinary importance of the issues that the Special Prosecutor tenders demands no
less.

Mandamus is generally withheld when relief is available
in another manner.[30] Our review of the President's contentions
will necessarily subsume the Special Prosecutor's present concerns.
Since we do not consider the question of jurisdiction of his petition essential to a full disposition of this consolidated proceeding,
we exercise our discretion[31] to dismiss the petition without deciding it.

III.

We turn, then, to the merits of the President's petition. Counsel
for the President contend on two grounds that Judge Sirica lacked
jurisdiction to order submission of the tapes for inspection. Counsel argue, first, that, so long as he remains in office, the President
is absolutely immune from the compulsory process of a court; and,
second, that Executive privilege is absolute with respect to
presidential communications, so that disclosure is at the sole
discretion of the President. This immunity and this absolute privilege are said to arise from the doctrine of separation of powers and
by implication from the Constitution itself. It is conceded that neither the immunity nor the privilege is express in the Constitution.

A.

It is clear that the want of physical power to enforce its
judgments does not prevent a court from deciding an otherwise
justiciable case.[32] Nevertheless, if it is true that the President is legally immune from court process, this case is at an end. The judiciary will not, indeed cannot, indulge in rendering an opinion to
which the President has no legal duty to conform. We must therefore, determine whether the President is *legally* bound to comply
with an order enforcing a subpoena.[33]
We note first that courts have assumed that they have the
power to enter mandatory orders to Executive officials to compel
production of evidence.[34] While a claim of an absolute Executive
immunity may not have been raised directly before these courts,
there is no indication that they entertained any doubts of their
power. Only last term in Environmental Protection Agency v.
Mink,[35] the Supreme Court stated that a District Court "may or-

der" *in camera* inspections of certain materials to determine
whether they must be disclosed to the public pursuant to the
Freedom of Information Act.[36]

The courts' assumption of legal power to compel production of
evidence within the possession of the Executive surely stands on
firm footing. Youngstown Sheet & Tube Co. v. Sawyer,[37] in which
an injunction running against the Secretary of Commerce was affirmed, is only the most celebrated instance of the issuance of
compulsory process against Executive officials. *See, e. g.*, United
States v. United States District Court, 407 U.S. 297, 92 S.Ct.
2125, 32 L.Ed.2d 752 (1972) (affirming an order requiring the
Government to make full disclosure of illegally wiretapped conversations); Kendall v. United States ex rel. Stokes, 37 U.S. (12
Pet.) 524, 9 L.Ed. 1181 (1828) (issuing a mandamus to Postmaster General, commanding him fully to comply with an act of
Congress); State Highway Commission v. Volpe, 479 F.2d 1099
(8th Cir. 1973) (enjoining the Secretary of Transportation).

It is true that, because the President has taken personal
custody of the tapes and is thus himself a party to the present action, these cases can be formally distinguished. As Judge Sirica
noted, however, to rule that this case turns on such a distinction
would be to exalt the form of *Youngstown Sheet & Tube* over its
substance. Justice Black, writing for the *Youngstown* majority,
made it clear that the Court understood its affirmance effectively
to restrain the President. There is not the slightest hint in any of
the *Youngstown* opinions that the case would have been viewed
differently if President Truman rather than Secretary Sawyer had
been the named party.[38] If *Youngstown* still stands, it must stand
for the case where the President has himself taken possession and
control of the property unconstitutionally seized, and the injunction would be framed accordingly. The practice of judicial review
would be rendered capricious—and very likely impotent—if jurisdiction vanished whenever the President personally denoted an
Executive action or omission as his own. This is not to say that
the President should lightly be named as a party defendant. As a
matter of comity, courts should normally direct legal process to a
lower Executive official even though the effect of the process is to
restrain or compel the President. Here, unfortunately, the court's
order must run directly to the President, because he has taken the
unusual step of assuming personal custody of the Government
property sought by the subpoena.

The President also attempts to distinguish United States
v. Burr,[39] in which Chief Justice Marshall squarely ruled that a
subpoena may be directed to the President. It is true that *Burr*
recognized a distinction between the issuance of a subpoena and
the ordering of compliance with that subpoena, but the distinction
did not concern judicial power or jurisdiction. A subpoena *duces
tecum* is an order to produce documents or to show-cause why

they need not be produced. An order to comply does not make the subpoena more compulsory; it simply maintains its original force. The Chief Justice's words merit close attention. His statement:

> Whatever difference may exist with respect to the power to compel the same obedience to the process, as if it had been directed to a private citizen, there exists no difference with respect to the right to obtain it[,]

is immediately followed by the statement:

> The guard, furnished to this high officer, to protect him from being harassed by *vexatious and unnecessary* subpoenas, is to be looked for in the conduct of a court after those subpoenas have issued; not in any circumstance which is to precede their being issued.[40]

The clear implication is that the President's special interests may warrant a careful judicial screening of subpoenas after the President interposes an objection, but that some subpoenas will nevertheless be properly sustained by judicial orders of compliance. This implication is borne out by a later opinion by the great Chief Justice in the same case. When President Jefferson did not fully respond to the subpoena issued to him, Colonel Burr inquired why the President should not comply. The Chief Justice's answer should put to rest any argument that he felt the President absolutely immune from orders of compliance:

> The president, although subject to the general rules which apply to others, may have sufficient motives for declining to produce a particular paper, and those motives *may be* such as to restrain the court from enforcing its production. * * * I can readily conceive that the president might receive a letter which it would be improper to exhibit in public * * *. The occasion for *demanding* it ought, in such a case, to be very strong, and to be fully shown to the court before its production could be *insisted* on. * * * Such a letter, though it be a private one, seems to partake of the character of an official paper, and to be such as ought not on *light ground* to be forced into public view.[41]

A compliance order was, for Marshall, distinct from an order to show cause simply because compliance was not to be ordered before weighing the President's particular reasons for wishing the subpoenaed documents to remain secret. The court was to show respect for the President in weighing those reasons, but the ultimate decision remained with the court.[42]

Thus, to find the President immune from judicial process, we must read out of *Burr* and *Youngstown* the underlying principles that the eminent jurists in each case thought they were establishing. The Constitution makes no mention of special presidential immunities. Indeed, the Executive Branch generally is afforded none. This silence cannot be ascribed to oversight. James Madison raised the question of Executive privileges during the Constitutional Convention,[43] and Senators and Representatives enjoy an express, if limited, immunity from arrest, and an express privilege from inquiry concerning "Speech and Debate" on the floors of Congress.[44] Lacking textual support, counsel for the President nonetheless would have us infer immunity from the President's political mandate, or from his vulnerability to impeachment, or from his broad discretionary powers. These are invitations to refashion the Constitution, and we reject them.

Though the President is elected by nationwide ballot, and is often said to represent all the people,[45] he does not embody the nation's sovereignty.[46] He is not above the law's commands: "With all its defects, delays and inconveniences, men have discovered no technique for long preserving free government except that the Executive be under the law . . . ."[47] Sovereignty remains at all times with the people, and they do not forfeit through elections the right to have the law construed against and applied to every citizen.

Nor does the Impeachment Clause imply immunity from routine court process.[48] While the President argues that the Clause means that impeachability precludes criminal prosecution of an incumbent, we see no need to explore this question except to note its irrelevance to the case before us. The order entered below, and approved here in modified form, is not a form of criminal process. Nor does it compete with the impeachment device by working a constructive removal of the President from office. The subpoena names in the alternate "any subordinate officer," and the tasks of compliance may obviously be delegated in whole or in part so as not to interfere with the President's official responsibilities.[49] By contemplating the possibility of post-impeachment trials for violations of law committed in office, the Impeachment Clause itself reveals that incumbency does not relieve the President of the routine legal obligations that confine all citizens. That the Impeachment Clause may qualify the court's power to sanction noncompliance with judicial orders is immaterial. Whatever the qualifications, they were equally present in *Youngstown*: Commerce Secretary Sawyer, the defendant there, was an impeachable "civil officer,"[50] but the injunction against him was nonetheless affirmed. The legality of judicial orders should not be confused with the legal consequences of their breach; for the courts in this country always assume that their orders will be obeyed, especially when addressed to responsible government officials. Indeed, the

President has, in this case, expressly abjured the course of setting himself above the law.

Finally, the President reminds us that the landmark decisions recognizing judicial power to mandamus Executive compliance with "ministerial" duties also acknowledged that the Executive Branch enjoys an unreviewable discretion in many areas of "political" or "executive" administration.[51] While true, this is irrelevant to the issue of presidential immunity from judicial process. The discretionary-ministerial distinction concerns the nature of the act or omission under review, not the official title of the defendant.[52] No case holds that an act is discretionary merely because the President is the actor.[53] If the Constitution or the laws of evidence confer upon the President the absolute discretion to withhold material subpoenaed by a grand jury, then of course we would vacate, rather than approve with modification, the order entered below. However, this would be because the order touched upon matters within the President's sole discretion, not because the President is immune from process generally. We thus turn to an examination of the President's claim of an absolute discretion to withhold evidence from a grand jury.

B.

There is, as the Supreme Court has said, a "longstanding principle" that the grand jury "has a right to every man's evidence" except that "protected by a constitutional, common law, or statutory privilege."[54] The President concedes the validity of this principle. He concedes that he, like every other citizen, is under a legal duty to produce relevant, non-privileged evidence when called upon to do so.[55] The President contends, however, that whenever, in response to a grand jury subpoena, he interposes a formal claim of privilege, that claim without more disables the courts from inquiring by any means into whether the privilege is applicable to the subpoenaed evidence. The President agrees that, in theory, the privilege attached to his office has limits; for example, he explicitly states that it "cannot be claimed to shield executive officers from prosecution for crime."[56] Nonetheless, he argues that it is his responsibility, and his alone, to determine whether particular information falls beyond the scope of the privilege. In effect, then, the President claims that, at least with respect to conversations with his advisers, the privilege is absolute, since he, rather than the courts, has final authority to decide whether it applies in the circumstances.

We of course acknowledge the longstanding judicial recognition of Executive privilege. Courts have appreciated that the public interest in maintaining the secrecy of military and diplomatic plans may override private interests in litigation.[57] They have further responded to Executive pleas to protect from the light of litigation "intra-governmental documents reflecting * * * deliberations comprising part of a process by which governmental decisions and policies are formulated."[58] In so doing, the Judiciary has been sensitive to the considerations upon which the President seems to rest his claim of absolute privilege: the candor of Executive aides and functionaries would be impaired if they were persistently worried that their advice and deliberations were later to be made public.[59] However, counsel for the President can point to no case in which a court has accepted the Executive's mere assertion of privilege as sufficient to overcome the need of the party subpoenaing the documents. To the contrary, the courts have repeatedly asserted that the applicability of the privilege is in the end for them and not the Executive to decide.[60] They have, moreover, frequently ordered in camera inspection of documents for which a privilege was asserted in order to determine the privilege's applicability.[61]

It is true, as counsel for the President stress, that Presidents and Attorneys General have often said that the President's final and absolute assertion of Executive privilege is conclusive on the courts.[62] The Supreme Court in United States v. Reynolds, however, went a long way toward putting this view to rest. The Reynolds Court, considering a claim based on military secrets, strongly asserted: "The court itself must determine whether the circumstances are appropriate for the claim of privilege;"[63] "judicial control over the evidence in a case cannot be abdicated to the caprice of executive officers."[64] It is true that, somewhat inconsistently with this sweeping language, the Court formally reserved decision on the Government's claim that the Executive has an absolute discretion constitutionally founded in separation of powers to withhold documents.[65] However, last term in Committee for Nuclear Responsibility, Inc. v. Seaborg,[66] we confronted directly a claim of absolute privilege and rejected it: "Any claim to executive absolutism cannot override the duty of the court to assure that an official has not exceeded his charter or flouted the legislative will."[67]

We adhere to the Seaborg decision. To do otherwise would be effectively to ignore the clear words of Marbury v. Madison,[68] that "[i]t is emphatically the province and duty of the judicial department to say what the law is."[69]

Seaborg is not only consistent with, but dictated by, separation of powers doctrine. Whenever a privilege is asserted, even one expressed in the Constitution, such as the Speech and Debate privilege, it is the courts that determine the validity of the assertion and the scope of the privilege.[70] That the privilege is being asserted by the President against a grand jury subpoena does not make the task of resolving the conflicting claims any less judicial in nature. Throughout our history, there have frequently been conflicts between independent organs of the federal government as well as between the state and federal governments. When such conflicts arise in justiciable cases, our constitutional system provides a means for resolving them—one Supreme Court. To leave the proper scope and application of Executive privilege to the President's sole discretion would represent a mixing, rather than a separation, of Executive and Judicial functions. A breach in the separation of powers must be explicitly authorized by the Constitution,[71] or be shown necessary to the harmonious operation of "workable government."[72] Neither condition is met here. The Constitution mentions no Executive privileges, much less any absolute Executive privileges. Nor is an absolute privilege required for workable government. We acknowledge that wholesale public access to Executive deliberations and documents would cripple the Executive as a co-equal branch. But this is an argument for recognizing Executive privilege and for according it great weight, not for making the Executive the judge of its own privilege.

If the claim of absolute privilege was recognized, its mere invocation by the President or his surrogates could deny access to all documents in all the Executive departments to all citizens and their representatives, including Congress, the courts as well as grand juries, state governments, state officials and all state subdivisions. The Freedom of Information Act could become nothing more than a legislative statement of unenforceable rights. Support for this kind of mischief simply cannot be spun from incantation of the doctrine of separation of powers.[73]

Any contention of the President that records of his personal conversation are not covered by the *Seaborg* holding must be rejected. As our prior discussion of United States v. Burr makes clear, Chief Justice Marshall's position supports this proposition. At issue in *Burr* was a subpoena to President Jefferson to produce private letters sent to him—communications whose status must be considered equal to that of private oral conversations. We follow the Chief Justice and hold today that, although the views of the Chief Executive on whether his Executive privilege should obtain are properly given the greatest weight and deference, they cannot be conclusive.

IV.

The President's privilege cannot, therefore, be deemed absolute. We think the *Burr* case makes clear that application of Executive privilege depends on a weighing of the public interest protected by the privilege against the public interests that would be served by disclosure in a particular case.[74] We direct our attention, however, solely to the circumstances here. With the possible exception of material on one tape, the President does not assert that the subpoenaed items involve military or state secrets;[75] nor is the asserted privilege directed to the particular kinds of information that the tapes contain. Instead, the President asserts that the tapes should be deemed privileged because of the great public interest in maintaining the confidentiality of conversations that take place in the President's performance of his official duties. The privilege, intended to protect the effectiveness of the executive decision-making process, is analogous to that between a congressman and his aides under the Speech and Debate Clause; to that among judges, and between judges and their law clerks;[76] and similar to that contained in the fifth exemption to the Freedom of Information Act.[77]

We recognize this great public interest, and agree with the District Court that such conversations are presumptively privileged.[78] But we think that this presumption of privilege premised on the public interest in confidentiality must fail in the face of the uniquely powerful showing made by the Special Prosecutor in this case. The function of the grand jury, mandated by the Fifth Amendment for the institution of federal criminal prosecutions for capital or other serious crimes, is not only to indict persons when there is probable cause to believe they have committed crime, but also to protect persons from prosecution when probable cause does not exist.[79] As we have noted, the Special Prosecutor has made a strong showing that the subpoenaed tapes contain evidence peculiarly necessary to the carrying out of this vital function—evidence for which no effective substitute is available. The grand jury here is not engaged in a general fishing expedition, nor does it seek in any way to investigate the wisdom of the President's discharge of his discretionary duties. On the contrary, the grand jury seeks evidence that may well be conclusive to its decisions in on-going investigations that are entirely within the proper scope of its authority. In these circumstances, what we said in Committee for Nuclear Responsibility v. Seaborg becomes, we think, particularly appropriate:

But no executive official or agency can be given absolute authority to determine what documents in his possession may be considered by the court in its task. Otherwise the head of an executive department would have the power on his own say so to cover up all evidence of fraud and corruption when a federal court or grand jury was investigating malfeasance in office, and this is not the law.[80]

Our conclusion that the general confidentiality privilege must recede before the grand jury's showing of need, is established by the unique circumstances that made this showing possible. In his public statement of May 22, 1973, the President said: "Executive privilege will not be invoked as to any testimony concerning possible criminal conduct or discussions of possible criminal conduct, in the matters presently under investigation, including the Watergate affair and the alleged cover-up."[81] We think that this statement and its consequences may properly be considered as at least one factor in striking the balance in this case. Indeed, it affects the weight we give to factors on both sides of the scale. On the one hand, the President's action presumably reflects a judgment by him that the interest in the confidentiality of White House discussions in general is outweighed by such matters as the public interest, stressed by the Special Prosecutor, in the integrity of the level of the Executive Branch closest to the President, and the public interest in the integrity of the electoral process—an interest stressed in such cases as Civil Service Commission v. National Association of Letter Carriers[82] and United States v. United Automobile Workers.[83] Although this judgment in no way controls our decision, we think it supports our estimation of the great public interest that attaches to the effective functioning of the present grand jury. As Burr makes clear, the courts approach their function by considering the President's reasons and determinations concerning confidentiality.

At the same time, the public testimony given consequent to the President's decision substantially diminishes the interest in maintaining the confidentialty of conversations pertinent to Watergate. The simple fact is that the conversations are no longer confidential. Where it is proper to testify about oral conversations, taped recordings of those conversations are admissible as probative and corroborative of the truth concerning the testimony.[84] There is no "constitutional right to rely on possible flaws in the [witness's] memory. * * * [N]o other argument can justify excluding an accurate version of a conversation that the [witness] could testify to from memory."[85] In short, we see no justification, no confidentiality grounds, for depriving the grand jury of the best evidence of the conversations available.[86]

The District Court stated that, in determining the applicability of privilege, it was not controlled by the President's assurance that the conversations in question occurred pursuant to an exercise of his constitutional duty to "take care that the laws be faithfully executed." The District Court further stated that while the President's claim would not be rejected on any but the strongest possible evidence, the Court was unable to decide the question of privilege without inspecting the tapes.[87] This passage of the District Court's opinion is not entirely clear. If, however, the District Judge meant that rejection of the claim of privilege requires a finding that the President was not engaged in the performance of his constitutional duty, we cannot agree. We emphasize that the grand jury's showing of need in no sense relied on any evidence that the President was involved in, or even aware of, any alleged criminal activity. We freely assume, for purposes of this opinion, that the President was engaged in performance of his constitutional duty. Nonetheless, we hold that the District Court may order disclosure of all portions of the tapes relevant to matters within the proper scope of the grand jury's investigations, unless the Court judges that the public interest served by nondisclosure of *particular* statements or information outweighs the need for that information demonstrated by the grand jury.

V.

The question remains whether, in the circumstances of this case, the District Court was correct in ordering the tapes produced for *in camera* inspection, so that it could determine whether and to what extent the privilege was properly claimed. Since the question of privilege must be resolved by the Court, there must be devised some procedure or series of procedures that will, at once, allow resolution of the question and, at the same time, not harm the interests that the privilege is intended to protect.

Two days after oral argument, this Court issued a Memorandum calling on the parties and counsel to hold conversations toward the objective of avoiding a needless constitutional adjudication. Counsel reported that their sincere efforts had not been fruitful.[88] It is our hope that our action in providing what has become an unavoidable constitutional ruling, and in approving, as modified, the order of the District Court, will be followed by maximum cooperation among the parties. Perhaps the President will find it possible to reach some agreement with the Special Prosecutor as to what portions of the subpoenaed evidence are necessary to the grand jury's task.

Should our hope prove unavailing, we think that *in camera* inspection is a necessary and appropriate method of protecting the grand jury's interest in securing relevant evidence. The exception that we have delineated to the President's confidentiality privilege depends entirely on the grand jury's showing that the evidence is directly relevant to its decisions. The residual problem of this case derives from the possibility that there are elements of the subpoenaed recordings that do not lie within the range of the exception that we have defined.

This may be due, in part, to the fact that parts of the tape recordings do not relate to Watergate matters at all. What is apparently more stressed by the President's counsel is that there are items in the tape recordings that should be held confidential yet are inextricably interspersed with the portions that relate to Watergate. They say, concerning the President's decision to permit testimony about possible criminal conduct or discussions thereof, that testimony can be confined to the relevant portions of the conversations and can be limited to matters that do not endanger national security. Recordings cannot be so confined and limited, and thus the President has concluded that to produce the recordings would do serious damage to Presidential privacy and to the ability of that office to function.[89]

The argument is not confined to matters of national security, for the underlying importance of preserving candor of discussion and Presidential privacy pertains to all conversations that involve discussion or making policy, ordinary domestic policies as well as matters of national security, and even to personal discussion with friends and advisers on seemingly trivial matters.[90] Concerning the inextricability problem, the President's counsel say:

Recordings are the raw material of life. By their very nature they contain spontaneous, informal, tentative and frequently pungent comments on a variety of subjects inextricably intertwined into one conversation. * * * The nature of informal, private conversations is such that it is not practical to separate what is arguably relevant from what is clearly irrelevant.[91]

The "inextricable intermingling" issue may be potentially significant. The District Court correctly discerned that *in camera* inspection is permissible, even though it involved what the President's counsel agree is a "limited infraction" of confidentiality, in order to determine whether there is inextricable intermingling. In EPA v. Mink, the Supreme Court declared that *in camera* inspection was an appropriate means of determining whether and to what extent documents sought in litigation were disclosable as factual information even though the Government argued that the documents "submitted directly to the President by top-level Government officials" were, by their very nature, a blending of factual presentation and policy recommendations that are necessarily "inextricably intertwined with policymaking processes."[92] The Supreme Court stated that it had no reason to believe that the District Judge directed to make *in camera* inspection "would go beyond the limits of the remand and in any way compromise the confidentiality of deliberative information." The Court acknowledged that "the encouragement of open expression of opinion as to governmental policy is somewhat impaired by a requirement to submit the evidence even [*in camera*]." Yet the Court stated: "Plainly, in some situations, *in camera* inspection will be necessary and appropriate."[93] It further noted: "A representative document of those sought may be selected for *in camera* inspection." And it suggested that the agency may disclose portions of the contested documents and attempt to show, by circumstances, "that the excised portions constitute the barebones of protected matter."[94]

In this case, the line of permissible disclosure is different from that in *Mink*, since even policy and decisional discussions are disclosable if they relate to Watergate and the alleged cover-up. But *Mink* confirms that courts appropriately examine a disputed item *in camera*, even though this necessarily involves a limited intrusion upon what ultimately may be held confidential, where it appears with reasonable clarity that some access is appropriate, and *in camera* inspection is needed to determine what should and what should not be revealed.[95]

Mink noted that the case might proceed by the Government's disclosing portions of the contested documents,[96] and also noted an instance in which the "United States offered to file 'an abstract of factual information.' contained in the contested documents (FBI reports)."[97] We think that the District Judge and counsel can illuminate the key issue of what is "inextricable" by cultivating the partial excision and "factual abstract" approaches noted in *Mink*.

The District Court contemplated that "privileged portions may be excised so that only unprivileged matter goes before the grand jury." Even in a case of such intermingling as, for example, comment on Watergate matters that is "pungent," once counsel, or the District Judge, has listened to the tape recording of a conversation, he has an ability to present only its relevant portions, much like a bystander who heard the conversation and is called to testify. He may give the grand jury portions relevant to Watergate, by using excerpts in part and summaries in part, in such a way as not to divulge aspects that reflect the pungency of candor or are otherwise entitled to confidential treatment. It is not so long ago that appellate courts routinely decided cases without an exact transcript, but on an order of the trial judge setting what was given as evidence.

VI.

We contemplate a procedure in the District Court, following the issuance of our mandate, that follows the path delineated in *Reynolds, Mink,* and by this Court in Vaughn v. Rosen.[98] With the rejection of his all-embracing claim of prerogative, the President will have an opportunity to present more particular claims of privilege, if accompanied by an analysis in manageable segments.

Without compromising the confidentiality of the information, the analysis should contain descriptions specific enough to identify the basis of the particular claim or claims.

1. In so far as the President makes a claim that certain material may not be disclosed because the subject matter relates to national defense or foreign relations, he may decline to transmit that portion of the material and ask the District Court to reconsider whether *in camera* inspection of the material is necessary. The Special Prosecutor is entitled to inspect the claim and showing and may be heard thereon, in chambers. If the judge sustains the privilege, the text of the government's statement will be preserved in the Court's record under seal.

2. The President will present to the District Court all other items covered by the order, with specification of which segments he believes may be disclosed and which not. This can be accomplished by itemizing and indexing the material, and correlating indexed items with particular claims of privilege.[99] On request of either counsel, the District Court shall hold a hearing in chambers on the claims. Thereafter the Court shall itself inspect the disputed items.

Given the nature of the inquiry that this inspection involves, the District Court may give the Special Prosecutor access to the material for the limited purpose of aiding the Court in determining the relevance of the material to the grand jury's investigations. Counsels' arguments directed to the specifics of the portions of material in dispute may help the District Court immeasurably in making its difficult and necessarily detailed decisions. Moreover, the preliminary indexing will have eliminated any danger of disclosing peculiarly sensitive national security matters. And, here, any concern over confidentiality is minimized by the Attorney General's designation of a distinguished and reflective counsel as Special Prosecutor. If, however, the Court decides to allow access to the Special Prosecutor, it should, upon request, stay its action in order to allow sufficient time for application for a stay to this Court.

Following the *in camera* hearing and inspection, the District Court may determine as to any items (a) to allow the particular claim of privilege in full; (b) to order disclosure to the grand jury of all or a segment of the item or items; or, when segmentation is impossible, (c) to fashion a complete statement for the grand jury of those portions of an item that bear on possible criminality. The District Court shall provide a reasonable stay to allow the President an opportunity to appeal.[100] In case of an appeal to this Court of an order either allowing or refusing disclosure, this Court will provide for sealed records and confidentiality in presentation.

VII.

We end, as we began, by emphasizing the extraordinary nature of this case. We have attempted to decide no more than the problem before us—a problem that takes its unique shape from the grand jury's compelling showing of need.[101] The procedures we have provided require thorough deliberation by the District Court before even this need may be satisfied. Opportunity for appeal, on a sealed record, is assured.

We cannot, therefore, agree with the assertion of the President that the District Court's order threatens "the continued existence of the Presidency as a functioning institution."[102] As we view the case, the order represents an unusual and limited requirement that the President produce material evidence. We think this required by law, and by the rule that even the Chief Executive is subject to the mandate of the law when he has no valid claim of privilege.

The petition and appeal of the United States are dismissed. The President's petition is denied, except in so far as we direct the District Court to modify its order and to conduct further proceedings in a manner not inconsistent with this opinion.

The issuance of our mandate is stayed for five days to permit the seeking of Supreme Court review of the issues with which we have dealt in making our decision.

So ordered.

12. "The Supreme Court and all courts established by Act of Congress may issue all writs necessary or appropriate in aid of their respective jurisdictions and agreeable to the usages and principles of law." 28 U.S.C. § 1651(a) (1970).

13. Will v. United States, 389 U.S. 90, 95, 88 S.Ct. 269, 273, 19 L.Ed.2d 305 (1967), *quoting* Roche v. Evaporated Milk Ass'n, 319 U.S. 21, 26, 63 S.Ct. 938, 87 L.Ed. 1185 (1943). For a full discussion of the general rules governing our authority to issue the writ, *see* Donnelly v. Parker, 158 U.S.App. D.C. 335, 338, 340–343, 486 F.2d 402, 405, 407–410 (1973).

14. Will v. United States, *supra* note 13, 389 U.S. at 95, 88 S.Ct. at 273, *quoting* De Beers Consol. Mines v. United States, 325 U.S. 212, 217, 65 S.Ct. 1130, 89 L.Ed. 1566 (1945).

Opinions by Circuit Judge MacKinnon, concurring in part and dissenting in part, and Circuit Judge Wilkey concurring in part and dissenting in part, are omitted.

15. Parr v. United States, 351 U.S. 513, 520–521, 76 S.Ct. 912, 100 L.Ed. 1377 (1956).

16. Will v. United States, *supra* note 13, 389 U.S. at 96–98, 88 S.Ct. 269.

17. United States v. Ryan, 402 U.S. 530, 532, 91 S.Ct. 1580, 1581, 29 L.Ed.2d 85 (1971). *See also* Cobbledick v. United States, 309 U.S. 323, 60 S.Ct. 540, 84 L.Ed. 783 (1940). *But see* Carr v. Monroe Mfg. Co., 431 F.2d 384 (5th Cir. 1970).

18. *Compare* Schlagenhauf v. Holder, 379 U.S. 104, 110–111, 85 S.Ct. 234, 13 L.Ed.2d 152 (1964).

19. *Id.*

20. Bankers Life & Cas. Co. v. Holland, 346 U.S. 379, 385, 74 S.Ct. 145, 98 L.Ed. 106 (1953), *quoting* Ex parte Fahey, 332 U.S. 258, 260, 67 S.Ct. 1558, 91 L.Ed. 2041 (1947).

21. In so concluding, we do not discard the direct appeal as an alternative basis for review in the particular situation before us. The final-order doctrine, as a normal prerequisite to a federal appeal, is not a barrier where it operates to leave the suitor "powerless to avert the mischief of the order." Perlman v. United States, 247 U.S. 7, 13, 38 S.Ct. 417, 419, 62 L.Ed. 950 (1918). In the case of the President, contempt of a judicial order—even for the purpose of enabling a constitutional test of the order—would be a course unseemly at best. To safeguard against any possible miscarriage of justice, we make known our view that our jurisdiction exists by way of appeal if for any reason the President's application is not properly before us on the jurisdictional predicate he invokes.

22. *See* United States v. United States District Court, 444 F.2d 651, 655–656 (6th Cir. 1971), aff'd, 407 U.S. 297, 301, n.3, 92 S.Ct. 2125, 32 L.Ed.2d 752 (1972).

23. We think it clear, in any event, that the District Court's August 29th order is unappealable at the instance of the Special Prosecutor, either under 28 U.S.C. § 1291 or § 1292 (1970). In addition, since the order in no way finally decides that any of the subpoenaed material must be denied the grand jury, it cannot be deemed an order "suppressing or excluding evidence," or otherwise within the contemplation of the Criminal Appeals Act, 18 U.S.C. § 3731 (1970). *But see* note 100, *infra.*

24. Will v. United States, *supra* note 13, 389 U.S. at 98, 88 S.Ct. at 275.

25. *Id.*

26. *Supra* note 18.

27. *Supra* note 18, 379 U.S. at 110, 85 S.Ct. 234.

28. *Id.* at 111, 85 S.Ct. at 239.

29. *Id.*

30. *See* Ex parte Republic of Peru, 318 U.S. 578, 584, 63 S.Ct. 793, 87 L.Ed. 1014 (1943).

31. *See, e.g.,* Ex parte Skinner & Eddy Corp., 265 U.S. 86, 95–

96, 44 S.Ct. 446, 68 L.Ed. 912 (1924).

32. Glidden v. Zdanok, 370 U.S. 530, 568–571, 82 S.Ct. 1459, 8 L.Ed.2d 671 (1962); Baker v. Carr, 369 U.S. 186, 208–237, 82 S.Ct. 691, 7 L.Ed.2d 663 (1962). *See also* South Dakota v. North Carolina, 192 U.S. 286, 318–321, 24 S.Ct. 269, 48 L.Ed. 448 (1904); La Abra Silver Mining Co. v. United States, 175 U.S. 423, 461–462, 20 S.Ct. 168, 44 L.Ed. 223 (1898).

33. If the judiciary's want of *de facto* power to enforce its judgment has any relevance, it is that the third branch of government, posing little physical threat to coordinate branches, need not hesitate to reject sweeping claims to *legal* immunity by those coordinate branches. *See* United States v. Lee, 106 U.S. (16 Otto) 196, 223, 1 S.Ct. 240, 27 L.Ed. 171 (1882).

34. *See, e. g.,* United States ex rel. Touhy v. Ragen, 340 U.S. 462, 465–466, 472, 71 S.Ct. 416, 95 L.Ed. 417 (1951) (Frankfurter, J., concurring); Westinghouse Electric Corp. v. City of Burlington, Vermont, 122 U.S.App. D.C. 65, 351 F.2d 762 (1965); Boeing Airplane Co. v. Coggeshall, 108 U.S.App.D.C. 106, 280 F.2d 654 (1960).

35. 410 U.S. 73, 93, 93 S.Ct. 827, 35 L.Ed.2d 119 (1973).

36. *See* text at notes 92–97 *infra*

37. 343 U.S. 579, 72 S.Ct. 863, 96 L.Ed. 1153 (1952).

38. In Land v. Dollar, 89 U.S.App.D.C. 38, 190 F.2d 623 (1951), vacated as moot, 344 U.S. 806, 73 S.Ct. 7, 97 L.Ed. 628 (1952), as well, it was clear that the court realized that its order countered the executive will of the President. The *Land* court acknowledged that the President had directed the cabinet officials to disregard the initial judicial decision. *Id.* at 54, 190 F.2d at 639.

39. 25 Fed.Cas. p. 30 (Case No. 14,692d) (1807).

40. *Id. at 34.* (Emphasis supplied.)

41. United States v. Burr, 25 Fed.Cas. pp. 187, 190, 191–192 (Case No. 14,694) (1807). (Emphases supplied.)

42. In 1818, several years after the *Burr* case, a subpoena was also issued to President James Monroe. It summoned the President to appear as a defense witness in the court martial of Dr. William Burton, naming a specific date and time. A copy of the summons is in Attorney General's Papers: Letters received from State Department, Record Group 60, National Archives Building. Attorney General Wirt advised Monroe, through Secretary of State John Quincy Adams, that a subpoena could "properly be awarded to the President of the United States," but suggested that the President indicate on the return that his official duties precluded a personal appearance at the court martial. William Wirt to John Quincy Adams, Jan. 13, 1818, Records of the Office of the Judge Advocate General (Navy), Record Group 125, (Records of General Courts Martial and Courts of Inquiry, Microcopy M-272, case 282), National Archives Building. In conformance with this advice, Monroe wrote on the back of the summons that he would "be ready and willing to communicate, in the form of a deposition any information I may possess, relating to the subject matter in question." President James Monroe to George M. Dallas, Jan. 21, 1818, *id.* Subsequently, President Monroe did in fact submit answers to the interrogatories forwarded to him by the court. President James Monroe to George M. Dallas, Feb. 14, 1818, *id.*

43. 11 Farrand. The Records of the Federal Convention of 1787, 502–503 (1967).

44. U.S.Const., art. I, § 6, ¶ 1.

45. Myers v. United States, 272 U.S. 52, 123, 47 S.Ct. 21, 71 L.Ed. 160 (1926).

46. *See, e. g.,* United States v. Burr, *supra* note 39, 25 Fed.Cas. at 34.

47. Youngstown Sheet & Tube Co. v. Sawyer, *supra* note 37, 343 U.S. at 655, 72 S.Ct. at 880 (1952) (Jackson, J., concurring).

48. U.S.Const., art. I, § 3, ¶ 7:
Judgment in Cases of Impeachment shall not extend further than to removal from Office, and disqualification to and enjoy any Office of Honor, Trust or Profit under the United States: but the Party convicted shall nevertheless be liable and subject to Indictment, Trial, Judgment and Punishment, according to Law.

49. On this point, too, Chief Justice Marshall was instructive:
If, upon any principle, the president could be construed to stand exempt from the general provisions of the constitution, it would be, because his duties as chief magistrate demand his whole time for national objects. But it is apparent that this demand is not unremitting.
United States v. Burr, *supra* note 39, 25 Fed. Cas. at 34.

50. Because impeachment is available against all "civil Officers of the United States," not merely against the President, U.S.Const. art. II, § 4, it is difficult to understand how any immunities peculiar to the President can emanate by implication from the fact of impeachability.

51. *See, e. g.,* Marbury v. Madison, 5 U.S. (1 Cranch) 137, 165, 2 L.Ed. 60 (1803); Kendall v. United States ex rel. Stokes, 37 U.S. (12 Pet.) 524, 610, 9 L.Ed. 1181 (1838).

52. [T]he question, whether the legality of an act of the head of a department be examinable in a court of justice or not, must always depend on the nature of that act.
Marbury v. Madison, *supra* note 51, 5 U.S. (1 Cranch) at 165. The mandamus does not seek to direct or control the postmaster general in the discharge of any official duty, partaking in any respect of any executive character; but to

enforce the performance of a mere ministerial act, which
neither he *nor the President* had any authority to deny or
control.

>   Kendall v. United States ex rel. Stokes, *supra* note 51, 37
>   U.S. (12 Pet.) at 610. (Emphasis supplied.)

53. In this regard, the President's reliance on Mississippi v.
Johnson, 71 U.S. (4 Wall.) 475, 18 L.Ed. 437 (1866), is mis-
placed. In that case, the State of Mississippi sought to enjoin
President Johnson from enforcing the Reconstruction Acts.
Though Attorney General Stanbery argued that the President
was immune from judicial process, the Court declined to
found its decision on this ground, choosing instead to deny
the bill of injunction as an attempt to coerce a discretionary,
as opposed to ministerial, act of the Executive. The Attorney
General rehearsed many of the arguments made by the
President in this case, claiming that the President's dignity as
Chief of State placed him above the reach of routine judicial
process and that the President was subject only to that law
which might be fashioned in a court of impeachment. *Id.* at
484. We deem it significant that the Supreme Court declined
to ratify these views. *Compare* Georgia v. Stanton, 73 U.S. (6
Wall.) 50, 18 L.Ed. 721 (1867), where the Court declined jurisdiction of a similar bill of injunction even though sub-
presidential Executive Branch officials were named as
defendants.

54. Branzburg v. Hayes, 408 U.S. 665, 688, 92 S.Ct. 2646, 2660,
33 L.Ed.2d 626 (1972). We reject the contention, pressed by
counsel for the President, that the Executive's prosecutorial
discretion implies an unreviewable power to withhold evidence relevant to a grand jury's criminal investigation. The
federal grand jury is a constitutional fixture in its own right,
legally independent of the Executive. *See* United States v.
Johnson, 319 U.S. 503, 510, 63 S.Ct. 1233, 87 L.Ed. 1546
(1943). A grand jury may, with the aid of judicial process,
Brown v. United States, 359 U.S. 41, 49–50, 79 S.Ct. 539, 3
L.Ed.2d 609 (1959), call witnesses and demand evidence
without the Executive's impetus. Hale v. Henkel, 201 U.S. 43,
60–65, 26 S.Ct. 370, 50 L.Ed. 652 (1906). If the grand jury
were a legal appendage of the Executive, it could hardly serve
its historic functions as a shield for the innocent and a sword
against corruption in high places. In his eloquent affirmation
of unfettered prosecutorial discretion in United States v. Cox,
342 F.2d 167, 189 (5th Cir.), cert. denied, 381 U.S. 935, 85
S.Ct. 1767, 14 L.Ed.2d 700 (1965), Judge Wisdom recognized
the grand jury's independent and "plenary power to inquire,
to summon and interrogate witnesses, and to present either
findings and a report or an accusation in open court by
presentment." As a *practical*, as opposed to legal matter, the

Executive may, of course, cripple a grand jury investigation
by denying staff assistance to the jury. And the Executive
may refuse to sign an indictment, thus precluding prosecution
and, presumably, effecting a permanent sealing of the grand
jury minutes. United States v. Cox, *supra*. These choices remain open to the President. But it is he who must exercise
them. The court will not assume that burden by eviscerating
the grand jury's independent legal authority.

55. Brief of Petitioner Nixon at 84; Reply Brief of Petitioner,
    Nixon at 30 n.6.

56. Brief of Petitioner Nixon at 69; citing Gravel v. United
    States, 408 U.S. 606, 627, 92 S.Ct. 2614, 33 L.Ed.2d 583
    (1972).

57. Totten v. United States, 92 U.S. 105, 23 L.Ed. 605 (1875);
    United States v. Reynolds, 345 U.S. 1, 73 S.Ct. 528, 97 L.Ed.
    727 (1953); United States v. Burr, *supra* note 39.

58. Carl Zeiss Stiftung v. V.E.B. Carl Zeiss, Jena, 40 F.R.D.
    318, 324 (D.C.D.C.1966), aff'd on opinion below, 128
    U.S.App.D.C. 10, 384 F.2d 979, cert. denied, 389 U.S. 952,
    88 S.Ct. 334, 19 L.Ed. 2d 361 (1967).

59. *See, e. g., id.* 40 F.R.D. at 329–335; Kaiser Aluminum &
    Chemical Corp. v. United States, 157 F.Supp. 939, 141 Ct.Cl.
    38 (1958).

60. *See, e. g.,* United States v. Reynolds, *supra* note 57; Olson
    Rug Co. v. NLRB, 291 F.2d 655 (7th Cir. 1961); Timken
    Roller Bearing Co. v. United States, 38 F.R.D. 57 (N.D.Ohio
    1964); United States v. Procter & Gamble Co., 25 F.R.D. 485
    (D.N.J.1960); Kaiser Aluminum & Chemical Corp. v. United
    States, *supra* note 59; *see also* the cases cited at 8 C. Wright
    & A. Miller, Federal Practice & Procedure 167–173 (1970).
    Despite our peculiar constitutional tradition of judicial review,
    American law is not in fact unusual in subjecting claims of
    Executive privilege to court scrutiny. Indeed, no common law
    country follows the rule, urged by the President in this case,
    that mere executive assertions of privilege are conclusive on
    the courts. In Conway v. Rimmer, [1968] 1 A11 E.R. 874,
    the House of Lords explicitly reversed its long held view, as
    expressed in Duncan v. Cammell Laird & Co., [1842] 1 A11
    E.R. 587, that executive privilege is absolute. *Conway* held
    that proper adjudication of a privilege claim may require *in
    camera* inspection of documents over which the privilege is
    asserted. [1968] 1 A11 E.R. at 888 (opinion of Lord Reid),
    and 896 (opinion of Lord Morris of Borth-y-Gest). Similar
    recognition of judicial power to scrutinize claims of privilege
    may be found in almost every common law jurisdiction. *See,
    e. g.,* Robinson v. South Australia (No. 2), [1931] A11 E.R.
    333 (P.C.); Gagnon v. Quebec Securities Comm'n, [1965] 50
    D.L. R.2d 329 (1964); Bruce v. Waldron, [1963] Viet.L.R.

3; Corbett v. Social Security Comm'n, [1962] N.Z.L.R. 878; Amar Chand Butail v. Union of India, [1965] 1 India S.Ct. 243.

61. In Environmental Protection Agency v. Mink, *supra* note 35, the Supreme Court relied on cases in which claims of Executive privilege were reviewed by the court, often *in camera*, in interpreting how the judiciary should apply the intragovernmental communication exemption to the public disclosure mandate of the Freedom of Information Act. *Id.* at 88 & cases cited at notes 14 & 15.

62. *See, e. g.*, 40 Op.Atty.Gen. 45, 49 (1941) (Attorney General Jackson); 100 Cong.Rec. 6621 (1954) (President Eisenhower).

63. *Supra* note 57, 345 U.S. at 8, 73 S.Ct. at 532.

64. *Id.* at 9–10, 73 S.Ct. at 533.

65. *Id.* at 6 & note 9, 73 S.Ct. 528.

66. 149 U.S.App.D.C. 385, 463 F.2d 788 (1971).

67. *Id.* at 390, 463 F.2d at 793.

68. *Supra* note 51, 5 U.S. (1 Cranch) at 157.

69. The purpose of the explicit constitutional privilege against self-incrimination, like that of Executive privilege, is defeated by too much judicial inquiry into the legitimacy of its use, *see* United States v. Reynolds, *supra* note 57, 345 U.S. at 3–9, 73 S.Ct. 528, but the courts have never held the mere invocation of the privilege to be sufficient to free the invoker from questioning. The judge msut first determine whether the privilege is properly invoked. *See, e. g.*, Hoffman v. United States, 341 U.S. 479, 486–487, 71 S.Ct. 814, 95 L.Ed. 1118 (1951).

70. The Supreme Court has repeatedly made clear that it is for the courts to determine the reach of the Speech and Debate Clause, U.S.Const. Art. I, § 6, ¶ 1. *See, e. g.*, Gravel v. United States, *supra* note 56; United States v. Brewster, 408 U.S. 501, 92 S.Ct. 2531, 33 L.Ed.2d 507 (1972); United States v. Johnson, *supra* note 54. Indeed, very close judicial review is needed to determine whether the activities concerning which questioning or prosecution is sought are:

> integral part[s] of the deliberative and communicative processes by which Members participate in committee and House proceedings with respect to the consideration and passage or rejection of proposed legislation or with respect to other matters which the Constitution places within the jurisdiction of either House.

Gravel v. United States, *supra* note 56, 408 U.S. at 625, 92 S.Ct. at 2627. If separation of powers doctrine countenances such a close review of assertions of an express constitutional privilege, the doctrine must also comprehend judicial scrutiny of assertions of Executive privilege, which is *at most* implicit in the Constitution. *Gravel* deals on its facts only with an assertion of privilege by an individual legislator. As collective bodies, the Houses of Congress have frequently made unilateral declarations of an absolute privilege to withold documents in their custody from court process. *See, e. g.,* Senate Resolution, Oct. 4, 1972, 92nd Cong., 2d Sess. These claims have never been pressed to a judicial resolution, and we have no occasion here to decide them. It is sufficient to note that they rest on a footing different from the President's claim of absolute privilege in this case. The President's claim has been previously litigated, and repudiated, in United States v. Burr, *supra* note 39. Further, Congress' claims draw upon two express constitutional privileges unavailable to the President, the aforementioned Speech and Debate Clause, and the Secrecy Clause in Art. I, § 5, ¶ 3. Even so, we note that *Gravel* states that the scope of the Speech and Debate privilege cannot be unilaterally "established by the Legislative Branch," Gravel v. United States, *supra,* 408 U.S. at 624 n. 15, 92 S.Ct. 2614.

71. *See* Myers v. United States, 272 U.S. 52, 116, 47 S.Ct. 21, 71 L.Ed. 160 (1926).

72. See Youngstown Sheet & Tube Co. v. Sawyer, *supra* note 37, 343 U.S. at 635, 72 S.Ct. 863 (Jackson, J., concurring).

73. The doctrine of separation of powers was adopted by the Convention of 1787, not to promote efficiency but to preclude the exercise of arbitrary power The purpose was not to avoid friction, but, by means of the inevitable friction incident to the distribution of the governmental powers among three departments, to save the people from autocracy.

   Myers v. United States, *supra* note 71, 272 U.S. at 293, 47 at 85. (Brandeis, J., dissenting).

74. Chief Justice Marshall wrote two opinions concerning the production of the letters. In the first of these opinions, the Chief Justice ruled that a subpoena to produce the letters could be issued to the President and that the Chief Justice himself would consider and weigh any specific objections interposed by the President that the letters contained matter "which ought not to be disclosed." United States v. Burr, *supra* note 39, 25 Fed.Cas. at 37; *see* page 710 *supra.* Statements of the Chief Justice in the first *Burr* opinion suggest that he contemplated that he would actually inspect the letters *in camera.*

   If it contain matter not essential to the defense, and the disclosure be unpleasant to the executive, it certainly ought not to be disclosed. This is a point which will appear *on the return.* * * * If they contain matter interesting to the nation, the concealment of which is required by the public safety, that matter will appear *upon the return.*

United States v. Burr, *supra* note 39, at 37. The United States Attorney Hay seems to have read the Chief Justice's first opinion to contemplate inspection by the court. As Judge Wilkey notes in his dissent, after Burr had renewed his request for the letters, Hay offered to submit them to the court for copying of "those parts which had relation to the cause." Hay further expressed his willingness to transmit the letters to Burr's counsel so that they could form their own opinions on what portions should be kept confidential from Burr and the public. Hay anticipated that differences between the opinions of Burr's counsel and himself would be arbitrated by the court. United States v. Burr, *supra* note 41, 25 Fed.Cas. at 190. The prosecution in the *Burr* case thus seems to have read Chief Justice Marshall's first opinion to support a procedure analogous to *in camera* inspection by Judge Sirica and Special Prosecutor Cox. It was only after Burr's counsel rejected Hay's position and demanded direct submission of the entire letters to Burr himself that Marshall found it necessary to issue his second opinion. In this opinion the Chief Justice addressed the remaining question of whether the President should be ordered to release the letters directly to Burr or whether the court should first inspect the documents to screen out privileged portions. Marshall made clear that before frustrating Burr's efforts to obtain the letters, the court would have to balance the opposing interests:

> The president may himself state the particular reasons which may have induced him to withhold a paper, and the court would unquestionably allow their full force to those reasons. At the same time, the court could not refuse to pay proper attention to the affidavit of the accused.

Id. at 192.

75. *See* United States v. Reynolds, *supra* note 57.

76. Soucie v. David, 145 U.S.App.D.C. 144, 158, 448 F.2d 1067, 1081 (1971) (Wilkey, J., concurring).

77. 5 U.S.C. § 552(b)(5) (1970); *see* Environmental Protection Agency v. Mink, *supra* note 35.

78. *See* Carl Zeiss Stiftung v. V.E.B. Carl Zeiss, Jena, *supra* note 58, 40 F.R.D. at 324–325.

79. *E. g.,* Branzburg v. Hayes, *supra* note 54, 408 U.S. at 687–688, 92 S.Ct. 2646.

80. *Supra* note 66, 149 U.S.App.D.C. at 391, 463 F.2d at 794. (per curiam); *see* Gravel v. United States, *supra* note 56, 408 U.S. at 627, 92 S.Ct. 2614.

81. Statement by the President, May 22, 1973, *quoted* in Appendix to the Brief for the United States (Special Prosecutor), at 14, 24.

82. 413 U.S. 548, 93 S.Ct. 2880, 37 L.Ed.2d 796 (1973).

83. 352 U.S. 567, 575, 77 S.Ct. 529, 1 L.Ed.2d 563 (1957).

84. Lopez v. United States, 373 U.S. 427, 437–440, 83 S.Ct.

1381, 10 L.Ed.2d 462 (1963); Osborn v. United States, 385 U.S. 323, 326–331, 87 S.Ct. 429, 17 L.Ed.2d 394 (1966).

85. Lopez v. United States, *supra* note 84, 373 U.S. at 439, 83 S.Ct. at 1388.

86. Where, as here, a conversation attended by the President, Mr. Dean and Mr. Haldeman has been the subject of divergent accounts by Mr. Dean and by Mr. Haldeman, without any restriction by the President on their testifying on the ground of confidentiality, there is no objection to presentation by the tape recorder of that part of the conversation that relates to Watergate, any more than to testimony on his point by another witness who had perfect auditory memory.

87. In re Subpoena to Nixon, *supra* note 7, 360 F.Supp. at 21–22.

88. The Memorandum and replies of counsel are set forth in Appendix I, *infra*.

89. Brief of Petitioner Nixon at 69.

90. *Id.* at 41–43.

91. *Id.* at 61.

92. *Supra* note 35, 410 U.S. at 92, 93 S.Ct. at 838.

93. *Id.* at 93, 93 S.Ct. at 839.

94. *Id.*

95. Carl Zeiss Stiftung v. V.E.B. Carl Zeiss, Jena, *supra* note 58, 40 F.R.D. at 331.

96. *Supra* note 35, 410 U.S. at 93, 93 S.Ct. at 827.

97. *Id.* at 88, 93 S.Ct. at 836, *citing* United States v. Cotton Valley Comm., 9 F.R.D. 719, 720 (W.D.La.1949), aff'd by equally divided court, 339 U.S. 940, 70 S.Ct. 793, 94 L.Ed. 1356 (1950).

98. 157 U.S.App.D.C. 340, 484 F.2d 820 (1973).

99. *See id.* at 348, 484 F.2d at 828.

100. Since the subpoenaed recordings will already have been submitted to the District Court, the opportunity to test the court's ruling in contempt proceedings would be foreclosed. And any ruling adverse to the Special Prosecutor would clearly be a pre-trial "decision or order . . . suppressing or excluding evidence . . . in a criminal proceeding . . . ." Thus the District Court's rulings on particularized claims would be appealable by the President as final judgments under 28 U.S.C. § 1291 (1970), and by the Special Prosecutor under 18 U.S.C. § 3731 (1970). *See* United States v. Ryan, 402 U.S. 530, 533, 91 S.Ct. 1580, 29 L.Ed.2d 85 (1971); Perlman v. United States, 247 U.S. 7, 12–13, 38 S.Ct. 417, 62 L.Ed. 950 (1918); United States v. Calandra, 455 F.2d 750, 751–753 (6th Cir. 1972).

101. Judge Wilkey, in dissent, adheres to the abstract in his discussion of who has the right to decide; he makes no reference to the facts before us framing that issue. John Marshall

addressed it in the context of President Jefferson's decision to reveal the contents of a private letter to the extent of characterizing it, in a message to Congress, as containing overwhelming evidence of Burr's treason. So here, we must deal with that issue not in a void but against the background of a decision by the President, made and announced before the existence of the tapes was publicly known, to permit participants in private conversations with him to testify publicly as to what was said about Watergate and its aftermath. That decision—and the resulting testimony containing conflicts as to both fact and inference—has made it possible for the Special Prosecutor to make a powerful showing of the relevance and importance of the tapes to the grand jury's discharge of its responsibilities. What the courts are now called upon primarily to decide, as distinct from what the President has already decided with respect to the relative importance of preserving the confidentiality of these particular conversations, is how to reconcile the need of the United States, by its grand jury, with the legitimate interest of the President in not disclosing those portions of the tapes that may deal with unrelated matters.

102. Brief of Petitioner Nixon at 94.

Opinion on Releasing Evidence to the House Judiciary Committee, March 18, 1974, by Judge Sirica

In re REPORT AND RECOMMENDATION OF JUNE 5, 1972 GRAND JURY CONCERNING TRANSMISSION OF EVIDENCE TO the HOUSE OF REPRESENTATIVES.

Misc. No. 74–21.

United States District Court,
District of Columbia.
March 18, 1974.

OPINION

SIRICA, Chief Judge.

On March 1, 1974, in open court, the June 5, 1972 Grand Jury lodged with the Court a sealed Report. The materials comprised

Reproduced from *Federal Supplement*, vol. 370 (1974), by permission of the West Publishing Company, St. Paul, Minnesota.

in that Report were filed by the Court and ordered held under seal pending further disposition. The materials were accompanied by a two-page document entitled *Report and Recommendation* which is in effect a letter of transmittal describing in general terms the Grand Jury's purpose in preparing and forwarding the Report and the subject matter of its contents. The transmittal memorandum further strongly recommends that accompanying materials be submitted to the Committee on the Judiciary of the House of Representatives for its consideration. The Grand Jury states it has heard evidence that it regards as having a material bearing on matters within the primary jurisdiction of the Committee in its current inquiry, and notes further its belief that it ought now to defer to the House of Representatives for a decision on what action, if any, might be warranted in the circumstances.

After having had an opportunity to familiarize itself with the contents of the Report, the Court invited all counsel who might conceivably have an interest in the matter, without regard to standing, to state their positions concerning disposition.[1] The President's position, through counsel, is that he has no recommendation to make, suggesting that the matter is entirely within the Court discretion.[2] He has requested that should the Report be released, his counsel have an opportunity to review and copy the materials.[3] The House Judiciary Committee through its Chairman has made a formal request for delivery of the Report materials.[4] The Special Prosecutor has urged on behalf of the Grand Jury that its Report is authorized under law and that the recommendation to forward the Report to the House be honored.[5] Finally, attorneys for seven persons named in an indictment returned by the same June, 1972 Grand Jury on March 1, 1974, just prior to delivery of the Grand Jury Report,[6] have generally objected to any disclosure of the Report, and in one instance recommended that the Report be expunged or returned to the Jury.[7]

Having carefully examined the contents of the Grand Jury Report, the Court is satisfied that there can be no question regarding their materiality to the House Judiciary Committee's investigation. Beyond materiality, of course, it is the Committee's responsibility to determine the significance of the evidence, and the Court offers no opinion as to relevance. The questions that must be decided, however, are twofold: (1) whether the Grand Jury has power to make reports and recommendations, (2) whether the Court has power to disclose such reports, and if so, to what extent.

I.

Without attempting a thorough exposition, the Court, as a basis for its discussion, notes here some principal elements in the development and authority of the grand jury. Initially, the grand

jury, or its forerunner, was employed to supply the monarch with
local information regarding criminal conduct and was wholly a
creature of the crown. As the grand jury gained institutional
status, however, it began to act with a degree of independence,
and in some cases refused to indict persons whom the state
sought to prosecute.[8] Thereafter it became common for grand
juries to serve the dual function of both charging and defending.
By virtue of the Fifth Amendment, grand jury prerogatives were
given institutional status in the United States, and grand juries
have ever since played a fundamental role in our criminal justice
system.[9]

The grand jury is most frequently characterized as an
adjunct or arm of the judiciary. While such a characterization is
in the general sense accurate, it must be recognized that within
certain bounds, the grand jury may act independently of any
branch of government. The grand jury may pursue investigations
on its own without the consent or participation of a prosecutor. [10]
The grand jury holds broad power over the terms of charges it returns,[11] and its decision not to bring charges is unreviewable. Furthermore, the grand jury may insist that prosecutors prepare
whatever accusations it deems appropriate and may return a draft
indictment even though the government attorney refuses to sign
it.[12]

We come thus to the question of whether grand jury prerogatives
extend to the presentation of documents that disclose evidence the
jury has gathered but which do not indict anyone. The sort of
presentment mentioned above, where government attorneys decline to start the prosecutorial machinery by withholding signature from a draft indictment, is in the correct sense such a report
since grand jury findings are disclosed independent of criminal
proceedings, and it appears that nowhere has grand jury authority
for this practice been denied, particularly not in this Circuit.[13]
Nevertheless, where the jury's product does not constitute an indictment for reasons other than an absent signature, there is some
disagreement as to its propriety.

It should be borne in mind that the instant Report is not the
first delivered up by a grand jury, and that, indeed grand juries
have historically published reports on a wide variety of subjects.[14]
James Wilson, a signer of both the Declaration of Independence
and the Constitution and later an Associate Justice of the Supreme Court made these pertinent observations in 1791:

> The grand jury are a great channel of communication, be-
> tween those who make and administer the laws, and those for
> whom the laws are made and administered. All the operations
> of government, and of its ministers and officers, are within the
> compass of their view and research. They may suggest publick
> improvements, and the modes of removing publick incon-

veniences: they may expose to publick inspection, or to publick punishment, publick bad men, and publick bad measures.[15]

On this historical basis, with reliance as well upon principles of sound public policy, a number of federal courts have upheld and defined the general scope of grand jury reportorial prerogatives. In In Re Presentment of Special Grand Jury Impaneled January, 1969, 315 F.Supp. 662 (D.Md.1970), Chief Judge Thomsen received a "presentment" describing the course of an investigation by a Baltimore grand jury into possible corruption related to a federal construction project. The "presentment" also outlined indictments which the grand jury was prepared to return in addition to other indictments handed up with the "presentment," but noted that the United States Attorney had been directed not to sign them. The "presentment" was held under seal while interested parties argued its disposition, and was then released publicly in modified form. The grand jury's common law powers, Chief Judge Thomsen ruled, "include the power to make presentments, sometimes called reports, calling attention to certain actions of public officials, whether or not they amounted to a crime."[16]

Chief Judge Thomsen also cited Judge Wisdom's concurring opinion in United States v. Cox, 342 F.2d 167 (5th Cir.) cert. denied 381 U.S. 935, 85 S.Ct. 1767, 14 L.Ed.2d 700 (1965), for the proposition that, whether used frequently or infrequently, there is no reason to suppose that the powers of our constitutional grand jury were intended to differ from those of its "English progenitor."[17] In the Cox case four of the seven judges of the Fifth Circuit sitting en banc held that courts may order the United States Attorney to assist a grand jury by drafting "forms of indictment" according to the jury's wishes, while a different four-three combination ruled that the prosecutor could not be compelled to sign the presentment and thereby concur, on behalf of the executive branch, in prosecution. Judge Brown observed, without challenge from his brethren,

> To me the thing [is] this simple: the Grand Jury is charged to report. It determines what it is to report. It determines the form in which it reports.[18]

The Fifth Circuit recently had an opportunity to consider the specific question of grand jury reports, but was able to "pretermit the issue" as raised by a state court judge unfavorably mentioned in the report. In Re Grand Jury Proceedings, 479 F.2d 458 (5th Cir. 1973). The court found that the portions of the report dealing with purely local affairs were of no concern to a federal grand jury and should be expunged. The remainder of the report was left intact, however, and Judge Ainsworth writing for the court observed, citing a lengthy footnote:

We point out . . . that there is persuasive authority and considerable historical data to support a holding that federal grand juries have authority to issue reports which do not indict for crime, in addition to their authority to indict and to return a no true bill.[19]

The Seventh Circuit, in an opinion by Judge Barnes, In Matter of Application of Johnson et al., 484 F.2d 791, (7th Cir. 1973), recently upheld the authority of federal grand juries to issue reports. Chief Judge Robson of the Northern District of Illinois there permitted public distribution of a printed report based on the grand jury investigation into a confrontation between Chicago police and members of the Black Panther Party in which two persons were killed. Fifteen months after the report had been printed and distributed at the Government Printing Office, persons named in the report sought to have it expunged from court records. On appeal following denial of the motion, the Circuit Court noted that any harm was an accomplished fact, but more importantly, that the appellants were not charged with illegal activity. The court stated plainly, "the grand jury had the authority to make the report."[20]

The cases most often relied upon in denying reportorial powers are Application of United Electrical, Radio & Machine Workers of America, et al., 111 F.Supp. 858 (S.D.N.Y.1953), and Hammond v. Brown, 323 F.Supp. 326 (N.D. Ohio), affirmed 450 F.2d 480 (6th Cir. 1971).[21] Yet each of these decisions is careful to enumerate the factors militating against approval of the specific reports at issue and refrains from a blanket denial of reporting powers, although the Hammond court goes so far as to dub reports "as unnecessary as the human appendix."[22] Of these opinions, only that of Judge Weinfeld in United Electrical Radio and Machine Workers speaks from a fact situation involving a federal grand jury. In that case, petitioners, United Electrical and union officers, moved to expunge from court records the "presentment" of a 1952 grand jury in the Southern District of New York. The grand jury had investigated possible violations of perjury and conspiracy laws with reference to non-Communist affidavits filed with the National Labor Relations Board. Because leaks to newspapers revealed the names of persons referred to by the "presentment" or report, including petitioners, Judge Weinfeld treated the report as identifying its targets in derogatory contexts. The jury indicted no one, although its allegations could have been the basis for criminal proceedings. While recognizing that "reports of a general nature touching on conditions in the community . . . may serve a valuable function and may not be amenable to challenge,"[23] the court strongly disapproved of accusatory pronouncements which publicly condemn and yet bar their victim from a judicial forum in which to clear his name.

The widespread publication of the charges and the identification of petitioners as the offenders subjected them to public censure to the same degree as if they had been formally accused of perjury or conspiracy. At the same time it deprived them of the right to defend themselves and to have their day in a Court of Justice—their absolute right had the Grand Jury returned an indictment.

* * * * * * * *

". . . [I]f under the guise of a presentment, the grand jury simply accuse, thereby compelling the accused to stand mute, where the presentment would warrant indictment so that the accused might answer, the presentment may be expunged; . . ." [Jones v. People] 92 N.Y.S. at page 277.[24]

Judge Weinfeld also viewed the report in question as tantamount to an advisory opinion infringing upon matters exclusively within the province of another branch of government. The report recommended that the National Labor Relations Board "revoke the certification of the unions involved" and consider "including in each non-Communist affidavit a waiver by the signer of his Fifth Amendment privilege."[25]

In *Hammond*, the court was also troubled about separation of powers problems and concluded that "a grand jury is without authority to issue a report that advises, condemns or commends, or makes recommendations concerning the policies and operation of public boards, public officers, or public authorities."[26] There petitioners sought to defeat Ohio state indictments in which a number of them were charged, citing the prejudicial impact of a concurrent well-publicized report into which the grand jury had woven derogatory accusations against them. Among other things the jury stated that a group of 23 faculty members must share "responsibility for the tragic consequences of May 4, 1970" at Kent State University; it assigned major responsibility for the May, 1970 incident to "those persons who are charged with the administration of the University"; and it rendered "moral and social judgments on policies, attitudes, and conduct of the university administration, and some faculty and students."[27] *Hammond* relied upon Ohio law for the proposition that the grand jury lacked statutory authority to return a report of that kind in that case, noting further that common-law crimes and common-law criminal procedures were nonexistent in Ohio.[28]

The Report here at issue suffers from none of the objectionable qualities noted in *Hammond* and *United Electrical*. It draws no accusatory conclusions. It deprives no one of an official forum in which to respond. It is not a substitute for indictments where indictments might properly issue. It contains no recommendations, advice or statements that infringe on the prerogatives of other branches of government. Indeed, its only recommendation is to the Court, and rather than injuring separation of powers principles, the Jury sustains them by lending its aid to the House in the exercise of that body's constitutional jurisdiction. It renders no moral or social judgments. The Report is a simple and straightforward compilation of information gathered by the Grand Jury, and no more.

Having considered the cases and historical precedents, and noting the absence of a contrary rule in this Circuit, it seems to the Court that it would be unjustified in holding that the Grand Jury was without authority to hand up this Report. The Grand Jury has obviously taken care to assure that its Report contains no objectionable features, and has throughout acted in the interests of fairness. The Grand Jury having thus respected its own limitations and the rights of others, the Court ought to respect the Jury's exercise of its prerogatives.

II.

Beyond the question of issuing a report is the question of disclosure. It is here that grand jury authority ends and judicial authority becomes exclusive.[29]

As Chief Judge Thomsen observed regarding disclosure, "Each case should be decided on its own facts and circumstances."

The Court is the agency which must weigh in each case the various interests involved, including the right of the public to know and the rights of the persons mentioned in the presentment, whether they are charged or not. The Court should regulate the amount of disclosure, to be sure that it is no greater than is required by the public interest in knowing "when weighed against the rights of the persons mentioned in the presentment."[30]

There, the "presentment" or report was publicly released in summarized form after the court had noted the rampant speculation about the report and had weighed "the public interest in disclosure" against "the private prejudice to the persons involved, none of whom are charged with any crime in the proposed indictment."[31] Judge Ainsworth, in the 1973 Fifth Circuit case, posed the following criteria governing disclosure decisions:

. . . whether the report describes general community conditions or whether it refers to identifiable individuals; whether the individuals are mentioned in public or private capacities; the public interest in the contents of the report balanced against the harm to the individuals named; the availability and efficacy of remedies; whether the conduct described is indictable.[32]

There, portions of a report relating to federal narcotics control were left in the public record. Chief Judge Bryan in In Re Petition for Disclosure of Evidence, 184 F.Supp. 38 (E.D.Va.1960), cited the public interest, a particularized need for information and traditional considerations of grand jury secrecy in granting disclosure of a report to one agency and denying it to others. The Seventh Circuit Court of Appeals in the Chicago police—Black Panther report case considered, among other criteria, judicial discretion over grand jury secrecy, the public interest, and prejudice to persons named by the report.

We begin here with the fact that the Grand Jury has recommended disclosure; not public dissemination, but delivery to the House Judiciary Committee with a request that the Report be used with due regard for the constitutional rights of persons under indictment. Where, as here, a report is clearly within the bounds of propriety, the Court believes that it should presumptively favor disclosure to those for whom the matter is a proper concern and whose need is not disputed. Compliance with the established standards here is manifest and adds its weight in favor of at least limited divulgence, overbalancing objections, and leading the Court to the conclusion that delivery to the Committee is eminently proper, and indeed, obligatory. The Report's subject is referred to in his public capacity, and, on balance with the public interest, any prejudice to his legal rights caused by disclosure to the Committee would be minimal. As noted earlier, the Report is not an indictment, and the President would not be left without a forum in which to adjudicate any charges against him that might employ Report materials. The President does not object to release.

The only significant objection to disclosure, is the contention that release of the Report beyond the Court is absolutely prohibited by Rule 6(e), Federal Rules of Criminal Procedure. The text of Rule 6(e) is set forth in the margin.[33] Counsel objecting to release draw particular attention to the statement "[persons may disclose matters occurring before the grand jury] only when so directed by the court preliminarily to or in connection with a judicial proceeding . . . ."

In their "Notes" accompanying Rule 6(e)[34] the Advisory Committee on Rules, responsible for drafting Federal Rules, explains the intent of that paragraph as follows:

1. This rule continues the traditional practice of secrecy on the part of members of the grand jury, *except when the court permits a disclosure*, Schmidt v. United States, 115 F.2d 394, C.C.A. 6th; United States v. American Medical Association, 26

F.Supp. 429, D.C.; *Cf.* Atwell v. United States, 162 F. 97, C.C.A. 4th; and see 18 U.S.C. former § 554(a) ....[35]

It is apparent from an analysis of the Advisory Committee's authorities that the "traditional practice of secrecy" there codified covers a rather narrow area.[36] At most, the cases cited establish only that secrecy must prevail during deliberations, and that any later disclosure will occur at the court's discretion. The phrase in the Rule, "preliminarily to or in connection with a judicial proceeding," evidently derived from the fact that the Advisory Committee had in mind only cases where the disclosure question arose at or prior to trial. It left the courts their traditional discretion in that situation and apparently considered no others. If affirmed judicial authority over persons connected with the grand jury in the interest of necessary secrecy without diminishing judicial authority to determine the extent of secrecy. The Court can see no justification for a suggestion that this codification for a "traditional practice" should act, or have been intended to act, to render meaningless an historically proper function of the grand jury by enjoining courts from any disclosure of reports in any circumstance.

Since its enactment, these cases interpreting Rule 6(e) have varied widely on its disclosure provision. It has been held that "judicial proceeding" refers only to a proceeding in a United States District Court.[37] Other courts balancing need for disclosure against benefits of secrecy have both granted and denied disclosure of matters before a grand jury to state officials.[38] Administrative proceedings have been found to fit within the Rule's terms,[39] and not to fit.[40]

In the Second Circuit, Judge Learned Hand wrote that "the term 'judicial proceeding' includes any proceeding determinable by a court, having for its object the compliance of any person, subject to judicial control, with standards imposed upon his conduct in the public interest, even though such compliance is enforced without the procedure applicable to the punishment of crime."[41] He added, "an interpretation that should not go at least so far, would not only be in the teeth of the language employed, but would defeat any rational purpose that can be imputed to the rule."[42] Matters occurring before the grand jury were thus made available for use in a disbarment proceeding. More recently in an opinion written by Chief Judge Friendly, the Second Circuit held that Rule 6(e) did not bar public disclosure of grand jury minutes, wholly apart from judicial proceedings, when sought by the grand jury witness.[43]

This difficulty in application of Rule 6(e) to specific fact situations likely arises from the fact that its language regarding "judicial proceedings" can imply limitations on disclosure much more extensive than were apparently intended. As the *Biaggi* decision just cited implies, Rule 6(e) which was not intended to create new law, remains subject to the law or traditional policies that gave it birth. These policies are well established, and none of them would dictate that in this situation disclosure to the Judiciary Committee be withheld.

In two well-known antitrust cases, Pittsburgh Plate Glass Co. v. United States, 360 U.S. 395, 79 S.Ct. 1237, 3 L.Ed.2d 1323 (1959) and United States v. Proctor & Gamble Co., 356 U.S. 677, 78 S.Ct. 983, 2 L.Ed.2d 1077 (1958), the Supreme Court has listed in summary form the bases of grand jury secrecy:

(1) To prevent the escape of those whose indictment may be contemplated; (2) to insure the utmost freedom to the grand jury in its deliberations, and to prevent persons subject to indictment or their friends from importuning the grand jurors; (3) to prevent subornation of perjury or tampering with the witnesses who may testify before [the] grand jury and later appear at the trial of those indicted by it; (4) to encourage free and untrammeled disclosures by persons who have information with respect to the commission of crimes; (5) to protect [the] innocent accused who is exonerated from disclosure of the fact that he has been under investigation, and from the expense of standing trial where there was no probability of guilt.[44]

Upon the return of an indictment, the first three and the fifth reasons for secrecy are rendered inapplicable. The interest represented by the fourth, encouraging free disclosure by those who possess information regarding crimes, must be protected, but as these and other cases have asserted[45] a compelling need and the ends of justice may still mandate release.

Here, for all purposes relevant to this decision, the Grand Jury has ended its work. There is no need to protect against flight on anyone's part, to prevent tampering with or restraints on witnesses or jurors, to protect grand jury deliberations, to safeguard unaccused or innocent persons with secrecy. The person on whom the Report focuses, the President of the United States, has not objected to its release to the Committee. Other persons are involved only indirectly. Those persons who are not under indictment have already been the subject of considerable public testimony and will no doubt be involved in further testimony, quite apart from this Report. Those persons who are under indictment have the opportunity at trial for response to any incidental references to them. And although it has not been emphasized in this opinion, it should not be forgotten that we deal in a matter of the most critical moment to the Nation, an impeachment investigation involving the President of the United States. It would be difficult to conceive of a more compelling need than that of this country for an unswervingly fair inquiry based on all the pertinent information.

These considerations might well justify even a public disclosure of the Report, but are certainly ample basis for disclosure to a body that in this setting acts simply as another grand jury. The Committee has taken elaborate precautions to insure against unnecessary and inappropriate disclosure of these materials.[46] Nonetheless, counsel for the indicted defendants, some having lived for a considerable time in Washington, D. C., are not persuaded that disclosure to the Committee can have any result but prejudicial publicity for their clients. The Court, however, cannot justify non-disclosure on the basis of speculation that leaks will occur, added to the further speculation that resultant publicity would prejudice the rights of defendants in United States v. Mitchell et al. We have no basis on which to assume that the Committee's use of the Report will be injudicious or that it will disregard the plea contained therein that defendants' rights to fair trials be respected.

Finally, it seems incredible that grand jury matters should lawfully be available to disbarment committees and police disciplinary investigations and yet be unavailable to the House of Representatives in a proceeding of so great import as an impeachment investigation. Certainly Rule 6(e) cannot be said to mandate such a result. If indeed that Rule merely codifies existing practice, there is convincing precedent to demonstrate that common-law practice permits the disclosure here contemplated. In 1811, the presentment of a county grand jury in the Mississippi Territory, specifying charges against federal territorial Judge Harry Toulmin, was forwarded to the House of Representatives for consideration in a possible impeachment action.[47] Following a committee investigation, the House found the evidence inadequate to merit impeachment and dismissed the matter. Though such grand jury participation appears not to have occurred frequently, the precedent is persuasive.[48] The Court is persuaded to follow the lead of Judges Hastings, Barnes and Sprecher speaking for the Seventh Circuit, Judges Friendly and Jameson of the Second Circuit, Judge Wisdom of the Fifth Circuit, and Judge Thomsen of the District of Maryland.[49] Principles of grand jury secrecy do not bar this disclosure.[50]

III.

Consistent with the above, therefore, the Court orders that the Grand Jury *Report and Recommendation,* together with accompanying materials be delivered to the Committee on the Judiciary, House of Representatives. The only individuals who object to such order are defendants in the United States v. Mitchell et al. case currently pending in this court. Their standing is dubious at best given the already stated facts that (1) their mention in the Report is incidental, (2) their trials will provide ample opportunity for response to such references, none of which go beyond allegations in the indictment, and (3) considerations of possible adverse publicity are both premature and speculative. Their ability to seek whatever appellate review of the Court's decision might be had, is therefore questionable. Nevertheless, because of the irreversible nature of disclosure, the Court will stay its order for two days from the date thereof to allow defendants an opportunity to pursue their remedies, if any, should they desire to do so.

The President's request to have counsel review the Report's contents has not received comment from the Committee counsel due to their feeling that such comment would be inappropriate.[51] It is the Court's view that this request is more properly the Committee's concern, and it therefore defers to the Chairman for a response to the President's counsel.

Having ruled that the Recommendation of the Grand Jury and request of the House Judiciary Committee should be honored, the Court relinquishes its own control of the matter, but takes advantage of this occasion to respectfully request, with the Grand Jury, that the Committee receive, consider and utilize the Report with due regard for avoiding any unnecessary interference with the Court's ability to conduct fair trials of persons under indictment.

1. The Special Prosecutor notified the Court shortly before delivery of the Report that the Grand Jury intended to take such action. The Court had opportunity only for a brief review of relevant authorities, and decided to receive and hold the Report under seal. The Court's first opportunity to peruse the Grand Jury materials came on Monday, March 4th, and a hearing was scheduled for Wednesday, March 6th, to include all those who might possibly have an interest in the matter.

    The President's counsel has been permitted to review the two-page *Report and Recommendation*. Other counsel were offered a similar opportunity, but with one exception declined. See Transcript of Proceedings, March 6, 1974, Misc. 74–21 at pp. 63–68, 86–89, [hereinafter cited as Transcript].

2. Transcript at pp. 2, 3, 31, 32.

3. Letter to the Honorable John J. Sirica from James D. St. Clair dated March 7, 1974 and filed in Misc. No. 74–21.

4. Letter to the Honorable John Sirica from the Honorable Peter W. Rodino, Jr., dated March 8, 1974, and filed in Misc. No. 74–21. See also Transcript at p. 30.

5. Memorandum of the United States on Behalf of the Grand

Jury filed in Misc. No. 74–21 under seal. See also Transcript at pp. 68–85.

6. United States v. John N. Mitchell, et al., Criminal Case No. 74–110.

7. Letter to the Honorable John J. Sirica from John J. Wilson, Esq., dated March 4, 1974 and filed in Misc. No. 74–21. See also Transcript at pp. 4–21, 51–61, 90–102.

8. The most celebrated cases in England involved ignoramus returns to charges against Stephen Colledge [8 How.St.Tr. 550 (1681)] and the Earl of Shaftesbury [8 How.St.Tr. 759 (1681)]. In the United States, the grand jury action favoring Peter Zenger is equally prominent [Morris, Fair Trial 69–95 (1952)]. *See also*, Kuh, The Grand Jury "Presentment": Foul Blow or Fair Play, 55 Colum. L. Rev. 1103, 1107–09 (1955).

9. See generally Branzburg v. Hayes, 408 U.S. 665, 92 S.Ct. 2646, 33 L.Ed.2d 626 (1972) and Hale v. Henkel, 201 U.S. 43, 26 S.Ct. 370, 50 L.Ed. 652 (1906).

10. United States v. Thompson, 251 U.S. 407, 413–415, 40 S.Ct. 289, 64 L.Ed. 333 (1920); Blair v. United States, 250 U.S. 273, 282, 39 S.Ct. 468, 63 L.Ed. 979 (1919); Hale v. Henkel, *supra* note 9; Frisbie v. United States, 157 U.S. 160, 163, 15 S.Ct. 586, 39 L.Ed. 657 (1895).

11. Gaither v. United States, 134 U.S.App.D.C. 154, 413 F.2d 1061, 1066 (1969).

12. United States v. Cox, 342 F.2d 167 (5th Cir.) cert. denied 381 U.S. 935, 85 S.Ct. 1767, 14 L.Ed.2d 700 (1965); Gaither v. United States, *supra* note 11; In Re Miller, 17 Fed.Cas. p. 295 (No. 9,552) (D.C.D.Ind.1878); In Re Presentment of Special Grand Jury, January 1969, 315 F.Supp. 662 (D.Md.1970); United States v. Smyth, 104 F.Supp. 283 (N.D.Cal.1952).

13. See Gaither v. United States, *supra* note 11.

14. See, 55 Colum.L.Rev., *supra* note 8 at 1109–1110 citing examples both in England and the American colonies.

15. The Works of James Wilson, ed. R. G. McCloskey, vol. II at 537 (1967).

16. 315 F.Supp. at 675. Chief Judge Thomsen quotes at length from the eloquent statement of New Jersey Chief Justice Vanderbilt regarding the reasons for allowing such presentments. *Id.*

17. 342 F.2d 167, 186 (5th Cir. 1965).

18. *Id.* at 184. See also 342 F.2d at 180 (opinion of Rives, Gewin & Bell, JJ.), and 342 F.2d at 189 (opinion of Wisdom, J.): "No one questions the jury's plenary power to inquire, to summon and interrogate witnesses, and to present either findings and a report or an accusation in open court by presentment."

19. 479 F.2d at 460 (footnote omitted).

Counsel for two of the defendants in United States v. Mitchell, et al., CC 74–10, suggests that the action of Congress in specifically conferring reporting powers on special grand juries under 18 U.S.Code § 3331 et seq. is probative of the contention that grand juries lacked such powers at common law. This proposal, however, overlooks the fact that power to report was there made explicit simply to be certain that there could be no question in light of Judge Weinfeld's decision in *United Electrical* (111 F.Supp. 858). Congressman Poff, a sponsor of the bill creating special grand juries explained that since

> . . . the precise boundaries of the reporting power have not been judicially delineated . . . , the authority to issue reports relevant to organized crime investigations has been specifically conferred upon the special grand juries created by this title. The committee does not thereby intend to restrict or in any way interfere with the right of regular Federal grand juries to issue reports as recognized by judicial custom and tradition. (Congressional Record, Vol. 116, part 26, 91st Cong., 2d Sess., October 7, 1970 at 35291.)

20. 484 F.2d at p. 797.
21. Counsel have cited a further federal decision in this Circuit, Poston v. Washington, Alexandria & Mt. Vernon R.R., 36 App.D.C. 359 (1911), as ruling that in the District of Columbia a regular federal grand jury "has no power other than to indict or ignore." That decision, however, involved a state grand jury, and ruled only as to "the practice in the State of Virginia." 36 App.D.C. at 369.

Within state judicial systems, the dissent in Jones v. People 101 App.Div. 55, 92 N.Y. S. 275 (2d Dep't.), appeal dismissed 181 N.Y. 389, 74 N.E. 226 (1905) is often cited by courts rejecting grand jury reports, although the majority opinion which approved such reports in certain circumstances is apparently still the law in New York. For the proposition that state grand juries have legal authority to issue reports, Chief Justice Vanderbilt's opinion in In Re Camden County Grand Jury, 10 N.J. 23, 89 A.2d 416 (1952) has become a landmark. The author of the Note, The Grand Jury as an Investigatory Body, 74 Harv.L.Rev. 590, 595–96 (1961), suggests that a majority of state courts have disallowed reports unaccompanied by indictments, but have carved out exceptions for reports criticizing public officials, and for those which address general conditions and do not necessarily identify specific individuals. Consistent with federal decisions, the author further notes that state courts unanimously disallow reports made up solely of opinions and those which undertake to do nothing but advise the legislative or executive branches.

22. 323 F.Supp. 326, 351 (N.D.Ohio 1971).

23. 111 F.Supp. 858, 869 (S.D.N.Y. 1953). The court noted that at least 14 reports had been filed by grand juries in the Southern District of New York without challenge in the 16 years prior to its decision. 111 F.Supp. at 869.

24. *Id.* at 861, 867.

25. *Id.* at 860

26. 323 F.Supp. 326, 345 (N.D.Ohio 1971).

27. *Id.* at 336.

28. *Id.* at 343–344.

29. In Re Grand Jury Proceedings, 479 F.2d 458 (5th Cir. 1973); In Matter of Application of Johnson et al., 484 F.2d 791, (7th Cir. 1973); In Re Special Grand Jury Impaneled January, 1969, 315 F.Supp. 662 (D.Md.. 1970); In Re Petition for Disclosure of Evidence, 184 F.Supp. 38 (E.D.Va. 1960). Orfield, The Federal Grand Jury, 22 F.R.D. 343, 446–447 (1959).

30. 315 F. Supp. at 678.

31. *Id.* at 679

32. 479 F.2d at 460 n. 2.

33. Rule 6(e) *Secrecy of Proceedings and Disclosure.* Disclosure of matters occurring before the grand jury other than its deliberations and the vote of any juror may be made to the attorneys for the government for use in the performance of their duties. Otherwise a juror, attorney, interpreter, stenographer, operator of a recording device, or any typist who transcribes recorded testimony may disclose matters occurring before the grand jury only when so directed by the court preliminarily to or in connection with a judicial proceeding or when permitted by the court at the request of the defendant upon a showing that grounds may exist for a motion to dismiss the indictment because of matters occurring before the grand jury. No obligation of secrecy may be imposed upon any person except in accordance with this rule. The court may direct that an indictment shall be kept secret until the defendant is in custody or has given bail, and in that event the clerk shall seal the indictment and no person shall disclose the finding of the indictment except when necessary for the issuance and execution of a warrant or summons. (18 U.S.C., Federal Rules of Criminal Procedure, Rule 6.)

34. 18 U.S.Code Ann., Rule 6, p. 234.

35. *Id.* (emphasis added.)

36. The *Schmidt* case cited was an appeal by two attorneys from a conviction of contempt for having authorized their clients, in a criminal case, to privately obtain the affidavits of grand jurors who had voted on their indictment, in violation of the jurors oath of secrecy. The affidavits were filed in an attempt to overturn the indictments. In its holding the court stated:

Logically the responsibility for relaxing the rule of secrecy and of supervising any subsequent inquiry should reside in the court, of which the grand jury is a part and under the general instructions of which it conducted its "judicial inquiry." It is a matter which appeals to the discretion of the court when brought to its attention . . . and we think it is sound procedural law. (115 F.2d at 397, citations omitted.)

In the *American Medical Association* case, indicted defendants sought court permission to obtain the affidavits of grand jurors in support of pleas in abatement and motions to quash. The court stated in its holding, "Neither indictment, arrest of the accused, nor expiration of the jury term will operate to release a juror from the oath of secrecy, as the defendants here contend. That can only be done by a court acting in a given case when in its judgment the ends of justice so require." 26 F.Supp. at 430 (citations omitted). In Atwell v. United States, the Fourth Circuit reversed the contempt conviction of a grand juror who had given statements regarding grand jury proceedings to defense counsel following indictments and dismissal of the grand jury. The court analyzed the jurors oath and held as follows:

This oath required him (a) diligently to inquire and true presentment make of all such matters and things as were given him in charge; (b) to present no one for envy, hatred, or malice; (c) to leave no one unpresented for fear, favor, or affection, reward, or hope of reward; (d) the United States' counsel, his fellows', and his own to keep secret. It may well be said that the first three obligations of this oath relate to the positive duty required of the grand juror, while the latter relates to and defines the rule of conduct to be followed by him in the discharge of these positive duties. The first three are demanded by direct mandate of the law; *the latter only by its policy, and solely in order that the first three may be more thoroughly and effectively performed.* (162 F. at 99, emphasis added).

Former § 554(a) of Title 18, U.S. Code simply barred pleas or motions to abate or quash indictments on the ground that unqualified jurors voted whenever at least twelve qualified jurors concurred in the indictment. 18 U.S. Code § 554(a), 1946 edition.

37. United States v. Downey, 195 F.Supp. 581 (D.Ill.1961); United States v. Crolich, 101 F.Supp. 782 (D.Ala.1952).

38. Compare In re Petition for Disclosure of Evidence, *supra* note 28 with In re Holovachka, 317 F.2d 834 (7th Cir. 1963) and Petition of Brooke, 229 F.Supp. 377 (D.Mass.1964).

39. Jachimowski v. Conlisk, 490 F.2d 894 (7th Cir. 1973), authorizing release of grand jury evidence for a police disciplinary investigation; In re Grand Jury Investigation William

H. Pflaumer & Sons, Inc., 53 F.R.D. 464 (E.D.Pa.1971), permitting disclosure to agents of the Internal Revenue Service; In Re Bullock, 103 F.Supp. 639 (D.D.C.1952).

40. In Re Grand Jury Proceedings, 309 F.2d 440 (3rd Cir. 1962).

41. Doe v. Rosenberry, 255 F.2d 118, 120 (2nd Cir. 1958).

42. Id.

43. In Re Biaggi, 478 F.2d 489 (2nd Cir. 1973). Biaggi, a New York City mayoral candidate at the time, wanted minutes released to answer charges made in the campaign that he had invoked his Fifth Amendment privilege as a witness before the grand jury.

44. 356 U.S. at 681 n. 6, 78 S.Ct. at 986. See also 1 Wright, Federal Practice and Procedure, § 106 at 170 (1969).

45. See, e.g., United States v. Socony-Vacuum Oil Co., 310 U.S. 150, 234, 60 S.Ct. 811, 849, 84 L.Ed. 1129 (1940): "But after the grand jury's functions are ended, disclosure is wholly proper where the ends of justice require it."

46. See, Procedures for Handling Impeachment Inquiry Material, Committee on the Judiciary, House of Representatives, 93rd Cong., 2d Sess., February, 1974, House Committee Print, at 1, 2.

47. 3 Hinds' Precedents of the House of Representatives § 2488 at 985, 986 (1907).

48. In Deschler's words, "In the House of Representatives there are various methods of setting an impeachment in motion: ... by charges transmitted from the legislature of a State ... or from a grand jury ...." Deschler Constitution, Jefferson's Manual, and Rules of the House of Representatives, H.R. Doc. 384, 92d Cong. 2d Sess., § 603 at 296.

49. In Matter of Application of Johnson et al., supra at p. 1224, In Re Biaggi, supra note 43, United States v. Cox, supra note 12 (concurring opinion), and In Re Presentment of Special Grand Jury Impaneled January, 1969, supra at p. 1223, respectively.

50. The Court's holding renders unnecessary a consideration of Mr. Jenner's argument on behalf of the Committee that insofar as Rule 6(e) conflicts with the constitutional powers of impeachment, the Rule is pro tanto overridden. See Transcript at 32–39.

51. Letter to the Honorable John J. Sirica from John Doar, Esq., dated March 12, 1974, and filed in Misc. 74–21.

Opinion on the Release of Tapes,
Supreme Court, July 24, 1974,
by Chief Justice Warren E. Burger

UNITED STATES
v.
NIXON, PRESIDENT OF THE UNITED STATES, et. al.

Certiorari Before Judgment to the United States Court of
Appeals for the District of Columbia Circuit No. 73–176.

Argued July 8, 1974
Decided July 24, 1974

I
JURISDICTION

The threshold question presented is whether the May 20, 1974,
order of the District Court was an appealable order and whether
this case was properly "in" the Court of Appeals when the petition for certiorari was filed in this Court. 28 U.S.C. § 1254. The
Court of Appeals' jurisdiction under 28 U.S.C. § 1291 encompasses only "final decisions of the district courts." Since the appeal
was timely filed and all other procedural requirements were met,
the petition is properly before this Court for consideration if the
District Court order was final. 28 U.S.C. §§1254 (1), 2101 (e).

The finality requirement of 28 U.S.C. § 1291 embodies a strong
congressional policy against piecemeal reviews, and against obstructing or impeding an ongoing judicial proceeding by interlocutory appeals. See, *e. g.*, *Cobbledick* v. *United States*, 309 U.S.
323, 324–326 (1940). This requirement ordinarily promotes judicial efficiency and hastens the ultimate termination of litigation.
In applying this principle to an order denying a motion to quash
and requiring the production of evidence pursuant to a subpoena
duces tecum, it has been repeatedly held that the order is not final
and hence not appealable. *United States* v. *Ryan*, 402 U.S. 530,
532 (1971); *Cobbledick* v. *United States*, *supra*; *Alexander* v.
United States, 201 U.S. 117 (1906). This Court has

"consistently held that the necessity for expedition in the administration of the criminal law justifies putting one who seeks
to resist the production of desired information to a choice between compliance with a trial court's order to produce prior to
any review of that order, and resistance to that order with the

Reprinted from *United States Reports*, vol. 418 (1974), Washington,
D.C., U.S. Government Printing Office.

concomitant possibility of an adjudication of contempt if his claims are rejected on appeal." *United States* v. *Ryan, supra,* at 533.

The requirement of submitting to contempt, however, is not without exception and in some instances the purposes underlying the finality rule require a different result. For example, in *Perlman* v. *United States,* 247 U.S. 7(1918), a subpoena had been directed to a third party requesting certain exhibits; the appellant, who owned the exhibits, sought to raise a claim of privilege. The Court held an order compelling production was appealable because it was unlikely that the third party would risk a contempt citation in order to allow immediate review of the appellant's claim of privilege. *Id.,* at 12–13. That case fell within the "limited class of cases where denial of immediate review would render impossible any review whatsoever of an individual's claims." *United States* v. *Ryan, supra,* at 533.

Here too, the traditional contempt avenue to immediate appeal is peculiarly inappropriate due to the unique setting in which the question arises. To require a President of the United States to place himself in the posture of disobeying an order of a court merely to trigger the procedural mechanism for review of the ruling would be unseemly, and would present an unnecessary occasion for constitutional confrontation between two branches of the Government. Similarly, a federal judge should not be placed in the posture of issuing a citation to a President simply in order to invoke review. The issue whether a President can be cited for contempt could itself engender protracted litigation, and would further delay both review on the merits of his claim of privilege and the ultimate termination of the underlying criminal action for which his evidence is sought. These considerations lead us to conclude that the order of the District Court was an appealable order. The appeal from that order was therefore properly "in" the Court of Appeals, and the case is now properly before this Court on the writ of certiorari before judgment. 28 U.S.C. § 1254; 28 U.S.C. § 2101(e). *Gay* v. *Ruff,* 292 U.S. 25, 30 (1934).[1]

II

JUSTICIABILITY

In the District Court, the President's counsel argued that the court lacked jurisdiction to issue the subpoena because the matter was an intra-branch dispute between a subordinate and superior officer of the Executive Branch and hence not subject to judicial resolution. That argument has been renewed in this Court with emphasis on the contention that the dispute does not present a "case" or "controversy" which can be adjudicated in the federal courts. The President's counsel argues that the federal courts should not intrude into areas committed to the other branches of Government. He views the present disput as essentially a "jurisdictional" dispute within the Executive Branch which he analogizes to a dispute between two congressional committees. Since the Executive Branch has exclusive authority and absolute discretion to decide whether to prosecute a case, *Confiscation Cases,* 7 Wall. 454 (1869); *United States* v. *Cox,* 342 F.2d 167, 171 (CA5), cert. denied *sub nom. Cox* v. *Hauberg,* 381 U.S. 935 (1965), it is contended that a President's decision is final in determining what evidence is to be used in a given criminal case. Although his counsel concedes that the President has delegated certain specific powers to the Special Prosecutor, he has not "waived nor delegated to the Special Prosecutor the President's duty to claim privilege as to all materials . . . which fall within the President's inherent authority to refuse to disclose to any executive officer." Brief for the President 42. The Special Prosecutor's demand for the items therefore presents, in the view of the President's counsel, a political question under *Baker* v. *Carr,* 369 U.S. 186 (1962), since it involves a "textually demonstrable" grant of power under Art. II.

The mere assertion of a claim of an "intra-branch dispute," without more, has never operated to defeat federal jurisdiction; justiciability does not depend on such a surface inquiry. In *United States* v. *ICC,* 337 U.S. 426 (1949), the Court observed, "courts must look behind names that symbolize the parties to determine whether a justifiable case or controversy is presented." *Id.,* at 430. See also *Powell* v. *McCormack,* 395 U.S. 486 (1969); *ICC* v. *Jersey City,* 322 U.S. 503 (1944); *United States ex rel. Chapman* v. *FPC,* 345 U.S. 153 (1953); *Secretary of Agriculture* v. *United State*s, 347 U.S. 645 (1954); *FMB* v. *Isbrandtsen Co.,* 356 U.S. 481, 483 n. 2 (1958); *United States* v. *Marine Bancorporation, ante,* p. 602; and *United States* v. *Connecticut National Bank, ante,* p. 656.

Our starting point is the nature of the proceeding for which the evidence is sought—here a pending criminal prosecution. It is a judicial proceeding in a federal court alleging violation of federal laws and is brought in the name of the United States as sovereign. *Berger* v. *United States,* 295 U.S. 78, 88 (1935). Under the authority of Art. II, § 2, Congress has vested in the Attorney General the power to conduct the criminal litigation of the United States Government, 28 U.S.C. § 516. It has also vested in him the power to appoint subordinate officers to assist him in the discharge of his duties. 28 U.S.C. §§ 509, 510, 515, 533. Acting pursuant to those statutes, the Attorney General has delegated the authority to represent the United States in these particular matters to a Special Prosecutor with unique authority and tenure.[2]

The regulation gives the Special Prosecutor explicit power to contest the invocation of executive privilege in the process of seeking evidence deemed relevant to the performance of these specially delegated duties.[3] 38 Fed.Reg. 30739, as amended by 38 Fed.Reg. 32805.

So long as this regulation is extant it has the force of law. In *United States ex rel. Accardi* v. *Shaughnessy,* 347 U.S. 260 (1954), regulations of the Attorney General delegated certain of his discretionary powers to the Board of Immigration Appeals and required that Board to exercise its own discretion on appeals in deportation cases. The Court held that so long as the Attorney General's regulations remained operative, he denied himself the authority to exercise the discretion delegated to the Board even though the original authority was his and he could reassert it by amending the regulations. *Service* v. *Dulles,* 354 U.S. 363, 388 (1957), and *Vitarelli* v. *Seaton,* 359 U.S. 535 (1959), reaffirmed the basic holding of *Accardi.*

Here, as in *Accardi,* it is theoretically possible for the Attorney General to amend or revoke the regulation defining the Special Prosecutor's authority. But he has not done so.[4] So long as this regulation remains in force the Executive Branch is bound by it, and indeed the United States as the sovereign composed of the three branches is bound to respect and to enforce it. Moreover, the delegation of authority to the Special Prosecutor in this case is not an ordinary delegation by the Attorney General to a subordinate officer: with the authorization of the President, the Acting Attorney General provided in the regulation that the Special Prosecutor was not to be removed without the "consensus" of eight designated leaders of Congress. N. 2, *supra.*

The demands of and the resistance to the subpoena present an obvious controversy in the ordinary sense, but that alone is not sufficient to meet constitutional standards. In the constitutional sense, controversy means more than disagreement and conflict; rather it means the kind of controversy courts traditionally resolve. Here at issue is the production or nonproduction of specified evidence deemed by the Special Prosecutor to be relevant and admissible in a pending criminal case. It is sought by one official of the Executive Branch within the scope of his express authority; it is resisted by the Chief Executive on the ground of his duty to preserve the confidentiality of the communications of the President. Whatever the correct answer on the merits, these issues are "of a type which are traditionally justiciable." *United States* v. *ICC,* 337 U.S., at 430. The independent Special Prosecutor with his asserted need for the subpoenaed material in the underlying criminal prosecution is opposed by the President with his steadfast assertion of privilege against disclosure of the material. This setting assures there is "that concrete adverseness which sharpens the presentation of issues upon which the court so largely depends for illumination of difficult constitutional questions." *Baker* v. *Carr*, 369 U.S., at 204. Moreover, since the matter is one arising in the regular course of a federal criminal prosecution, it is within the traditional scope of Art. III power. *Id.*, at 198.

In light of the uniqueness of the setting in which the conflict arises, the fact that both parties are officers of the Executive Branch cannot be viewed as a barrier to justiciability. It would be inconsistent with the applicable law and regulation, and the unique facts of this case, to conclude other than that the Special Prosecutor has standing to bring this action and that a justiciable controversy is presented for decision.

III

RULE 17(c)

The subpoena *duces tecum* is challenged on the ground that the Special Prosecutor failed to satisfy the requirements of Fed. Rule Crim. Proc. 17(c), which governs the issuance of subpoenas *duces tecum* in federal criminal proceedings. If we sustained this challenge, there would be no occasion to reach the claim of privilege asserted with respect to the subpoenaed material. Thus we turn to the question whether the requirements of Rule 17(c) have been satisfied. See *Arkansas Louisiana Gas Co.* v. *Dept. of Public Utilities*, 304 U.S. 61, 64 (1938); *Ashwander* v. *TVA*, 297 U.S. 288, 346–347 (1936) (Brandeis, J., concurring).

Rule 17(c) provides:

"A subpoena may also command the person to whom it is directed to produce the books, papers, documents or other objects designated therein. The court on motion made promptly may quash or modify the subpoena if compliance would be unreasonable or oppressive. The court may direct that books, papers, documents or objects designated in the subpoena be produced before the court at a time prior to the trial or prior to the time when they are to be offered in evidence and may upon their production permit the books, papers, documents or objects or portions thereof to be inspected by the parties and their attorneys."

A subpoena for documents may be quashed if their production would be "unreasonable or oppressive," but not otherwise. The leading case in this Court interpreting this standard is *Bowman Dairy Co.* v. *United States*, 341 U.S. 214 (1951). The case recognized certain fundamental characteristics of the subpoena *duces tecum* in criminal cases: (1) it was not intended to provide a means of discovery for criminal cases, *id.*, at 220; (2) its chief innovation was to expedite the trial by providing a time and place *before* trial for the inspection of subpoenaed materials,[5] *ibid*. As both parties agree, cases decided in the wake of *Bowman* have generally followed Judge Weinfeld's formulation in *United States* v. *Iozia*, 13 F.R.D. 335, 338 (SDNY 1952), as to the required showing. Under this test, in order to require production prior to trial, the moving party must show: (1) that the documents are evidentiary[6] and relevant; (2) that they are not otherwise procurable reasonably in advance of trial by exercise of due diligence; (3) that the party cannot properly prepare for trial without such production and inspection in advance of trial and that the failure to obtain such inspection may tend unreasonably to delay the trial; and (4) that the application is made in good faith and is not intended as a general "fishing expedition."

Against this background, the Special Prosecutor, in order to carry his burden, must clear three hurdles: (1) relevancy; (2) admissibility; (3) specificity. Our own review of the record necessarily affords a less comprehensive view of the total situation than was available to the trial judge and we are unwilling to conclude that the District Court erred in the evaluation of the Special Prosecutor's showing under Rule 17(c). Our conclusion is based on the record before us, much of which is under seal. Of course, the contents of the subpoenaed tapes could not at that stage be described fully by the Special Prosecutor, but there was a sufficient likelihood that each of the tapes contain conversations relevant to the offenses charged in the indictment *United States* v. *Gross*, 24 F.R.D. 138 (SDNY 195). With respect to many of the tapes, the Special Prosecutor offered the sworn testimony or statements of one or more of the participants in the conversations as to what was said at the time. As for the remainder of the tapes, the identity of the participants and the time and place of the conversations, taken in their total context, permit a rational inference that at least part of the conversations relate to the offenses charged in the indictment.

We also conclude there was a sufficient preliminary showing that each of the subpoenaed tapes contains evidence admissible with respect to the offenses charged in the indictment. The most cogent objection to the admissibility of the taped conversations here at issue is that they are a collection of out-of-court statemens by declarants who will not be subject to cross-examination and that the statements are therefore inadmissible hearsay. Here, however, most of the tapes apparently contain conversations to which one or more of the defendants named in the indictment were party. The hearsay rule does not automatically bar all out-of-court statements by a defendant in a criminal case.[7] Declarations by the one defendant may also be admissible against other defendants upon a sufficient showing, by independent evidence,[8] of a conspiracy among one or more other defendants and the declarant and if the declarations at issue were in furtherance of that conspiracy. The same is true of declarations of coconspirators who are not defendants in the case on trial. *Dutton* v. *Evans*, 400 U.S. 74, 81 (1970). Recorded conversations may also be admissible for the limited purpose of impeaching the credibility of any defendant who testifies or any other coconspirator who testifies. Generally, the need for evidence to impeach witnesses is insufficient to require its production in advance of trial. See, *e. g.*, *United States* v. *Carter*, 15 F.R.D. 367, 371 (DC 1954). Here, however, there are other valid potential evidentiary uses for the same material, and the analysis and possible transcription of the tapes may take a significant period of time. Accordingly, we cannot conclude that the District Court erred in authorizing the issuance of the subpoena *duces tecum*.

Enforcement of a pretrial subpoena *duces tecum* must necessarily be committed to the sound discretion of the trial court since the necessity for the subpoena most often turns upon a determination of factual issues. Without a determination of arbitrariness or that the trial court finding was without record support, an appellate court will not ordinarily disturb a finding that the applicant for a subpoena complied with Rule 17(c). See, *e. g.*, *Sue* v. *Chicago Transit Authority*, 279 F.2d 416, 419 (CA7 1960); *Shotkin* v. *Nelson*, 146 F.2d 402 (CA10 1944).

In a case such as this, however, where a subpoena is directed to a President of the United States, appellate review, in deference to a coordinate branch of Government, should be particularly meticulous to ensure that the standards of Rule 17(c) have been correctly applied. *United States* v. *Burr*, 25 F.Cas. 30, 34 (No. 14,692d) (CC Va. 1807). From our examination of the materials submitted by the Special Prosecutor to the District Court in support of his motion for the subpoena, we are persuaded that the District Court's denial of the President's motion to quash the subpoena was consistent with Rule 17(c). We also conclude that the Special Prosecutor has made a sufficient showing to justify a subpoena for production *before* trial. The subpoenaed materials are not available from any other source, and their examination and processing should not await trial in the circumstances shown. *Bowman Dairy Co.* v. *United States*, 341 U.S. 214 (1951); *United States* v. *Iozia*, 13 F.R.D. 335 (SDNY 1952).

IV

THE CLAIM OF PRIVILEGE

A

Having determined that the requirements of Rule 17(c) were

satisfied, we turn to the claim that the subpoena should be quashed because it demands "confidential conversations between a President and his close advisors that it would be inconsistent with the public interest to produce." App. 48a. The first contention is a broad claim that the separation of powers doctrine precludes judicial review of a President's claim of privilege. The second contention is that if he does not prevail on the claim of absolute privilege, the court should hold as a matter of constitutional law that the privilege prevails over the subpoena *duces tecum*.

In the performance of assigned constitutional duties each branch of the Government must initially interpret the Constitution, and the interpretation of its powers by any branch is due great respect from the others. The President's counsel, as we have noted, reads the Constitution as providing an absolute privilege of confidentiality for all Presidential communications. Many decisions of this Court, however, have unequivocally reaffirmed the holding of *Marbury* v. *Madison*, 1 Cranch 137 (1803), that "[i]t is emphatically the province and duty of the judicial department to say what the law is." *Id.*, at 177.

No holding of the Court has defined the scope of judicial power specifically relating to the enforcement of a subpoena for confidential Presidential communications for use in criminal prosecution, but other exercises of power by the Executive Branch and the Legislative Branch have been found invalid as in conflict with the Constitution. *Powell* v. *McCormack*, 395 U.S. 486 (1969); *Youngstown Sheet & Tube Co.* v. *Sawyer*, 343 U.S. 579 (1952). In a series of cases, the Court interpreted the explicit immunity conferred by express provisions of the Constitution on Members of the House and Senate by the Speech or Debate Clause, U.S. Const. Art. I, § 6. *Doe* v. *McMillan*, 412 U.S. 306 (1973); *Gravel* v. *United States*, 408 U.S. 606 (1972); *United States* v. *Brewster*, 408 U.S. 501 (1972); *United States* v. *Johnson*, 383 U.S. 169 (1966). Since this Court has consistently exercised the power to construe and delineate claims arising under express powers, it must follow that the Court has authority to interpret claims with respect to powers alleged to derive from enumerated powers.

Our system of government "requires that federal courts on occasion interpret the Constitution in a manner at variance with the construction given the document by another branch." *Powell* v. *McCormack, supra*, at 549. And in *Baker* v. *Carr*, 369 U.S., at 211, the Court stated:

"Deciding whether a matter has in any measure been committed by the Constitution to another branch of government, or whether the action of that branch exceeds whatever authority has been committed, is itself a delicate exercise in constitutional interpretation, and is a responsibility of this Court as ultimate interpreter of the Constitution."

Notwithstanding the deference each branch must accord the others
the "judicial Power of the United States" vested in the federal
courts by Art. III, § 1, of the Constitution can no more be shared
with the Executive Branch than the Chief Executive, for example,
can share with the Judiciary the veto power, or the Congress
share with the Judiciary the power to override a Presidential veto.
Any other conclusion would be contrary to the basic concept of
separation of powers and the checks and balances that flow from
the scheme of a tripartite government. The Federalist, No. 47, p.
313 (S. Mittell ed. 1938). We therefore reaffirm that it is the
province and duty of this Court "to say what the law is" with respect to the claim of privilege presented in the case. *Marbury* v.
Madison, supra, at 177.

B

In support of his claim of absolute privilege, the President's
counsel urges two grounds, one of which is common to all governments and one of which is peculiar to our system of separation of
powers. The first ground is the valid need for protection of communications between high government officials and those who advise and assist them in the performance of their manifold duties;
the importance of this confidentiality is too plain to require further discussion. Human experience teaches that those who expect
public dissemination of their remarks may well temper candor
with a concern for appearances and for their own interests to the
detriment of the decisionmaking process.[9] Whatever the nature of
the privilege of confidentiality of Presidential communications in
the exercise of Art. II powers, the privilege can be said to derive
from the supremacy of each branch within its own assigned area of
constitutional duties. Certain powers and privileges flow from the
nature of enumerated powers;[10] the protection of the confidentiality of Presidential communications has similar constitutional
underpinnings.

The second ground asserted by the President's counsel in support of the claim of absolute privilege rests on the doctrine of
separation of powers. Here it is argued that the independence of
the Executive Branch within its own sphere, *Humphrey's Execu-
tor* v. *United States,* 295 U.S. 602, 629–630 (1935); *Kilbourn* v.
Thompson, 103 U.S. 168, 190–191 (1881), insulates a President
from a judicial subpoena in an ongoing criminal prosecution, and
thereby protects confidential Presidential communications.

However, neither the doctrine of separation of powers, nor the
need for confidentiality of high-level communications, without
more, can sustain an absolute, unqualified Presidential privilege of
immunity from judicial process under all circumstances. The
President's need for complete candor and objectivity from advisers
call for great deference from the courts. However, when the privi-

lege depends solely on the broad, undifferentiated claim of public interest in the confidentiality of such conversations, a confrontation with other values arises. Absent a claim of need to protect military, diplomatic, or sensitive national security secrets, we find it difficult to accept the argument that even the very important interest in confidentiality of Presidential communications is significantly diminished by production of such material for *in camera* inspection with all the protection that a district court will be obliged to provide.

The impediment that an absolute, unqualified privilege would place in the way of the primary constitutional duty of the Judicial Branch to do justice in criminal prosecutions would plainly conflict with the function of the courts under Art. III. In designing the structure of our government and dividing and allocating the sovereign power among three co-equal branches, the Framers of the Constitution sought to provide a comprehensive system, but the separate powers were not intended to operate with absolute independence.

> "While the Constitution diffuses power the better to secure liberty, it also contemplates that practice will integrate the dispersed powers into a workable government. It enjoins upon its branches separateness but interdependence, autonomy but reciprocity." *Youngstown Sheet & Tube Co* v. *Sawyer*, 343 U.S., at 635 (Jackson, J., concurring).

To read the Art. II powers of the President as providing an absolute privilege as against a subpoena essential to enforcement of criminal statutes on no more than a generalized claim of the public interest in confidentiality of nonmilitary and nondiplomatic discussions would upset the constitutional balance of "a workable government" and gravely impair the role of the courts under Art. III.

C

Since we conclude that the legitimate needs of the judicial process may outweigh Presidential privilege, it is necessary to resolve those competing interests in a manner that preserves the essential functions of each branch. The right and indeed the duty to resolve that question does not free the Judiciary from according high respect to the representations made on behalf of the President. *United States* v. *Burr*, 25 F.Cas. 187, 190, 191–192 (No. 14,694)(CC Va. 1807).

The expectation of a President to the confidentiality of his conversations and correspondence, like the claim of confidentiality of judicial deliberations, for example, has all the values to which we accord deference for the privacy of all citizens and, added to those values, is the necessity for protection of the public interest in candid, objective, and even blunt or harsh opinions in Presidential decisionmaking. A President and those who assist him must be free to explore alternatives in the process of shaping policies and making decisions and to do so in a way many would be unwilling to express except privately. These are the considerations justifying a presumptive privilege for Presidential communications. The privilege is fundamental to the operation of Government and inextricably rooted in the separation of powers under the Constitution.[11] In *Nixon* v. *Sirica*, 159 U.S. App.D.C. 58, 487 F.2d 700 (1973), the Court of Appeals held that such Presidential communications are "presumptively privileged," *id.*, at 75, 487 F.2d, at 717, and this position is accepted by both parties in the present litigation. We agree with Mr. Chief Justice Marshall's observation, therefore, that "[i]n no case of this kind would a court be required to proceed against the president as against an ordinary individual." *United States* v. *Burr*, 25 F.Cas., at 192.

But this presumptive privilege must be considered in light of our historic commitment to the rule of law. This is nowhere more profoundly manifest than in our view that "the twofold aim [of criminal justice] is that guilt shall not escape or innocence suffer." *Berger* v. *United States*, 295 U.S., at 88. We have elected to employ an adversary system of criminal justice in which the parties contest all issues before a court of law. The need to develop all relevant facts in the adversary system is both fundamental and comprehensive. The ends of criminal justice would be defeated if judgments were to be founded on a partial or speculative presentation of the facts. The very integrity of the judicial system and public confidence in the system depend on full disclosure of all the facts, within the framework of the rules of evidence. To ensure that justice is done, it is imperative to the function of courts that compulsory process be available for the production of evidence needed either by the prosecution or by the defense.

Only recently the Court restated the ancient proposition of law, albeit in the context of a grand jury rather than a trial,

> "that 'the public . . . has a right to every man's evidence,' except for those persons protected by a constitutional, common-law, or statutory privilege, *United States* v. *Bryan*, 339 U.S. [323, 331 (1950)]; *Blackmer* v. *United States*, 284 U.S. 421, 438 (1932). . . ." *Branzburg* v. *Hayes*, 408 U.S. 665, 688 (1972).

The privileges referred to by the Court are designed to protect weighty and legitimate competing interests. Thus, the Fifth Amendment to the Constitution provides that no man "shall be compelled in any criminal case to be a witness against himself." And, generally, an attorney or a priest may not be required to disclose what has been revealed in professional confidence. These and other interests are recognized in law by privileges against forced disclosure, established in the Constitution, by statute, or at common law. Whatever their origins, these exceptions to the demand for every man's evidence are not lightly created nor expansively construed, for they are in derogation of the search for truth.[12]

In this case the President challenges a subpoena served on him as a third party requiring the production of materials for use in a criminal prosecution; he does so on the claim that he has a privilege against disclosure of confidential communications. He does not place his claim of privilege on the ground they are military or diplomatic secrets. As to these areas of Art. II duties the courts have traditionally shown the utmost deference to Presidential responsibilities. In *C. & S. Air Lines* v. *Waterman S. S. Corp.*, 333 U.S. 103, 111 (1948), dealing with Presidential authority involving foreign policy considerations, the Court said:

"The President, both as Commander-in-Chief and as the Nation's organ for foreign affairs, has available intelligence services whose reports are not and ought not to be published to the world. It would be intolerable that courts, without the relevant information, should review and perhaps nullify actions of the Executive taken on information properly held secret."

In *United States* v. *Reynolds*, 345 U.S. 1 (1953), dealing with a claimant's demand for evidence in a Tort Claims Act case against the Government, the Court said:

"It may be possible to satisfy the court, from all the circumstances of the case, that there is a reasonable danger that compulsion of the evidence will expose military matters which, in the interest of national security, should not be divulged. When this is the case, the occasion for the privilege is appropriate, and the court should not jeopardize the security which the privilege is meant to protect by insisting upon an examination of the evidence, even by the judge alone, in chambers." *Id.*, at 10.

No case of the Court, however, has extended this high degree of deference to a President's generalized interest in confidentiality. Nowhere in the Constitution, as we have noted earlier, is there any explicit reference to a privilege of confidentiality, yet to the extent this interest relates to the effective discharge of a President's powers, it is constitutionally based.

The right to the production of all evidence at a criminal trial similarly has constitutional dimensions. The Sixth Amendment explicitly confers upon every defendant in a criminal trial the right "to be confronted with the witnesses against him" and "to have compulsory process for obtaining witnesses in his favor." Moreover, the Fifth Amendment also guarantees that no person shall be deprived of liberty without due process of law. It is the manifest duty of the courts to vindicate those guarantees, and to accomplish that it is essential that all relevant and admissible evidence be produced.

In this case we must weigh the importance of the general privilege of confidentiality of Presidential communications in performance of the President's responsibilities against the inroads of such a privilege on the fair administration of criminal justice.[13] The interest in preserving confidentiality is weighty indeed and entitled to great respect. However, we cannot conclude that advisers will be moved to temper the candor of their remarks by the infrequent occasions of disclosure because of the possibility that such conversations will be called for in the context of a criminal prosecution.[14]

On the other hand, the allowance of the privilege to withhold evidence that is demonstrably relevant in a criminal trial would cut deeply into the guarantee of due process of law and gravely impair the basic function of the courts. A President's acknowledged need for confidentiality in the communications of his office is general in nature, whereas the constitutional need for production of relevant evidence in a criminal proceeding is specific and central to the fair adjudication of a particular criminal case in the administration of justice. Without access to specific facts a criminal prosecution may be totally frustrated. The President's broad interest in confidentiality of communications will not be vitiated by disclosure of a limited number of conversations preliminarily shown to have some bearing on the pending criminal cases.

We conclude that when the ground for asserting privilege as to subpoenaed materials sought for use in a criminal trial is based only on the generalized interest in confidentiality, it cannot prevail over the fundamental demands of due process of law in the fair administration of criminal justice. The generalized assertion of privilege must yield to the demonstrated, specific need for evidence in a pending criminal trial.

D

We have earlier determined that the District Court did not err in authorizing the issuance of the subpoena. If a President concludes that compliance with a subpoena would be injurious to the public interest he may properly, as was done here, invoke a claim of privilege on the return of the subpoena. Upon receiving a claim of privilege from the Chief Executive, it became the further duty of District Court to treat the subpoenaed material as presumptively privileged and to require the Special Prosecutor to demonstrate that the Presidential material was "essential to the justice of the [pending criminal] case." *United States* v. *Burr*, 25 F.Cas., at 192. Here the District Court treated the material as presumptively privileged, proceeded to find that the Special Prosecutor had made a sufficient showing to rebut the presumption, and ordered an *in camera* examination of the subpoenaed material. On the basis of our examination of the record we are unable to conclude that the District Court erred in ordering the inspection. Accordingly we affirm the order of the District Court that subpoenaed materials be transmitted to that court. We now turn to the important question of the District Court's responsibilities in conducting the *in camera* examination of Presidential materials or communications delivered under the compulsion of the subpoena *duces tecum.*

E

Enforcement of the subpoena *duces tecum* was stayed pending this Court's resolution of the issues raised by the petitions for certiorari. Those issues now having been disposed of, the matter of implementation will rest with the District Court. "[T]he guard, furnished to [the President] to protect him from being harassed by vexatious and unnecessary subpoenas, is to be looked for in the conduct of a [district] court after those subpoenas have issued; not in any circumstance which is to precede their being issued." *United States* v. *Burr*, 25 F.Cas., at 34. Statements that meet the test of admissibility and relevance must be isolated; all other material must be excised. At this stage the District Court is not limited to representations of the Special Prosecutor as to the evidence sought by the subpoena; the material will be available to the District Court. It is elementary that *in camera* inspection of evidence is always a procedure calling for scrupulous protection against any release or publication of material not found by the court, at that stage, probably admissible in evidence and relevant to the issues of the trial for which it is sought. That being true of an ordinary situation, it is obvious that the District Court has a very heavy responsibility to see to it that Presidential conversations, which are either not relevant or not admissible, are accorded that high degree of respect due the President of the United States. Mr. Chief Justice Marshall, sitting as a trial judge in the *Burr* case, *supra,* was extraordinarily careful to point out that

"[i]n no case of this kind would a court be required to proceed against the president as against an ordinary individual." 25 F.Cas., at 192.

Marshall's statement cannot be read to mean in any sense that a President is above the law, but relates to the singularly unique role under Art. II of a President's communications and activities, related to the performance of duties under that Article. Moreover, a President's communications and activities encompass a vastly wider range of sensitive material than would be true of any "ordinary individual." It is therefore necessary[15] in the public interest to afford Presidential confidentiality the greatest protection consistent with the fair administration of justice. The need for confidentiality even as to idle conversations with associates in which casual reference might be made concerning political leaders within the country or foreign statesmen is too obvious to call for further treatment. We have no doubt that the District Judge will at all times accord to Presidential records that high degree of deference suggested in *United States* v. *Burr, supra,* and will discharge his responsibility to see to it that until released to the Special Prosecutor no *in camera* material is revealed to anyone. This burden applies with even greater force to excised material; once the decision is made to excise, the material is restored to its privileged status and should be returned under seal to its lawful custodian.

Since this matter came before the Court during the pendency of a criminal prosecution, and on representations that time is of the essence, the mandate shall issue forthwith.

Affirmed.

MR. JUSTICE REHNQUIST took no part in the consideration or decision of these cases.

1. The parties have suggested that this Court has jurisdiction on other grounds. In view of our conclusion that there is jurisdiction under 28 U.S.C. § 1254(1) because the District Court's order was appealable, we need not decide whether other jurisdictional vehicles are available.

2. The regulation issued by the Attorney General pursuant to his statutory authority, vests in the Special Prosecutor plenary authority to control the course of investigations and litigation related to "all offenses arising out of the 1972 Presidential Election for which the Special Prosecutor deems it necessary and appropriate to assume responsibility, allegations involving the President, members of the White House staff, or Presidential appointees, and any other matters which he consents to have assigned to him by the Attorney General." 38 Fed.Reg. 30739, as amended by 38 Fed.Reg. 32805. In particular, the Special Prosecutor was given full authority, *inter alia,* "to contest the assertion of 'Executive Privilege' . . . and handl[e] all aspects of any cases within his jurisdiction." *Id.,* at 30739. The regulation then goes on to provide:

   "In exercising this authority, the Special Prosecutor will

have the greatest degree of independence that is consistent with the Attorney General's statutory accountability for all matters falling within the jurisdiction of the Department of Justice. The Attorney General will not countermand or interfere with the Special Prosecutor's decisions or actions. The Special Prosecutor will determine whether and to what extent he will inform or consult with the Attorney General about the conduct of his duties and responsibilities. In accordance with assurances given by the President to the Attorney General that the President will not exercise his Constitutional powers to effect the discharge of the Special Prosecutor or to limit the independence that he is hereby given, the Special Prosecutor will not be removed from his duties except for extraordinary improprieties on his part and without the President's first consulting the Majority and the Minority Leaders and Chairmen and ranking Minority Members of the Judiciary Committees of the Senate and House of Representatives and ascertaining that their consensus is in accord with his proposed action."

3. That this was the understanding of Acting Attorney General Robert Bork, the author of the regulation establishing the independence of the Special Prosecutor, is shown by his testimony before the Senate Judiciary Committee:

"Although it is anticipated that Mr. Jaworski will receive cooperation from the White House in getting any evidence he feels he needs to conduct investigations and prosecutions, it is clear and understood on all sides that he has the power to use judicial processes to pursue evidence if disagreement should develop."

Hearings on the Special Prosecutor before the Senate Committee on the Judiciary, 93d Cong., 1st Sess., pt. 2, p. 450 (1973). Acting Attorney General Bork gave similar assurances to the House Subcommittee on Criminal Justice. Hearings on H. J. Res. 784 and H. R. 10937 before the Subcommittee on Criminal Justice of the House Committee on the Judiciary, 93d Cong., 1st Sess., 266 (1973). At his confirmation hearings, Attorney General William Saxbe testified that he shared Acting Attorney General Bork's views concerning the Special Prosecutor's authority to test any claim of executive privilege in the courts. Hearings on the Nomination of William B. Saxbe to be Attorney General before the Senate Committee on the Judiciary, 93d Cong., 1st Sess., 9 (1973).

4. At his confirmation hearings, Attorney General William Saxbe testified that he agreed with the regulation adopted by Acting Attorney General Bork and would not remove the Special Prosecutor except for "gross impropriety." *Id.*, at 5–6,

8–10. There is no contention here that the Special Prosecutor is guilty of any such impropriety.

5. The Court quoted a statement of a member of the advisory committee that the purpose of the Rule was to bring documents into court "in advance of the time that they are offered in evidence, so that they may then be inspected in advance, for the purpose . . . of enabling the party to see whether he can use [them] or whether he wants to use [them]." 341 U.S., at 220 n. 5. The Manual for Complex and Multidistrict Litigation published by the Federal Judicial Center recommends that use of Rule 17(c) be encouraged in complex criminal cases in order that each party may be compelled to produce its documentary evidence well in advance of trial and in advance of the time it is to be offered. P. 150.

6. The District Court found here that it was faced with "the more unusual situation . . . where the subpoena, rather than being directed to the government by defendants, issues to what, as a practical matter, is a third party." *United States* v. *Mitchell*, 377 F.Supp. 1326, 1330 (DC 1974). The Special Prosecutor suggests that the evidentiary requirement of *Bowman Dairy Co.* and *Iozia* does not apply in its full vigor when the subpoena *duces tecum* is issued to third parties rather than to government prosecutors. Brief for United States 128–129. We need not decide whether a lower standard exists because we are satisfied that the relevance and evidentiary nature of the subpoenaed tapes were sufficiently shown as a preliminary matter to warrant the District Court's refusal to quash the subpoena.

7. Such statements are declarations by a party defendant that "would surmount all objections based on the hearsay rule . . ." and, at least as to the declarant himself, "would be admissible for whatever inferences" might be reasonably drawn. *United States* v. *Matlock*, 415 U.S. 164, 172 (1974). *On Lee* v. *United States*, 343 U.S. 747, 757 (1952). See also C. McCormick, Evidence § 270, pp. 651–652 (2d ed. 1972).

8. As a preliminary matter, there must be substantial, independent evidence of the conspiracy, at least enough to take the question to the jury. *United States* v. *Vaught*, 485 F.2d 320, 323 (CA4 1973); *United States* v. *Hoffa*, 349 F.2d 20, 41–42 (CA6 1965), aff'd on other grounds, 385 U.S. 293 (1966); *United States* v. *Santos*, 385 F.2d 43, 45 (CA7 1967), cert. denied, 390 U.S. 954 (1968); *United States* v. *Morton*, 483 F.2d 573, 576 (CA8 1973); *United States* v. *Spanos*, 462 F.2d 1012, 1014 (CA9 1972); *Carbo* v. *United States*, 314 F.2d 718, 737 (CA9 1963), cert. denied, 377 U.S. 953 (1964). Whether the standard has been satisfied is a question of admissibility of evidence to be decided by the trial judge.

9. There is nothing novel about governmental confidentiality.

The meetings of the Constitutional Convention in 1787 were conducted in complete privacy. 1 M. Farrand, The Records of the Federal Convention of 1787, pp. xi-xxv (1911). Moreover, all records of those meetings were sealed for more than 30 years after the Convention. See 3 Stat. 475, 15th Cong., 1st Sess., Res. 8 (1818). Most of the Framers acknowledged that without secrecy no constitution of the kind that was developed could have been written. C. Warren, The Making of the Constitution 134–139 (1937).

10. The Special Prosecutor argues, that there is no provision in the Constitution for a Presidential privilege as to the President's communications corresponding to the privilege of Members of Congress under the Speech or Debate Clause. But the silence of the Constitution on this score is not dispositive. "The rule of constitutional interpretation announced in *McCulloch* v. *Maryland*, 4 Wheat. 316, that that which was reasonably appropriate and relevant to the exercise of a granted power was to be considered as accompanying the grant, has been so universally applied that it suffices merely to state it." *Marshall* v. *Gordon*, 243 U.S. 521, 537 (1917).

11. "Freedom of communication vital to fulfillment of the aims of wholesome relationships is obtained only by removing the specter of compelled disclosure. . . . [G]overnment . . . needs open but protected channels for the kind of plain talk that is essential to the quality of its functioning." *Carl Zeiss Stiftung* v. *V. E. B. Carl Zeiss, Jena*, 40 F.R.D. 318, 325 (DC 1966). See *Nixon* v. *Sirica*, 159 U.S. App. D. C. 58, 71, 487 F.2d 700, 713 (1973); *Kaiser Aluminum & Chem. Corp.* v. *United States*, 141 Ct. Cl. 38, 157 F.Supp. 939 (1958)(Reed, J.); The Federalist, No. 64 (S. Mittell ed. 1938).

12. Because of the key role of the testimony of witnesses in the judicial process, courts have historically been cautious about privileges. Mr. Justice Frankfurter dissenting in *Elkins* v. *United States*, 364 U.S. 206, 234 (1960), said of this: "Limitations are properly placed upon the operation of this general principle only to the very limited extent that permitting a refusal to testify or excluding relevant evidence has a public good transcending the normally predominant principle of utilizing all rational means for ascertaining truth."

13. We are not here concerned with the balance between the President's generalized interest in confidentiality and the need for relevant evidence in civil litigation, nor with that between the confidentiality interest and congressional demands for information, nor with the President's interest in preserving state secrets. We address only the conflict between the President's assertion of a generalized privilege of confidentiality and the constitutional need for relevant evidence in criminal trials.

14. Mr. Justice Cardozo made this point in an analogous con-

text. Speaking for a unanimous Court in *Clark* v. *United States*, 289 U.S. 1 (1933), he emphasized the importance of maintaining the secrecy of the deliberations of a petit jury in a criminal case. "Freedom of debate might be stifled and independence of thought checked if jurors were made to feel that their arguments and ballots were to be freely published to the world." *Id.*, at 13. Nonetheless, the Court also recognized that isolated inroads on confidentiality designed to serve the paramount need of the criminal law would not vitiate the interests served by secrecy:

"A juror of integrity and reasonable firmness will not fear to speak his mind if the confidences of debate are barred to the ears of mere impertinence or malice. He will not expect to be shielded against the disclosure of his conduct in the event that there is evidence reflecting upon his honor. The chance that now and then there may be found some timid soul who will take counsel of his fears and give way to their repressive power is too remote and shadowy to shape the course of justice." *Id.*, at 16.

15. When the subpoenaed material is delivered to the District Judge *in camera*, questions may arise as to the excising of parts, and it lies within the discretion of that court to seek the aid of the Special Prosecutor and the President's counsel for *in camera* consideration of the validity of particular excisions, whether the basis of excision is relevancy or admissibility or under such cases as *United States* v. *Reynolds*, 345 U.S. 1 (1953), or *C. & S. Air Lines* v. *Waterman S. S. Corp.*, 333 U.S. 103 (1948).

Opinion on Liddy's Motion for Reduction of Sentence, June 20, 1975, by Judge Sirica

UNITED STATES of America

v.

George Gordon LIDDY et. al.
Crim. No. 1827–72.

United States District Court,
District of Columbia.
June 20, 1975.

MEMORANDUM OPINION AND ORDER

SIRICA, District Judge.

This matter comes before the Court on the motion of the defendant George Gordon Liddy for a reduction of sentence, filed May 19, 1975. The Court has carefully reviewed this motion and the memorandum filed in support thereof, and has taken into consideration all of those factors which are usually considered by most judges when passing upon such motions.

The provision for such a motion under Rule 35 of the Federal Rules of Criminal Procedure is intended to provide a means by which a convicted defendant may have a second chance before a sentencing judge, while giving the judge an opportunity to reconsider the initial sentence imposed in light of any further information concerning the defendant or the case which might have arisen and been brought to the attention of the Court in the interim. *United States* v. *Ellenbogen*, 390 F.2d 537, 543 (2 Cir.) *cert. denied* 393 U.S. 918, 89 S.Ct. 241, 21 L.Ed.2d 206 (1968).

When this defendant was sentenced, the Court mentioned the four principal reasons for imposing sentences. It was noted at that time that reprisal was not an appropriate purpose for which to sentence this defendant, and that rehabilitation, although considered, was not the principal consideration. The Court, however, emphasized the purposes of imposing just punishment for the grave offenses committed and of deterring others from engaging in such reprehensible conduct.

The deterrent effect of the sentences, as one of the primary reasons for prescribing the term of incarceration for the defendant, is no less important now than it was at the time of his initial sentencing. As the prosecutor stated at that time:

". . . What these defendants have done . . . is not only violate the freedom of association of a major political party but perhaps more important . . . what they have done is to generate a fear . . . that this illegal activity, wiretapping, bugging and burglary for political purposes, is both widespread and condoned.

. . . [I]t is important that the sentences imposed in this case . . . respond to this fear by deterring future conduct of this kind and by demonstrating that this kind of conduct will not be tolerated."[1]

Similarly, the purpose of imposing punishment appropriate for the grave offenses of which the defendant was convicted has not been negated by the facts, circumstances or events which have come to the attention of the Court in the interim.

The rehabilitative purpose to be served by Mr. Liddy's sentence must also be reconsidered. The need for the personal rehabilitation of this defendant has assumed even greater importance than it had two years ago due to the events that have occurred in the interim. A review of his present criminal record is revealing. When this defendant first appeared before the Court he had no criminal record, having never before been sentenced to jail or even having been convicted of an offense more serious than a traffic violation. However, on March 23, 1973, when he stood before this Court to be sentenced, he stood convicted of two counts of burglary, two counts of intercepting wire communications, one count of intercepting oral communications and one count of conspiracy. Since then, the defendant has been convicted by another jury of another felony charge, namely, conspiracy to violate the rights of a citizen; he has been found guilty of statutory contempt of court for refusing to testify before a Federal Grand Jury; and has been found guilty by another federal judge of contempt of Congress for refusing to testify before a Congressional Committee. With the exception of the statutory contempt conviction, the sentences the defendant received for his other convictions were either suspended or made to run concurrently with the sentences imposed by this Court.

Subsequent to his conviction and sentencing in this case, the defendant had several opportunities to provide valuable assistance to governmental investigating units by testifying as to his knowledge of certain alleged illegal activities. He was even granted immunity from prosecution for the testimony which he was subpoenaed to give. Yet, he refused to cooperate. It is reasonable for the Court to assume that this defendant had reason to know and believe that any further consideration he might receive from the Court concerning his sentence might be affected by his conduct after sentencing. In fact he was present in the courtroom when his co-defendants were specifically informed that their cooperation with the grand jury and the Senate Select Committee would be a relevant factor which the Court would consider in determining their final sentences.

At that time this court stated to all the defendants in the presence of Mr. Liddy:

". . . [N]one of you have been willing to give the government or other appropriate authorities any substantial help in trying this case or in investigating the activities which were the subject of this case.

I think under the law, the Court is entitled to consider this fact in determining sentences.

*   *   *   *   *   *

I believe I may also properly suggest to you that in the interval between now and the time when the Bureau of Prisons studies are completed, you give serious consideration to lending your full cooperation to investigating authorities.

Now I want to speak plainly about this matter. You will, no doubt, be given an opportunity to provide information to the grand jury which has been, and still is, investigating the Watergate affair and to the Senate Select Committee on Presidential Campaign Activities.

I sincerely hope that each one of you will take full advantage of any such opportunity . . . .

*   *   *   *   *   *

Now I believe that the Watergate [Break-in] affair . . . should not be forgotten. Some good can and should come from a revelation of sinister conduct whenever and wherever such conduct exists. I am convinced that the greatest benefit that can come from this prosecution will be its impact as a spur to corrective action so that the type of activities revealed by the evidence at trial will not be repeated in our nation.

For these reasons, I recommend your full cooperation with the grand jury and the Senate Select Committee. You must understand that I hold out no promises or hopes of any kind to you in this matter but I do say that should you decide to speak freely I would have to weigh that factor in appraising what sentence will be finally imposed in this case. Other factors will, of course, be considered, but I mention this one because it is one over which *you have control* and I mean each and every one of you."[2]

Yet, despite this admonition by the Court and the fact that the Court subsequently gave consideration to other defendants on this basis, this defendant chose to continue to refuse to cooperate with the government investigations.

In short, this defendant has not shown the Court the slightest remorse or regret for his actions, and has not given the Court even a hint of contrition or sorrow, nor has he made any attempt to compensate for his illegal actions by trying to aid our system of justice in its search for the truth.

This defendant's obstinate disregard for the processes of law is difficult for the Court to comprehend. As was acknowledged on the day of sentencing, this defendant "has throughout his adult life been very interested and involved with the law . . . [and] been deeply involved in the law."[3] Clearly this is not the case in which one who is disadvantaged or uneducated breaks the law. This defendant is a well-educated man who has had considerable experience with the law and politics, having been a lawyer, an assistant district attorney, an FBI special agent, a Congressional candidate, a special assistant in the Organized Crime Section of the Treasury Department, and a White House aide. The Court noted when it sentenced the defendant:

> "Now it is true that 'ignorance of the law is no excuse,' and that one may be held accountable for a failure to obey the law whether he has read the statute books or not. Despite this fact, however, the Court believes that the knowing and deliberate violation of laws deserve a greater condemnation than a simple careless or uncomprehending violation."[4]

Mr. Liddy, in his motion for reduction of sentence, also specifically requests that the fines imposed at the time of sentencing be vacated. However, the Court notes that the defendant has not cooperated with investigators even so much as to try to explain whatever became of the approximately $199,000 which testimony at trial indicated was dispersed to Mr. Liddy.[5]

> The Court sees no reason to vacate the fine. Should the defendant be unable to pay the fine at the time when he has served his sentence, he will then have the opportunity to take a pauper's oath under the applicable statute (18 U.S.C. § 3569). At that time he will be able to satisfy this portion of his sentence by serving an additional thirty days imprisonment.

In conclusion, the mitigating factors inherent in those cases in which a defendant has displayed some personal remorse or regret for his actions and has demonstrated a desire to reform his conduct to conform to the simple standards of a lawful society are absent in this case.

In the interim which has passed since the Court sentenced the defendant in this case, no information has been brought to the attention of the Court which would move this Court to reduce the sentence of the defendant. The Court can only repeat what it stated at the initial sentencing of Mr. Liddy:

> "I shall not attempt to enumerate every item which the Court has pondered. Numerous other considerations, both favorable and unfavorable to the defendants, have played a part in the Court's decisions. Suffice it to say that the sentences which the Court will now impose, are the result of careful thought extending over a period of several weeks. I think the sentences are appropriate and just."[6]

For the reasons above stated, it is this 20th day of June, 1975,
Ordered that the defendant's motion for reduction of sentence be, and the same hereby is, denied.

1. Transcript of March 23, 1973, pp. 13, 14 (attached hereto as an appendix and hereinafter referred to as "Transcript").
2. Transcript, pp. 35–36, 39–40 (emphasis added).
3. Transcript, pp. 11, 12.
4. Transcript, p. 15.
5. Transcript of Trial, *United States v. George Gordon Liddy, et al.,* Criminal No. 1827–72, pp. 1448–1449.
6. Transcript, pp. 16, 17.

Index

About the Author

JOHN J. SIRICA was born in Waterbury, Connecticut, on March 19, 1904, the son of Fred and Rose Sirica. He attended public schools in Jacksonville, Florida, and New Orleans, Louisiana. He received the degree of LL.B. from Georgetown University Law School in 1926, was admitted to the bar of the United States District Court for the District of Columbia in October 1926, and was subsequently admitted to the bars of the United States Court of Appeals for the District of Columbia Circuit and of the Supreme Court of the United States. He engaged in private practice in the District of Columbia until August 1, 1930, when he was appointed assistant United States attorney for the District of Columbia. After his resignation on January 15, 1934, he resumed the practice of law. In 1944 he served as general counsel to the House Select Committee to Investigate the Federal Communications Commission, and between 1949 and 1957 was a member of the law firm of Hogan and Hartson. On February 26, 1952, he married Lucile M. Camalier, their children are John J., Jr., Patricia Anne, and Eileen Marie. On February 25, 1957, President Eisenhower nominated him a judge of the United States District Court for the District of Columbia, and he entered upon the duties of that office on April 2, 1957. He became chief judge of the court on April 2, 1971, and as required by law, stepped down as chief judge on March 18, 1974, to resume duties as a full-time United States district judge. He assumed senior judge status effective on November 1, 1977.

A member of the American Bar Association, he served as state chairman of the Junior Bar Conference of the American Bar Association for the District of Columbia during 1938–39. He is a member of Phi Alpha Delta law fraternity, the Congressional Country Club, and the Board of Regents of Georgetown University; and is an honorary member of the District of Columbia Bar Association, the National Lawyers Club, and the Lido Civic Club.

Judge Sirica has received honorary degrees from the following colleges and universities: College of New Rochelle, New Rochelle, N.Y.; Brown University, Providence, R.I.; New England School of Law, Boston, Mass.; Fairfield University, Fairfield, Conn.; City University of New York, New York, N.Y.; Duke University, Durham, N.C.; Georgetown University, Washington, D.C.; Mt. St. Mary's College, Emmitsburg, Md.; Gettysburg College, Gettysburg, Pa.

He has also received the following awards and honors: Award of Merit, American Judges Association (1973); *Time* Man of the Year, *Time Magazine* (1973); Touchdown Club of Washington "Timmie" award (local boy makes good) (1974); the John Carroll Award, Georgetown University Alumni Association (1974); Key West (Florida) Jaycee Good Government Award, (1974); Certificate of Achievement, Italian Historical Society of America (1974); Certificate of Outstanding Contribution to the Judiciary, Phi Alpha Delta international law fraternity (1974); Brien McMahon Memorial Award, Fordham University Club of Washington (1975); Outstanding Trial Judge of 1975, Association of Trial Lawyers of America (1975); Award of Merit, Federal Administrative Law Judges' Conference (1975); James Cardinal Gibbons Medalist, Catholic University of America Alumni Association (1975); Award of Merit, United States Department of Justice, Drug Enforcement Administration (1975); Award of Merit, American Justinian Society of Jurists (1975); Outstanding Achievement Award, National Association of Secondary School Principals (1976); Italian American Bicentennial Tribute, Award of Merit (1976); Association of Federal Investigators, Judiciary Award (1976); Award of Merit, American Academy of Achievement (1977); Kappa Alpha Psi Humanitarian Award (1977); Jurisprudence Father of the Year, National Father's Day Committee (1978); Award of Merit, Jewish National Fund (1978); award in recognition of outstanding and distinguished service by District of Columbia Bar (1978); Centennial Medal, Vanderbilt University (1978).

SIGNET and MENTOR Books You'll Want to Read